Death in Quotation Marks

HARVARD STUDIES IN COMPARATIVE LITERATURE
Founded by William Henry Schofield

41

Svetlana Boym ▪▪

Death
in
Quotation
Marks

▪▪

Cultural Myths of the Modern Poet

▪▪

Harvard University Press

Cambridge, Massachusetts
London, England
1991

*This book is printed on acid-free paper, and its binding materials have
been chosen for strength and durability.*

Library of Congress Cataloging-in-Publication Data

Boym, Svetlana, 1959–
    Death in quotation marks: cultural myths of the modern poet /
Svetlana Boym.
        p.   cm.—(Harvard studies in comparative literature; 41)
    Includes bibliographical references and index.
    ISBN 0-674-19427-6
    1. Death in literature. 2. Survival in literature. 3. Authors—Psychology. 4. Criticism, Textual.
5. Psychology in literature. 6. Literature, Modern—History and criticism. I. Title.
II. Series.
    PN56.D4B6 1991
    809.1'9354—dc20   90–44306
                    CIP

Acknowledgments

In writing *Death in Quotation Marks* I have relied on the generous help and knowledge of many people. First, I wish to thank Jurij Striedter and Barbara Johnson for kindly encouraging me throughout the writing of the book and not letting it die in the process. Jurij Striedter provided invaluable intellectual stimulation and shared with me his love and knowledge of Russian Formalism. Barbara Johnson taught me how to practice theory, use puns seriously, and take as many intellectual risks as I dared.

I am grateful to Donald Fanger for supporting me during my years at Harvard with creative insight, intellectual generosity, and good humor. To Susan Suleiman my special thanks for broadening my intellectual horizon and making me think about the subversive relationship between women and the avant-garde.

I benefited greatly from conversations with Margaret Higonnet, who read my chapter on Tsvetaeva and encouraged me to examine death and suicide in the most challenging and open-ended way. Elizabeth Bronfen made me think further about death and representation as well as about the "beautiful corpses" that are produced in the artistic process.

I owe a particular debt to my first American teacher—the writer and critic Alicia Borinsky—who inspired me to think about theoretical fables in life and literature.

My friends were my most generous interlocutors: Inna Galperina, Florence Dumora, Marya Schechtman, Norbert Bonenkamp, Clare Cavanagh, Leslie Dunton-Downer, Andrew Wachtell, and Clive Dilnot. I am also grateful to Liz Scarlett, John Henriksen, and Lily Parrot for taking care of all the details and the missing English articles.

My warm thanks to Lindsay Waters and Alison Roberts of Harvard University Press for helping the book come alive.

And finally I am greatly indebted to my parents, Musa and Yury Goldberg, whose coming to the United States has pleasantly interrupted my work.

A note on transliteration: I have standardized Russian proper names to make them look more "comfortable" in English, but use a more scholarly system for Russian words and phrases.

Contents

Introduction

Literature, Biography, and the Modern "Death of the Author"

Жизнь и смерть давно беру в кавычки,
как заведомо пустые сплеты.

I have long put life and death in quotation marks,
like fabrications known to be empty.
    Marina Tsvetaeva, "New Year's Eve"

Marina Tsvetaeva's address to Rilke, already deceased, poetically expresses the desire that motivated my work—a desire to shift, reopen, or make visible the numerous quotation marks around the words "life," "death," and "art," and expose critical "fabrications" about them. A reconsideration of the relationship between a literary *persona*, a biographical *person*, and a cultural *personage* will help me to elaborate cultural mythologies of the life of a modern poet and the connections between the making of poetry and the making of self.

I will try to develop alternative strategies of reading "life," "text," and "culture" together, without subordinating one to another. While rethinking the boundaries between them, I will begin to trace the intellectual history and politics behind the establishment of critical frontiers between different disciplines, different discourses, and different spheres of human experience. The relationship between literature and everyday life, between literariness and literalness, between giving a figure and disfiguring, between textualizing and living out, between stopping writing and stopping living will be at the center of my discussion. What is at stake for the critic in consolidating these boundaries and distinctions? What does one risk in the attempt to question or historicize them? How is one's cultural self both fashioned and disfigured in the process of self-conscious writing? What is the relationship between subjectivity and the body? Does the writer live his or her own fictions or, on the contrary, simply write the story of a life? Finally, what is the nature of the uncanny relationship between artistic *corpus* and *corps*, and why is it celebrated by contemporary critics?

All these issues are closely linked to the problematics of modernism. In the 1990's, when "modern" is no longer new, when the word "modern" has acquired a prefix and turned into an object of intense critical nostalgia, the time has come for reconsideration of many modernist myths. The

critical vocabulary of "modernism"—understood as a self-conscious artistic response to the modern condition, that is, to specific historical, cultural, and economical changes that have occurred in Western society during the past two centuries—depends on such terms as "autonomy of art," "dehumanization of art," and "death of the author." It makes the question of the interrelationships between life, text, and culture particularly urgent, since with the advent of modernity, the prestige of artistic institutions has been seriously shaken and poets themselves have turned into endangered creatures. Modernist writers rediscovered the paradoxical logic of language, which precludes simple oppositions between past and present, linearity and circularity, history and theory. And yet it is still of extreme critical importance to circumscribe (albeit artificially) the modern project within a historical context and defy its uniformity and universality by examining a variety of modernisms that emerge in different cultural contexts. Inescapably, my own critical writing will not only describe but often unwillingly act out all the aporias of modern discourse—the tensions between theorizing and historicizing, between "reporting life" and narrating fictions, between consolidating the boundaries of texts, genres, and figures and questioning them, between circumscribing the texts within cultural, historical, or critical "contexts" and "facts of life" and exploding those contexts and circumstances from within, through the subversive logic of writing.

The relationship between what are called "literature and biography" (Tomashevsky), or "l'homme et l'oeuvre" (Sainte-Beuve), or the author's person and persona (American New Critics) has shifted and developed through history, reflecting the changing conception of subjectivity and the relationship between writing and the self. Before the Romantic discovery of "genius" and the conception of art as a revelation of personality, literature and biography were not viewed as necessarily co-dependent; they were judged according to the laws of different genres. The biography of a poet, like the biography of any "great man," was regarded not as "personal" but rather as mythical, communal, and almost archetypal. It had a certain cultural iconography that guaranteed both fame and anonymity to the author. This was perhaps at the root of the paradoxes of Homer and Shakespeare—two embodiments of a profoundly anti-Romantic view of the life of the artist that puzzled many naive biography lovers because of a conspicuous lack of picturesque and delicious gossip about the authors. The fiction even emerged that Shakespeare and Homer, in fact, never existed and that their works were composed by someone else, hiding behind their names. They also both became the fantastic heroes of Jorge

Luis Borges, who turned them into predecessors of the modern depersonalized and defaced authors, perfect prototypes for "somebody and nobody."[1]

The question of autobiography as it emerged after Rousseau's *Confessions* could hardly be posed regarding the texts of Homer and Shakespeare, despite various critical attempts to identify the addressees of Shakespeare's sonnets and to regard them as a key to his personality. Interesting as it might be for historical and cultural reasons, Shakespeare's biography cannot be seen as a revealing metaphor for his work or vice versa because in his particular culture there simply was no myth of a cause-and-effect relationship between an artist's life and work. As Stephen Greenblatt has demonstrated, the elements of "self-fashioning" had emerged in Renaissance writing, but the reader's expectations of what the poet's life should be were not yet "structured."[2] What was most valued in authors was precisely their protean or chameleon-like quality, their ability to reveal universal laws of human and divine nature rather than personal and idiosyncratic ones.

The Romantic biographical use of literature can be traced to the neoclassical "interest in mankind" and to the famous rhetorical conceit that "style is an image of mind."[3] Gradually, style becomes a man (or a woman—as we shall observe in examining the "poetess"), and the figuration of the author, in Romantic psychological terms, becomes the critic's main preoccupation. Critical interest in the unique (or rather the uniquely natural) individuality of the artist was fostered by the doctrine of genius. Genius, according to Schleiermacher, is a spirit that turns upon itself to find "the divine source of all plastic arts and poetry."[4] Geniuses are endowed with the ability to read "natural laws"; moreover, they themselves create according to natural laws with the help of grace and inspiration. Hence, in Romanticism art and the artist's personality turn into "correlated variables." Similarly, they can be viewed as metaphors of one another, with tenor and vehicle thoroughly blurred. The poet is transformed into a spectacular figure, his own romantic hero. Romantics conscientiously worked on self-stylization, cultivating a limited repertoire of stock characters—from a demonic Byronesque type to a melancholic "sensitive man."[5] Thus, Romanticism creates a new iconography, a new repertoire of images, the indispensable element of which is the connection between art and life—making life poetic while making art autobiographical. The poet has to love tragically and sentimentally, like Werther, and die tragically and heroically like Shelley, Byron, Lermontov, or Pushkin. He can be a solitary figure, like Vigny or Keats, but he

is preferably a public persona, a distinguished politician and revolutionary, like Hugo or the Russian poets—Decembrists who spoke in verse with their wives and beloveds who followed them to Siberia or to the place of their execution.[6] Of course, Romanticism produced its own "cure"— romantic irony. The Romantic poets pioneered the parodying of Romantic attitudes in life and art. But the passion for individual figuration prevailed, a passion for picture galleries in which the Romantic poet with all his spectacular visual attributes rivaled Napoleon, himself the exemplary Romantic in life.

The relationship between the Romantic poet and his reader, most often represented as a "mob" incapable of comprehending the suffering of the tragic outcast, or as a rare "soul-mate" who shares the poet's sorrows, was in fact that of a double bind. The grotesque description of the mob was indispensable for the poet's heroic self-depiction while the configuration of the reader as a soul-mate provided a necessary chain reaction of Romantic imitations, a guarantee of the poet's vitality. Close attention on the part of the reader to the poet's own persona can have many adverse effects. Even when the poet emphasizes that he is different from his characters, the reader often turns him into one, expecting to see the poet himself in every Romantic hero he creates and judging the poet's life with high Romantic standards. The elements of this popular reading practice which emerged with Romanticism, the period that coincided with the birth of mass culture, proved to be very pervasive and survives today. It manifests itself, for instance, in the common practice of television and film fans who often identify the characters of their favorite soap operas and movies with the actors, turning them into larger-than-life quasi Romantic supermen and wonderwomen.

There is a crucial paradox in Romantic image making: It is a self-conscious process, and yet it is "the image of personality and not the mechanism that sets it in motion that is important."[7] In other words, the image can be satirized and rejected for the sake of another, but the very practice of imaginative self-stylization is not called into question. We may apply to the Romantics the term first employed by the Russian Symbolists and then elaborated by their critics: "life-creation," in Russian "zhiznetvorchestvo." It is usually understood as an imposition of an ideal or idealized grid upon everyday behavior in an attempt to achieve a perfect aesthetic organization of life.[8] Life-creation is a double-edged phenomenon. On the one hand, it reveals a highly stylized organization of everyday behavior that contributes to the literary image and thus might exclude or even reverse certain features of the poet's "real-life" charac-

ter, as in the case of Lermontov. On the other hand, by virtue of certain uncanny mechanisms, a literary image can turn into a poet's "second nature," and the poet's "real life" might become indistinguishable from the created one. Some of these mechanisms will be examined more closely in the discussion on Mayakovsky.

The middle of the nineteenth century can be regarded as a period of gradual demise of the Romantic legend and a transition to what have been called "realistic" codes of behavior, at once more eclectic and less stylized than what preceded them.[9] It led to some significant changes in the relationship between the author's life and text. The emphasis shifted from the poet—Romantic unique natural genius—to the writer, a professional author, or what in turn-of-the-century France was called "an intellectual." The direct relationship between the author's life and art became less apparent, less "metaphorical," so to speak. The author no longer cultivated the image of the Romantic hero, but rather preferred to be an invisible omniscient narrator behind the "realistic and objective" depiction of a world, someone without a personal legend. Obviously, as Donald Fanger has demonstrated, Realism hardly ever existed in its pure form, without additional qualifiers such as Romantic realism or poetic realism, and it often bordered on Naturalism and Symbolism, which makes it particularly difficult to draw clear distinctions between the movements.[10] At times the shift from Romanticism to Realism did not signify a plurality of genres or a reaction against the conventional Romantic pose, but rather a shift from Romantic idealism to Realist social determinism. In Russia this was particularly true for the writers called *raznochinets* (lower-middle-class intelligentsia) such as Nikolay Chernyshevsky, Vissarion Belinsky, Nekrasov, and others. This kind of social writing preserved the Romantic structure of image making but supplanted the figure of a Romantic individualist with that of a noble sufferer for humankind. On the whole, Realist aesthetics, in spite of its seeming antirhetorical and antitheatrical emphasis and its tendency to avoid excessive Romantic self-stylization, should not be regarded as lacking in life-creation. Still, its mechanisms and devices were less self-conscious, or less self-consciously exposed, and less spectacular and more subtle in their appeal to the reader than Romantic devices of self-fashioning.

One of the most interesting and symptomatic figures in nineteenth-century biographical criticism is Charles Augustin Sainte-Beuve. Sainte-Beuve in France, like Belinsky in Russia, shaped literary institutions and literary tastes of the time. His criticism presents an interesting mixture of the Romantic fascination for biography, the moralist preoccupa-

tion of the Enlightenment, and the scientific developments of the mid nineteenth century. It was he who coined the expression "l'homme et l'oeuvre," which dominated critical discourse for a long time. Sainte-Beuve formulated the kernel of his famous "scientific" method in this way:

> La littérature, la production littéraire n'est point pour moi distincte ou séparable du reste de l'homme et de l'organisation; je puis goûter une oeuvre, mais il m'est difficile de la juger indépendamment de la connaissance de l'homme même; et je dirais volontiers: tel arbre, tel fruit. L'étude littéraire me mène ainsi tout naturellement à l'étude morale.[11]

> Literature and literary production for me are not at all separate from the rest of the man and the organization; I can enjoy the work, but it is difficult for me to judge it independently of my knowledge of the man himself; and I will admit willingly, the fruit does not fall too far from the tree. Thus the literary study naturally leads me to the moral study.

Thus, in the center of Sainte-Beuve's method is not the study of the text, but of the portrayal of a "superior man, distinguished by his work," leading critics to analyze Sainte-Beuve's "families of spirits." Sainte-Beuve violently attacks the excessive rhetoric of traditional "unscientific" criticism and promotes a "natural method" based on the model of the natural sciences. As a result, the fear of rhetoric and a taste for scientific moderation often leads Sainte-Beuve to ignore the new preoccupation with language that becomes particularly crucial in the second half of the nineteenth century. A famous example of this is his blindness vis-à-vis the work of one of the major poets of modernity, Charles Baudelaire, to whom Sainte-Beuve dedicates only a brief appendix, after having written extensive studies and eulogies for many mediocre, conventional, and now-forgotten poets and writers. Thus, modernism in criticism starts with the attack against Sainte-Beuve, that is, with Proust's *Contre Sainte-Beuve*, a mixture of criticism, autobiography, and fiction in which Proust charges Sainte-Beuve with having missed the fundamental nature of the artistic process—depersonalization, precisely the loss of "l'homme" in "l'oeuvre."[12]

The term "modernist" is as problematic as the term "romantic" or "realist." As Romantics were often more classicist than they wished and Realists more illusionist than they admitted, modernists were often quite traditional.[13] Modern has been used in opposition to classical, traditional, or even romantic, particularly in the French and American tradi-

tions, while in the German context this opposition did not quite hold. Twentieth-century use of the term varies from country to country. For instance, the Spanish and Latin American term *modernismo*, which originated with Rubén Darío, refers more to a belated symbolist tradition, while in the Russian context "modern" is a style of turn-of-the-century architecture prone to Western influences and visually similar to northern European art nouveau. Moreover, in Soviet criticism from the 1930's till the early 1980's, the term had strong derogatory connotations; regarded as an ideologically incorrect "ism," it had to be combated with the proper "isms"—Socialist Realism and patriotism. Thus, "modern" is a modern term with numerous and diverse, sometimes contradictory, significations: by virtue of its controversial nature, it preserves its theoretical validity.

Several factors in the development of European and American capitalism through the nineteenth century affected the situation of literature and art in general.[14] The development of technology, the flourishing of newspapers and journals, and the birth of photography (later film) influenced the status of art or text, conditioned a new perception and new habits of reception, and threatened to extinguish the figure of the "homme de lettres," encyclopedic writer, and poet-prophet and turn them into mere specialists. With the decline of the patronage system and a shift toward the new market, artists were forced to fashion themselves as small businesspeople who were encouraged to produce original and creative work in exchange for fame and money. Fragmentation and separation of spheres of experience, and pluralization of worldviews and of social discourses, further consolidated the alienation and isolation of artists. Their repertoire of cultural roles changed: the genius was challenged by the engineer and scientist; the artist was threatened by the photographer; and the poet was superseded by the professional politician, professional writer, and professional journalist. The poet became an almost anachronistic figure—an alienated martyr of writing, an apolitical dandy, or an antisocial bohemian.

The question of modernity is at the very heart of the literary matter, since on the one hand the impulse to confront modernity stimulates the search for a new language, and on the other it can lead beyond the boundaries of the literary. A paradoxical self-destructive impulse marks all the waves of modern writers from the seventeenth-century author Charles Perrault, whose arguments against Classical literature often mix with arguments against literature-as-such, to Arthur Rimbaud, the major nineteenth-century precursor of the twentieth-century avant-garde, who stops practicing literature and lives out his desire for newness. The ten-

sion and interdependence of literature and life constitutes the central aporia of modernity: in the modern writer "the man of letters" always wrestles with "the man of action." As we shall see in Mallarmé, Maya-kovsky, and Tsvetaeva, both are threatened and seduced by the "woman of fashion," fashion often being regarded as the frivolous and superficial double of modernity and its infatuation with newness.

Modern artistic making of the self is marked by experiences of negativ-ity: the so-called death of the author, disfiguration, and de-facement of the artist, a gradual recognition of the subject's failure to impose poetic order upon a chaotic world. As far as biographical myths are concerned, the moderns rebelled against the glamorous figure of the Romantic poet and proclaimed his unglamorous death through writing. At the same time, unlike the Realists, they did not wish to hide the process of linguis-tic myth making or perpetuate the reader's mystification by means of the seemingly objective, omniscient pose of an invisible narrator. The figu-rative "death of the poet"—on the one hand, the erasure of the spectac-ular Romantic subject through the process of writing, and, on the other, the exposure of the invisible mask of the omnipotent, unselfconscious narrator of the nineteenth-century psychological novel—becomes essen-tial to modern(ist) self-fashioning. We encounter these features in West-ern European and American writings, as well as in Russian and Soviet ones: in Proust's *Contre Sainte-Beuve*, in Flaubert's *Correspondance*, in Mallarmé's *Crise de vers*, in the critical writings of T. S. Eliot and Wallace Stevens, in Mandelstam's *The Noise of Time*, and Pasternak's *Safe Con-duct*—to give just a few characteristic examples. At the same time, the new wave of moderns inherited a large and eclectic arsenal of images and representations of the artist's life and of the relationship between life and text.

The concept of the "autonomy of art," which dominates contemporary discussions of modernism, comes from different critical contexts, specif-ically from Russian Formalism and the German Frankfurt School. Here I will only touch upon the major cultural differences of the various theoret-ical elaborations of this concept. In the later reinterpretation of Peter Bürger, "autonomy of literature" presents a serious methodological prob-lem: it is a "category of bourgeois society" that at the same time reflects the actual state of things, the apartness of art from the praxis of life and refuses to acknowledge this state of things as part of a predetermined historical process.[15] Moreover, the artist can use his or her imposed de-tachment from society as a critical stronghold, from which accepted con-ventions of language and representation can be subverted, and the bour-

geois cultural myth of the objectivity, transparency, and anonymity of language can be dismantled. Furthermore—and this is where Bürger sees the difference between what he calls Aestheticism and the Avant-Garde—the artist can attempt to organize a new praxis of life from a basis in art.

The problem inherent in Bürger's and many other theories of modernism and the avant-garde lies in their often unconscious universalizing of one kind of European modernism. This results from privileging "major" European nations—England, France, and Germany—and excluding the others, thus consolidating a kind of cultural imperialism that the theorists themselves often criticize. For instance, in the Russian context, as will be examined in the discussion on Jakobson and Mayakovsky, the notion of the autonomy of literature never quite reflected the actual state of things and functioned more as a utopian construct. The process of economic and social modernization develops in diverse ways within the European continent—to say nothing of in the rest of the world. The artist as a cultural figure is much more important in countries fighting for national independence; in such countries as Poland, Italy, Spain, Greece, and others, Romantic myths surrounding the poet usually survive longer. In Russia and throughout the Soviet Union, where the cult of personality whether in reference to a tsar or a communist leader survives all ideological wars, the modern aporia of writing and life adopts quite different manifestations. Here the role of the artist or poet remains crucial both in the sphere of unofficial cultural myths and in that of the official ideology. The poet is perceived as the voice, vision, and conscience of the nation. In popular culture, poets are worshiped as much as, if not more than, tsars and party leaders. The autonomy of art, proposed and defended by the Russian Formalists immediately after the revolution and during the early 1920's, was an attempt to rebel against the burden of overpoliticization and excessive moralization of art.[16] Instead of being apolitical, as it has been perceived in later criticism, this notion was in fact politically subversive, exposing important political dimensions of the poetic language as well as rhetorical devices of ideological discourse. In the late 1920's and early 1930's the fight for the autonomy of literature turned into a strategy for the literature's survival, a way of protecting the poets—not from the figurative death of the author but from actual human death during the Stalinist purges of intellectuals.

In my reading the supposedly autonomous boundaries of literature will be consciously and continuously invaded. The autonomy of art and life will be regarded as one of the modern myths, one stylization of everyday

behavior among many. An attempt will be made to investigate the nature (or the nature and the culture) of the connection between "art" and "life" of the modern poet and describe their possible rhetorical relationship. Are they metaphorically or metonymically related to each other? How does this relationship shift through history, and within individual texts and individual lives? Which rhetorical devices in the texts themselves indicate a certain attitude toward life, or, rather, how do the texts influence the author's "pact with the reader?" How does one "read" an author's life? Should it be "read" at all?

My investigation of the modern author will be restricted to the poet for several reasons. Since Romanticism, the *poet* has been the primary example of the intersection of work and life and its poetic mythification. The poet as a figure continues to fascinate the reader. The power of the Romantic image of the poet still operates in the minds of readers and authors alike, setting up certain conflicting expectations. The poet's text plays with and pushes to their limits the conventions of language. The poetic function of language, according to Jakobson, makes linguistic signs palpable and visible, challenging the belief in the transparency and linearity of language.[17] (However, this slightly Romantic distinction between poetry and prose does not always hold true in modernist writing, which conflates genre conventions and juxtaposes various conflicting and disparate discursive codes.)

If the poet's text is an experiment in writing, the poet's life, as Yeats put it, is "an experiment in living." Therefore, it often presents in a more condensed form certain "conventions of living" that are characteristic for a specific time. In addition, the moment of modernity presents a vital challenge to poets and poetry, jeopardizing the very foundation of their existence. By the 1980's poets seemed to be more and more out of fashion culturally; a few exceptions such as the Russian émigré poet Brodsky, who received the Nobel Prize for Literature, only confirmed the rule. The role traditionally played by literature has been usurped by film and television, and the poet is substituted by an actor or, in the youth culture, by a rock singer.[18] The turn of the century and period between the two world wars were among the last crucial decades for poetic myth making, a myth making which dramatizes some tragic foreboding concerning the fate of poetry.

Gradually I will move away from the terms life and art and try to find a new way of speaking about their relationship, to elaborate a new (in most cases contextually new, but technically unoriginal) vocabulary to discuss peculiar cultural paradigms that traverse life and art, blurring their op-

position. I will seek alternative terms such as performance, theatricality, fashioning, figure, obscenity, and excess that do not constitute a single grid, a single semiotic or any other system, but rather function as slots of suggestiveness capturing, each in its own context, a similar transgressive interaction between life and art. One word, however, will be privileged— the infinitely suggestive word *death*, which disrupts many systematic orders.

Perhaps there is a fundamental link between the Western understanding of aesthetics and that of death. Since the Renaissance the anatomic theater has become the workshop of the artist and the theater of representation par excellence, which, in turn, demands an "anatomy of criticism." In the Western tradition, the creation of the artistic corpus seems to be predicated on the creation of the corps, be it the death of the other—re-presented, objectified, allegorized, as in Edgar Allan Poe's image of a beautiful woman whose death is the ideal poetic subject—or the death of the self, a self-effacement in the process of artistic production.[19]

In this book death and more specifically the death of the poet will be regarded in both figurative and literal terms. On the one hand, I will discuss the Mallarméan "elocutionary disappearance of the poet," the figurative murder of the "all-too-human" poet/Romantic hero, and the victory of omnipotent modern writing, in which the subject is endlessly sacrificed for the sake of the pure *oeuvre*. This figurative "death of the author" emphasizes the irrelevance of the poet's biography, its almost accidental or insignificant relationship to the text, which develops according to its own textual laws. Similarly, Flaubert proclaims the artist a monster in daily life, who must exist outside of any political, religious, or moral consideration. Thus, he stresses this exteriority of political, religious, and moral concerns to the magical craft of writing, proclaiming the necessity of the sacrificial murder of the artist's social persona and advocating self-inflicted monstrosity for the sake of the semisacred impersonality of writing. Figurative death can also be written in the plural and regarded—to use Tsvetaeva's expression—as the poet's own "self-defense," the figurative murder of poetic alter egos (biographically or culturally imposed images of the poet). Thus, Pushkin, in his "novel in verse" *Eugene Onegin*, kills the Romantic poet Lensky; Mayakovsky, in one of his manifestos, proclaims the "death of Mayakovsky-Futurist," and Marina Tsvetaeva attempts to murder "the poetess," a culturally inferior, parodic image of literary femininity.

On the other hand, the figure of death will reveal to us the instability

of other figures, which subverts any attempt to sustain clear, purely figurative boundaries. I will discuss several suicides of poets and examine what kind of cultural narratives, or "biographical legends," their tragic deaths generate and the ways in which they challenge critics and make problematic the relationship between "art and life." In other words, as Jakobson suggested, paraphrasing Mayakovsky, the actual death of the poet might turn into a *literary fact*.[20] Yet, it is a *literary fact* that prohibits clear boundaries between literature and life, revealing the uncanny "literariness" of life and the transgressive vitality of texts. The death of the poet is the ultimate act of "defamiliarization" that unearths complexities and contradictions of any seemingly coherent poetic, ideological, or critical system.

From the Death of the Author to a Poetics of Everyday Life

It is curious to note that in contemporary Structuralist (and post-Structuralist) critical vocabulary the expression "death of the poet" or "death of the author" is immediately associated with the figurative murder of the poet's biography by the critic—one of the cruel clichés of modernity. Since the 1960's the discussion of the artist's life has become outmoded in theoretical circles, an obvious and partly justifiable reaction to the simplistic examinations of poets' lives and the infatuation with picturesque biographic paraphernalia of time past.[21] At the same time, biography still flourishes as a popular nonfiction genre. Book stores feature biographies and periodicals and even local newspapers regularly review biographies of writers, actors, and politicians, whereas they review very few books of literary criticism. Although some of the biographies are quite interesting and well written, most of them are guided by the principles of popular psychology which help to explain the author's innermost crisis (that incidentally makes him or her create a masterpiece). They are also spiced with Romantic kitsch and descriptions of the author's sentimental attachment. The story of a writer's life is influenced by the biographer's own double bind of patronizing self-effacement and irreverent reverance toward the great genius, treated as a misbehaving child who has been generously forgiven. In American popular mythology, biography exists in the "real world" while literary criticism is written only for "academia." Thus, genre distinctions between more popular (or popularized) writing about the life of the author—a tribute to the tradition of Romantic readership and the general taste for literary gossip—and the

highbrow "scholarly," professionally textual analysis of the author's works are perpetuated by commercial publishers and academics alike, thereby protecting both the established boundaries of disciplines and their spheres of influence.

Three traditions of criticism have capitalized on the death of the author—Russian Formalism, American New Criticism, and French Structuralism. Within contemporary American academia both Russian Formalists and French Structuralists were read from the perspective of New Criticism, resulting in an interesting cultural appropriation. In fact, if we attempt to trace the national origins of the death of the author, the situation becomes increasingly confusing. The American New Critics were strongly influenced by the work of Eliot, who in turn was influenced by Valéry, Laforgue, and other French Symbolists who explored the fundamental links between death and representation in the Western tradition. In his "Tradition and the Individual Talent" Eliot makes a number of prophetic statements, such as "the progress of the artist is a continual self-sacrifice, a continual extinction of personality," and furthermore that "poetry is not a turning loose of emotion, but an escape from emotion; it is not the expression of personality, but an escape from personality."[22] Eliot uses two words in describing the poet's sacrifice of his or her personality to the written medium: "depersonalization" and "impersonality." Ultimately, he is much less interested in the enactment of the process of depersonalization than with the achievement of impersonality, which allows one to focus on poetry and tradition rather than on individual emotions and eccentricities. Eliot's tradition has been followed not only by a generation of American poets but also by professional academic critics— Ransom, Tate, Blackmur, Beardsley, Brooks, Wimsatt, and others through the 1940's and 1950's. They pioneered the concept of the "poetic persona" that still dominates critical discourse, which otherwise considers itself post–New Critical.

W. K. Wimsatt opens his programmatic book *The Verbal Icon* with the discussion of two fallacies—the "intentional fallacy" and the "affective fallacy."[23] Wimsatt attempts to trace very clear boundaries between what he calls criticism of poetry or cognitive science and the author's physiology, which is the subject of another, parallel discipline, that of literary biography, thus giving a theoretical justification for the separation of the nonfictional, popular genre of biography and the academic explanation of the texts. He makes a clear distinction between what he considers to be internal to the poem, that is, its verbal meaning—that which is at once public, democratic, shared by the community of readers, and explicable

by the discerning literary critic—and the "external, private and idiosyncratic evidence," which is "elitist" and exclusive in nature. The latter reveals "how and why the poet wrote the poem, to what lady, while sitting on what lawn, or at the death of what friend or brother."[24] We notice that even in that ironic description of a simplistic biographical account, which supposedly has nothing to do with the poem's meaning, there are certain presuppositions about the conventions of poetry writing, about the gender of the poet, and *his* leisure habits. Supposedly, these are so commonplace that they can be easily excluded from critical inquiry. New Critics created their own strong canon of what constitutes exemplary poetry, concentrating almost exclusively on the Anglo-American tradition, particularly the English metaphysical poets, and Eliot. They shaped their own idiosyncratic poetic tradition, which was to pass for public, democratic, and universal.

In one sense, the New Critical project was an attack on popular, simplistically Romantic notions about the figure of the poet and the poet's self-expression and an attempt to teach readers how to read poetry and pay attention to its linguistic devices instead of indulging in impressionistic descriptions and personal emotions. Also when considered in the context of the postwar American society and the educational reform of the 1950's, especially the GI bill which allowed new masses of students to attend college, the New Critics provided excellent pedagogical techniques for teaching literature that no longer relied on vast erudition and historical knowledge. In another sense, New Criticism while promoting the study of literature has also perpetuated American cultural myths of ahistoricity, objectivity, and the pragmatic value of "cognitive sciences" over "arts."[25] It consolidated the boundaries between different realms of inquiry and strengthened the opposition between subject and object, mind and body, reason and emotion. Perhaps there was also a personal stake in this criticism of the "personal heresy" of the poet: it guaranteed the professional identity of an academic critic.

Among American new New Critics (more diverse as a group than the old New Critics), there has been much questioning of the unity of the verbal icon with the development of the concept of intertextuality, with reexamination of Romantic subjectivity, with an interest in psychoanalysis and a renewed attention to the rhetorical devices that reveal the operations of desire, as well as with broadening of cross-cultural references.[26] However, apart from the Feminist critics, very few critics of poetry address the issues of biography and text. For the most part they rely on more sophisticated, contemporary elaborations of the figurative

death of the author, such as Roland Barthes's "Death of the Author," Michel Foucault's "What Is an Author?" (both authors draw from an early Maurice Blanchot text, "The Death of the Last Writer"), and Paul de Man's "Autobiography as De-facement," all influenced by the development of French Structuralism.[27]

De Man offers the most radical critique of the Romantic notion of the relationship between life and art. He makes problematic the very possibility of the genre of autobiography and rephrases the central question of classical mimesis. He skillfully demonstrates that at a certain rhetorical level it becomes undecidable whether life produces autobiography or vice versa: "We assume that life produces autobiography as an act produces its consequences, but can we not suggest with equal justice that the autobiographical project may itself produce and determine the life and that whatever the writer does is in fact governed by the technical demands of self-portraiture, and thus determined in all its aspects by the resources of his medium?"[28]

The demands of self-portraiture affect and shape the author's conception of life. Moreover, they deprive "life" of its "liveliness," permanently secluding it within deadly quotation marks. It is no accident that the exemplary autobiographical texts, texts which produce and are produced by what de Man calls life, are in fact inscriptions about death—for example, Wordsworth's *Essays upon Epitaphs*. And de Man's statement has a peculiar syntax: it is uttered without taking a breath, as if fearing to end the sentence, and it reflects a sense of existential urgency: "The language of tropes (which is a specular language of autobiography) is indeed like the body, which is like its garments, the veil of the soul as the garment is the sheltering veil of the body."[29]

This sentence is a rhetorical tour de force in itself. By means of the problematic expression "is indeed like"—technically, a simile, but with an excessive logic of persuasion that makes it *almost* an equation—de Man designs a metaphorical chain of linguistic garments, covering up the singularity of their folds and cultural fashions, to say nothing of all the potentially erotic excesses of the body. Later de Man demonstrates how "the garment," "the veil," and "the language of tropes" are potentially "deadly and violent as the poisoned coat of Jason or of Nessus."

But what happens to the famous concept of *difference?* How is it erased by the persuasive simile? What are the demands of self-portraiture and what kind of body is culturally accepted as normal? How does this rhetoric violate the abnormal body—female or foreign, for instance? Is there any tension between body, image, and writing? Are they, indeed, *trans-*

latable into one another? The question of body/writing translatability is not addressed by de Man. There is nothing in his text suggesting that body might exceed textual inscription or that its representation depends on a combination of languages—visual, cinematographic, sculptural, verbal—and a fluency in cultural mythologies. According to de Man, rhetoric provides a universal code of translatability. Thus, it is writing—the verbal language—that by means of the rhetorical device of prosopopoeia can posit voice, face, or body. Prosopopoeia, that is, personification or "impersonalization of an absent or imaginary speaker," is a violent weapon which helps verbal language take revenge against the body and nonverbal images, producing multiple body-look-alikes, phantasms, garments, imaginary incarnations that ultimately disembody the author. Writing has the power to personify the inanimate and to reify and disembody the person who produces it. What is called in everyday speech the "real-life" *person* and the literary *persona* becomes conflated in de Man, and the *persona* always wins, allowing the *person* a realization of the tragic existential, or rather linguistic, predicament—the predicament of mortality. ("Death is a displaced name for a linguistic predicament.") The last sentence of de Man's article carries the apocalyptic message in his usual mysterious and mystifying way, not without some grim irony: "Autobiography veils a defacement of the mind of which it itself is the cause."[30]

If for Barthes the text that precipitates the death of the author is at least erotic, for de Man it is completely deprived of seductive allure. Why multiply the illusions of liveliness? De Man's famous "undecidability" (in this case, the posited undecidability whether life produces the autobiography or vice versa) is usually rhetorically decided in his texts, his strategy being to push forcefully the most paradoxical, anticommonsensical, and anti-Romantic solution. The direction is always toward metonymy, allegory, and the recognition of the accidental, chaotic, and inanimate—the direction of death. The double movement, which undecidability or specularity should entail, is never enacted in de Man's own critical readings. Defacement and disembodiment are given much more space than the possibility of playful body language or a proliferation of faces. Mixing some blood, tears, or sweat with the ink is never considered. One can "play it safe" with the text, erasing—with the same irony and desperation that motivated Romantic figuration—the excesses of the body.

In earlier texts by Barthes and Foucault we find a similar passion for disfiguration. Michel Foucault ends his famous article "What Is an Author?" (published in French in 1969) with a radical replacement of one

set of questions with another: "No longer tiresome repetitions of 'What is the real author? Have we proof of his authenticity and originality? What has he revealed of his most profound self in his language?' . . . New questions will be heard: 'What are the modes of existence of this discourse? Where does it come from; how is it circulated; who controls it?' Behind all these questions we would hear little more than a murmur of indifference: 'What matter who is speaking?'"[31]

Repeating the Nietzschean gesture, Foucault proclaims the death of the author, the death of the Romantic demiurge as a necessary, *modern* sacrifice. But this strange excess—"little more than a murmur of indifference"—points to certain erasures in the critic's argument. From the outset, Foucault proposes to set aside the sociohistorical analysis of the author which involves an investigation into the systems of valorization and the development of literary institutions, focusing instead exclusively on the author as a function of discourse.

Foucault both shares the general Structuralist reaction against biographical criticism and goes one step further. For the historian of discursive practices the death of the author marks the modern condition. As if to follow Borges's aphorism that "every writer invents his own precursors," Foucault chooses the writings of Flaubert, Mallarmé, Proust, and Kafka to exemplify *the* modern work of art, a work of art in which "the writing subject endlessly disappears." Obviously Foucault's focus on discourse is different from the New Critical objectification of the text and the privileged pedagogical exercise of close reading. Not only does Foucault foreground the historicity of discursive practices but also, in his later work, he develops the notion of power, or rather, *powers* that manipulate discourses. And yet even in his later writings Foucault never discusses the problem of the author's making of the self, the myths of the writer, and the variety of modernisms throughout the world that might present alternatives to the Western European *episteme*.

Roland Barthes's argument of the "de-sacralization of the Author" and the subversion of the "Author's empire" develops along the same lines as Foucault's. Barthes elaborates the modern theory of writing (*écriture*) not as an emanation of the Romantic genius but as an anonymous performance, "a field without origin—or at least with no origin but language itself, i.e., the very thing which ceaselessly calls any origin into question."[32] The opposition between the body of the author and that of the text is traced in the first paragraph of the essay and is shaped by the definition of Barthesian "writing": "Writing is that neuter, that composite, that obliquity into which our subject flees, the black and white where all identity is lost, beginning with the very identity of the body that writes."[33]

The survivor in Barthes's ritual killing of the author is the reader, who is finally liberated from extratextual authority and who can now become a new kind of writer. One wonders, however, whether this reader of the "scriptible" text becomes as disembodied as the author.

In Barthes's and Foucault's later writings, however, which are considered less in American literary criticism, one observes a significant shift toward a further acknowledgment of subjectivity and—in the case of Foucault—its cultural development and techniques. Thus Foucault in his *History of Sexuality* is not so much concerned with sexuality per se, that is, in the nineteenth-century conceptualization of it, but rather with the "techniques of self" and more generally with the "aesthetics of existence." Moreover, in his interview Foucault emphasizes the need to put "the so called literature of the self . . . into the general and very rich framework of these practices of the self." [34] And yet the techniques of self of the modern defaced author remain undescribed. Perhaps, writing as a practice, which like the practice of sexuality continuously stages a conflict between eroticism and asceticism, deserves a history of its own parallel to the history of sexuality.

Barthes's critical rediscovery of pleasure in the early 1970's—first the pleasures of the text and then those of the writing subject—leads him away from the radical murder of the author. In *The Pleasure of the Text* the "erotic body" that occupies the critic is the body of the text itself, which gradually opens the space for the erotic figuration of the author who is "dead as an institution" but alive as the object of the reader's desire. [35] In *Roland Barthes*, Barthes's antiautobiographical writing that could be subtitled "Fragments of Autoerotic Discourse," the critic seeks the author's body which resists textualization. He attempts to capture what he calls the "unfashionable subject"—the subject "subtracted from the book"—and the subject "not banalized by literature." [36] Instead of representing the author's (or his own) body through a series of mythical images, Barthes wishes to inscribe it from within with all its unique tastes, drives, obsessions, desires, and appetites. What interests Barthes is not a gregarious, collective subjectivity but an individual body.

Interestingly, among the proposals for future books suggested in *Roland Barthes* we find, together with the "Encyclopedia of Food" and "The Discourse of Homosexuality," the following projects: " 'A Life of Illustrious Men' (read a lot of biographies and collect certain features, *biographèmes*, as was done for Sade and Fourier) and 'The Book/Life' (take some classical book and relate everything in life to it for a year)." [37] And yet there is one important factor that prevented Barthes from writing a book of writer's "biographemes"—his constant aversion to the "phantoms

of theater," which would be hard to avoid in figuring someone's life, as well as his resistance to the "image repertoire" especially in regard to literary figures. We can in fact trace a kind of dominant drama of the whole of Barthes's fragmented critical corpus from the 1950's to the 1970's: his fascination/repulsion for the cultural image is perpetually in conflict with his search for "writing degree zero" and the "neuter."

Already in the 1950's, parallel with the elaboration of the theories of "writing degree zero," Barthes explores "cultural mythologies" using mostly iconic visual images such as the face of Garbo or the emblematic cover of *Paris Match.*[38] In contrast to de Man, Barthes openly confronts the problem of the image, its power to fascinate, and its difference from the verbal message.[39] In his late essay "The Image," the image is to be regarded as a "social military service" from which one cannot be completely exempted, but which one can try to thwart.[40] Ultimately, the critic desires to "unstick" and "suspend" the image, especially as far as the personal "image-repertoire" is concerned, which can be easily canonized and manipulated by ideologists or sociologists. In the end Barthes insists that it is the text—disfiguring and playful—that remains the only antidote to cultural icons. In *Mythologies* Barthes demystifies the bourgeois author, the "writer on vacation" whose widely publicized humanity only highlights the divinity of his genius, but he never explores the biographical myth of modernist writers, who aimed at a utopian "degree zero" of the image. It is always extremely difficult to argue with Barthes, who himself anticipates his own traps and limitations and finds suggestive ways to circumvent them. My argument with Barthes is not really an argument, but rather an attempt to recover the artfully blurred figure of the martyr of modern writing that is self-consciously or unselfconsciously darkened on the background of Barthes's page.

But what kind of image of the author can be easily suspended? What are the conventional attributes of the supposedly neutral, "disposable" biography of the modern writer? What happens to those who do not die natural deaths? What is the closet drama of life bracketed by Foucault, suspended by Barthes, and ironically erased by de Man by means of persuasive simili? Why is the drama of writing considered to be in better critical taste? To examine these issues it is important to raise the curtain on the Russian Formalists—the critical predecessors of the French Structuralists and perhaps the most misread critics of the twentieth century—who more than fifty years ago anticipated many contemporary theoretical dramas.

In 1919 Roman Jakobson wrote that "to superimpose upon the poet

the thoughts expressed in his works" and "to incriminate the poet with ideas and emotions is as absurd as the behavior of the Medieval audience that beats the actor who played Judas."[41] Jakobson expresses the major concerns of the early Formalists—the desire to disengage the poet from his poetry and to place the major critical emphasis on the intrinsic qualities of the literary work, on its "literariness." Shklovsky made a similar "bloody" statement: "Art is fundamentally transemotional. 'Blood' in poetry is not blood . . . it is a component of a sound pattern, or an image."[42] These cruel scenes are familiar in the Western tradition of interpreting the Formalists and are correlated with the French Structuralist murder of the author. These pronouncements—shocking and radical in their own time—have become clichés of contemporary literary theory. They conform to the established view of Russian Formalism in the criticism of Western Europe and the United States, which tends to regard this movement as in opposition to both the biographical and the historical (or Marxist) approaches to literature.[43]

Obviously, in translating the Russian Formalists into Western European critical discourse much of the contextual foreignness has been disregarded. Here I am referring to the Formalist reactions against not only the dominant nineteenth-century Romantic and Realist "psychologism," which was a European turn-of-the-century trend, but also against the specific postrevolutionary Soviet Russian circumstances. What is often translated as the Formalist apolitical stance is in fact a reaction to the overpoliticized official bureaucratic jargon, a revolutionary discourse which became the discourse of power. Thus, at that time, protecting the autonomy and literariness of literature was a politically subversive gesture, not simply a reaffirmation of existing literary institutions. The Formalists' creative defacement through language was often directed against the official iconic uniformity, an imposed ideological defacement which crippled the writer and led to a death much more bloody and tragic than the figurative murder.

Moreover, due to the peculiar circumstances of the rediscovery of Formalist theory in the West, which coincided with the flourishing of New Criticism in the United States and the emergence of Structuralism in France, certain aspects of the Formalists' thought, particularly its diversity and its self-critical evolution, were often overlooked or underestimated. Thus, such distinguished Formalists as Yury Tynyanov, Boris Tomashevsky, and Boris Eikhenbaum, as well as their later disciple, Lidiya Ginsburg, and Soviet semioticians Yury Lotman and Boris Gasparov, attempted to elaborate new approaches to the writer's life. There is, how-

ever, no systematic corpus of Formalist work addressing the issue of "how the writer's life is made." I attempted to assemble a montage of various terms and fragments from the Formalist texts, usually known only by specialists and often not translated into English.

Yury Tynyanov, in the essays "Literary Fact," "On the Literary Evolution," and "On Parody," introduces the concept of "literary personality."[44] It coincides neither with the actual personality of the writer nor with his lyrical persona. The literary personality reveals the dynamic boundaries between literature and *byt* (here this refers to daily existence and "extra-literary" genres), showing how some facts of the poet's personal life can turn into literary facts and vice versa. Tynyanov's interest in the relationship between literary and other discourses demonstrates that contrary to many popular critical beliefs, the cultural project of the Formalists is not in opposition to that of Bakhtin. Tynyanov is concerned with what he calls cultural poetics of the author's life, rather than in psychological or psychoanalytical approaches. The literary personality is a product of literary evolution; it is shaped by the changing cultural myths surrounding the poet. Tynyanov writes: "The author's individuality is not a static system; the literary personality is as dynamic as the literary period in which and together with which it shifts. It is not a closed space that impersonates something or reveals something. Rather it is a broken line, broken and directed by the literary period."[45]

Tynyanov argues against the reemerging (or never-erased) Romantic cult of the genius, and yet, aware of the particularly important role of the poet and his mission in the Russian culture, he does not go to the other extreme of turning the author into a mere "function of the discourse." The issue is politically urgent and Tynyanov cannot bracket the sociohistorical considerations. In an extremely suggestive parenthetical comment in "Literary Fact" we find an interesting political comparison. Tynyanov remarks that "to attribute the peculiarity of the event and its evolutionary significance to the personal psychology of the creator is the same as to attribute the genesis and the importance of the Russian revolution to the personal idiosyncrasies of the leaders of the opposing camps."[46] Remembering that the essay was originally published in 1924—a crucial transitional year in Russian history, the year of Lenin's death and the emergence of his monumental personal cult—we observe how this comment highlights the political dimension of Formalism. In the Soviet Russian context of 1924, literary and ideological discourses were rivals, viewed as intimately linked and co-dependent, even when the political referent appears to be technically absent from the literary or critical text. At issue

was the question of which discourse to privilege, which to view as primary and paradigmatic for the other. For Tynyanov it is "literary evolution," a perpetual flux of discourses and boundaries of discourses, that shapes literary texts, literary personalities, and literary ideology. "Literary" always comes first in his concerns, not as a defacement of the author but rather as his cultural refashioning.

With de Man in mind perhaps we can ask where the genesis of the "literary personality" occurs—in life, in the text, or in the lore of cultural mythology. Tynyanov avoids the slippery question of origins. He suggests that there are certain "phenomena of style," however, such as confessional intonation, emotionalism, devices of personification or parody, that contribute to the poet's legend, helping the poet to form a peculiar "pact" with the reader.[47] In the example of the poet Alexander Blok, whose major literary theme is Blok, Tynyanov traces how style becomes the man, how style invites personifications (*olicenija*), which then transgress the boundaries of literature and are transferred to the person.[48] Unlike the New Critics, Tynyanov emphasizes the devices of personification rather than the structures of impersonality, perhaps because of the peculiar literary personality of Russian literary history and its cult of poets.

One of the central devices that helps to define literary personality is parody. Similar to the device of parabasis, often used in the Romantic drama when instead of a Romantic hero the audience contemplates an actor, the discourse of parody (parody of the self or of the other) forces the reader to see the author's person with his or her everyday gestures, in place of the literary persona. The parodied author is not murdered, but rather resurrected or reincarnated, styled as an actor in the estranging theater of Berthold Brecht or Vsevolod Meyerhold.

Boris Tomashevsky starts his article "Literature and Biography" with a parody of dogmatic Formalism.[49] He creates a literary personality of simplistic Formalism according to which any analysis of biography is "unscientific propaganda" and a "back-door" approach to literature. Unfortunately, it is this literary personality of Formalism that has been adopted in the West and has influenced most critical readings of the Formalists. Tomashevsky concentrates on the "literary functions of biography" that exist in the readers' minds as a traditional concomitant of the artist's work. What he calls a "documentary biography" does not concern him, since these biographies "belong to the domain of cultural history, on a par with the biographies of generals and inventors."[50] Tomashevsky elaborates on the notion of the "biographical legend"—"a literary conception of the author's life," a fiction co-authored by the poet and the

literary period. The biographical legend is perceptible as background for the literary work, as a premise which the author himself took into account during the creative process. Often, as Tomashevsky points out, "the poet considers as a premise for his creation not his actual curriculum vitae, but his ideal biography."[51] ("The reader" who perpetuates the author's legend according to Tomashevsky is usually the author's contemporary and compatriot, who shares the same core of cultural myths, expectations, and conventions of literary representation.) The obvious difficulty in Tomashevsky's approach is to demarcate between "documentary biography" and "biographical legend." My examination will show that it is not always possible to preserve unviolated the boundaries of different systems and fields of expertise. The documentary facts and the literary facts are co-dependent; they often intrude into one another's territory and blur the frontiers between the poet's "life" and "art."

Tomashevsky points to the historicity of the relationship between literature and biography and distinguishes between "writers with a biography," that is, those who like the Romantics demanded a legend, and "writers without a biography," that is, professional writers who did not need to be romantically heroic. However, unlike Foucault, he does not see the "death of the author" as an obligatory modern sacrifice. In fact, Tomashevsky observes how the Symbolists—Blok and Bely, among others—brought back the confessional lyrical autobiographic mode, while the Futurists "boldly inserted" their legendary biographies into the works themselves and did so in quite a hyperbolic fashion. Perhaps Tomashevsky would have argued that Foucault privileges writers without a biography and creates his theory exclusively on the basis of French and a few other Western European examples. Viewed from the cross-cultural perspective, it appears that behind Foucault's erasure of life, the Mallarméan *blanc*, there is an assumed normative middle-class, eventless life and an assumed historical context that makes it possible. It is not accidental that the first criticism of the Structuralist resistance to biography came from Feminist critics and from scholars of non-Western cultures or countries with a totalitarian regime, who refute a single model of modernism emphasizing cultural, gender, and historical differences. Interestingly, both Foucault and Barthes propose subtle distinctions between the terms "author" and "writer," the author being the one who writes "with the intransitive verb," who is a language professional, while the writer, alias intellectual, is someone who posits goals "of which language is merely a means."[52] However, the fact that the ability to trace those differences might vary greatly depending on the context remains overlooked.

In other contexts—such as, for instance, the Russian one—there is a different conception of what Eikhenbaum calls "the writer's fate," that is, a sense of the extreme importance of the writer's civic and spiritual mission, which cannot be erased from the Russian or Soviet collective cultural consciousness.

Among contemporary Soviet semioticians who already in the 1960's and 1970's went beyond the official Soviet rhetorical-ideological criticism and primitive biographical gossip, Yury Lotman and Lidiya Ginsburg appear to be the most faithful followers of Tynyanov and Tomashevsky. Lidiya Ginsburg examines the literary models for such personality types as the "natural man," "superfluous man," "romantic hero," and so on, proposing to use literary patterns and conventions in an interpretation of life, particularly the life of a poet.[53] Developing further the idea of the biographical legend, Lotman analyzes the "theatricality of daily life," and what he calls "the poetics of everyday behavior," using the example of the eighteenth- and nineteenth-century Russian culture.[54] In his new "biography" of Pushkin, Lotman discusses Romantic and Realist lifestyles and demonstrates how Pushkin plays with the plurality of styles in his life, as well as in his art.

Lotman's valorization of the Realist, or what he sometimes calls the prosaic approach to life, which goes beyond the Romantic or poetic pur- and monological unity of style in all existential activities, is somewhat similar to Bakhtin's privileging of the *heteroglossia*, that is, multivoicedness, which he finds in Dostoevsky's novels. Lotman concludes that Pushkin "entered Russian culture not only as a poet-genius, but also as a genius-master of life."[55]

Boris Gasparov, in his introduction to *The Semiotics of Russian Cultural History*, which includes works by Lotman and Ginsburg, examines the theoretical foundations of the Soviet disciples of the Formalists that lead to what can be called a "reverse mimesis" of life and art.[56] He argues that literature, unlike everyday life, possesses a high degree of internal organization. Consequently, while operating within a single cultural system the paradigms of the literary text can be imposed upon the chaos of everyday life (*byt*) and reveal within that chaos a certain model having a distinct structure and meaning. The examination of the literary text allows the critic to discern important cultural configurations recognizable by the members of that culture.

In the relationship between art and life, Gasparov emphasizes literature's twofold influence upon life. On the one hand, the structures of literature influence life directly. Lidiya Ginsburg gives us an example of

this phenomenon in her discussion of the nineteenth-century Russian revolutionary Decembrists whose politics and everyday behavior were shaped by Romantic poetics. On the other hand, artistic structures offer an ideal model for describing the multifaceted processes of society. Texts are a kind of crystallization of floating, formless cultural codes that exist in a society.

But what happens to the literary text when it is reduced to the ideal metaliterary model? What kinds of literary texts would best qualify for modeling? What happens to modernist texts, for instance, Mallarmé's "Coup de dés" or Mandelstam's *The Egyptian Stamp,* which self-consciously dramatize the eruption of chaos within textual structures? It seems that what one can extrapolate from them, if one wishes to remain a faithful reader, is not the paradigm but the very tension between structuring and entropy, the very impossibility of creating clear-cut paradigms and critical systems.

Although the work of Lotman, Ginsburg, Gasparov, and Bakhtin was a great inspiration to me, I notice a conspicuous absence or scarcity of twentieth-century examples in their critical investigations. In his discussion of the poetics of everyday behavior Lotman limits himself mostly to what he calls Romantic and Realist conventions, avoiding the consideration of distinctly modern and modernist texts of life and literature, texts characterized by—to quote Foucault—the "radical shattering of the discourse." There is, of course, an obvious "contextual" explanation for this—the difficulty that any Soviet critic of the 1970's encountered in using contemporary examples, considering the dangers of both external and internal (internalized) censorship. However, apart from political circumstances, but also to some extent conditioned by them, there has been, at least until very recently, a general tendency in all branches of Soviet criticism to deface the literary personality of modernism, to disregard it contemptuously as a fashion and see it as yet another Romantic disguise, or as another exemplification of the Romantic/Realist tension. It is at these critical crossroads—between French and Soviet Russian critics, between the modernist, disfiguring practice of writing and the proliferation of ancient and modern biographical legends—that I would like to elaborate the distinctly modern cultural mythologies of the poet's life and death.

The Theater of the Self: Myth, Fashion, and Writing

The examination of the nuances and complexities of the modern death of the poet in writing and in life requires a construction (or a reinvention) of

a dynamic critical vocabulary. We have observed that "modernism" is defined by a peculiar practice of writing which explores the boundaries of language and of the writing subject and questions linear temporality and chronology. This practice of language aims at the suspension of the cultural image repertoire, especially that of the author, who, as in the case of Mallarmé, confronts the reader with a frightening disfiguration. There develops a certain preconception of a privileged interiority of writing, which is then celebrated by the critics as the author's successful escape from the iconic profanations and popular theater of everyday life. Hence there is a need to reestablish the cultural framing of this modernist practice of writing—not to inscribe it completely within a rigid historical and ideological frame but to be able to describe it adequately from a broader cultural perspective. I would argue that the modernist resistance to framing and the privilege of the interiority of writing might be regarded as myths. The death of the author can be seen as a proclamation of his immortality, the erection of a peculiarly modernist monument.

Barthes's *cultural myth* will be a crucial concept in my discussion. Barthes did not apply his concept of cultural myth to the life of the author, or to the problem of the self in general. The Formalist notions of "literary personality" and "biographical legend" help to bridge this gap.

Cultural myth is neither an archetypal, universal, Jungian myth, nor a personal myth, a whimsical product of the individual subconscious. It is an unwritten law shared by the community, a law that is difficult to repudiate because it seems to be natural, unauthorized, given. It transforms culture into nature and aims to mask its ideological implications by erasing its historicity. According to Barthes, cultural myth constitutes a kind of anonymous depoliticized discourse which pretends to be nonideological and transparent. It masks its historicity under the disguise of universality and atemporality. As Barthes says, "Myth does not deny things, on the contrary, its function is to talk about them; it simply purifies them, it makes them innocent, it gives them a natural and eternal justification, it gives them a clarity which is not that of an explanation, but that of a statement of fact."[57]

In the first edition of his *Mythologies*, Barthes proposes a graphic model of the cultural myth whose object is the linguistic sign; accordingly it becomes a metalanguage. Later he abandoned this hierarchical model, although it survived much longer in the studies of Barthes's disciples. In my opinion, the cultural myth should not be regarded as a secondary semiotic system, that is, as a cultural sign built on the linguistic (Saussurian) sign, like a Russian doll (*matreshka*). Linguistic and cultural spheres are interdependent and culture cannot be examined as a large

wooden dummy which has a smaller but identical wooden dummy (language) inside it, or even as several wooden dummies, one inside the other (subculture, sub-subculture, language, dialect, subdialect, and so on and so forth).

Cultural myth is neither a secondary linguistic system nor a metalanguage describing another language; the student of cultural myths is not a metacritic. Barthes revised his earlier conception of myth in the preface to the 1971 edition of *Mythologies*.[58] Here Barthes indicates that the problem lies not in demystifying or demythifying "bourgeois myths," which has become a convenient critical myth, but in the fissures of the representation itself, in the fluctuation of the sign. The task now consists not of *naming the myth*, but of *retracing the mythical* in phraseology, stereotypes, and references. There is a certain parallelism between the Barthesian critique of Barthes's early notion of myth and Bakhtin's critique of semiotics. The Soviet semioticians developed their own theories of the "typology of cultures." Culture is regarded as a system of information or a system of social codes that permits communication of this information by means of signs. Bakhtin criticizes the notion of code because it allows for both the development of a hierarchy of systems and the concept of metalanguage. Instead he proposes the notion of a dialogical utterance that collapses the levels of discourse and does not allow the cultural critic to establish an absolute scientific distance from the object of analysis.[59]

There is continuous dialogue, interaction, interpenetration, and superimposition of various "systems," or discourses, as well as close intertextual ties, between the linguistic and the cultural elements of myth. In fact, what are often considered to be purely linguistic conventions, such as the uses of masculine and feminine pronouns, the uses of "I," and the rhetoric of clarity, can have broad cultural implications.

Thus the cultural mythologist has to experience a perpetual identity crisis. The cultural mythologist (who should always be a cross-cultural mythologist) is not a distant, objective scientist; he or she must take a borderline position, neither inside nor entirely outside the culture. This position involves a continuous interplay of distance and involvement, estrangement and engagement.[60]

However, individual experience is obviously limited both temporally and spatially. Thus, in my attempt to discern the cultural myths of poets, I will usually rely on a superimposition of several texts, which reveals a certain cluster of significations. This cluster of meaning might be found in a fixed, idiomatic phrase such as "pure poet" or "revolutionary poet,"

or even the single word "poetess," that has important cultural connotations. I attempt to trace some of its history and try to see how it operates in the modern period and how it is reshaped by the modernist practice of writing. The clusters which I have chosen to examine certainly do not exhaust all the possibilities of cultural repertoire available to poets. They do expose, however, crucial issues of modernism, such as the relationship between poetry and politics, poetry and gender, as well as the emergence of a poetry that refuses to be regarded in relation to anything other than itself.

What is particularly elusive about cultural myth is the fact that it does not depend entirely on written language. It is both difficult and challenging for students of literary criticism to see the limits of the verbal empire they construct around themselves. The cultural myth largely relies on unwritten but widely accepted, naturalized nonverbal discourse, on the power of the image and its semivisible, heavily codified iconography, as well as on cultural fashioning and social masks used in the "theater of everyday life."

The metaphor of the theater will be crucial in my examination of the cultural self of the poet. I assume that there is a limited cultural repertoire of roles, with their necessary visual and dramatic attributes, which are enacted and reshaped in each individual performance. There is no script for these roles, no compendium of cultural myths of the self written in the ideal metalanguage, a sort of critical Esperanto. The roles are not written anywhere in anything resembling a paradigmatic language of pure codes. Rather, they are realized in the course of individual performances, and their common attributes can be traced through their mutual superimposition. Hence, the relationship between life, art, and culture is not that of a mimesis, or a hierarchy, but rather that of a chain of rehearsals based on a certain limited repertoire (which, nevertheless, can offer a relatively unlimited number of combinations). This chain of rehearsals neither starts with the definitive original script nor ends with a final master performance. It is in a process of constant modification. Certain roles can be provisionally reified and described in order to understand the ongoing process. The death of the poet is a crucial poetic act and a crucial critical metaphor. It can be seen as an ultimate fulfillment of certain strategies and potentialities in the text, or as a provocative disruption of any unifying critical system.

To focus on the cultural myth of the poet might be particularly illuminating, because the poet is someone who is both creative and created, who is directly in touch with the language and therefore possesses maxi-

mum flexibility in role playing. At the same time, poets might stylize themselves excessively, making their attributes and theatrical makeup more visible. I wish to elaborate the notions of cultural image, cultural fashions, self-fashionings, and theatricality further, since they have been frequently excluded from the iconoclastic accounts of modernist writing.

The metaphor of the theater has emerged in various contexts in the examination of both the French and American critics, as well as the Soviet Russian Formalists and semioticians.[61] The French Structuralists and post-Structuralists focus primarily on the drama of writing, which protects its interiority and autonomy, while the Formalists begin to examine the "literary masks" of the writer and acknowledge their inescapability. The use of theatrical metaphors in everyday life and in literary criticism is tremendous. The very terms which apply both to the real-life self and to the literary self of the author (literary persona or personality) are etymologically related to the Latin word *persona*, theatrical mask. Perhaps, person, persona, personage, and personality are only different kinds of masks that suggest various degree of self-dramatization. In French *personne* also signifies "nobody," while in English "person" means precisely the opposite—"somebody." The etymological development of the two languages reflects two opposite ways of looking at the theatrical predicament of a human being, two opposites that paradoxically converge, as in the title of the Borges story about Shakespeare entitled "Somebody and Nobody."

"Mask" here does not imply a superficial disguise that hides the "real self." In fact, in traditional theatrical performances the interaction between actor and mask is very complex. The Kabuki actor, for instance, studies himself wearing the mask before a mirror for several days, for "one feels like a bamboo when one looks at a bamboo."[62] In other words, the actor identifies with his new image and becomes it (a sort of adult reenactment of the Lacanian "mirror-stage," during which a child identifies with his or her ideal flat mirror image). Greek and Roman actors undertook long silent communions with their masks before putting them on, in order to be receptive to them. Contemporary actors who work with masks note that they both hide and reveal. While they seem objects behind which one can physically hide and characterizations that "mask" one's emotions, they reveal crucial human features which go beyond individual character traits. Thus, in ancient rituals, as well as in the twentieth-century avant-garde theater of Artaud, Meyerhold, and others, the mask is often regarded as a typified image, closer to the intersubjective "self" than an actual face. In this conception the mask is no longer

"outside" but rather a representation of the "inside." The paradox of the mask consists precisely in its ambivalence: in different moments in history and in different theaters it has been seen as a metaphor of exteriority, as an exterior superficial disguise, and by contrast as a metaphor of a deep, hidden, depersonalized inner self, an image of intersubjectivity.[63]

Furthermore, there are different intermediate states between being totally masked and completely unmasked. Wearing makeup, which can be subtle or ostentatious, is one example. It is no accident that one of the first major statements of modern poetics—Baudelaire's "Le Peintre de la vie moderne" ("The Painter of Modern Life")—includes a praise of makeup, in which feminine makeup is regarded as a metaphor for modern art.[64] The masks of the commedia dell'arte, for instance, are also half-masks; they reveal the mouth and chin and allow interaction between parts of the face and the mask. Thus, the metaphor of the mask, always incomplete, always in the process of transforming and being transformed by the body and face of the actor, the mask that hides and reveals all the complex interrelationships between persona, personality, and the French personne, serves as a useful metaphor in the discussion of literature and life. One of the central questions that will be explored in my book is precisely whether a complete "unmasking," a complete "laying bare" of cultural clothing, is possible. I will try to follow the traces of blurred makeup on the poet's defaced figure.

In fact, the Western concepts of identity and individuality are closely linked to the metaphor of the theater. Even Freud uses Sophocles' play to tell his revelatory psychoanalytical story of the self; moreover, he calls the unconscious "another theater." Elizabeth Burns writes in *Theatricality* that the actor mimes the dominant concept of "identity" in a given period, or in other words the actor's craft reflects the existential human condition.[65] The movement is from sacred to social, from the medieval notion of acting as an allegorical "personification" of moral virtues and vices that refers to human beings in relation to the unseen world of spiritual reality, to the Renaissance "impersonation" of various social types— "a portrayal of a person through imitation of behavior, derived from observation and experience of ordinary life"—from "homo sub specie aeternae" to "uomo singolare e unico."[66] It is no accident that the metaphor of *theatrum mundi* becomes a philosophical cliché precisely in the Shakespearean Renaissance world, when people become acutely aware of the theater of everyday life—not only a transcendental tragedy of the human predicament written in heaven but also a secular comedy of manners, and later even a sentimental melodrama that is acted and directed

by the characters themselves. "Theatricality" here does not simply refer to the theater as one of the artistic genres or media; rather, it points to a certain ontological and social condition. In other words, it points to the "vital" element in theater, to what theater dramatizes and foregrounds in life, and to what makes us call "life" theatrical and theater "lifelike"— an interaction between playfulness and conventionality, prescriptiveness of roles and the singularity of acts.

It is curious, however, that through the centuries the obvious linguistic link between "persona" and "personality" became culturally veiled. Moreover, they were viewed in opposition to each other, the mask turning into a cover-up, a superficial disguise of the "person." On the nineteenth-century theatrical stage this opposition is reflected in the growing negative attitude toward the use of masks—they are preserved only in popular spectacles such as the commedia dell'arte. Twentieth-century theater witnesses the return of the stylized mask, as a sign of the alienated, depersonalized self and, according to Artaud, as an expression of the desire for a new, universal reintegration through the reenactment of a cruel primitive spectacle.

As Jonas Barish demonstrated in his fascinating book *The Antitheatrical Prejudice*, the "antitheatrical prejudice" runs through the whole of Western intellectual history from Plato to Artaud.[67] The argument against theatricality is at the cornerstone of Plato's *Republic*. Theatricality is a kind of human malaise, a superficial fondness of spectatordom, posing, grimacing, affection, in short, a fondness for the transient world of appearances, for the aberrant imitation of imitations. Plato builds his own utopian republic—a totalitarian philosopher-state—in opposition to what he calls "an evil sort of theatrocracy," a rein of superficially innovative poets and decadent theater people who are incapable of capturing the essential archetypes.[68] This paraphrase is an obvious vulgarization of Plato, but it helps to summarize the antitheatrical legend, a cultural prejudice that keeps reappearing throughout European intellectual history under varying disguises. My hypothesis is that the modernist practice of language—as elaborated by Flaubert, Mallarmé, and the contemporary French theorists, especially Barthes—the practice of language in which the drama of writing displaces the social theatricality of life and the "phantoms of the theater" in general, can be seen as a variation on the antitheatrical prejudice that dates back to Plato.[69]

Another term that is related to theater as well as to modernism is "fashion," both as a verb and as a noun. The attention to fashion allows us to highlight the visual attributes and characteristic attire in the cultural myth of the poet, pointing beyond the distinctions of life and art.

A problematic configuration of modernism and fashion deserves a special consideration. The word "modernism" from the Latin *modo*, "just now," which emphasizes the immanence of the present tense and capitalizes on newness, is also related to "mode" as in way of thinking, behaving, dressing, and, in Romance languages, to *mode/moda* (feminine), meaning "fashion"—an association that generates many derogative connotations, usually activated by self-righteous satirists of the "moderns." Fashion, especially in the German tradition, is seen as a "false newness," or false sublation. Even de Man insists on preserving the distinctions between "fashion" and "modernity." His description of fashion sounds rather Romantic: "Fashion (*la mode*) can sometimes be only what remains of modernity after the impulse has subsided—as soon—and it can be almost at once—as it has changed from being an incandescent point in time into a reproducible cliché . . . Fashion is like the ashes left behind by the uniquely shaped flames of the fire, the trace alone revealing that the fire has actually taken place."[70] Fashion, especially in the context of German criticism, is seen as a monstrous double of the modern quest for newness, deprived of the aura of uniqueness and converted into a "reproducible cliché."

The history of the usages of the word fashion demonstrates a spectacular cultural degradation. Stephen Greenblatt examines its cultural etymology and remarks that it gains a particular significance in the sixteenth century, concurrently with the spread of the metaphor of *theatrum mundi*: "As a term for action, or a process of making, for particular features or appearances, for a distinct style or pattern, the word has been long in use, but it is in the sixteenth century that *fashion* seems to come into wide currency as a way of *designing* and forming the self."[71]

Fashioning and self-fashioning are a kind of secular/social "self-creation," distinct from the medieval "imitation of Christ." They presuppose an increasing recognition of the theatricality of daily life and of the possibility to choose one's own repertoire, to represent oneself. Greenblatt notes that "self-fashioning derives its interest precisely from the fact that it functions without regard for sharp distinctions between literature and social life."[72] It is enacted across the border, through representations and self-representations in all the spheres of human activity. In other words, certain similar fashions traverse the culture of the period, and operate in literature and life—interlocking them and preventing the critic from compartmentalizing them. A Romantic poet, a revolutionary poet, a poetess, a martyr of writing, a poet-pariah, a poet engagé, an *enfant terrible*, a prophet, a *voyant*, a voyeur, a dandy, a bohemian, a professional writer, a poet without biography, a poet-functionary of the

State, a poet-monument, an academic—these are only some of the imprecise names for cultural fashioning. Fashion designates that peculiar
space of vital intertextuality, or, as Shoshana Felman puts it, "vitality of
texts" and "textuality of life," that might help us reshape the figure of the
poet, and give us a broader insight into the making of the self in general.
The study of fashions might unveil some spectacular theatrical underwear
of the self, the self that can never be "layed bare" and exempt from everyday dramas. Even the pure poet is not completely unfashionable.

In fact, "fashion" originates from the same verb as "poetry," "to
make"—*facere* in Latin and *poein* in Greek. Thus in my paradigm poetry
and fashion are related like person and personality, or like person and
personne. This correspondence further complicates the distinctions between the "self" and the "mask," between the writing self and the everyday persona, between writing and acting, between the disfiguration and
proliferation of images.

In this book I will examine further the modern conjunction of poetry
and fashion. The poet's cultural fashionings present an extreme case, a
knot of contradictory representations, which exaggerate, intensify, "defamiliarize," and help to reveal fundamental elements of any human ad-
aptation to our theatrical predicament. The contemporary meaning of the
word fashion—"the current style or custom in dress and behavior"—is
not foregrounded in Greenblatt's illuminating readings. At times fashion
appears too superfluous and transient for analysis. My readings, however,
will explore how clothes signify in poetry and in the development of the
biographical legend. I will combine *clothes reading* and *close reading*,
demonstrating the impossibility of a complete "disclosure" or laying
bare of the poetic text. This way a certain double movement will be
established between dressing literary texts in cultural attire and
inscribing cultural images of poets onto the subversive practice of
writing.

My focus will be precisely on the tension between the cultural image/
mask/myth and the individual practice of writing. I will regard the practice of writing as one of the outstanding everyday practices that both contributes to and resists self-theatricalization. What interests me here is not
biography, but rather life in quotation marks and biographical legend. I
will show how poets articulate the relationship between their life and art
and how the poet's writing both depends upon and challenges his or her
intentionally created, unintentionally assumed, or forcefully imposed,
cultural mask. Although my investigation of "life" will be limited to the
biographical legend or to life as a literary fact, I will emphasize with

specific examples the difficulties of drawing clear boundaries and of defining which one is primary: writing or experience, literary fact or fact of daily life. The death of the poet, both figurative and nonfigurative, will challenge the stability of the boundaries between disciplines, the spheres of experience and texts, and expose the fragility of a figure—rhetorical or otherwise.

Lidiya Ginsburg describes the conflict that inspired her discussion of the poetics of everyday behavior as between "individual interior life and the historic character." [73] Instead, the conflict at the center of my examination is between the individual practice of language, particularly the modernist practice of language with all its abysmal gaps and depersonalization, and the cultural mask of the practitioner of that language. Cross-cultural readings of the plurality of modernisms will prevent us from constructing a "strawman" modernist martyr as a single and universal model, revealing instead that the "modernist" self-fashioning has more "Romantic," "Realist," and "postmodern" features than we are often accustomed to acknowledge.

In each of the chapters I examine a specific instance of the death of the author that challenges the practice of close reading. I regard each poet as a poet-plus-qualifying-adjective, even if he or she was a "pure poet." In Chapter 1 I focus on the legend of a poet without a biography—the legend of Mallarmé's "defacement" and some peculiar figurations of this defacement created by his contemporaries. From Mallarmé's self-effacement in text I move to Rimbaud's stopping writing and explore the relationship between text and body and the limits of literary practice.

In Chapter 2 I investigate the relationship between poetry and politics, centering on the myth of the revolutionary poet and exposing the tension between poetry and engagement, writing and acting, literariness of politics and politicization of text. Also, my analysis will show how Mayakovsky's transgressive theatricality, a self-conscious and unself-conscious role playing that spreads throughout all his activities, becomes contagious and infects his critics and readers. Often, they end up using Mayakovsky's favorite device, that of omnipotent metaphor, of making the most accidental details of daily life significant and signifying (such as Mayakovsky's yellow blouse). In this way his critics turn certain elements in the poet's life and art into key metaphors to expose their own political and poetic positions.

In Chapter 3 I explore the relationship between poetry and gender, focusing on the cultural figuration of literary femininity, on the grotesque

image of the "poetess" and her gaudy attire. I will attempt to reveal what is hidden behind both the claim of a universal poetic genius and the genderless impersonality of modernist writing. At the center of my discussion is the figurative and nonfigurative death of the Russian woman-poet Marina Tsvetaeva, who hanged herself in the small Siberian town of Elabuga and whose place of burial remains unknown. I will explore how the cultural mask of the poetess can entrap, challenge, and seduce the woman-poet and how the poet's death can be written in the transcendental neuter (which in some cases veils the masculine) and in the tragic feminine.

Finally, I will add a few questions to the end of Foucault's essay "What Is an Author?": What are the limitations of the critical discourse that excludes the poet's "biographical legend" from the scope of inquiry? Does it presuppose a certain normative, eventless modernist biography? Can it be regarded as a cultural luxury? What is the context of the poet's death? What cultural myths and critical narratives does it generate? What are the politics and poetics of constructing a biography? What happens when the poetic and political myths characteristic of one culture are transplanted to another? Does it lead to universalism, internationalism, or mistranslation? Is there a connection between myth making and misreading? What kind of vital interaction exists between making a life and making a work of art?

Edouard Manet, Portrait of Stéphane Mallarmé. *Paris Louvre. Courtesy Giraudon/Art Resource* (top)

Ernest Pignon Ernest, Rimbaud in Paris. *Courtesy Editions Hazan* (bottom)

· 1 ·

The Death of the Author: Stopping Living and Stopping Writing

The "Book" and the "Life": Mallarmé and Rimbaud

Je suis parfaitement mort.
Stéphane Mallarmé

Je suis réellement d'outre tombe.
Arthur Rimbaud

The myths of Mallarmé and Rimbaud represent two extremes of the modern crisis of literature and are often seen as opposites. For Stéphane Mallarmé, the poet's life is supposed to be ritually sacrificed for the sake of the drama of writing. Mallarmé leads what he calls the eventless life of a professional English teacher and family man, and he proudly claims that his life lacks extraordinary romantic adventures. Meanwhile, he aspires to compose the universal book, "le Livre," one that would present an ultimate explanation of the world.

The opposite is the case for Arthur Rimbaud. He abandons poetry for the sake of the drama of life. The poet stops writing at the age of twenty, after having created extraordinarily innovative and precocious works, and undertakes a series of journeys in search of true modern life ("la vraie vie"). He attempts to enlist in the army, then goes to the Orient and to Abyssinia where he makes a living as a trader and occasionally as an arms dealer. At his death he leaves a bundle of prosaic, nonliterary letters full of pragmatic details and descriptions of Abyssinian ennui.

Mallarmé, crowned as the Prince of Poets, dies at the age of fifty-six in his country home in Valvins. Rimbaud, at thirty-seven, dies in the Marseilles hospital, known only to a small group of friends and Abyssinian arms dealers.

Mallarmé elaborates his theory of modernity in the form of the intergeneric poetic essay "Crise de vers" ("Crisis of Verse"). Rimbaud, having proclaimed that "one must be absolutely modern," feels the need to abandon literature and to seek modernity in extreme vital experiences following "the march of progress."[1] If Mallarmé capitalizes the book, which in its foldings and infinite expansion of letters will express the complexities of the world, Rimbaud capitalizes life and questions the power of literature as a practice and as an institution.

One can write two different histories of modernity starting from Mallarmé or Rimbaud. The path of Mallarmé would lead us to the figure of the autonomous author, the author without a biography, whose self end-

lessly disappears in the text. At the same time, this "writerly text" (to use Barthes's expression) endlessly reproduces the scripts of metaphorical suicide, ensuring the survival of the literary establishment. This path will extend from Mallarmé through Paul Valéry, T. S. Eliot, Wallace Stevens, and Jorge Luis Borges to the author's critical tombs recreated by Michel Foucault, Roland Barthes, and the American New Critics.

The other path might be slightly less comfortable for the academic institution of literary criticism. The path of Rimbaud, full of vital and literary discontinuities, will lead us to the avant-garde tradition, not so much the tradition of the death of the author, but rather that of the death of literature. Obviously, the very expression "avant-garde tradition" is problematic: it reveals a failure of the utopian avant-garde project by merging artistic and social revolutions and points to the incorporation— even if problematic—of the avant-garde into the history of art. Rimbaud was a mythical precursor of the Surrealists, one of the rare precursors who can claim to be both a "Surrealist in writing" and a "Surrealist in life." The myth of Rimbaud presents a constant threat to the modern literary institution. If read in Rimbaud's fashion, the very expression "modern literature" is in danger of being oxymoronic. Rimbaud challenges the myth of the poet as a privileged spokesman for modernity or for modern self-consciousness. He demonstrates that the myth of the poet can coexist with many other modern myths—the myth of the explorer, of the scientist, or of the "man of action."

Mallarmé, on the contrary, wishes to make modern synonymous with literary by modeling the crisis of modernity on the crisis of verse. He reacts against positivistic discourse and sociological theories of historical progress, which tend to present themselves as linguistically transparent and do not problematize the complexities of language and representation. Mallarmé challenges both the romantic myth of life as literature and the positivist myth of "real life" (or in the contemporary American version, "the real world"), which has nothing to do with fiction. In Mallarmé's terms, literature (especially free-verse poetry practiced by a creatively self-effacing subject) is the only real life, and the most vital action takes place in the process of writing. Thus, according to Mallarmé, the expression "modern literature" is almost pleonastic, since both modernity and literature force one to confront the linguistic manipulations and the complexities of representation.

Yet Mallarmé and Rimbaud were both informed by the same historical and cultural context. Both reacted to the fading role of the poet in their society and to the fragmentation of social discourses that raised linguistic

awareness. The superimposition of the myth of Mallarmé and the myth of Rimbaud will force us to question the radical quality of the modernist gesture of each—Mallarmé's attempt to erase his everyday biography, which is, figuratively speaking, an attempt to stop living outside one's texts, and Rimbaud's attempt to forget his poetic past and to stop writing literature altogether. What kind of life can one consider eventless, neutral, and historically insignificant, and what kind of literature can one cease to practice? In other words, when does literature stop being vital and when does life stop being literary? Is the gap between the two starting points critically unbridgeable? Why do the founders of the critical death of the author, Foucault and Barthes, avoid the path of Rimbaud? Why is Rimbaud excluded from the revolution in poetic language elaborated by Julia Kristeva? Why is Mallarmé conspicuously absent from the Surrealists' obligatory reading lists of the true modern poets? How do these two figurative deaths contribute to the critical myth of the death of the author and in what way do they contradict it?

First we will examine a departure from life—the myth of the author without a biography, a pure poet composing his universal book, and the ways in which this myth is both constituted by and contradicted by the poetic texts of Mallarmé. Then we will look at the departure from literature and examine what is at stake when one lives out the violence of poetic tropes and no longer composes what one's contemporaries view as works of art.

Theoretical Necrophilia: The Tomb of Mallarmé Revisited

It is possible to say that Mallarmé was one of the pioneers of the modern myth of the death of the author that is passionately elaborated in contemporary criticism. Mallarmé wrote endlessly about the end of the poet and poetry. His works—composed of funeral toasts, tomb dedications to illustrious dead geniuses, and multiple rehearsals of suicide in different genres and genders, from the metaphysical suicide of Elbehnon to the heroic, feminine self-sacrifice in "Victorieusement fui le suicide beau" ("Victoriously fled beautiful suicide")—present an interesting case of literary necrophilia. Indeed, Mallarmé nurtures his poetry with the allegorical corpses of a poet. He continuously stages the poet's death, reenacts depersonalization and disfiguration, and performs a ritual purification of his poems to eliminate the anecdotes related to personal biography or history. Mallarmé's encounter with nothingness and his questioning of the boundaries of poetry did not lead him, as they later did Rimbaud, to

definitely end his writing. "The infinite is at last fixed" ("L'infini est enfin fixé"), wrote Mallarmé in "Igitur," as though anticipating Rimbaud's desire "to fix the vertigo" ("fixer les vertiges").[2] And yet, that instance of the successful fixation of the infinite in the act of Igitur's metaphysical suicide was only a temporary mastery, only an illusion of a definitive poetic textualization of the infinite (*infini-enfin*). In each new poetic act Mallarmé pushes himself to the limits of poetry, tempts his "Muse of Impotence" with a final rupture, but never follows through. Paradoxically, it is precisely Mallarmé's fixation on death that guarantees his poetic survival.

In the case of many poets and writers, the theme of suicide in writing becomes tragically prophetic; a repeated literary suicide culminates with actual physical self-destruction. Nerval, Crevel, Mayakovsky, Tsvetaeva, and Plath are some examples. For Mallarmé, on the contrary, the poetic suicide—both as a theme and as a rhetorical performance—has a therapeutic effect. The words of Spanish poet and mystic Santa Teresa—"I am dying because I am not dying"—reflect very well the dialectics of the death of the poet in Mallarmé. In this chapter I will discuss some problematic aspects of this dialectic—that of not dying while dying and dying while not dying. My examination will touch upon the following issues: What is involved in the poetic staging of the suicide and what kind of relationship between the literature and biography does it presuppose? What are the dangers of conflating the figurative death of the poet and his actual death? How is this suicide related to the myth of the "pure poet"? What biographical and historical evidence is erased in this purification? What are the figurations of the self-disfiguring pure poet? What clothes does he wear? In what theater does he perform? What are his impurities? And finally, what is the conjunction between the poetic suicide and the myth of modernity?

Mallarmé's death of the poet has been lavishly celebrated by literary critics. In fact, the changing reception of Mallarmé reflects important shifts in French cultural history, as well as in the European and American practice of reading. Right after Mallarmé's death in 1898, he was monumentalized by Valéry, who was later to transform some of Mallarmé's painful experiments into ones accepted by the Académie Française.[3] In reaction to Valéry's official monument to the "pure poet," the French avant-garde artists, specifically, the Surrealists, tried to silence Mallarmé. André Breton creates his own version of the progression of French literary history and—to paraphrase Borges—invents his own precursors of modernity. Among them are Sade, Lautréamont, and Rimbaud.[4] As for

Mallarmé, he is absent from both the Surrealists' list of "authors to be read" and their list of "authors never to be read." He is conspicuously erased from the Surrealist conscious memory (or perhaps he is only masterfully hidden on the white margins of the Surrealist *cadavre exquis*). In any case, the official avant-garde version of the history of modernity does not present Mallarmé as one of its founders.

At the same time, among critics and readers Mallarmé is considered to be obscure, difficult, precious, and apolitical. Early scholarly attempts to approach the poet focus on explaining his obscurity. The critics concentrate primarily on the structuring of Mallarmé's themes into a psychoanalytical or some other "imaginary universe."[5] In the words of Leo Bersani, this kind of criticism "proposes a technique by which Mallarmé's difficulty can be reduced." In other words, while attempting to "portray a coherent personality in literature," this criticism reconstructs "the self" behind Mallarmé's disfigurations and thus disregards Mallarmé's staging of the death of the poet.[6]

The critics of the 1960's and 1970's revisit the tomb of Mallarmé, and his works become primary texts for major theoretical concepts, most of which start with "de" or "dis"—Jacques Derrida's "dissemination," de Man's "defacement," Barbara Johnson's "défiguration," and, of course, Barthes's and Foucault's "death of the author." From an apolitical poet, Mallarmé becomes a revolutionary in poetic language whose repeated figurative death signals the first ritual of modernity. ▪

The difficulty in reading Mallarmé is viewed as paradigmatic of modern logic, which subverts the binary principles of Western metaphysics as well as the preconceptions of the unity of the self and of the text. Furthermore, this logic undermines the very possibility of an unproblematic linear unfolding of writing and its meaning. Mallarmé's figurative suicide, regarded not so much as a theme but rather as a rhetorical performance, is pivotal for a new French and American criticism. The emphasis is no longer on themes or images but rather on Mallarmé's capitalized *Syntaxe* and on the *practice* of writing and reading: "Lire—/Cette practique . . ." ("To read—/This practice . . ."). These readings of Mallarmé, which ushered in an important intellectual revolution, called into question the very possibility of an independent existence of theme and syntax. However, for strategical reasons, since these critical readings had to combat the domain of simplistic or neo-Platonic thematicism, they tended to be radically antithematic. Mallarmé's art nouveau Swan (*Cygne*), aristocratically aesthete and nostalgically old-fashioned, was sacrificed (strategically "put under erasure," defaced, and gradually

made invisible) for the sake of the up-to-date semiotic Sign (*Signe*) in the style of the 1960's.

Each critic celebrated the death of Stéphane Mallarmé in his or her own specific fashion. Derrida regards what he calls "masturbatory suicide," acted out in Mallarmé's "Mimique" ("Mimicry"), from a philosophical angle.[7] According to Derrida, Mallarmé's paradoxical poetic logic presents a crucial challenge to the Platonic concept of mimesis. This logic proceeds through the folding and grafting of contradictory double-edged words, such as "hymen," which signifies at once a virginal membrane which separates and a marriage which unites. Derrida juxtaposes Mallarmé's "Mimique" with the Platonic discussion on writing and painting, and he foregrounds the philosopher's difficulty in determining which of the two arts imitates which and which one is closer to "the writing of the soul." Derrida critically rethinks the Platonic distinction between good and bad repetition, as well as between verbal and visual language, and reinscribes both of them as a certain kind of writing. This writing endlessly displaces its origins and does not allow one to trace anything outside the text. Mallarmé's mime imitates nothing in the Platonic sense; he plays both the part of Pierrot the murderer and of Colombina the victim, and mimes only "the supreme spasm, the rising of ecstatic hilarity," which appears to be beyond good and evil.[8] "Mimique" presents a challenge to Platonic "mimesis." Mallarmé's text displaces or "puts under erasure" the very opposition between internal and external, between the original and the copy, between the artistic act and its external referent.

We note that Derrida does not "deconstruct" the "masturbatory suicide" of Mallarmé's mime. On the contrary, he reaffirms it and uses it didactically as a "good example." The critic examines the poet's suicidal self-destructive theatrical performance with much less critical suspicion than the dialogical performance of the philosopher. Obviously, the poet's suicide here is completely figurative or rather completely disfigured by poetic textuality. It is radically unreferential (although not necessarily antireferential): it refuses to transfer into life, biography, or personal history. In fact, according to Derrida, Mallarmé's masturbatory suicide precludes any consideration of a nontextual or extraliterary sphere. It mimes itself rather than any "external" scene.

One might argue that Derrida's notion of text and writing potentially subverts the rigid, critical, and commonsensical understanding of both and does not allow one to construct a binary opposition between the self-referential and the referential functions of language. There is no "hors texte" (outside the text) in Derrida, but there is "hors d'oeuvre" (outside

the work).[9] "Oeuvre" is a masterpiece confined to the limits of a book, while the "text" subverts the logocentric boundaries of the book. However, the very choice of material that exemplifies Derrida's complex notion of the text is symptomatic of certain exclusions. In "The Double Session," Derrida does not transgress Mallarmé's carefully delineated stage and avoids mixing genres. In other words, the critic does not confuse Mallarmé's self-miming literary persona with Mallarmé as a person, that is, with Mallarmé the English teacher, father, husband, and lover who casually glanced at the playbills of the theater on his way to the lycée.

My purpose will be to foreground and push further some of these insights and to bring into focus what has been strategically marginalized, even by one of the best critics of marginalization. I will demonstrate that Mallarmé's texts both question and reaffirm the notion of the literary oeuvre, protecting not so much the autonomy of literature as the autonomy of the poet's life. In the same respect, a textual (in a broad Derridean sense) reading of biography and history would not be entirely against Derrida's enterprise. In fact, Derrida effectively attempts this in his essay on Freud.[10] As for Mallarmé, he remains spared of a lively "hors d'oeuvre." In his case, the main course is too exciting for the critic, too sacred to be spiced by the vital sauces. Besides, Mallarmé's hors d'oeuvre, or biography, lacks an obviously picturesque quality. One finds there no exile, no particularly interesting sexual transgressions, no venereal diseases, no revolutionary involvements.

Yet Derrida's description of Mallarmé's masturbatory suicide defies easy textual closure. It is full of erotic playfulness. The erotic drive, which determines the choice of Derrida's key double-edged word "hymen" as exemplification of Mallarmé's paradoxical poetic logic, can potentially link literature and biography, persona and person, or even the critic and the reader. In fact, the whole discussion of hymen is full of double entendres with which the critic attempts to seduce the reader. Moreover, the surface of Derrida's textuality, which defies any depth, remains as multilayered as Mallarmé's folding laces and as whimsical as sea foam, dense enough to hold the entire poem ["Rien, cette écume, vierge vers" ("Nothing, this foam, virgin verse")]. Its excess of suggestivity excites the reader, allowing him or her to explore the connections and the paths not taken by the critic himself, but in some way inspired by the paradoxes of his poetic logic.

Paul de Man's "Lyric and Modernity" also celebrates Mallarmé's figurative suicide.[11] But this critical funeral is seen as much less pleasurable

and much more intellectual and austere. At the center of de Man's discussion is Mallarmé's poem "Tombeau de Verlaine" ("Verlaine's Tomb"), and indirectly "Tombeau de Baudelaire" ("Baudelaire's Tomb") is key as well. According to de Man, Mallarmé's modernity consists of his radical disfiguration of both the Christian and the Romantic images of a martyr and a poet. De Man writes: "Verlaine's death and poetic transfiguration prefigure in a naive tonality the highly self-conscious repetition of the same experience by Mallarmé himself. Like all *true* poets, Verlaine is a poet of death, but death for Mallarmé means precisely the discontinuity between the personal self and the voice that speaks in the poetry from the other bank of the river, beyond death." [12] (Italics here and in the following discussion are mine.)

We observe how de Man displaces the actual physical death of the person (in this case, Verlaine), which served as a pretext for writing the poem, with the figurative death of the poet. According to de Man, this figurative death of the poet signals a radical break, or rather the acknowledgment of radical discontinuity between the person and the poet, the personal history and biography and the text. The paradoxical historical continuity from Baudelaire to Mallarmé is regarded as "a *genetic* movement of gradual allegorization and depersonalization." Mallarmé's heroic poetic death is alternatively described as "the sacrificial death of life into work," as a radical defacement of the poet, as impersonality, or as a substitution of "the logic of nature and representation by a purely intellectual and allegorical logic." [13] De Man insists that the "*authentic* poetic immortality" is "entirely devoid of any personal circumstances." In his critical paradigm it is opposed to what he calls the false kind of transcendence which relies on the Romantic myth of the poet's exceptional *personal* destiny, which, in the case of Verlaine, would be the redeeming sacrifice of the suffering sinner.

Now we can observe the difference between Derrida's and de Man's murderous textuality. Derrida suggests (although he does not necessarily explore) possible vital excesses of the textual "hymen." On the one hand, the critic's hymen separates life and text, protecting the virginity of each, and on the other hand, it invites the reader to what might be a marriage between the two. De Man's "true" poetic textuality demands the murder of the poet's extraliterary life: in fact, the text defines itself against life, as the poet defines himself against the person. In other words, Derrida's paradoxical logic is based on *a Möbius-strip–like continuity* between the inside and the outside of the text;[14] strictly speaking, there is no "hors texte" in Derrida but a rigorous free play of traces and effects of writing—

grafted, folded, and superimposed upon one another. One might still argue that the use of linguistic metaphor, even with the purpose of revealing the blind spots of linguistics, does not escape certain "linguistification" of diverse phenomena, to which for lack of better definition we will refer with their traditional names—experience, life, image. They generate their own logic, which is often irreducible to even the most sophisticated concept of writing proposed by Mallarmé or Derrida.

In de Man, the "text" is radically severed from the "hors texte." There is a *radical discontinuity* between the logic of language, which functions like a machine generating tropes, and the logic of life, which is based on organic development. For strategic reasons—in order to avoid a dangerously Romantic organic view of language—de Man emphasizes the radical break between life and text, denying any possible superimposition of the two, or any motivation or cause and effect relationship between them. And yet the idea of "radicality" (which has as its root the word "root"), as well as the impossibility of escaping the use—even when parodic—of organic metaphors (as in "a *genetic* movement of gradual allegorization"), reveals the blind spots of de Man himself and works against his passionate anti-Romanticism. The language machine regenerates human errors. The very idea of radicality—strategically crucial for the development of criticism—always points to the closures that can lead to intellectual dead ends.

The insistence upon the radical discontinuity between text and life, and the obsession with "authentic" poetic immortality forces de Man to exclude the erotic temptation of Mallarmé's text. For de Man, the "Mort des Artistes" (Death of Artists) has nothing to do with "la petite mort" ("orgasm," literally "little death"). It is curious to note that Derrida and de Man choose the examples of Mallarmé's double-edged words—"nubile (plis)" and "hymen"—that have somewhat similar connotations. De Man masterfully confines the erotic connotations of "nubere" in parenthesis: "But 'nubere,' aside from erotic associations (*that can be sacrificed for the economy of the exposition*), the bad etymological but very Mallarméan pun on 'nubere' (to marry) and 'nubere' (clouds)."[15]

Unlike Derrida, de Man refuses to marry potentially different meanings of the word and places the major emphasis on "clouds," which, after Baudelaire's opening poem of *Le Spleen de Paris*, "L'Etranger" ("The Stranger"), have become a poetic thing par excellence. Where Derrida explores ("disseminates") multiple possible meanings of hymen, de Man advocates an ascetic allegory of the modern "linguistic predicament." There is an analogy between the attitude toward the extraliterary life and

toward eroticism. While in de Man life and eroticism are thought to be sacrificed in a similar fashion, in Derrida "erotic openness" might be read as the potential openness of the text.

The immediate context of de Man's polemics is obvious: he argues against a simplistic version of literary history and biography, advocating a slow and careful reading of the poetic text. De Man proposes a kind of subversive close reading that would capture the logic of the text, explore its self-differences and contradictions without sacrificing them for the sake of the rigid coherence of a historical, sociological, or naive biographical grid. As Barbara Johnson points out, de Man's text is caught in the same paradox of simultaneous blindness and insight, an assertion of authority and the antiauthoritative gesture, which the critic exposes in the poetic texts. [16] We see that de Man's own text, obsessed with the "authenticity" of death and the "truth" of the linguistic predicament, reveals both the intellectual vitality and dead ends of a radical practice of rigorous close reading.

Thus, Mallarmé's textual death produces chain effects for his readers. It becomes an exemplary modern allegory, a promise of modern immortality for the price of textual flagellation of the flesh. The allegory of the pure poet, the story of his death and immortality, is at the center of a new gospel of modernity, propagated by both poets and critics, a paradoxical modernity that wishes to abolish history.

In her early book *Défigurations du langage poétique* (*Disfigurations of Poetic Language*) Barbara Johnson places Mallarmé's "interregnum," which requires the death of the poet, between two actual deaths, those of Baudelaire and Hugo. She writes:

> De même que la mort de Baudelaire a coïncidé avec le commencement du silence de l'interrègne mallarméen, de même ce n'est peut être pas un hasard si c'est une deuxième "mort du père" qui semble au contraire dénouer son écriture. [17]

As Baudelaire's death coincided with the beginning of the Mallarméan interregnum, it is probably not by accident if it is indeed a second "death of the father" which seems to unravel his writing.

The second death is that of the great father figure of French poetry, Victor Hugo, who according to Mallarmé was "le vers personnellement" ("verse in person"). On the one hand, *Défigurations du langage poétique* establishes a connection between the actual deaths of the poets Baudelaire and Hugo and a figurative death of Mallarmé. Mallarmé is placed

within a certain literary history, and his text is culturally contextualized. Mallarmé's poetic death is regarded as a murder of the cultural myth of Hugo, who exemplifies a Romantic cult of the personality of the poet, whose heroic life authorizes his texts. In Mallarmé the poet is neither a glamorous Romantic hero, nor a national hero, but a will of language itself. On the other hand, Johnson insists upon a "figurative structure" of what can be seen as the oedipal relationship between Hugo and Mallarmé, emphasizing that the name of Hugo "désigne moins une personne qu'une personnification du vers, alors tuer Hugo, ce n'est tuer qu'une figure, un Père-Vers" ("designates less a person than a personification of verse; thus, killing Hugo is killing only a figure, a personage, a p(at)erversity").[18] Ultimately, what is crucial for Johnson in Mallarmé's per-verse murder and suicide is neither the oedipal structure, nor the shifting cultural myth of the poet and the shifting role of the poet in society. Rather, it is the fact that the suicide lays bare the modern linguistic predicament: It "met à nu la structure essentiellement linguistique, fondamentalement figurée, de toute violence oedipienne" ("lays bare the essentially linguistic and fundamentally figurative structure of all oedipal violence").[19] Later in my analysis I will return to Johnson's metaphor of the "laying bare" of the linguistic structures and of the "allegory's triptease." But before stripping the text, I will examine how it is dressed up and how it reproduces the latest fashions ("les dernières modes") of the time.

In the later works of Johnson, Bersani, Mehlman, and others there is a shift toward a closer examination of what is disfigured and how. Johnson disfigures Mallarmé's own name in "Les Fleurs du Mal-Armé" ("The Flowers of Evil Armed," invoking Baudelaire's *Les Fleurs du mal* ["The Flowers of Evil"]), and points to the dangers and traps of excessive allegorization and a too-quick erasure of a woman and of historical facts perpetuated by Mallarmé and Mallarmé's deconstructive criticism. Bersani, while still perpetuating the poetic death of Mallarmé as a guarantee of poetic immortality in his book *The Death of Stéphane Mallarmé*, claims that for him the poet's death can be regarded as a prolegomenon for a new theory of sublimation.[20] Thus the critic looks beyond Mallarmé's text, not so much into culture, but rather into a new revisionist psychoanalysis.

My analysis, informed and inspired by the 1960's and 1970's deconstructive readings of Mallarmé—the readings which emphasize Mallarmé's philosophy of syntax and suicidal laying bare of the linguistic and

figurative structures—will also present a contextual response to these versions of Mallarmé's death. I will focus on both figuration and disfiguration in Mallarmé's text and attempt to recover, from underneath the erasure, what has been for a long time sacrificed for many strategic reasons, specifically for the noble cause of posthistorical (or antihistorical) modernity. In other words, I will concentrate on the tension between laying bare and refashioning, between syntax and image.

Writing and Domestic Sacrifice

Mallarmé's "Autobiographie" (1885), a rather unusual autobiographical text, articulates the relationship between art and life, as well as between writing and domestic sacrifice, in a uniquely friendly fashion. In fact, "Autobiographie" is a personal letter to Verlaine written in response to Verlaine's request for some biographical information to appear in the volumes *Hommes d'aujourd'hui* and *Poètes maudits*. The title "Autobiographie" does not belong to Mallarmé; it was added in the 1924 Bonniot edition of the letter. Indeed it would be very difficult to imagine Mallarmé writing a Rousseau-like autobiographical confession with a detailed description of childish pranks and domestic adventures. The three roots of the word "auto-bio-graphy" are radically problematized by Mallarmé: the extraliterary "self" and personal life supposedly disappear in the writing, which endlessly displaces and disfigures them. Thus Mallarmé's unique autobiographical text has a problematic status: it is both a personal letter to a friend and fellow poet and a peculiar self-fashioning as a contemporary man ("homme d'aujourd'hui"); at once an article of circumstance, not written out of any internal poetic necessity but for a specific use, and a carefully structured document for posterity.

"Autobiographie" is not simply *about* a problematic relationship between the poet and the man; it in fact exemplifies the problems that it discusses. As a letter, a peculiar genre of writing, it occupies a borderline position between literature and everyday life. Mallarmé is quite aware of the genre problem. He self-consciously describes his letter to Verlaine as "noté au crayon pour laisser l'air d'une de ces bonnes conversations d'amis à l'écart et sans éclat de voix" ("jotted down in pencil to give it the appearance of one of those nice little private conversations between friends without the burst of voices").[21] Thus he places the letter in between oral and written communication, as well as between the writer and the reader, allowing the reader to breathe some fresh air and

fill the gaps at his or her ease while selecting and reorganizing the biographical details disseminated in the text. Mallarmé refuses to take his extraliterary person with a solemn seriousness. He stresses the casual, fragmentary character of his writing, which defies a unified, coherent, programmatic, or pure image of himself. Mallarmé's fragmentary "Autobiographie" is typical of his written work, which he describes as a collection of elegant and precious "scraps, bits, trinkets." This text, like the literary life that it relates, lacks the architectonic structure of the ideal *Livre*, "orphic explanation of the earth."[22] "Life" according to Mallarmé is the most disjointed and discontinuous amalgam of details and fragments that can be temporarily arranged by a poet-friend.

Mallarmé claims that his life is deprived of the anecdotal ("la vie denuée d'anecdote"). "Denuer" is a curious verb here; it relates poetically to "nu(e)," both clouds and nudity. Instead of erasing, Mallarmé "clouds" (waters down, makes vague and shapeless) the potential anecdotes in his life, stressing the quotidian insignificance of some of them and turning the others into "poèmes"; "anecdotes ou poèmes" ("anecdotes or poems") is the subtitle of one of Mallarmé's collections of prose poems. In "Autobiographie," Mallarmé describes himself as belonging to a dynasty of Parisian clerks and functionaries of the state: "Mes familles paternelle et maternelle présentaient, depuis la Révolution, une suite ininterrompue du fonctionnaires dans l'Administration de l'Enregistrement" ("Since the Revolution, both the paternal and maternal sides of my family have shown themselves as an uninterrupted series of functionaries of the Registry").[23]

However, he immediately recovers the traces of those of his relatives who experienced the pleasure of holding a pen "pour autre chose qu'enregistrer des actes" ("for some other purpose than to register transactions"). Among them is his distant cousin, who even published a romantic volume entitled *Ange ou démon* (*Angel or Demon*). Mallarmé classifies his ancestors first and foremost according to their relation to writing, not according to their ethnic or class origins. The mention of his mother's early death and of his own early marriage takes up less space in "Autobiographie" than the account of his first experience of writing poetry à la Beranger.

We notice that there is no search for romantic or exotic ancestors: Mallarmé classifies his family as typical Parisian bourgeoisie of Burgundian, Lorrainian, and Dutch origins and does not spend time elaborating any flattering genealogical tree. Also, unlike a Romantic autobiography,

Mallarmé's text lacks any mythology of love. In fact, the poet's official mistress, the salon hostess Méry, born Marie-Rose (who incidently shared the name with his wife and sister), is not even mentioned.

Mallarmé presents himself as a writer by origins and a language professional, a modest English teacher in the lycée, who composed many precious poetic fragments but failed to create the unique *Livre*. Thus, this biography of a Parisian bourgeois, a typical writer's biography shared by many, is one that can be safely erased from literary history and sacrificed for the sake of writing. This biography lacks eccentricity: Mallarmé was not an outsider to Parisian letters—he was neither a woman, nor a foreigner, nor a political exile. There was no need to describe "the old interior of the familial Parisian bourgeoisie," because it was familiar to most of the writers, critics, and readers of the time.

But it is important to remember that a biography that can be harmlessly erased and sacrificed for the sake of the text, as it has been done by many critics, is not "neutral." The antithesis of a Romantic biography is a middle-class professional life with a few familial deaths and too many internal poetic dramas. But this kind of life is a cultural luxury, available to a minority of poets who happened to live between great wars and revolutions, in the time when one could afford to have vaguely apolitical and anarchic beliefs and not be persecuted for "formalism," "cosmopolitanism," or "decadentism." In short, this was a time when one could live safely in the familiar bourgeois interiors, first, being able to afford this minimum of comfort, and, second, taking for granted that this refuge of domesticity could only be exploded from inside and not "expropriated" or taken away by some kind of "committee," as happened to many Russian poets in the first half of the twentieth century.

There is a curious insistence upon furnishings in Mallarmé's text which will dictate the "interior design" of my own critical reading. Two scenes with furniture will present the central issues of "Autobiographie," that is, the relationship between poetry and life, between the poet's internal drama and his domestic interior. In the first the old Parisian furniture and the familiar bourgeois environment are described with a mixture of irony and nostalgia. We learn that even the purest poet, whose life is deprived of anecdotes, is not deprived of furniture. Here is how Mallarmé describes his favorite occupation:

> Je vague peu, préférant à tout, dans un appartement défendu par la famille, le séjour *parmi quelques meubles anciens et chers*, et la feuille de papier souvent blanche.[24]

I wander little, preferring to all else to stay in an apartment shielded by the family, among some dear old furniture, and the frequently white piece of paper.

Thus, the wrestling with the white page, the drama of writing with which Mallarmé displaces the Romantic drama of life, takes place in a certain familiar Parisian interior, which is not entirely disfigured.

The other scene with furniture is much less comfortable. In fact, it violently disrupts the harmony of writing and domestic life, of poet and person. Let us compare the everyday scene of writing cited above with the poet's violent dream.

J'ai toujours rêvé et tenté autre chose, avec une patience d'alchimiste, prêt à y sacrifier toute vanité et toute satisfaction, *comme on brûlait jadis son mobilier et les poutres de son toit,* pour y alimenter le fourneau du Grand Oeuvre. Quoi? c'est difficile à dire: un livre . . . qui soit un livre, architectural et prémedité, et non un recueil des inspirations du hasard, fussent-elles merveilleuses . . . J'irai plus loin, je dirai: le Livre.[25]

I always dreamed and attempted the other thing, with an alchemist's patience, ready to sacrifice to it all vanity and satisfaction, just as in the old days people used to burn their furniture and the girders of their roof to feed the stove of the Great Oeuvre. What? it is hard to say: a book . . . that is a book, architectural and premeditated, and not a collection of haphazard inspirations, as marvelous as they could be . . . I will go further; I will say; the Book.

In the first scene, the ordinary encounter with the white page, the relationship between poetry writing and domestic life can be described as a relationship by metonymy or by contiguity: the poet sits among his domestic furniture, in some ways protected by the familiar coziness. In the second case, the situation is drastically different. *Le Livre* can only be written at the price of a domestic sacrifice, only after the inquisition of domesticity. The two cannot coexist in one space: one has to displace violently or destroy the other. "Furniture" here stands for more than bourgeois comfort. The poet does not simply wish to burn his middle-class milieu. This would be a romantic rebellion, something that would lead not to the impersonal *Livre* but to the complete works of Victor Hugo and to a simplistic version of Marxist criticism.[26] "Furniture" and "roof" here are spatial metaphors for the "person."

Hence it is crucial to differentiate between these two scenes in Mal-

larmé: the ordinary scene that depicts the poet meditating on the white page in peaceful coexistence with his familiar bourgeois interiors and the dream scene that describes the domestic fire. It is difficult to determine which of the two is a "primal scene," and it is precisely the tension between writing and dreaming of writing that creates the dynamics of Mallarmé's text. In my opinion, de Man and other Structuralists and post-Structuralists focus exclusively on the second scene—self-purification with fire. For strategic reasons, they pushed one tendency of the Mallarméan text to a radical extreme. And yet, for Mallarmé himself the architectural and ideally premeditated *Livre*, which deserves a total sacrifice, existed only as pure potentiality. *Le Livre*, a total victory of modern impersonality, was a dream that sustained the poet through his routine encounters with the white page in the midst of the familiar interior.

The relationship between Mallarmé's utopian Grand Oeuvre, the ideal architectural *Livre*, which wins over chance, subjectivity, and arbitrariness, and the poet's actual work called alternatively "mille bribes connues" ("a thousand known scraps"), "collection de chiffons d'étoffe séculaire ou précieuses" ("a collection of rags of old or precious fabric"), "lambeaux" ("shreds"), or named with the condemnatory word "Album," follows two rhetorical paradigms that remind us of the paradigms of the two scenes. (In the description of the latter we notice the abundance of clothing metaphors, which contrast with the architectural metaphors related to *le Livre*.) This collection of materials exists beside ("à côté") the potential *Livre*, the most intense personal dream of the poet.

> Avec ce mot condamnatoire d'*Album* dans le titre . . . cela contiendra plusieurs séries, pourra même aller indéfiniment (*à côté* de mon travail personnel qui je crois, sera anonyme, le Texte y parlant de lui-même et sans voix d'auteur).[27]

> With this condemnatory word 'Album' in the title . . . this will contain several series, it can even go on indefinitely (beside my own personal work, which I believe will be anonymous, the Text speaking of itself and without the voice of the author).

Le Livre seems to be only metonymically related to the everyday verse making of the poet. At the same time, however, the poet confesses that he will never be able to complete his Grand Oeuvre in its entirety, and therefore he hopes at least to demonstrate fragments of it that would prove its existence. His modest goal is "à en faire scintiller par une place

l'authenticité glorieuse, en indiquant le reste tout entier auquel ne suffit pas une vie" ("to make glorious authenticity glitter in one spot, indicating the rest in its entirety, for which a life does not suffice").[28]

The poet suggests that one of the fragments, one of the pieces of materials from his eclectic and impure collection can serve as a metaphor for *le Livre*. The fragment can be regarded as a part for the whole, a part illuminating the entire utopian structure, turning synecdoche into metaphor. Here the fire is not destructive, but illuminating; the conjunction of the two contradictory meanings reveals again a polysemantic functioning of Mallarmé's vocabulary.

A particularly illuminating juxtaposition in the text of "Autobiographie" is that of *le Livre*, called ironically and with much less solemnity "despotique bouquin" ("despotic little book"), and Mallarmé's fashion magazine *La Dernière Mode* (*The Latest Fashion*), a collection of all sorts of textures and materials, in all multiple meanings of both words. Mallarmé appears to be quite proud of his accomplishment in the world of fashion. In confessing the "vice" of dreaming about *le Livre*, Mallarmé uses the verb "mettre à nu": "Voilà l'aveu de mon vice, mis à nu" ("That is the confession of my depravity, laid bare"). When he describes his affectionate treatment of his fashion magazine he employs a synonymous verb "devêtir": "Les huit ou dix numéros parus servent encore quand je les devêts de leur poussière à me faire longtemps rêver" ("The eight or ten issues already published still serve to make me dream a long while when I take off [un-dress] their dust").[29] The juxtaposition of *Le Livre* and *La Dernière Mode* will reveal some of the paradoxes of Mallarmé's self-fashioning and dress making.

Thus the text of "Autobiographie" stages crucial paradigms and controversies of Mallarmé's work. Suggestive biographical and antibiographical details in the text raise many important questions. What is the relationship between life and text? Is the poet's life metonymic to his text, that is, does it simply go on "beside" the work? Or is the poet's life to be metaphorically burned like the familiar furniture for the sake of purifying the work? What kind of life can be easily murdered by the poet or by his critics? What are the familiar interiors that some critics take for granted? What is the relationship between the "pure" and the "impure" oeuvre of Mallarmé?

It is ironic that the text of "Autobiographie" appeared in the collection *Hommes d'aujourd'hui* (*Men of Today*) accompanied by a cartoon-like picture depicting Mallarmé the poet. Mallarmé was represented as a faun with a nimbus and a lyre. Hence, paradoxically, the text that advocates

disfiguration and anonymity is placed beside a cartoonish image of the poet. Indeed, the life of the text goes beyond the intentions of the author.

My further analysis will proceed in two directions, toward black and white—Mallarmé's two favorite colors. First, I will examine the color of the pure poet's costume and the setting of his internal drama in "Igitur," "Sur Poe" ("On Poe"), and "Action restreinte" ("Restrained Action"). Then, I will trace Mallarmé's "impurities," following the flight of the white butterfly from "Le Livre, instrument spirituel" ("The Book, the Spiritual Instrument") to *La Dernière Mode.*

Black Velvet of Talent, or the Figuration of the Pure Poet

"Igitur" portrays one of the most radical suicide attempts in literary history. It both thematizes and dramatizes a suicide, exploring the limits of language and consciousness. The genre and title of this peculiar work reflect its problematic character. "Igitur" is variously called "Conte" ("Tale"), "Ancienne Etude" ("Ancient Study"), and "Scène de théâtre ancien" ("Scene of Ancient Theater"). As a conte it reminds us of the fantastic stories of Poe, their fascination with death, dying, and postmortem revelations. Yet "Igitur" lacks the uncanny or fantastic hesitation of Poe stories that stirs up our primitive fears and instincts. "Ce Conte s'adresse à l'Intelligence du lecteur qui met les choses en scène, elle-même" ("This Tale is addressed to the Intelligence of the reader which stages the things itself"), writes Mallarmé in his dedication.[30] His conte is about an intellectual suicide, a suicide of "indifference," a victory over any "all-too-human" manifestation of consciousness. It is "Intelligence" itself, capitalized and depersonalized, the intelligence of the writer and the reader (if the reader flatters himself or herself with the capital "I"), that directs the drama.

As a piece of theater "Igitur" is intentionally antitheatrical and unperformable, at least on the conventional stage. It is interesting that Mallarmé consistently usurps theatrical metaphors in order to subvert the very nature of theater as a collective social spectacle. Barash calls it "an unattainable quixotic attempt on the part of the anti-theatrical principle to capture the theater."[31] Mallarmé's drama unfolds as a spectacular annihilation of costumes, props and actors, as well as of the very possibility of a social stage. The poet, according to Mallarmé, is a "histrion spirituel" ("spiritual histrion"), a "pitre" ("buffoon"), laughing and crying in front of a white page in the empty interior. It is "Le Spectacle de Soi" ("The Spectacle of Oneself") that Mallarmé stages, a monodrama and a

linguistic performance that murders figuration. It is a drama of personifications, and not of persons. The identities of "he," "I," and "you" in "Igitur" are interchangeable. The monologues and the commentaries of the narrator are superimposed upon each other like the shadows on the screen, which "you" has to remake.

The madness suggested in the subtitle of the drama—"La Folie d'Elbehnon" ("The Madness of Elbehnon")—is at once schizophrenia and paranoia, the identification with multiple others and the obsession with the self, the folding of the same mechanism of depersonalization upon itself. "Igitur" consists of the text of four fragments, glossa and "scholium," a commentary upon the fragments, but in fact all of them replay one another, just like "I," "he," and "you." They depict the same intellectual suicide, the same encounter with nothingness and absurdity. In his unperformable piece of theater Mallarmé wishes to stage the experience of "pure negativity," a monologue of "réciproques néants" ("reciprocal nothingnesses").

"Igitur" personifies the "elocutionary disappearance of the poet" described in Mallarmé's later programmatic article "Crise de vers" ("Crisis of Verse"): "l'oeuvre pure implique la disparition élocutoire du poète qui cède l'initiative aux mots" ("the pure oeuvre implies the elocutionary disappearance of the poet who yields the initiative to words").[32] In "Igitur," the human hero is on the verge of being displaced by the flickering dance of the words. The most significant recurring words of the text, such as "folie" ("madness"), "nuit" ("night"), "lumière" ("light"), are disseminated through the text by way of multiple anagrams: *folie/fiole, lumière/ lui-même, nuit/a nui, ennui,* and so on. In this way the text approaches the ideal "oeuvre pure" it acts out the figurative suicide of the poet and reveals a purely linguistic predicament. In many respects, "Igitur" is one of the most successful self-fashionings of the pure poet, one of the most emblematic recreations of "the death of the author."

In fact, the name of the main character, Igitur, is a paradoxical embodiment of syntax itself. Igitur—in Latin, *therefore, hence*—is a conjunction, an element which does not signify in itself, but which can only acquire signification within syntactical structure. It is synonymous with the Cartesian "ergo" in "cogito ergo sum," or as Barbara Johnson paraphrases it à la Mallarmé, "I write therefore I disappear." This device of making a character into a personification of syntax is obviously twofold: on the one hand, it suggests a radical depersonalization and dehumanization of the dramatic hero. On the other hand, it reveals the impossibility of escaping figures, especially when one wishes to illustrate or to stage the process of disfiguration.[33]

In a way, "Igitur" is also one of Mallarmé's last attempts to present the drama of the death of the author in a theatrical or existential manner. Later in his writing it becomes a drama of the syntax itself, without any dramatis personae. In "Le Mystère dans les lettres" ("The Mystery in Letters") Mallarmé writes: "Quel pivot, j'entends, dans ces contrastes, à l'intelligibilité? Il faut une garantie—La Syntaxe" ("What pivot, in these contrasts, I understand, for intelligibility? A guarantee is necessary—Syntax").[34] It is this "Syntaxe," the pivot of intelligibility, which is regarded by Derrida, de Man, Johnson, and others to be Mallarmé's privileged force of disfiguration and depersonalization.

And yet, one wonders, why is "Syntaxe" capitalized in Mallarmé's quote? "Syntaxe," with a capital S, functions in Mallarmé's text in the same way as suggestive symbolist images, such as "Nuit," "Cygne," or "Azur." Is "Syntaxe" on the verge of becoming a "Symbol," even if it is a dynamic and transgressive symbol? Does it suggest, then, that image and syntax, personification and depersonalization, are always co-dependent? Instead of focusing on the disfiguring tendency, which has been privileged in recent criticism, I will examine the figurations of the drama of suicide and the ways in which death in writing can be life-affirming.

In fact, "Igitur" is not entirely self-referential; it establishes intertextual ties with other self-referential literary suicides. Its prototypical drama is *Hamlet*. In *Crayonné au théâtre* (*Sketched at the Theater*), Mallarmé detheatricalizes and decontextualizes the Shakespearean play, seeing it as a "solitary drama" and "an intimate tragedy." "L'oeuvre de Shakespeare est si bien façonnée selon le seul théâtre de notre esprit, prototype du reste" ("Shakespeare's work is so well styled according to the sole theater of our spirit, the prototype of the rest").[35] According to Mallarmé, the character of Hamlet escapes the specific Rennaissance ambience "spirituellement émbrumée d'un rien de fourrures septentrionales" ("spiritually hazed over with a bit of northern fur") and approaches "le théâtre sublime et pur" ("the pure and sublime theater") of the spirit itself. Hamlet is an emblematic hero, "à demi mêlé à l'abstraction" ("partially mixed with abstraction"). Hamlet transcends a specific context, be it the English Renaissance stage or the Parisian stage of the second half of the nineteenth century. The actor playing Hamlet relives the destiny of the pure spirits and is marked by a stamp of an almost hermetic ahistoricity—"le sceau d'une époque suprême et neutre" ("the stamp of a supreme and neuter epoch").

And yet, even the most avant-garde theater director would have to dress the actor playing Hamlet. According to the poet, Hamlet escapes the contextuality of the costumes: "Hamlet, lui, évite ce tort, dans sa

traditionnelle presque nudité sombre, un peu à la Goya" ("Hamlet, in his Goyaesque, *traditional, almost dark nudity,* avoids this wrong").[36] (Italics are mine.) This "almost" of Mallarmé's is crucial. Is it possible to be nude and clothed at the same time? Is "atemporal" synonymous with "traditional?" Can one be at once neutral, abstract, and styled after Goya? Is Mallarmé's pure poet only *almost* pure?

Traditionally, Hamlet wears a costume of black velvet. Black can be seen as the absence of color, as a pure, reflective screen. The shining, thick, black velvet is a perfect Mallarméan surface, dense and suggestive. In the Shakespearean play, Hamlet's costume is described as an "inky suit." This is yet another crucial connotation of blackness. It is the color of ink, the color of writing itself, writing that affirms its victory over chance disseminated on the white page. In *La Dernière Mode,* while discussing the fashions for bride and groom (traditionally white and black), white is described as "feminine par excellence."[37] Thus, the colors of the poet's drama of writing are also the colors of sexual difference. The unselfconscious suicide of Ophelia and the tantalizingly unfinished self-erasure of Hérodiade are styled in white, while the two creatively accomplished masculine suicides—those of Hamlet and Igitur—are written in black.

Igitur's midnight drama is depicted in somber colors. It is dominated by Hamlet's shadow. We find here the same constellation of the words "pur," "neutre," "abstrait," which are at the heart of Mallarmé's legendary poetic suicide. The tomb is regarded as the ultimate neutrality. Thus, Igitur's journey to the tomb is a gradual self-neutralization, the erasure of emotions and even intelligence. The purity of Igitur consists in his spiritual "racial" purity, "pureté de sa race." And the uniform of this spiritual elite is a luxurious inky suit in rich black velvet. In his journey to the tomb, despite his mother's interdiction, Igitur encounters "le buste du génie supérieur, vêtu de velours, et dont l'unique frisson était le travail arachnéen d'une dentelle qui retombait sur le velours: le personnage parfait de la nuit" ("the bust of a superior genius, clothed in velvet, and whose sole shivering was the gossamer work of a piece of lace which was draped on the velvet: the perfect character of the night").[38] In this place, the clothes of the genius seem to acquire subjectivity, or to rob it from the characters; they mirror themselves—black on black. "Le propre miroitement du velours sur le buste" ("The proper mirroring of the velvet on the bust") dominates the other shadows of the old interior.

Genius is used both in the singular and in the plural. It evokes at once the Romantic superior genius and the classic image of geniuses of place,

referring to the Roman cult of ancestors. Here the two converge: the only pedigree of Igitur is his spiritual pedigree, as the only pedigree of a "man of today." Mallarmé is the forebear of professional writers and scribblers. The classic bust of the genius is hardly neutral, abstract, and atemporal, but it is definitely traditional. It reveals the traditional Classic-Romantic figuration reestablished by the pure poet and, if anything, only reaffirmed by the metaphysical suicide. The neutrality is culturally specific, gender-marked, and representational. Hence, the poet performs a double gesture: on the one hand, he wishes to murder Hugo and destroy his Romantic ghost, and, on the other, he resurrects the genius, a traditional figuration of artistic creation. Why is this bust of genius conspicuously absent from the post-Structuralist picture of Mallarmé? Why does the bust of the genius survive Mallarmé's syntax? Why is it not disfigured? Is the bust of genius a part of the old Victorian furniture, or is he (it is definitely "he," a masculine creative force, as demonstrated by Robert Greer Cohn) an emblem of the new, shady interior in which the furniture has been burnt?

The obsession with furniture continues through this spiritual autobiography. At a certain point the familiar furniture becomes grotesque: "les meubles tordent leur chimère dans le vide" ("the furniture twist their chimera in the void"). One imagines the whimsical *fin de siècle* furniture, with its neorococo curves. Remembrances of it periodically intrude upon the pure poetic voice, and the poet's erasing completely the setting and reproducing the ideal "absence of atmosphere." The character, surrounded by the whimsical furniture, agonizes in a pure and chimeric dream in front of a deceptive mirror. Thus Mallarmé's purity is both a product of intelligence and of a chimeric nightmare. Purity and chimera ironically mirror each other, and a flickering shadow of the "pure poet" at times appears as a grotesque, as part of some neorococo ornament.

In fact, if we look closer, "Igitur" presents at once a clever, almost architectonic linguistic paradigm—a paradise of self-engendering words—and a chimeric visual spectacle. The tension between the visual and linguistic inspirations of "Igitur" mirror the tension between image and syntax. Many words and images of the text have a syncretic dimension. They evoke different media—visual, verbal, and musical—and appeal to different senses. For instance, the title of one of the fragments is "touches," which refers both to the piano keys and to the brushstrokes. The same goes for "étude" ("study") and "ébauches" ("sketches"). It is a common practice in Symbolist poetry to attempt to expand into the other arts. Verlaine desired to write "grey songs," music paintings, which

would escape what he called derogatively "literature," while Rimbaud invented the color of vowels. Mallarmé was tortured by the relationship between music and writing, as well as between literature and ballet, poetry and mystery. Cohn suggests a "tetrapolarity"—not a binary but a plural (paragraphic) paradigm—to approach Mallarmé, and this multimedia dimension would be quite a good example to support his approach.[39]

The peculiar medium of "Igitur," designed to be unperformable theater, the theater of depersonalized shadows and dropped curtains, reminds us of another art form, ingeniously prefigured by Mallarmé—the art of film. Indeed, this nervous movement of the shadows projected by blowing on a candle ("bougie," which suggests both the source of light and the movement itself—"bouger") is an interesting recreation of the operation of the camera obscura. Mallarmé, with his acute poetic sensitivity toward numerous media of expression, was indeed one of the first among his contemporaries to write about the effect of the newly invented cinematograph upon literature. In a brief response to the questionnaire on the book illustration written in 1898, the year of Mallarmé's death—almost thirty years after the composition of "Igitur" (1869) and only four years after the invention of the cinematograph by the brothers Lumière—the poet writes:

> Je suis pour—aucune illustration, tout ce qu'évoque un livre devant se passer dans l'esprit du lecteur: mais si vous remplacez la photographie, que n'allez-vous droit au cinématographe, dont le déroulement remplacera, images et texte, maint volume, avantageusement.[40]

> I am for—no illustrations, all that a book evokes should take place in the mind of the reader: but if you replace it with photography, simply go straight to the cinematograph, the unfolding of which will replace, images and text, many a volume, advantageously.

Like Victor Hugo in *Notre-Dame de Paris*, who wrote that the book had displaced the Gothic cathedral as a locus of cultural communication par excellence, Mallarmé prophetically anticipated that film would displace the book—the process which we are witnessing in postmodern culture, the culture which relies more and more upon simulacra projected on the screen or blinking electronic video dots. Mallarmé would have liked the word "film," which suggests a thin transparent surface that can hold an infinite number of images. The film screen is a modern folding upon the Mallarméan profound surface. "Igitur" is a script for the first "film noir,"

with long shots, whimsical camera movements, and at the same time quite traditional imagery—Victorian furniture and the classical busts of the ancestors—*genii loci*, a commonplace of literary tradition.

These busts of geniuses dressed in Hamlet's black velvet play a crucial role in "Igitur," both in refiguring the traditional images and in reaffirming creative immortality. In fact, at the very beginning of "Ancienne Etude" ("Old Study"), "he"—before he is even given a euphonic syntactical name—pays homage to and challenges his mythical ancestors. As if wishing to take control over his metaphysical suicide and keep the ancestors from snuffing out his poetic life, "Igitur" discovers his creative powers:

> Lui-même à la fin, quand les bruits auront disparu, tirera une preuve de quelque chose de grand. . . . de ce simple fait qu'il peut causer l'ombre en soufflant sur la lumière.[41]

> He himself, in the end, when the noises have disappeared, will extract a proof of something grand. . . . from this simple fact that he can bring about a shadow by blowing on the light.

Obviously "lui-même" linguistically echoes "lumière" and reinscribes a traditional Romantic metaphor of the light as a source of creation. But what is even more important is the act of breathing, of blowing upon the light. This is obviously one of the best-known metaphors of giving life— "breathing life," so to speak—that appears in the Bible. Mallarmé himself also associated the rhythm of breathing with the incantatory rhythm of the pure oeuvre which he describes in "Crise de vers." Here, however, I resist the temptation of intertextuality and the seduction of literariness, and instead of quoting more instances of breathing metaphors in Mallarmé or other texts of Western culture, I will look at Mallarmé's life.

When he was writing "Igitur," Mallarmé experienced a metaphysical and physical crisis. We know from his letters that he was paralyzed for a while by an encounter with nothingness and existential absurdity. He also suffered the first attacks of the disease that would cause his death thirty years later—severe difficulty in breathing. It often seems that writers' diseases and the causes of writers' deaths are very literary. Thus, for instance, the Russian symbolist poet Andrey Bely prophetically wrote about his symbolic death after being pierced by sunbeams. He later dies as a consequence of excessive exposure to the sun, of a kind of sunstroke. In a similar way, Mallarmé was to die when he was no longer capable of breathing and uttering words.

In this respect, the literary birth of Igitur is a deferral of the poet's death. Igitur's simple recognition that he can breathe on the candle and cause an infinite fluttering of shadows on the curtain is a recognition of creative potential. As long as the self can still be projected and exhaled on its own conscious will, "the spectacle of oneself" continues. The reenactment of the ritualized metaphysical death of the poet is an exercise in poetic capability, a life-affirming act. The suicide of Igitur is a therapeutic mystery play which indicates that the poet can still breathe both physically and metaphysically.

The figurative suicide is a deferral of actual death and a literary cure for any suicidal attempts in life. As long as nothingness and absurdity can still be inscribed, projected, and reflected by the readers, the poet lives. Walter Benjamin, in his essay on Proust, wrote about almost self-inflicted Proustian asthma which stimulated Proustian writing and shaped his style.[42] Extremely long, Proustian sentences seemed to defer the ending; they engender one another endlessly as if precluding closure. The rhythm of writing is made urgent by the instinct of self-preservation, of survival. Something similar happens in the nervous rhythm of breathing in "Igitur."

Perhaps it is precisely this obsession with creativity, this urgency of writing, which precludes the delineation of clear boundaries between the literary and the extraliterary, between writing and living. Living and writing are conditioned by the same rhythms of breathing, and, paradoxically, it is the ritual death of the author acted out in the text that makes the poet's life possible. It is a therapeutic exorcism which reaffirms the frontiers between figurative and actual death. Therefore, the classical busts of the geniuses—solid figurations of creativity and a guarantee of the continuity of literary production (even if this production is in itself discontinuous)—cannot be disfigured. The black velvet of the genius mirrors the poet's creative impulses and promises survival.

A somewhat similar gesture, a simultaneous enactment of the disfiguration of the writing subject and the refiguration of the pure poet, occurs in "Action restreinte." The text is typical of Mallarmé's anecdotes and poems. It relates the encounter between poet and comrade and their debate on writing and acting. The piece appeared both as a journal article in *Revue Blanche*, in the series "Variation sur un sujet" ("Variation on a Subject") (1895), and in the book *Divagations (Ramblings)*. Here again the biography of the text indicates that Mallarmé, in spite of his notorious contempt toward the contemporary situation which he considered to be the poet's interregnum, in fact actively participated in the contemporary debates. "Action restreinte," as well as "Conflit" and "Confrontation," is

a response to the socialist and social-democratic discourse of the day. Mallarmé's strategy is to enter into dialogue with those discourses, to inscribe their vocabulary into his multivoiced poetic discourse and place them in the context of his labor of writing. In these three articles (or prose poems) Mallarmé uses such words as "class struggle," "proletariat," "bourgeoisie," "comrade," and "action" (specifically referring to political action) and decontextualizes them, depriving them of the univocal meaning they assume in socialist discourse.

Socialist theorists' choice of terminology was guided by the desire to employ a reliable scientific language stripped of any kind of "literariness." Scientific socialism, according to Engels, was supposed to be the "ideal reflection" of the objective conflict between "productive forces and the modes of production."[43] This kind of conflict is obviously different from Mallarmé's. The social(ist) scientist's claim of scientific objectivity presupposes a certain transparency of language, or at least it implies that the speaker possesses the language of truth, which allows him to represent reality adequately without staging the self-conscious drama of writing. In fact, the sociological or scientific text is dominated by the invisible presence of the omniscient narrator, whose authority is taken for granted.

Depersonalization, according to Mallarmé, is the opposite of this scientific objectivity. In contrast to the conflict which takes place in objective reality outside the speaker, Mallarmé's conflict makes the drama of "I," and the very process of depersonalization, visible. Moreover, it forces us to be suspicious of the claim of scientific objectivity. Mallarmé's "divagation sans sujet" ("rambling without a subject") or "variation sur un sujet" ("variation on a subject") plays on different meanings of "subject" (as a cause, as the speaking or writing subject, and as the matter about which one is speaking) and entwines them. The writing subject is inseparable from the subject of his writing.

Mallarmé advocates a restrained practice of reading, a reading which has to dramatize the difficulties of writing on any subject. "Action" in Mallarmé always applies to writing. For a professional author, writing remains one of the most difficult acts. Here is how Mallarmé stages the ritual depersonalization, the ritual sacrifice of the writing subject:

> L'écrivain de ses maux, dragons qu'il a choyés, ou d'une allégresse, doit s'instituer au texte, le spirituel histrion.
>   Plancher, lustre, obnubilation des tissus, et liquéfaction de miroirs, en l'ordre réel, jusqu'aux bonds excessifs de notre forme gazée, autour d'un arrêt sur pied, de la virile stature, un Lieu se présente, scène, majoration

devant tout du spectacle de Soi; là en raison des intermédiares de la lumière de la chair et des rires le sacrifice qu'y fait, relativement à sa personnalité, l'inspirateur, aboutit complet ou c'est sans une résurrection étrangère, fini de celui-ci; de qui le verbe répercuté et vain désormais s'exhale par la chimère orchestrale.[44]

The writer of his sorrows, of dragons which he has cherished, or of a gladness, should establish himself in the text, the spiritual histrion.

Floor, lustre, obnubilation of tissues, and liquefaction of mirrors, in the real order, up to the excessive leaps of our gauzed shape, around a halt at the foot of the virile stature, a Place presents itself, scene, culmination of the spectacle of the Self before all; there, by reason of the intermediaries of the light of the flesh and the laughter, the sacrifice, which the inspirer makes there, relative to his personality, ends complete or it is finished without a strange resurrection of him, whose word, reverberated and vain, is henceforth breathed by the orchestral chimera.

We recognize here all the attributes of Mallarmé's sacrifice of the poet's personality: the darkening of the tissues, the liquefaction of reflective mirrors into foamy surfaces, and of course the grotesque breathing of the chimera. This appears to be a most radical depersonalization—there is nothing left but the empty stage, only the Place itself, with a capital P. This reminds us of another memorable place of the poet's death—"Un Coup de dés" ("A Throw of the Dice"): "Rien n'aura eu lieu que le lieu" ("Nothing but the place will have taken place"). And yet after the blank space following this paragraph of "Action restreinte" there comes a strange recuperation of representation:

Une salle, il se célèbre, anonyme, dans le héros.

Tout, comme fonctionnement de fêtes: un peuple témoigne de sa transfiguration en vérité.

Honneur.[45]

A room, he celebrates himself, anonymous, in the hero.

All, as the functioning of holidays: a people truly witnesses his transfiguration.

Honor.

Thus it turns out that the anonymous Place encloses the classical, colossal statue of a hero. His clothes (all the feminine gauzes, folds, and tissues) are obscured only to reveal his virile figure. The people are present to render him honors. Julia Kristeva sees the hero in Mallarmé

as the figure of a demi-god, the son of the phallic mother, someone who evokes the ancient mysteries in the utilitarian bourgeois republic.[46] In other words, according to Kristeva, the hero rebels against bourgeois law, with its division of labor and pragmatism, and seeks to recreate a communal, cathartic experience even at the price of self-sacrifice. The hero has a very precise gender—he is not androgynous or gender-neutral; he is a god's son, the masculine creative principle. Thus, in spite of Mallarmé's fascination with the feminine, which has been consistently emphasized by contemporary critics, the poet remains virile, even when he is disfigured in a modern and classical fashion. The text, the pure work, and the book might be compared to a female dancer (*danseuse*), who as Mallarmé hastens to remark is no longer a woman, but an allegory "crayonné au théâtre." But the pure poet, son of geniuses, a creatively self-sacrificial national hero, is masculine. Therefore, when a contemporary critic sees "the death of the author" as a modern sacrifice, and assumes the absence of figuration, in fact (even if unconsciously), he or she is paying a tribute to the virile aristocratic statue of the classical poet.

The hero as a figure for the pure poet appears also in Mallarmé's tomb poems. "Le Tombeau d'Edgar Poe" describes the Poet "with a naked sword," who, like Heracles, is ready to attack the Hydra. De Man analyzes some of the "tombeau" poems in his "Lyric and Modernity," but completely disregards their heroic bas-reliefs. In general, tomb poetry and dedications to dead poets occupy a significant part of Mallarmé's corpus. In these works, disfiguring devices co-exist with a strong instinct for poetic self-preservation and an emphasis on sculpting true poetic immortality.

In fact, Mallarmé actively participates in contemporary rituals in honor of dead poets and assists in their institutionalization. For instance, he reads the speech at the opening of the monument to Theodore de Banville, "prince of poets," now remembered only as Mallarmé's contemporary.[47] The image of Banville in Mallarmé's text strangely reminds us of when the cartoonish frontispiece appeared in Mallarmé's "Autobiographie," a time when Mallarmé himself became a "prince of poets." Although one might argue that the poet's utopian, classical kingdom is much less harmful than some political utopias, it is still quite different from the empty place, *le Lieu*, or from the neutral, abstract, and pure operation of syntax. Neither the "classic" nor the "ancient" is synonymous with neutral, universal, or archetypal.[48] Mallarmé's classicism is nostalgic; it is a sort of neo-neoclassicism, enclosed within many art nouveau frames with grotesque ornaments and arabesques.

Besides the classical hero, there is another, more contemporary part to be played by the pure poet—the part of *dandy*. Let us look at another "médaillon" poem, "Edgar Poe," which appeared in the same collection as the one about Banville. Paradoxically, Mallarmé describes Poe as "the pure among the Spirits" and "the absolute literary case."[49] At the same time he uses a portrait by Whistler to illustrate this absolute literary case. In "Igitur" he exemplifies the antitheatrical in the theater itself, while here, in talking about absolute literariness, he relies on an image. Obviously, this is not a psychological but a cosmic portrait, with astral eyes and serpentine mount. And yet we notice that Mallarmé's Poe wears the familiar black clothes in "the black coquetry." Why does the purest of spirits have to wear a coat? What are the purest spiritual fashions? Obviously the hot color of the season, "la dernière mode," of the pure poets is black.

Moreover, Mallarmé represents the painter himself in the same attire as his model. According to Mallarmé, Whistler's refinement, natural grace, and sarcasm are heightened by his favorite clothes—"l'habit noir" ("black outfit"). The black clothes of the painter mirror the black clothes of his model. In fact, as follows from the correspondence between Mallarmé and Whistler, Whistler reminded Mallarmé of Poe.[50] In this case it is difficult to determine who is imitating whom and who is fashioning whom. It appears that on the one hand Whistler creates his own image of a Poe/aesthete who wears black and speaks with a French Symbolist accent, and on the other hand he borrows the style for both life and painting from Poe. The issue is further complicated by yet another layer of clothes and textuality—that of Mallarmé himself. The late friendship of Whistler and Mallarmé was a peculiar syncretic artistic symbiosis: Whistler made a black and white engraving of Mallarmé (or *crayonné au Mallarmé*) while Mallarmé wrote a "note" to Whistler, in which he creates a French rhyme for the painter's English name (*Whistlér/air*) and which Whistler finds "très dandy."[51]

The last word, "dandy," finally names this strange play of coincidences and the repeated reflection of black clothes in the mirror. Both Mallarmé and Whistler, as well as their character, Poe, participate in the same cultural myth—the myth of the dandy. At the center of this myth is "the making of the self." As the famous dandy Brummel put it: "It is my folly that is the making of me."[52] The dandy turns his life into an elegant fiction and himself into a character. And yet, as Charles Baudelaire tells us in "Le Peintre de la vie moderne" ("The Painter of Modern Life"), *dandysme* cannot be reduced to "an immoderate taste of dress and of

material elegance." According to Baudelaire, *dandysme* is a kind of religion, bordering on spiritualism and stoicism.[53] In this respect, the color of the dandy's clothes is crucial. Black attire helps to erase the physicality of the body, emphasizing spirituality; and at the same time it is uniquely flattering to the figure.

The black figure can function as a hieroglyph, an incorporeal sign of writing. Blackness might appear as a lack of color and as an oversaturation. It is an aristocratic sign, a sign of permanent spiritual mourning, and also a kind of coy poverty—false modesty, so to speak. It is pretentiously unpretentious, antiaristocratically aristocratic, asexually sexy. Black clothes disguise the very presence of clothing and help to highlight the whiteness of the face. They deindividualize the face by surrounding it with a uniform frame and at the same time emphasize individual facial features, causing them to stand out with particular clarity against the black background.

Baudelaire regarded *dandysme* not only as a cult of the self but also as a defiance of the institution of law. It is an elegant subversion, a revolutionary "action restreinte" that undermines utilitarian social principles, reducing to absurdity the theater of everyday life. Baudelaire sees in *dandysme* a modern heroism: "Le dandysme est le dernier éclat d'héroisme dans les décadences" ("Dandyism is the last outburst of heroism in decadence").[54] The dandy, "an unemployed Hercules," is a hero of an antiheroic age, a pathetic pastiche on his statuesque ancestor. Eventually, however, the subversive eccentricities of dandies become mythified, composing a certain code of "making of me" and "erasing of me."[55]

The folly of the dandy, "the making of me," is somewhat similar to the folly of Elbehnon-Igitur but in the dandy's case the medium is different: he does not write with language but with his body, and instead of depersonalization he practices impersonation. Or, rather, the folly of the dandy consists precisely of the impossibility of distinguishing between depersonalization and impersonation, between life and fiction, between the making of oneself in poetry and in everyday existence. As I pointed out earlier, "making," "fashion," and "poetry" signify similar actions etymologically. The dandy demonstrates in his self-fashioning the same formal principles that the poet demonstrates in his writing. The same anarchic and subversive syntax operates in both, but the limits of the "text" become dangerously open to transgression.

Baudelaire, however, differentiates between writer and dandy. A dandy is an ascetic and an aesthete; he is too aloof to love or to suffer, to be ecstatic or to be repulsed. He is not passionate about anything, even

art. In this respect, Mallarmé, for whom writing (the covering up of the white page with black signs) was an existential therapy and an obsession, would not quite qualify. As Michel Lemaire writes in *Le Dandysme de Baudelaire à Mallarmé*, there is always a tension between writer and dandy, between a writer/dandy and a dandy/writer. A writer often wishes to mask himself as a dandy/writer and to play down the seriousness of his literary profession.[56] Moreover, Mallarmé made his living as a professor of English (which might sound dandy, but in fact is not), and he is reported to have been modest, simple, and self-effacing, that is, the very opposite of the ostensible man of fashion. But the black clothes betray the dandy's uniform. Mallarmé was known for his black attire, in which he is represented in the famous portrait by Manet. The black suit here is not simply a pictographic convention but an everyday fact. Several other features of Mallarmé's daily behavior reveal the iconography of a dandy: his famous salon dialogues—"fumées"—and "mardis" on rue de Rome, a stylish love affair with one of the most fashionable women of the time, Méry Laurent, and finally the making of his unique cultural oeuvre, *La Dernière Mode*.

Hence we note again that together with the process of modern defacement and the fulfillment of the linguistic predicament described by de Man, the process of dynamic image making goes on. This is something that can be provisionally called a *cinematic predicament*—an act of recognizing cuts and discontinuities and at the same time of yielding to the erotic in an image, participation in a collective enjoyment of darkness and of the luminescent screen, of projection and identification.

Depersonalization in writing affects the personal life of a writer in boomerang fashion: it strikes back and forces one to impersonate the self-effacement and adopt its acceptable cultural expression, partaking in cultural myths. One can also say that the practice of spiritual dandyism pushed to the extreme might engender monsters and chimeras that are more extravagant and excessive than those allowed by dandy-ish ornamental iconography—textual monsters and verbal doppelgängers. In this case, the elegant bouquet of flowers, most probably orchids, on the encrusted table of the dandy, would turn into the scandalous *Fleurs du mal* or even into Mallarmé's abstract and spiritual flower in poetic crisis—the flower "absent of any bouquet."

Mallarmé's neutrality can be compared to "the neutral mask" ("masque neutre"), a certain conventional device which is used in the theater of masks and in the twentieth century specifically elaborated by Jacques Lecoq.[57] It is a white schematic mask that allows the actors to

lose their ordinary identity. Hence, it acts as a traditional theatrical disguise that helps the actors to dispose of their personal idiosyncratic outfits. In a similar way, Mallarmé's neutrality is always a mask, a cultural mark, and not the absence of one. Mallarmé practices a form of modern depersonalization, sponsored by the specific culture; it can be subversive, challenging, and transgressive, but it cannot entirely escape the cultural figuration. Mallarmé's radical syntax disfigures neither the classical bust with laurel and lyre nor the virile hero with sword. The richness and suggestiveness of Mallarmé's poetry comes precisely from its culturally specific ornamentation and its obsessive treatment of the tension between syntax and image, between the extraliterary and the literary, the fashionable and the outmoded. This modern suggestiveness resides in the erotic folding together of black textures—the chimeric fashion of the pure poet.

The White Butterfly, or the Erotics of Impurity

We have observed how the cultural attire of a pure poet is disguised by Mallarmé's subversive and self-effacing texture. The costume of Mallarmé's suicidal hero—the self-reflective heroic black velvet—is "traditional and neutral," a perfect mythical texture (in a Barthesian sense) that masks its historicity and cultural specificity by appealing to a certain supreme, classical primal scene of the sacrifice and rebirth of the poet/ hero. And yet Mallarmé's infatuation with the materiality of folds and textures, with the ornamentation of domestic furniture, finds its ultimate expression in the poet's peculiar oeuvre—*La Dernière Mode*, which Mallarmé wrote and edited almost single-handedly in 1874.

La Dernière Mode occupies a special place in Mallarmé's corpus. As we remember, Mallarmé dedicates an entire paragraph in his "Autobiographie" to the journal, expressing his pride and pleasure regarding this work, and placing it somewhat marginally both to his collection of poetry and to his utopian *le Livre*. A section of *La Dernière Mode* is entitled "Gazette du monde et de la famille" ("Gazette of the world and of the family"). "The world" here is not an orphic atemporal universe, but the glamorous world of 1870's Paris, "a small world." It seems that *La Dernière Mode* exemplifies everything Mallarmé would place under the derogative name "journal," a journal that deals with transient contemporary topics and completely lacks the premeditated, universal architectonics of *le Livre*. And yet Mallarmé's fashion magazine has a global ambition sim-

ilar to *le Livre*—"total expansion of the letter." It is an attempt to furnish an imaginary world in its entirety, prescribing everything from cooking recipes to ways of dreaming with a half-closed book on one's lap.

Here I will explore further the relationship between the hypothetical "Livre," which can only be written at the price of a total domestic sacrifice, the burning of familial furniture, and *La Dernière Mode*—"gazette de la famille," which erotically reconstructs all the whimsical ornaments and folds of the domestic interior, with its master and slave, the woman. I will examine *La Dernière Mode* together with the short text "Le Livre, instrument spirituel," which presents an interesting description of the mythical book viewed in opposition to the commercial journal. My focus will be on one suggestive poetic image—that of the white butterfly (papillon blanc) that circulates between the two texts, both reconstituting and blurring their boundaries.

"Le Livre, instrument spirituel" is an essay from the short collection *Quant au livre* (*As for the Book*), the title of which already suggests that *le Livre* will be treated within Mallarmé's syntax, in incomplete sentences with conditional clauses. The first paragraph of the essay describes the relationship between the book and the world, in which the book composed by the genius "à coup sûr" is regarded as an ultimate world masterpiece: "Une proposition qui émane de moi . . . que tout au monde existe pour aboutir à un livre" ("A proposition which emanates from me . . . that everything in the world exists to result in a book").[58]

The relation between "je" ("I") and "génie" ("genius") in this text is analogous to the relationship between the text of "Le Livre, instrument spirituel," signed by Stéphane Mallarmé, and "Le Livre" itself, a volume without signature, a postscript to the spiritual suicide of the poet. Although the title of the essay regards the book as a spiritual instrument, the essay itself elaborates on its material characteristics, such as typography, and on the spatial aspects that distinguish a book from a journal. The journal, which in Mallarmé's quotidian scene is abandoned on the garden bench, is described as "la feuille étalée," an exhibited, flat piece of paper with a typographical composition imprinted upon it. The book on the contrary is "le pliage," an infinite folding of letters and sheets upon themselves and each other, a folding that suggests a certain hermeneutic rhythm of revelation and concealment, of word and silence.

There is a suggestive white space that separates the ending from the rest of the essay—an example of Mallarmé's own exploration of modern typography. While the poet who composes in the "pure space" of the book becomes more and more depersonalized, the book itself in Mallarmé's

description acquires disturbing, anthropomorphic features. It is compared to a domestic bird, and then to a virgin, ready for ritual sacrifice:

> Voici dans le cas réel, que pour ma part, cependant au sujet de brochures à lire d'après l'usage courant, je brandis un couteau, comme le cuisinier égorgeur de volailles.
>
> Le reploiment vierge du livre, encore, prête à un sacrifice dont saigna la tranche rouge des anciens tomes; l'introduction d'une arme, ou coupe-papier, pour établir la prise de possession. Combien personnelle plus avant, la conscience, sans ce simulacre barbare: quand elle se fera participation, au livre pris d'ici, de là, varié en airs, deviné comme une énigme—presque refait par soi.[59]

> Here, in the real case, for my part—as regards brochures for reading, according to current usage—I brandish a knife, just as the cook, slaughterer of fowl.
>
> The virgin folding of the book, again, ready for a sacrifice in which will bleed the red edge of ancient volumes; the introduction of a weapon, or a paper knife, to establish taking possession. Further however personal, the conscience, without this barbarous simulacra: when it [she, the conscience] will partake in the book taken from here, from there, varied in airs, figured out as an enigma—almost redone by itself.

In the "real case," as opposed to the utopian fantasy of the "pure" composition of the book of the world, the poet resigns himself to the status of a creatively sadomasochistic reader. The act of reading is presented through physical action—the cutting of pages with a knife, the action that metamorphoses into the sacrifice of a domestic bird, and later into the ritual rape of a paper virgin. Something happens at the moment when, in the reader's sadistic fantasy, the edge of the book becomes tinged with red. The rape is suspended, and the potential "*prise* de possession" ("taking possession") turns into a perpetual "*surprise*," an unattainable enigma of the book folding upon itself, and a mocking of "the barbarous simulacra," the imaginary sacrifice. Mallarmé prefers the aesthetic of surprise to the aesthetic of transgression. "Le coup sûr" ("the stroke") of the genius, metamorphosed into a possible "coupe" ("cut") of "coupe-papier," is indefinitely deferred. The act of reading or writing *le Livre*, the ultimate act of "se livrer à livre" ("liberation and effacement of the self for the sake of the book") of the poet, as well as (as it usually happens in these heroic circumstances) the sacrifice of a female virgin for the noble cause of a male genius, is never completely accomplished. (Incidently, the correlation between the victoric us hymn of the poet/hero

and the virginal hymen of the text, which is obvious here, is not sufficiently explored by Derrida, who otherwise explored most of the meanings of the word "hymen," crucial to his anti-Platonic revisionist paradigm.)

Mallarmé's text always stops before the reading of the book. In the last
paragraph of the essay the reader is left with an ingenius flight of "le
papillon blanc."

> Attribuons à des songes avant lecture, dans un parterre, l'attention que
> sollicite quelque papillon blanc, celui-ci à la fois partout, nulle part, il
> s'évanouit, pas sans qu'un rien d'aigu et d'ingénu, où je réduisis le sujet,
> tout à l'heure ait passé et repassé, avec insistance, devant l'étonnement.[60]

> Let's attribute to the dreams before reading, the attention which a white
> butterfly solicits in a flower bed [parterre: flower bed, pit in the theater];
> the butterfly, at the same time everywhere and nowhere, vanishes, not
> without a keen and ingenious nothing, where I reduced the subject; it has
> just passed by and passed by again with insistence before astonishment.

The white butterfly, the last animation of the virginal fold of the book,
flies away from the writer and from the reader. Upon a rereading, one
recognizes its traces in each white space of the text. "Papillon blanc" is
a folding of the image and paper together, of the text and the writing
instrument. In a way this metaphysical white butterfly is also a personification of the "instrument spirituel," since in ancient mythology, both
Egyptian and Roman, the butterfly stands for the soul, or for Psyche,
searching for her invisible husband Cupid and escaping him. It is a
paradoxical materialization of the soul of Mallarmé's text, which both
desires the reader and defies him or her. (For Mallarmé the implicit
reader of this text is most likely male, while that of *La Dernière Mode* is
distinctly female.) It is the dream of an unviolated book, a never accomplished loss of virginity, and an enactment of yet another lost chance to
perform a supreme, depersonalizing "coup de génie." The flight of the
white butterfly signals the failure on the poet's part to prove his virility, a
virility required of the hero or genius. The butterfly is an incarnation of
Mallarmé's metaphysical frivolity, a *licencia poetica* that escapes the austere classical vigilance of the familial busts in black velvet. It flies between natural and theatrical space ("parterre," which refers both to the
flower bed and to the orchestral seats in the theater), disturbing the poet's
suicidal "spectacle de soi," threatening with impotence and promising
poetic pleasures.

The spiritual white butterfly reappears again on the page of Mallarmé's fashion magazine. *La Dernière Mode* seems to be the opposite of the murderous, poetic "one-man show." It describes the theater of everyday life, " la fête suprème et quotidienne," whose characters are elegantly dressed and coiffured female models. The journal is not about the poet's depersonalization, creative sterility, or his stripping of everyday attires. On the contrary, it exemplifies the poet's power of seduction—the imaginative power to dress and undress imaginary women. And yet, once we look at what happens to the author of this fashionable world, we discover a curious case of schizophrenia, somewhat similar to the folly of Elbehnon from "Igitur." Here the authorship is fragmented. Mallarmé, while almost single-handedly writing the editorial material for the magazine, consistently erases himself, hiding behind various female and male pseudonyms. Among his playful alter egos are "Marguerite de Ponty," or "Madame de P.," an elegant Parisian lady who writes erotic articles about fashion; "Miss Satin," a poignant Englishwoman (a humorous creation of the bored English professor) who writes the regular column "Gazette de la fashion" and frequently uses "les mots anglais"; "a Creole Lady" and "Zizi," "good mulatto of Surate," who kindly provide recipes for gumbo and coconut jam respectively; and finally the director of the entire magazine—Marasquin, who borrowed his name from the famous liqueur, maraschino.

Mallarmé's name appears on the cover, among the renowned fellow poets who contributed to the magazine—Théodore de Banville, Léon Claudel, Alphonse Daudet, Sully Prudhomme, Emile Zola, and others. Obviously, the great poet Mallarmé does not feature in the section "Dans la mode et le goût Parisien" ("In the Fashion and Taste of Paris") but in the section proudly entitled "En Littérature" ("In Literature") and under the French translation of Tennyson's poem "Marianne." Perhaps, this shows Mallarmé's attempt not to tarnish his pure poetic reputation by involvement in such an impure, worldly, and commercial affair. The whole issue of signature, raised in "Le Livre, instrument spirituel," or rather the insistence on the lack of signature as a stamp of genius, emerges again here with a new angle. In the context of *La Dernière Mode*, the "Stéphane Mallarmé" of literature, who appears in the distinguished company of Madame de Ponty, Miss Satin, and Zizi, can be read as yet another pseudonym—a persona of a pure poet and master of high culture. Moreover, in the context of *La Dernière Mode*, this "Mallarmé" is not a main hero, but a rather minor character.

The recourse to pseudonyms in this case is of both metaphysical and

commercial value. It is one of the strange convergences of the needs of high culture and commercial art. On the one hand, the plurality of pseudonyms reveals a special fragmentation of Foucault's "author function" in Mallarmé, a fragmentation deprived of deadly angst and embued with playfulness and eroticism. The feminine impersonation allows the poet to indulge his own fetishistic obsession with clothes without qualms of aesthetic conscience. If the fashions of the pure poet have to remain disguised and hermeneutic, the fashion of the woman of the world can be embellished with the minute precision of every ruffle. On the other hand, female masks are used by the male author for a practical purpose: to seduce female readers into erotic and aesthetic complicity, ultimately to help sell the journal. What are the politics of Mallarmé's erotic seduction in *La Dernière Mode?* Does the use of female pseudonyms in the discussion of fashion perpetuate the stereotypes of cultural femininity and leave the myth of the pure poet intact? Or, on the contrary, does it create a gender schizophrenia on the part of the male author? Does it solidify the boundaries between "feminine" and "masculine" domains of writing, between popular and high culture, between fashion and literature, or does it entail their blurring?

We remember that the imaginary editorial board of *La Dernière Mode*, in which the majority of contributors are women (and all of them impersonated by Mallarmé himself) is headed by the male director Marasquin.[61] The same hierarchical structure persists in the world of fashion described by Mallarmé, which is dominated by female dressmakers, "les faiseuses," but governed by the great and ingenious male designer Worth. Moreover, for the most important accessories such as jewelry, women are advised to consult a male artist, or an architect—and not one of their *modistes* or *faiseuses.*

On a less figurative level, we know that all the actual contributors of the journal were men. Even if Madame Mallarmé, or any other woman, helped Mallarmé to edit the texts or advised on the clothes, she remains anonymous. Her anonymity is quite different from Mallarmé's playful and self-conscious manipulation of pseudonyms and signatures, with their erasures, disguises, and reappearances. Her anonymity, as well as the anonymity of actual *faiseuses, liseuses* and *poetesses* (dressmakers, female readers, poetesses), is historically imposed and absolute, like the unframed white spaces and the folds of black velvet. In fact, when Mallarmé lost the journal in 1874, Rémy de Gourmont wrote, complaining about feminine authorship: "A la fin de 1874, *La Dernière Mode*, hélas! tombe aux mains d'une femme qui en fait la banale revue historiée de sottises

dont il n'y a que trop d'échantillons" ("At the end of 1874, *The Latest Fashion*, alas! falls into the hands of a woman who makes it a banal review decorated [historiée] with foolishness, of which there are too many examples").[62] In the hands of actual women the poetic trifles and charms turn into stupidities and banalities; Mallarmé's subversive "revue *historique*" degenerates into "revue *historiée*," full of meaningless decoration.

Thus *La Dernière Mode* is a fantastic communication between imaginary female authors and imaginary female readers carefully orchestrated for the voyeuristic and narcissistic enjoyment of a male poet. The *liseuse* of *La Dernière Mode* is a utopian construct of poetic femininity. (As opposed to *lectrice*, *liseuse* exists only in the feminine form and suggests *promeneuse* [female stroller] and *danseuse* [female dancer].) Like the *danseuse* in *Crayonné au théâtre*, she is not a woman but a metaphor, a metaphor for the ideally erotic reader, whom the author can fancy dressing and undressing. The author of this essay, "IX," fashions himself as a gentle friend of a lady who supervises her aesthetic surprises.

> On va répétant non sans vérité, qu'il n'y a plus de lecteurs, je crois bien ce sont des lectrices. Seule une dame, dans son isolement de la Politique et des soins moroses, a le loisir nécessaire pour que s'en dégage, sa toilette achevée, un besoin de se parer l'âme.[63]

> It is repeated, not untruthfully, that there are no more male readers; but I believe there are female readers. Only a lady, in her isolation from Politics and gloomy cares, has the necessary leisure time, once she has dressed, for a need to adorn [se parer] the soul.

This statement suggests that the ideal reader, not only of this specific journal, but in general, is an idle reader, placed outside politics and other routine chores (which sounds doubly ironic, since Mallarmé himself is involved here in tailoring the politics of gender). And a woman, due to her cultural situation, is the only candidate for the position. The other ideal feature of the *lectrices* and *liseuses* is that they actually do not read, but rather share transient erotic epiphanies with the author.[64] The descriptions of toilettes and recipes for coconut jam are saturated with the same persistent images of clouds, folds, interstices, threshold states, distractions, "divagations sans objet," and "actions restreintes" that permeate "Le Livre, instrument spirituel" and other strictly literary works of Mallarmé. In *La Dernière Mode*, literature and fashion exist side by side; they exchange metaphors and fold upon one another like the imaginary clothes of a *liseuse*.

La Dernière Mode is not so much about the linguistic predicament as about sight and the ways of seeing through the semitransparent gauze of a multilayered dress. This is how Marguerite de Ponty defines her subject: "Toilettes et toilettes encore, teintées et noires, *images placées hors du texte et dans le texte* et plusieurs écrites mêmes avec la plume" ("Costumes and costumes again, tinted and black, images placed outside the text and in the text and several writings themselves with the feather [pen]").[65] "Plume" as an accessory of a woman's costume and as a writing instrument puts together texts and toilettes, which turn upon each other like the pages of a half-closed book hidden in a woman's skirt. These double-edged words do not allow us to draw a clear-cut distinction between inside and outside the text, between the text itself and the costume, between the black costume of the poet and colorful feminine attire. The reading of the half-closed book cannot be a "close reading"; it is a simultaneous reading of clothes, body, and the text.

One image that ties together the inside and outside of the text, an image that serves not to *séparer* (separate) but to *se parer* (adorn oneself), is that of the "papillon." It appears first in one of the most erotic texts by Marguerite de Ponty in the issue of November 15. The essay is an erotic *tour de force*, an exercise in suspense and deferral of textual and extratextual pleasures.

> Fermant les yeux à d'adorables motifs dont me tente la description, je poursuis, stricte et brève.
> Que des noeuds papillon soient avec un heureux manque de symétrie, posés, pour compléter des volants espacés et plissés très fin; que des floraisons courent en girandoles et en espaliers: c'est là un luxe ordinaire et presque facile. *Le génie qui métamorphosa des tissus en papillons et en fleurs,* le cède encore devant la splendeur pure et simple des tissus eux-même, tulle blanc lamé d'argent à côté de bandes de satin blanc.[66]

> Closing the eyes to adorable motifs, the description of which tempts me, I pursue, strict and brief.
> May only butterfly knots be with a happy lack of symmetry, placed to complete the very finely spaced and pleated flounces; may the blooming hasten into clusters and espaliers: that is an ordinary and almost easy luxury. The genius which metamorphosed the tissues into butterflies and flowers yields it still before the pure and simple splendor of the tissues themselves, silver lamé white tulle beside the strips of white satin.

Here "papillon" is not a spiritual symbol but a detail of dress. (The meanings of the English word "butterfly" and the French "papillon" over-

lap but do not entirely coincide.) It is a carefully designed excess, what in *La Dernière Mode* is often called "un rien sérieux" ("a serious nothing"), something superfluous and elegant that adds the necessary poetic accent to already beautiful white textures—white tulle on white satin, a material version of Mallarmé's famous white-on-white. The appearance of the solemn genius in this fashionable context is rather remarkable. The description suggests that it takes a stroke of genius to perform a creative metamorphosis and design a sublime poetic thing out of meaningless folds. The ingenious simplicity and gracefulness of the "papillon" distinguishes it from the "vain overburdening" and "useless ornamentation" criticized later in the description.

And yet this stroke of genius is deferred in a way similar to, although much less violent than, "Le Livre, instrument spirituel." In fact, the creation of the "papillon" is so superfluous that the stroke of genius could be postponed and, as a result, the creative energy would be disseminated throughout the folds of the material without tying them together. The imaginary "papillon" serves only to foreground "the pure splendor" of the textures and tissues themselves, in the same way as Mallarmé's verse forces us to see infinite suggestiveness in the white space between the lines. The ending of Marguerite de Ponty's text is an excessive enumeration of elegant tissues, unviolated by any design.

Ultimately, the "papillon" is but a simulacrum; it emerges and vanishes only to reveal the endlessly erotic interplay of the textures themselves. Although on one level this text can be read as an exercise in male voyeurism, or as an elaborate seduction of the "lectrice," on another level, it is contaminated by the imaginary feminity that it depicts. The kind of eroticism that this text perpetrates with its vacillations, deferrals, excesses, and detours marks what in the late twentieth century is described as *écriture féminine*.[67]

In the subtitle of one of Marguerite de Ponty's essays of October 18 we read: "Le Papillon. Emblème? Non, Parure" ("The butterfly [bow]. Emblem? No, adornment"). A large part of the article is dedicated to the white dress of the bride. First, Marguerite de Ponty clearly establishes gender distinctions (in which she coincides with "Mallarmé"). She then insists on never mixing either the genres of fashions or the gender roles. She quickly dismisses as "le paradoxe charmant" the masculine outfit of a woman, as did Mallarmé in his response to a questionnaire concerning a woman's bicycling costume.[68] Thus we see that in the context of *La Dernière Mode* and the rest of Mallarmé's work, only one gender has a right to be self-consciously playful and assume the masks of the other gender without eliciting repulsion.

The white dress of the bride, a clear reminder of institutionalized gender roles, is turned into the ultimate aesthetic object. It is this dress that inspires the Papillon fantasy.

> Ce cachet [le cachet véritable de Fantasie], il lui sera donné surtout par une nouvelle, complétant les informations qui précèdent: c'est, quoi? l'annonce d'un emblématique Papillon qui, vaste, superbe, taillé dans ces tissus légers et délicieux, élèvera son vol immobile à hauteur, Mesdames, de l'une ou de l'autre de vos joues, remplaçant par son caprice la fraise historique de ces dernières années. Vos frisures feront tomber leurs anneaux dans l'intervalle de deux ailes. Brillante imagination, n'est-ce pas? qui rappelle les métamorphoses mêlant à gazes d'insectes un visage de femme dans les albums anciens de Granville: non, elle appartient au génie de ce magicien extraordinaire . . . le grand Worth.[69]

> This style [the true style of Fantasy], it will be given to her especially by a piece of news, completing the information which precedes: it is, what? the announcement of an emblematic Butterfly—vast, superb, cut in these light and delicious fabrics—which will elevate its immobile flight to the height, my dear ladies, of one or the other of your cheeks, replacing the historical ruff of the past years by its caprice. Your curls will let down their ringlets in the space between the two wings. Brilliant imagination, isn't it? which recalls the metamorphoses interweaving a woman's face from the old Granville albums with insect gauze: no, it belongs to the genius of that extraordinary magician . . . great Worth.

This paragraph recounts a proliferation of possibilities for metamorphosis. The wings of the butterfly displace the textures of a woman's elegant clothes, and then the woman's face itself. The author refuses to fix the butterfly in its "immobile flight." Even when the word is capitalized, it never becomes an emblem or a symbol of one specific displacement. Rather, it vacillates between becoming a symbol and turning into a graceful decorative trifle, "une parure," a figment of the imagination. "Papillon" is a metaphor par excellence, which exemplifies the very instability of the metaphoric process in its perpetual flight of displacements. It oscillates between the spiritual book and the commercial journal, and does not allow the drawing of a *pure* opposition between the two. It turns the pages of the book dreamed by a pure poet into the face of a woman, the folds of the paper into the folds of a dress, the images of extreme spirituality into fetishes of erotic seduction. The butterfly is both extremely illuminating of the dynamics of Mallarmé's text and completely superfluous; it emerges and vanishes only to foreground the semitransparent virginal white texture, the space between the lines.

Mallarmé is not the only fan of butterflies among poets, writers, and artists. His friend Whistler stylized his signature as a butterfly with wide-open wings, taking the first initial of his last name and juxtaposing it with its upside down double. The butterfly plays a game of hide-and-seek with the spectator, who is challenged to find the author's signature artfully concealed in the black background. Whistler's butterfly, an ornament of authorship, lurks behind in Mallarmé's text. A few decades after Mallarmé and Whistler, Vladimir Nabokov became the most famous collector of butterflies, but his butterflies were not metaphorical. In fact, the Museum of Comparative Zoology at Harvard University preserves an odd collection of the butterflies—particularly of the butterfly genitalia, carefully removed by a one-time research assistant of the museum, Vladimir Nabokov. These exotic, beautiful, and mutilated insects, exhibited with meticulous annotations composed in Nabokov's neat Russian handwriting, present a strange spectacle. The pinned and castrated butterfly appears as a perfect aesthetic and scientific object, an emblem of the author's perverse mastery over his subject. Mallarmé's textual butterfly, unlike that of Whistler, is anonymous and is not made to resemble the poet's signature (although, visually, Mallarmé's first initial is the exact image in reverse of Whistler's). Neither is it pinned down meticulously and sadistically like that of Nabokov. Rather it remains in perpetual flight and metamorphosis—one of those vertigoes that the poet refuses to fix.

The flight of the white butterfly is both the invention of a male genius and a deferral of his final stroke. The text manipulates cultural images of femininity and at the same time prepares their revision. On the one hand, as in the world of Mallarmé's *La Dernière Mode*, women are dispossessed of any power—aesthetic, intellectual, or political. "*La* mode," "fashion," might be feminine, but "*le* mode d'emploi," the way of using it and thinking about it, emanates from a male creative source. And yet, *la mode* contaminates the poet's mode of thinking not only about clothes but also about texts, history, and spirituality. Mallarmé's usurpation of the cultural metaphors of femininity—the making, especially dressmaking—of this feminine world, leads to the eventual reevaluation of these metaphors. As in Baudelaire's "Le Peintre de la vie moderne" in which the metaphor of female make-up serves to illustrate the modern conception of mimesis, in *La Dernière Mode* the scene of a distractive feminine reading, as well as a complex folding of images inside and outside the text, is a statement of Mallarmé's modern aesthetics. The recourse to feminine pseudonyms liberates the poet from the intellectual and aesthetic constraints of "high culture," allowing him to indulge in a popular occurrence of everyday life and juxtapose gossip, recipes, and advice on fashionable materials with

the discussion of serious poetic matter. Also, the very syntax of Mallarmé's text, with its "feminine" excesses, detours, and deferrals, as opposed to the strokes of a male genius, tailors a much more playful and less heroic costume for the modern poet. It allows for a richness and plurality of everyday fashions, instead of the exclusive and formal black costume of the pure poet. The erotics of impurity, the vacillation of the reader's and the writer's gaze, and the text's vacillation between high culture and commercial culture presents an alternative model for the modern text. This modern text is much less abstract, formal, austere, and suicidal than the text of the dead and disfigured author glorified by many contemporary critics.

The pure white butterfly, therefore, turns into a sign of aesthetic impurity and cultural eclecticism that are characteristic of modernism. It is Mallarmé's poetic thing par excellence, culturally specific and elusive at the same time, which does not allow us to fix the poet within any purely theoretical grids and makes us consider all of his pseudonyms and personae—a faceless poet and a dandy in black, a fashionable woman and an English professor, a radical innovator of syntax, and a faithful preserver of traditional cultural images.

The "Purest Poet": Myth Making and Mis-Reading

Au lieu d'écrire: cygne, or, azur, j'écris: vie, etc. Mon travail n'en est guère changé. On dit que je suis plus humain et plus à la mode.

Instead of writing: swan, gold, azure; I write: life, etc. My work is not changed by it. People say that I am more human and more fashionable.
Paul Valéry, *Cahiers*

Paul Valéry made his living as an author from the deaths of Stéphane Mallarmé. Both Mallarmé's actual death and his crisis of literature inspired Valéry to design the most perfect—and often, perfectly monstrous—figure of a modern *homme d'esprit*. Valéry authorized and institutionalized the iconography of a "pure poet," alternatively called "pure spirit" or, in Boris Tomashevsky's terminology, a "writer without a biography." This writer without a biography was destined to become a modern character par excellence: he pervaded diverse national traditions of modernism, reaching to the new world specifically in the aesthetic theories of T. S. Eliot and Jorge Luis Borges.

Here I will trace Valéry's strategies of reading Mallarmé's "death of the author." We can observe how, in Valéry's version, Mallarmé's text, with its multiple suggestive gaps and semantic ambiguities, becomes a precise and architectonic *figure of the text* and the poet, Mallarmé, becomes the exemplary poet's monument with an oversized head. Thus my focus will be on *the transformation of reading into myth making*, on the rhetoric of giving a figure—quite a monumental and anthropomorphic figure of a pure "homme d'esprit"—to the disfigured textual self and to the complex process of depersonalization and syntactic self-effacement enacted in Mallarmé's writings.

What is interesting in Valéry's position vis-à-vis Mallarmé's is its crucial ambiguity. Valéry is both a passionate reader of Mallarmé and his personal friend. After Valéry meets Mallarmé in 1890, an affectionate friendship gradually develops between the two. Because of the great difference in their ages and positions on the French literary Parnassus, this friendship is something like a father-son relationship—there is a filial reverence on the part of Valéry and a paternal kindness on the part of Mallarmé. And yet Valéry remarks in one of his later essays on Mallarmé that he cannot speak about Mallarmé "without *egotism*," putting the word in italics as if writing on Mallarmé gives him a pretext to expose his own poetic and antipoetic theories. [70] Mallarmé is both Valéry's privileged subject of writing and his privileged addressee, with whom Valéry wishes to share his own literary crisis.

Valéry wrote several letters and essays concerning Mallarmé's actual death and his figurative "death of the author." Among the letters we find a variety of genres: from the official letters for posterity, usually written from one famous writer to another (such as Mallarmé's letter to Verlaine, later entitled "Autobiographie"), to the informal, urgent letters composed at life's tragic moments. Valéry questioned the official conventions of literary genres, claiming that all criticism is autobiography and that the most lucid ideas can be best expressed in the form of fragmentary diary notes not suited for publication—which led to the posthumous publication of his multivolumed notebooks, "cahiers." And yet there is an obvious generic hierarchy among the various examples of Valéry's writings in the first person, which reveals an interesting politics of exclusion and inclusion crucial for the process of myth making. I will start with one of the most personal and "uncensored" (referring of course to internal censorship) letters written by Valéry just a few weeks after Mallarmé's death.

The letter is addressed to Valéry's close friend André Gide. It recounts the physical details of Stéphane Mallarmé's death:

> Voici comme il est mort. C'est un accident et unique. Depuis lundi il avait une amygdalite—aucune gravité—mais délicate de ce côté, il s'est couché. Vendredi le médecin vient le voir. Il se trouve mieux (naturellement) et voulait se lever. Tandis qu'il causait avec le docteur, un spasme de la glotte l'a tué net par asphyxie; il s'est dressé, s'est jeté à genoux en étreignant le médecin, et il est retombé mort. Il paraît que ces cas sont extraordinairement rares. Ce spasme mortel n'avait que fort peu rapport avec le mal de gorge existant. [71]

> This is how he died. It is an accident and an unparalled one. He had been suffering from tonsillitis since Monday—nothing serious—but being fragile in this respect, he went to bed. On Friday the doctor came to see him. Naturally, he was feeling better and wanted to get out of bed. While he was chatting with the doctor, a glottal spasm killed him right off by asphyxiation; he reared up, fell to his knees while clutching the doctor, and then fell dead. Apparently such cases are extremely rare. The fatal spasm had little to do with the existing sore throat.

Thus Mallarmé dies as the result of a tragic accident, of a tragic game of chance. The guttural spasm, the interruption in the rhythm of breathing that produced many creative shadows in "Igitur," turns out to be fatal. Mallarmé's death has been anticipated as well as deferred by his writing. Valéry's description strikes us with its detailed physicality. It describes the details of Valéry's last visit to Mallarmé, the last encounter with the poet's wife and his daughter, who was self-sacrificially dedicated to him, and the funeral. The letter starts and ends with a description of Valéry's own state of physical and emotional distress, which can only with difficulty be translated into words. "Mon cher André, voici des détails. Cela me soulagera un peu d'écrire car il'y a trois nuits que je ne dors plus, que je pleure comme un enfant et que j'étouffe" ("My dear André, I'm writing you the details. It will relieve me somewhat to write because for the past three nights I haven't been sleeping, I've been crying like a baby; I'm suffocating"). [72] The letter ends:

> Les derniers déchirements publics de sa fille ont en lieu, puis on l'a éloignée et nous sommes partis. Tout cela m'est revenu cette nuit et, ne pouvant plus respirer, je me suis levé, j'ai fait des fumigations, puis un orage énorme éclaté et j'ai dormi une heure. Je te prie de garder cette lettre qui est une description exacte d'hier. Je t'en demanderai plus tard une copie, car je n'ai pas envie ni courage d'écrire tout ceci pour moi, maintenant. [73]

His daughter's last public outbursts took place, someone then took her off and we were thus parted. This past night all of that came back to me, and no longer being able to breathe, I got up, inhaled some medicinal vapors, then a big storm broke and I slept for an hour. Please keep this letter, which is an exact description of yesterday. Later on I will ask you for a copy of it, as I don't feel like writing all this for myself right now.

Here Valéry appears to relive Mallarmé's symptoms preceding his death: he experiences shortage of breath and a respiratory spasm. Moreover, he confesses to Gide his inability to describe Mallarmé's death. The grief and the urgency of the physical pain can only be shared with another friend, can be communicated but not written. However, Valéry asks Gide to keep a copy of the letter, because he wishes to preserve this emotional document—if not for posterity, then at least for his own memory.

Valéry's essay "La Dernière Visite à Stéphane Mallarmé" ("The Last Visit to Stéphane Mallarmé") describes the same events—receiving the news of Mallarmé's death and Valéry's last visit to the poet. It is written in Valéry's privileged first person—the first person of a critic and an autobiographer. And yet we notice from the very beginning that the essay follows different codes of personal description, a different set of rules of inclusion and exclusion, than the letter to Gide. In spite of the highly personal framing of the article, Valéry's loss is depicted as a purely intellectual one, and the relationship between Valéry and Mallarmé is presented not so much as a human bond as a spiritual bond. The physicality of suffering, as well as all the details of Mallarmé's quotidian familial existence and references to his wife and daughter, are completely absent from the essay: it focuses exclusively on the spiritual friendship between two great intellects. This displacement of the physical by the spiritual, the erasure of femininity and eroticism, and the displacement of Mallarmé's text by Valéry's systematic interpretation of it will be at the center of Valéry's critical myth making.

At the beginning of "La Dernière Visite à Stéphane Mallarmé" Valéry describes his own literary crisis, one that is somewhat similar to what Mallarmé called the poet's interregnum. Like Mallarmé, Rimbaud, and later the Surrealists, Valéry goes through a period of deep questioning of the institution of literature and of literary production, an experience which leads him to interrupt his precociously successful poetic career. During the memorable, sleepless night of October 5, 1892, Valéry decides to abandon the artistic and sentimental endeavors that imprison his mental life and dedicate himself to a scientific search for lucidity and

rigor, of "la conscience de moi-même pour elle-même" ("the conscience of myself for itself"). It is this crisis of literary beliefs that Valéry wishes to share with Mallarmé, whose death appears as a tragic, irretrievable interruption of the lucid intellectual dialogue that is established between the two men.

Thus, paradoxically, Valéry meets Mallarmé, his literary idol and inspiration, at the moment when Valéry decides to abandon what he considers to be trivial literary pursuits. The effects of this central paradox resonate throughout his essay. There is a tension between the Mallarmé of literature and Mallarmé the person. Valéry cherishes Mallarmé's spirit, of which he made "a profound company," but criticizes Mallarmé's literary practice that lacks precision and rigor. Valéry comments explicitly on the different strategies of writing and interpretation used by Mallarmé and himself: "Il ne parlait jamais, d'ailleurs, de ses idées que par figures . . . Mais moi, en essayant de me résumer ses tendances, je me permettais intérieurement de les désigner à ma façon" ("Moreover, he never spoke about his ideas except figuratively . . . But I, trying to sum up his tendencies, let myself interpret them in my own way").[74] In Mallarmé's poetics, it is simply impossible to "speak about the ideas" without acting out the drama of writing and speaking, without capitalizing on syntax. Let us look at how Valéry reads and reshapes Mallarmé in his own writing. At the conclusion of the essay Valéry quotes one line from Mallarmé, a sentence that tragically prefigures the poet's own death:

> Mallarmé me montra la plaine que le précoce été commençait de dorer: *"Voyez,* dit-il, *c'est le premier coup de cymbale de l'automne sur la terre."*[75]

> Mallarmé showed me the plain which the precocious summer was beginning to gild: *"See,* he said, *it is the first stroke of the cymbal of autumn on earth."*

This is a typically Mallarméan sentence with a suggestive phonic ambiguity in the word "cymbale" (*cymbale/symbole*) and a beautiful syncretic image, a transference of autumn color into autumn sound. It is also laconic, casual, and unpretentiously poetic. Valéry does not let the words "speak" for themselves, but rather frames them with a pure atemporal landscape: "absolute splendor," "silence full of vertigo and of exchanges," "stunningly beautiful," "the pure sky." Moreover, he carefully analyzes his own sentiment and translates it into a rather solemn language of classical rhetoric and classical philosophy:

Je perdais le sentiment de la différence de l'être et du non-être. La musique parfois nous impose cette impression, qui est au-delà de toutes les autres. La poésie, pensais-je, n'est-elle point aussi le jeu suprême de la transmutation des idées?[76]

I lost the feeling for the the difference of being and not being. Music sometimes gives us this impression, which is above all others. Poetry, I thought, is it not also the supreme play of the transmutation of ideas?

In this way Valéry explains poetry as a "transmutation of ideas" and wishes to transpose it to a certain metalevel. According to Valéry, Mallarmé "intuitively" ("sans connaissances scientifiques") moved from ordinary literature (equivalent to simple arithmetic) to a sort of metaliterature—an investigation of the literary process and the process of consciousness in general—which Valéry equates with algebra. It is obvious that Valéry privileges the scientific model over the artistic one, preferring the precision of mathematical laws—the ultimate achievement of the human intellect—to the chaotic, arbitrary, and sentimental intuitions of the text. There is a gentle but arrogant condescension in Valéry's remark about Mallarmé's lack of scientific knowledge. Mallarmé appears as a literary martyr who transgresses the boundaries of literature, aiming at but never quite reaching the heights of systematic scientific knowledge to which Valéry aspires.

In other words, Valéry privileges the metapoetic moment in Mallarmé's poetry. Throughout his critical and autobiographical writings, Valéry wishes to establish a kind of universal "metaself" or "moi pur," retrieving it from the impurity of the poetic, intuitive, and personal elements. Valéry wishes to salvage the first part of the word "metapoetic." As a result, Mallarmé is elevated to a metalevel and turned into a sign of Valéry's own system of intellectually controlled subjectivity.

In fact, Mallarmé's central "idea"—if we employ Valéry's word paradoxically—consists precisely of the impossibility of straight, linear, and systematic expositions of "ideas," especially when one attempts to shed light upon the complexities of the modern crisis of literature.

In this respect Mallarmé is not "intuitive," "naive," or "prescientific" as Valéry claims. Rather, unlike Valéry, Mallarmé does not privilege the discourse of science over any other discourse. He stages a general modern crisis of language. Valéry attempts to systematize Mallarmé's "ideas" and to perform a purified metareading of his text and of his death. What are the reductions and dangers of this kind of metareading? How

does it affect the text and life of the poet who is subjected to this critical practice? What image of the poet emerges in the foreground of this landscape of pure sky and absolute splendor? How does it happen that the last encounter between two friends turns into a spiritual homage on the tomb?

We notice that the personal, anecdotal framework of "La Dernière Visite à Stéphane Mallarmé is gradually displaced by the conceptual and spiritual one. The actual subject of Valéry's description in the essay is not Mallarmé's revelatory text, but his person, his human self. The tension between Mallarmé as a person (in French, both somebody and nobody) and Mallarmé as a personage in Valéry's theater becomes particularly apparent. Mallarmé the person is depicted as "the most gentle, the most deliciously simple" person with the "smile of a sage." There is a certain inconsistency between the abundance of details—such as the date of the encounter between the two men (July 14, 1898), the exact place (Valvins office), and even the name of the press that published the first edition of "Coup de dés"—and the complete lack of specificity in the portrait of Mallarmé. This portrait is carefully purified by Valéry.

> Pauvre et sans honneurs, la nudité de sa condition avilissait tous les avantages des autres; mais il s'était assuré, sans les rechercher, des fidelités extraordinaires. Quant à lui, dont le sourire de sage, de victime supérieure, accablait doucement l'univers, il n'avait jamais demandé au monde que ce qu'il contient de plus rare et de plus précieux. Il le trouvait en soi. [77]

> Poor and without honors, the nudity of his condition degraded all the advantages of others; but he was assured of extraordinary fidelities without searching for them. As for him, whose smile of a sage, of a superior victim, gently overtook the universe, he never requested anything from the world except for that which was rarest and most precious. He found it in himself.

Mallarmé is well known for his modesty and a certain distrust for literary fame. Yet to consider his perfectly comfortable and quite fashionable literary career as "nudity" and a rejection of the world appears rather hyperbolic. The folding pages of *La Dernière Mode* and the exquisite black velvet of a dandy are obviously discarded by Valéry. In the essay "Stéphane Mallarmé" which again reiterates the story of Valéry's receiving the news of Mallarmé's death—Valéry goes one step further and claims that Mallarmé practiced a "sort of asceticism." Thus we notice that in the process of myth making and purification, Valéry gradually

displaces emotional pain with spiritual joy, the poetic with the metapoetic, the erotic (which is at the core of Mallarmé's poetic language) with the ascetic (to Valéry, synonymous with aesthetic), and Mallarmé's infatuation with fashions, textures, and clothes with a spiritual nudity.

In "Stéphane Mallarmé" Valéry recreates the hypothetical scene of the poet's sacrifice depicted in Mallarmé's "Autobiographie," but he presents it rather literally, depicting Mallarmé as a "superior victim" of the artist's requisite sacrifice of life. Moreover, Valéry pursues the opposition between body and spirit. The artist in a human body ("un artiste de corps humain") sacrifices his life in order to create a metalife—writing; but the true "homme d'esprit" has to go one step further—from simple writing to metawriting, sacrificing the immediate expression for the sake of his spiritual potential.

Moreover, the memory of a living Mallarmé is replaced by the insistence that the poet is always already dead. Valéry remarks several times throughout his essays on Mallarmé that he never thought of Mallarmé as mortal.[78] Even during his last conversation with Mallarmé, Valéry dreams of his "destin comme achevé" ("destiny as concluded"). It seems almost uncanny that Valéry projects death upon the living poet in order to design a perfect tomb for him, to purge him of impurities. Speaking figuratively, it appears that Valéry's system "kills" the poet Mallarmé, substituting the irreducible poetic element in the poet's life and text with deadening scientific immortality. What is the iconography of the absent poet? Why does Valéry so carefully delineate his portrait instead of practicing depersonalization and the disappearance of the subject in his writing? Why does the monument on the poet's tomb occupy Valéry more than the reenactment of the ritual death of the author?

Mallarmé in Valéry's system appears as a kind of superman ("surhumain"), a superhuman hero, which was hypothetically sketched by Mallarmé himself. Here his iconography is fixed and canonized; he is presented as the only true poetic god in the pantheon of idols. Valéry's purified Mallarmé appears as a statue of a Roman stoic: heroic, wise, and self-sacrificial. Valéry loves to employ Latin words and expressions (*testis, ars*)—Latin for him appears to be a language of eternal values. Here again we observe the conceptual conflation of antiquity and eternity, of historical classicism and atemporal spirituality that we traced in the writings of Mallarmé himself. In Valéry it reemerges much more straightforwardly, with less poetic ambiguity. The other image that influences Valéry's iconography of the pure poet is that of a Christian martyr, which is also prominent in Flaubert's description of the artist/monster, the artist

who sacrifices everything for his literary faith. In Valéry, Mallarmé appears as a sort of John the Baptist—and not at all as Hérodiade, Mallarmé's own privileged figure in his poetic texts. In "Lettre sur Mallarmé" one senses a certain obsession with Mallarmé's head that becomes central to Valéry's iconography.

> Me rendant plus heureux que Caligula, il m'offrait à considérer une tête en laquelle se résumait tout ce qui m'inquiétait dans l'ordre de la littérature, tout ce qui m'attirait, tout ce qui la sauvait à mes yeux. Cette tête si mystérieuse avait pesé tous les moyens d'un art universel.[79]

> Making me happier than Caligula, he offered to me for consideration a head in which everything that bothered me in the order of literature, all that attracted me, all that saved it in my eyes was summed up. This very mysterious head weighted all the means of a universal art.

The quote betrays Valéry's extreme interest in lobometry, one of the nineteenth-century pseudosciences whose evaluation of the intellect relies on measurements of the skull. This hyperbolic head of the poet stands for his body, becoming a powerful metaphor. From this "tête" of Mallarmé it is easy to move to Valéry's most celebrated work, *Monsieur Teste*. In fact, the first chapter of the book, "La Soirée avec M. Teste" ("The Evening with Mr. Teste") was written in 1892, around the time of Valéry's literary crisis and his first encounters with Mallarmé. According to Valéry, however, M. Teste should not be regarded as a pastiche on Mallarmé: M. Teste is not a pure poet; he is above or beyond literature altogether. He does not condescend to practice art and instead occupies himself with the pure exploration of consciousness. Yet as a mythological hero, "a chimera of intellectual mythology," M. Teste and the pure poet appear as twin monsters.[80]

Like Athena, goddess of wisdom born from Zeus's head, M. Teste was engendered in the head of his author in the "chamber of August Comte." This male fantasy of intellectual "immaculate conception" seriously preoccupies Valéry. It is a spiritual engenderment that happily escapes corporeal, feminine, and erotic impurity. The Latin epigraph to the work reads, "vita Cartesii est simplicissima," suggesting Valéry's crucial rewriting of the notion of "life." In the context of the book, life refers to the life of the mind, the interior being of consciousness. The other life, everyday existence, is regarded in Valéry's extremist intellectual poetics as a strange sentimental invention, a human aberration. Valéry tells us in his notebooks that this kind of life, not illuminated by Cartesian reason,

like "azure," "gold," and other poetic metaphors, is "de la littérature" in a derogatory sense. M. Teste is a "demon of possibility," an attempt to incarnate the interior being, to give it a figure, a shape. Again, we note that Valéry never follows Mallarmé in his staging of self-effacement and disfiguration, in the self-destructive, creative games of syntax. In fact, Valéry is not dealing at all with a problem of syntax, so crucially posed by Mallarmé. Valéry is much more interested in giving a figure to the disfigured, in creating a series of anthropomorphic characters to embody pure spirituality.

Valéry proliferates those monumental intellectual monsters and delineates their iconography in detail. We have, for example, a portrait of M. Teste, his log books, and the testimonies of his friends and wife: quite an extensive documentation for the figure of absence; quite a detailed description of an erased life and biography. Moreover, like a natural child, Valéry's M. Teste grows and develops throughout Valéry's literary career: Valéry keeps attaching new fragments to the biography of M. Teste, adding notes to M. Teste's log book, and sketching new portraits. M. Teste is both Valéry's ideal and his pastiche, his idol and his monster. [81]

The mythical relationship between Mallarmé and Valéry is somewhat parallel to the relationship between Valéry and M. Teste: Valéry reverses the roles of father and son and, figuratively speaking, engenders his spiritual father, whom he can now place under the complete control of reason, preventing any poetic impurity.

Following Harold Bloom's metaphor of the literary oedipal struggle, we can regard the engendering of M. Teste as a consequence of Valéry's extreme "anxiety of influence," a result of his wrestling with literature, specifically with its strongest and most challenging embodiment—Mallarmé. M. Teste exists on the pure metalevel which does not even require being metapoetic. His literary immaculate conception demonstrates that it is much easier to create a pure intellectual creature from scratch than to reshape it from contradictory fragments of the poetic text.

Yet in the description of M. Teste we discover a similar paradox of excessively present absence—"l'excès d'absence," as Mme. Teste puts it—to what we encountered in the description of Mallarmé. [82] On the one hand, Valéry insists on the absence of exterior characteristics in M. Teste. According to Valéry, his hero "killed his marionette," by which he means an idiosyncratic human personality. M. Teste neither smiles nor cries; he hardly ever changes his facial expression at all. His sacred color is obviously black: M. Teste prays his sacrilegious prayers to Blackness, calling upon the Supreme Thought. Valéry describes him as "être noir

mordoré par lumière" ("black being bronzed by light"), which reminds us again of the iconography of Mallarmé's hero, lgitur.

On the other hand, unlike Igitur, who remains a vacillating figure, nothing but a game of shadows always in the process of figuration and disfiguration, Valéry's M. Teste has many realistic attributes. In spite of his metaphysical searching and his prayers to universal Blackness, he leads a perfect French bourgeois lifestyle. He buys box seat tickets for the opera, takes walks on the boulevard, and is comfortably married. Mme. Teste shares with the reader her view that great souls "don't get married, except by accident; or just to make a warm room for oneself." The most endearingly pure (and not silly, poetic, or sentimental) names that M. Teste invents for his wife are "being," "thing," and, if he is in a particularly friendly mood, "oasis." The letter from M. Teste's wife—who is Valéry's more traditional novelistic creation—is quite illuminating; it sheds light upon M. Teste's not-so-glamorous everyday existence, which is not deprived of domestic violence nor marital alienation. Moreover, as Mme. Teste informs us with property humility and self-debasement, her husband does not dislike pineapple and jam.[83] Thus it turns out that the erasure of biography and life does not preclude a daily portion of delicate sweets.

M. Teste's excess of absence reveals the presence of certain things— the necessary attributes of bourgeois comfort—that are taken for granted. The excess of purity that Valéry desperately tries to achieve reflects his own anxiety of influence with respect to Mallarmé, for whom he wishes to design the perfect classical tomb in order to render harmless certain ambiguously erotic and subversive elements of his poetry.

M. Teste, thought to be more pure than the pure poet, no longer needs to write poetry. He is the ideal of a pure intellectual pushed to the limits of the possible and, at the same time, a reduction to absurdity of this construct of pure reason. Moreover, in spite of all theoretical displacements, and the author's desire to practice a metadiscourse divorced of superfluous and mundane elements, the historicity and cultural specificity of Valéry's monstrous child and his embodiment of pure spirit cannot be completely erased. His iconographic attributes include black clothes, tickets to the opera, and a delicious serving of jam and pineapple on a porcelain plate.

The last in this series of symbolic displacements is from Jorge Luis Borges's famous story "Valéry as a Symbol." Here it is not M. Teste but Valéry himself who appears as a character in one of Borges's inquisitions, "the other inquisitions." Valéry becomes Borges's privileged French pre-

cursor; he is regarded as the author of the most lucid modern and eternal creation—that of a defaced personality. Borges, a well-known literary francophobe, attempts to erase the French cultural specificity of Valéry. In fact, the only reference to the French language is derogatively italicized: "comerciantes del *surréalisme*" ("dealers of surrealism"). Crossing national boundaries, Borges compares Valéry to Whitman. The dubious similarity between the two men resides not in their poetic texts or artistic talent but rather in their ability to compose a "sign of an exemplary poet," in their talent for myth making. Furthermore, in his reading of Valéry, Borges emphasizes neither Valéry's impulse toward systematizing nor his French Cartesian return to rationalism. Instead he focuses on the paradoxical quality of Valéry's writings, especially the simultaneous death of the author and birth of a defaced hero.

Borges pushes this paradox further, creating a vertiginous series of reflections and doppelgängers. He writes:

> Para nosotros Valéry es Edmond Teste. Es decir, Valéry es una derivación de M. Dupin de Edgar Poe y del inconcebible dios de los teólogos. Lo cual, verosímilmente, no es cierto.[84]

> For us Valéry is Edmond Teste. Which is to say that Valéry is a derivation of M. Dupin from Edgar Poe and of the inconceivable God of theologians. Of which, most probably, one can never be sure.

Borges explores the relationship between creation and self-creation, between the author and his fiction, which turn out to be mutually replaceable. Valéry is the author and the fictional character, both self-perpetuating and self-effacing. Devoid of any national or individual specificity, he is every man and no man, everything and nothing. Once again, Borges demonstrates here his mastery in the manipulation of ironic repetitions which are destined to refute both temporality and a simplistic progressive understanding of history. Valéry and his double M. Teste become interchangeable symbols of modern lucidity, of the recognition of nonoriginality and the universal powers of reason.

In another story, "Pierre Menard, Autor del Quijote," Borges creates his own character à la Valéry—the French Symbolist from Nîmes, Pierre Menard. The story offers us a peculiar Borgesian version of the literary pedigree of a French Symbolist: Pierre Menard is presented as "devoto a Poe, que engendró a Baudelaire, que engendró a Mallarmé, que engendró a Valéry que engendró a Edmond Teste" ("Devotee of Poe, who gave birth to Baudelaire, who gave birth to Mallarmé, who gave birth to Valéry,

who gave birth to Edmond Teste").[85] Borges takes great pleasure in pointing out that his marionette French Symbolist author dates back not to the French but to the American poet, and what he rewrites is the great Spanish classic. Menard is the anti-original author par excellence, someone who makes us question the notions of authorship and originality. The list of Menard's so-called visible works includes the transposition in alexandrine verse of Valéry's "Cimetière Marin" ("Seaside Cemetery"), an invective against Valéry which, according to the narrator, is the absolute opposite of Menard's actual opinion. But Menard's most purely unoriginal work is a verbatim rewriting of *Don Quijote*, which becomes his life-long obsession. The story ends with the paragraph from *Don Quijote* about history as the mother of truth, which can be interpreted in quite different ways depending on the authorial attribution. The paragraph composed by "a secular genius," Cervantes in the seventeenth century, reads as mere rhetorical praise of history, while the one written by Pierre Menard, a contemporary of William James, presents an important philosophical view of history not as a consequence but as the origin of truth.

Thus, the story reduces to absurdity both the Romantic idea of originality and the modernist project of a completely accomplished nonoriginality. It ridicules both the passion for authorship and the passion for plagiarism. According to Borges, every extreme idea contains its opposite: self-erasure contains self-creation, the loss of individuality contains its recovery, ahistorical truth is inscribed in history. And yet certain dimensions of these paradoxes are not fully explored by Borges himself. In fact, the reading of the two Borges stories together reveals a contradiction; in one the French Symbolist poet becomes a modern symbol, a symbol of lucidity and the universal power of reason, while in the other the French Symbolist is the exponent of a certain style and certain culturally specific narrative mannerisms.

In Borges's "Pierre Menard," it is precisely this clash of writing styles between Cervantes and Menard that makes all the difference in our reading. In other words, the first story emphasizes the similarity and the universality of the symbol of lucidity, while the other foregrounds the historicity and the specificity of style. Is this only the same difference? What strategic political decisions determine our choice of emphasis? If we assume that any strategy of reading and writing involves a complex interplay of foreground and background, then what is at stake in Borges's focus on the universality of Valéry/M. Teste, as symbol and embodiment of clarity and reason?

Borges's own reading of Valéry contains a paradox that might have escaped even its paradox-loving author. The essay is written in 1945, the end of World War II and the year Valéry died. Valéry becomes not only a symbol of the ahistorical, eternal return of the defaced artistic doppelgänger but also an embodiment of Borges's specific political position.

> Proponer a los hombres la lucidez en una era bajamente romántica, en la era melancólica de nazismo y del materialismo dialéctico, de los augures de la secta de Freud y de los comerciantes del *surréalisme*, tal es la benemérita misión que desempeñó (que sigue desempeñando) Valéry.[86]

> To offer lucidity to the people in a debased romantic age, in the melancholic era of Nazism, of dialectical materialism, of the prophecies of the Freudian sect and of the dealers of surrealism, this is a worthy mission that Valéry accomplished (and continues accomplishing).

Valéry becomes a symbol of universal lucidity, a pure spirit, only in opposition to a strange army of romantics and melancholics, which includes Nazis, dialectical materialists, Surrealists, and the sect of Freud. Even with all due playfulness, not everyone will subscribe to Borges's political and literary myths, which put Nazis, dialectical materialists, and Surrealists in the same camp; not everyone will attribute complex political similarities and differences in quite the same manner as Borges. Borges's Valéry/M. Teste and the most pure spirit have the same degree of universality as Borges's point of view and his peculiar political position.

Thus, the words about history as the mother of truth, written first by Miguel de Cervantes and then by the most original and stylish of all plagiarists, Pierre Menard, teach us an important lesson in reading. In fact, what appears (visibly) to be identical—the same pure spirit, the same erasure of biography, the same exemplary modern defacement, the same understanding of modernism—hides invisible differences in their cultural contexts, myths of authorship, and theoretical frames of reference, differences which should be exposed with every critical reading.

Mallarmé's Embarrassment, or Rimbaud's Undressing

We will move from the myth of the poet without a biography to the myth of a biography of the ex-poet, from an attempted erasure of life to the attempted erasure of literature. In his letter-essay on Rimbaud, Mal-

larmé tells us a scandalous anecdote from Rimbaud's life. Once during dinner the inhabitants of the respectable Parisian hotel where Rimbaud lived heard screams and other noise coming from the young poet's room. A moment later—to their great astonishment—they saw Rimbaud throwing his clothes out of the window. "C'est . . . que je ne peux pas fréquenter une chambre si propre, virginale avec mes vieux habits criblés de poux" ("It's just . . . that I can't frequent a room so clean and virginal in my old clothes riddled with lice")—such was Rimbaud's explanation to Banville.[87]

This gesture of throwing away clothing and disrupting a comfortable bourgeois meal, as Mallarmé remarks, has a mythological quality to it. To some extent, it is a gesture against all fashions, it is both an appeal for and a mockery of propriety. Rimbaud's explanation is typical of his grotesque statements: the verb "cribler," which refers equally to wounds and scars, adds an element of violence to the scene. Moreover, it does not allow for a clear distinction between clothes and skin. Something in Rimbaud's purification ceremony, in the public disposal of his own clothes, is both humorous and scandalous, subversive and embarrassing. What could have been seen as an adolescent prank proved to be somewhat prophetic, especially when one thinks about Rimbaud's problematic relationship with the literary institution. Rimbaud is an embarrassment to professional, mature poets like Mallarmé. It is precisely this embarrassment, this challenging vitality, that Mallarmé wishes to hide between the elegant, self-reflective lines of his essay "Arthur Rimbaud."

Mallarmé writes about Rimbaud with a mixture of admiration and condescension. Mallarmé's primary desire is to inscribe Rimbaud into the literary institution: Rimbaud or rather Rimbaud's name serves as a poetic assonance "bercé à la fumée de plusieurs cigarettes" ("rocked in the smoke of several cigarettes"). It is nothing but a name pronounced with a gust of cigarette smoke, a name which designs a new wave of fashion for the distinguished literati gathered at Mallarmé's *mardis*. Mallarmé ridicules the frame of Rimbaud's "personnage," which profanes Rimbaud's mystery, "the broken thread of existence." He criticizes the proliferation of exotic masquerade costumes—all those beads and embroidered collars of "the black king."

Mallarmé does not completely restrain himself, however, from relating some of these anecdotes, including the story of Rimbaud's public undressing. He also presents his own description of Rimbaud, whom he met at the time of Rimbaud's precociously brilliant literary debut in the early 1870's. Mallarmé quotes in fact Paul Verlaine's description of Rimbaud's

adolescent beauty, which is at once boyish and feminine. Mallarmé pays special attention to the boy's hands and mouth. Both are elements of the portrait as well as directly related to the poetic vocation. This duality is reflected in both descriptions. Mallarmé focuses on the physical aspects of Rimbaud's hands, on their rough skin, and then mentions that they autographed beautiful verses. The very physicality of the hands appears to be a perfect Mallarméan texture, the texture of "rougis" ("reddened blotches") and "engelures" ("chilblains"). In a similar way, Rimbaud's mouth, which does not profer any poems, has a "pli boudeur et narquois" ("a sulky and derisive fold")—a typical Mallarméan fold.[88] This fixation on the hands and the mouth—the agencies of poetry writing and poetry reading—and their peculiar double-edged description reveals a characteristic Mallarméan gesture, a displacement of physicality by textuality, of a writer's body by the writing itself.

Mallarmé presents Rimbaud's life as a series of well-acted, exotic performances in which Rimbaud's hands, hands that hitherto caressed the pages of a book, at the end deal in ivory and oriental perfumes. Mallarmé interprets Rimbaud's silence as an interruption or "interregne" in literary production, but not as the end of it. Rimbaud's life is something like white space between "the great lines of destiny" of the great poet. Mallarmé refuses to accept Rimbaud's refusal of literature and prefers to believe in the future discovery of unknown and unedited poems composed by Rimbaud in Africa. In the essay Rimbaud is a poet/ghost, a character of Mallarmé's "Les Fenêtres" ("The Windows"), a sick man in the hospital paralyzed by his mutism. Rimbaud's life is nothing but a conspicuous absence of writing, an absence which can be incorporated into the modern "crise de vers." The end of Mallarmé's essay is the return of the repressed poet, or a revenge of the "impersonal ghost" ("le fantôme impersonnel") of the author. This impersonal ghost finally authorizes in literature all the painful silences, scandalous disruptions, and exotic life stories of the actual Arthur Rimbaud.

Incidentally, in 1896 the established "prince of poets" Stéphane Mallarmé received a letter from Rimbaud's mother asking his advice on a family matter and inquiring his distinguished opinion concerning the moral character of a certain Paterne Berrichon, "homme de lettres" and her daughter's fiancé. Mallarmé, the former editor of the "gazette de la famille," is quite flattered to dispense advice on such a delicate matter of family importance. He writes about Berrichon's dedication to the moral struggle and to literary production and expresses his sympathy to the widow Rimbaud:

Sans doute, pour vous, madame, dont le souvenir des commencements troublés de son admirable fils n'altère pas la piété que vous vouez, la première à Arthur Rimbaud, ce passé de quelqu'un, que prétend, aujourd'hui, au titre de votre gendre, ne garde rien d'alarmant.[89]

Undoubtedly, Madame, for you who doesn't let the memory of the troubled beginnings of your admirable son change the piety which you dedicate, first to Arthur Rimbaud, this past of someone, who today aspires to the title of your son-in-law, holds nothing alarming.

What does Mallarmé mean here by "commencements troublés" of Arthur Rimbaud? If Mallarmé were to share this notion with Madame Rimbaud, then these "troubled beginnings" would refer equally to Rimbaud's escapes from the family home, to his affair with Verlaine, and to the beginning of his transgressive practice of poetry. It is interesting that Berrichon, who receives a positive recommendation from Mallarmé, is the same Berrichon who would later—together with Rimbaud's sister Isabelle—rewrite the most acceptable version of his brother-in-law's troubled youth, regarding it as a sort of Christian martyrdom. The sheer conventionality of Mallarmé's letter, its politeness and self-complacent moralism, is very illuminating: it reveals the close link between the bourgeois institution of literature and that of morality. It also signals the hierarchy between Mallarmé, prince of the poets, and a brilliant, but definitely troubled, dead adolescent poet, Arthur Rimbaud.

Thus Mallarmé both acknowledges his own embarrassment in the face of Rimbaud's myth and wishes to cover it up. He attempts to reduce Rimbaud's death toward literature to a kind of death of the author, a self-effacement with a literary purpose that he himself propagates. In his essay Mallarmé desires to convince us that there is only one model for the relationship between the author's life and his writing—that of Mallarmé. It erases the otherness of Rimbaud. In my reading of Rimbaud I will attempt to avoid Mallarmé's narcissistic trap without falling into another extreme—the melodramatic exoticism of a Romantic biography. Hence I will vacillate between literary and literal reading. If in the case of Mallarmé my emphasis was on the tension between syntax and image, here the tension will be between multiple significations of the word "figure"— figure as a rhetorical trope, an element of representation, and figure as the shape and form of the human body that exceeds the discourse. These different meanings raise many questions: How can we examine Rimbaud's figure(s) in life and text without one necessarily being subsumed by the other? Is it possible to preserve both the otherness of literature

and the otherness of life? What are the main figures in Rimbaud's poetics and how do they punctuate the end of poetics? What is his understanding of life? Is the life described in his transgressive literary works really livable?

The Violence of Poetics: The Scars of Arthur Rimbaud

Rimbaud italicized the sentence "Je ne sais plus parler" ("I no longer know how to speak") in his *Une Saison en enfer* (*A Season in Hell*).[90] This sentence, which might have led Mallarmé to create beautiful sonnets addressed to his "muse of impotence" or to act out this impotence in typographic tours de force, inspired Rimbaud to stop writing. It would be an oversimplification to regard Rimbaud's departure from literature as a radical one, a final exit. In fact, in "Alchimie du verbe," Rimbaud puts the verb "to say farewell to the world" in the imperfect tense, suggesting a repeated or prolonged activity: "Je disais adieu au monde dans l'espèce de romances" ("I was saying good-bye to the world in some kind of romances").[91] Moreover, even the last poem of *Une Saison en enfer*, entitled "Adieu," does not necessarily signify the end of his writing. In fact, the dating of Rimbaud's collections *Une Saison en enfer* and *Illuminations* has been a source of ongoing critical debate. It would be convenient for critics to regard "Adieu" as Rimbaud's last literary text. However, it remains uncertain whether *Illuminations* was written before, after, or even simultaneously with *Une Saison en enfer*. It is obvious that Rimbaud's farewell was far more complex than a one-time written declaration. For Rimbaud, as in the case of Mallarmé, there are a series of reenactments of the ending, but with a significant difference. Rimbaud's stopping writing points to the radical instability of the figures of his text, including the figure of the self and the figure of death—the instability which aims beyond masterfully performed textual disfiguration. Rimbaud's death toward literature forces us to rethink the very boundaries between literature and life and the status of the text. Perhaps it gives us a chance to treat "literature" and "life" as equal critical possibilities, without subjugating one to the tyranny of the other.

Most of Rimbaud's published texts are of an ambiguous status. The only text that he himself arranged for publication was *Une Saison en enfer*, a violent spiritual autobiography. Thus the whole issue of what we are to consider as Rimbaud's "texts" and "literary works," and where we are to draw their limits, remains extremely complicated.

In my opinion, one of Rimbaud's most characteristic written genres,

the only one that he did not abandon until the very end, is the letter. In letters he expressed the fundamental principles of his poetics and his ideas about life, which as the letters from Abyssinia show grow less literary. The letter preserves an urgency of communication, or at least a structural illusion of it, and allows one to mix genres.

As Yury Tynyanov observes in his essay "On Literary Evolution," "the history of the epistolary genre exemplifies literary evolution, i.e., the shifting boundaries between literary and non-literary genres."[92] Specifically, the conventions of letter writing developed in the seventeenth through eighteenth centuries and were codified as literary by the emergence of the epistolary novel. Toward the end of the nineteenth century the epistolary novel for the most part falls from grace, but the structure of literary circles stimulates the emergence of the letter-essay, a mixture of personal address and critical aesthetic statement. We saw it in the examples of Mallarmé and Valéry. The letters of Rimbaud do not exactly fit this emerging convention; some of them go beyond letter-essays to letter-manifestos, while others are nothing but utilitarian notes. Both challenge critics and readers either by promising too much or by disappointing all expectations. Rimbaud's letters exemplify his view of life and act out an aesthetic of rupture.

In his 1870 letter to Théodore de Banville, one of the founders of *Parnasse Contemporain*, Rimbaud mocks his own image of a *poète-enfant*.

> Cher Maître:
> Nous sommes aux mois d'amour; j'ai dix-sept ans. L'âge d'espérances et des chimères, comme on dit, et voici que je me suis mis, enfant touché par le doigt de la Muse—pardon si c'est banal—à dire mes bonnes croyances, mes espérances, mes sensations, toutes ces choses des poètes—moi j'appelle cela du printemps.[93]

> Dear Master:
> We are in the months of love; I am seventeen years old. The age of hopes and of chimeras, as they say, and here I—a child touched by the Muse's finger (sorry if it's banal)—have undertaken to speak my beliefs, my hopes, my sensations, all these things of poets—I would say it's the influence of spring.

Rimbaud's playful use of the traditional tropes of spring, youth, love, and poetry betrays his extreme awareness of conventional literary myths, what one calls "things of poets." He both rewrites the poetic clichés and lays them bare, both enthusiastically plays the role of a young poet in love with love, spring, and poetry and distances himself from this trivial

image. A similar gesture of self-objectification can be found in Rimbaud's poems, specifically in "Les Poètes de sept ans" ("The Poets of Seven Years") and "Roman" (Romance") which present the poet of seventeen. Instead of depersonalization à la Mallarmé, Rimbaud proliferates the conventional figures and images of the poet as a person, those that might be seen as his own highly stylized autobiographical personae. Rimbaud is engaged in poetic role playing, or rather in playing the role of a poet. In both the letter and the poem "Roman" we find an interesting use of the impersonal form *on*, which expresses public opinion and the existing cultural myth of a child and a poet: in the letter "comme on dit" introduces the conventional poetic tropes, while in the poem the same *on*—"on n'est pas sérieux quand on a dix-sept ans" ("one isn't serious at age seventeen")—provides the conventional view of a young poet. In Rimbaud this relationship between *je* (I) and *on* (one, they), a relationship that vacillates between playful interaction and violent rupture, is crucial for both his poetics and for an understanding of his position on the contemporary French Parnassus, from which he eventually escapes, as he escaped from his mother's home earlier.

From the mockingly conventional letter to Banville we move to the famous "lettre du voyant" ("letter of the seer") in fact a series of letter-manifestos addressed to his school teachers, Georges Izambard and Paul Demeny, and written in May of 1871. One of Rimbaud's most quoted statements, "je est un autre" ("I is another"), usually taken out of context, comes from these letters.[94] "Je est un autre" is a radical rewriting of Baudelaire's "moi c'est tous, tous sont moi" ("I is everyone, everyone is I") and of Mallarmé's "disparition élocutoire du poète" ("elocutionary disappearance of the poet"). Moreover, as Shoshana Felman demonstrates in her article "Tu as bien fait de partir, Arthur Rimbaud" ("You did well to leave, Arthur Rimbaud"), Rimbaud's statement presents a "violent and rigorous deconstruction" of the Cartesian "ego."[95] But what kind of otherness does Rimbaud articulate here? Is this an encounter with the otherness of language, with the disfiguring practice of modern writing, as Felman suggests? Or does it point beyond textual deconstruction, beyond Mallarmé's self-effacement?

In approaching these problems, one might consider the contexts and the circumstances surrounding the writing of the letters of the seer. They were composed during Rimbaud's third escape to Paris. Apparently, left without any material means of existence, he lives in the barracks of the French communards where he experiences both emotional and physical tumult.[96] The experience of revolt as well as of violence, sexual and po-

litical, is transmitted in the letter, especially in the earlier one addressed to Izambard. The syncopal rhythm of the sentences reveals the urgency of communication and, at the same time, the urgency to allegorize the painful experience, to transform it into a poetic fiction, into "tout ce que je *puis inventer* de bête, de sale, de mauvais, en action et en paroles" ("all that is stupid, dirty, bad, which I *can invent* in action and in speech").[97]

Also, if we look at the syntax of the letter, which is similar to the syntax of Rimbaud's prose poems, particularly in *Une Saison en enfer*, we notice the abundance of incomplete, abrupt phrases, exclamations, and hyphens, and a continuous appeal to presence which manifests itself in Rimbaud's abundant use of demonstrative pronouns—"voici," "voilà." The first sentence of the letter is introduced by "revoilà," a paradoxical demonstrative pronoun that expresses both a desire for physical presence and a recognition that writing is only a mere representation of presence. Rimbaud's syntax (in the letter and in the prose poems) is quite different from Mallarmé's: the sentences do not fold upon each other creating a complex self-referential nonlinear texture. Rather, they disrupt one another, perform an anarchist attack on literature, and constantly reach toward something other than the text.

Each of Rimbaud's letters of the seer includes poems that in the letter to Paul Demeny are introduced as "hors du texte" (outside the text). How are we to read this expression of Rimbaud's? What is Rimbaud's "text" and what would be outside it? Does the text itself simply suggest that it is outside a specific conventional genre, or does it point to something other than textuality as such? How are we supposed to read it? The poem included in the letter to Izambard is the famous "Le Coeur supplicié" ("The Tortured Heart"), later renamed "Le Coeur volé" ("The Stolen Heart") and "Le Coeur du pitre" ("The Heart of the Fool"). Although "Le Coeur supplicié" follows obvious metric conventions, Rimbaud himself calls into question its poetic status: "Est-ce de la poésie? C'est de la fantaisie toujours—Mais je vous en supplie, ne soulignez ni du crayon, ni trop de la pensée" ("It is poetry? It's always fantasy—but I beg you, don't underline [that] with pencil nor with too much thought").[98] Here is the text of the poem:

> Mon triste coeur bavé à la poupe,
> Mon coeur est plein de caporal:
> Ils y lancent des jets de soupe,
> Mon triste coeur bave à la poupe:

Sous les quilibets de la troupe
Qui pousse un rire general,
Mon triste coeur bave à la poupe,
Mon coeur est plein de caporal!

Ithyphalliques et piopiesques
Leurs insultes l'ont depravé!
A la vesprée ils font des fresques
Ithyphalliques et piopiesques
Ô flots abracadabrantesques
Prenez mon coeur, qu'il soit sauvé:
Ithyphalliques et piopiesques
Leurs insultes l'ont depravé!

Quand ils auront tari leurs chiques,
Comment agir, ô coeur volé?
Ce seront des refrains bachiques
Quand ils auront tari leurs chiques,
J'aurais des sursauts stomatiques
Si mon coeur triste est ravalé:
Quand ils auront tari leurs chiques,
Comment agir, ô coeur volé?[99]

My sad heart driveled to the stern,
My heart is full of caporal:
There they launch streams of soup,
My sad heart drivels to the stern:
Under the quilibets of the troops
Which let out general laughter,
My sad heart drivels to the stern,
My heart is full of caporal!

Ithyphallic and piopiesque
Their insults corrupted it!
In the vespers they make frescoes
Ithyphallic and piopiesque
O abracadabric waves
Take my heart so that it may be saved:
Ithyphallic and piopiesque
Their insults corrupted it!

When they exhaust their tobacco chews,
How should I act, o stolen heart?
There will be bacchic refrains
When they exhaust their tobacco chews,

> My stomach will turn somersaults
> If my sad heart is choked back:
> When they exhaust their tobacco chews,
> How should I act, o stolen heart?

Rimbaud begs his former teacher not to underline his poem, not to touch "le coeur supplicié" with pencil or excessive intellectualization. Rimbaud's final statement about his verses—"ça ne veut pas rien dire" ("that doesn't mean nothing": what appears to be an error in the French is Rimbaud's)—expresses his fear that a conventional literary interpretation would miss his meaning, only deepening a painful wound which perhaps had just started to heal through the process of writing.[100] Although Izambard himself saw the poem as a literary joke, many critics, starting with Colonel Godshot and Enid Starkie, were led to believe that during the days of the Paris Commune and Rimbaud's brief stay with the *communards* he experienced a homosexual rape.[101] It is impossible to determine whether Rimbaud actually experienced, or only witnessed or fantasized, the scene of the rape. But the fact that the poem invites us to think about a violent experience, and not just an existential nausea allegorized in the image of seasickness (the view of Antoine Adam, the editor of the Pléiade edition of Rimbaud's works), is crucial.[102]

Obviously the biographical reading is partly due to the critic's desire to imbue the poems with life (Enid Starkie), instead of performing their close textual examination. In this case, however, the rhetoric of the poem itself invites one to examine the limits of the text. Its central device is synecdoche, especially in the description of the parts of the body—*coeur, sursauts stomatiques*. But as Tzvetan Todorov has argued, this is a kind of "sabotaged synecdoche" that resists metaphorization.[103] Rimbaud's body-part synecdoches in this poem violate the figurative level of reading and suggest some sort of physical mutilation. On the whole, the poem combines the details of explicit physical violence with rhetorical tours de force. Hence violence shapes both the referential (literal, or thematic) reading as well as the rhetorical (literary) reading. In the last stanza, the heart (*le coeur volé/violé*) is apostrophized; the poem ends with a rhetorical question which points beyond literature. This question can be paraphrased as a sort of "to act or not to act," and if "to act," then how? "Comment agir, ô coeur volé?"

It is interesting that what the Pléiade editor considered to be "obscene" in the poem, particularly the word "ithyphalliques" ("with erect penis"), is a Latin derivative.[104] Rimbaud's use of Latin is quite peculiar.

We remember how Valéry created a Latin name for his Mr. Consciousness (M. Teste from the Latin *testis*), and how Saussure used the Latin *arbor* to designate the concept of a tree in his famous diagram of the sign.[105] Unlike numerous French writers and scientists who resort to Latin for abstract theoretical notions, Rimbaud uses Latin obscenities. It is at once a rhetorical indiscretion, a subversion of the styles of language, a schoolboy prank, and an interesting philological fact. In "Alchimie du verbe," Rimbaud comments on his extravagant literary and linguistic taste.

> J'aimais les peintures idiotes, dessus de porte décors, toiles de saltimbanques, enseignes, en luminures démodée, latin d'église, livres érotiques sans orthographie, romans de nos aïeules, contes de fées, petits livres d'enfance, opéras vieux, refrains niais, rhythmes naïfs.[106]

> I liked idiotic paintings, decorations over doorways, clown's backdrops, billboards, popular prints, old-fashioned books, Church Latin, erotic books which do not observe any rules of spelling, the novels of our grandmothers, fairy tales, little children's books, old operas, silly refrains, naive rhythms.

This is strange cultural marginalia, which Mallarmé would have criticized in his *La Dernière Mode*. In fact, what Rimbaud enjoys is precisely what is outside fashion and outside the norms of established good taste. The paragraph is an amazing description of nineteenth-century kitsch. Rimbaud's vocabulary is less pure than that of Mallarmé or Baudelaire: it comprises many neologisms, popular expressions, slang, and even Latin obscenities. This "impure" poetic diction comes from diverse sources: from highly stylized, elegant Parnassian poetry and from popular culture—all things outmoded and eclectic from the old orthography of erotic books to the most unclassical Latin used in provincial churches. Hence Rimbaud's discourse is characterized not simply by literary "intertextuality" but by a broad social heteroglossia, an incorporation of many literary and everyday dialects and a disruption of their boundaries. Although Rimbaud was a master in imitating classical poetic forms, he quickly abandons the established traditional genres of poetic writing and practices a variety of prose poetry discovered by Baudelaire, but a more violently autobiographical version than his.

The linguistic experimentation and pattern of violent and vital disruptions that outline many of Rimbaud's works make it very difficult to determine Rimbaud's notion of the text and of the relationship between writing and living, between the text and the body. In the letter to Demeny, Rim-

baud describes the poet-seer as a monster, using Victor Hugo's image of a mutilated child from "Un Homme qui rit" ("A Laughing Man"): "Mais il s'agit de faire l'âme monstrueuse: à l'instar des comprachicos, quoi! Imaginez un homme s'implantant et se cultivant des verrues sur le visage" ("But it is about making the monstrous soul: in the manner of the baby brokers, what! Imagine a man taking root and cultivating warts on his face").[107] In *Une Saison en enfer* this image of bodily writing is explored further. In "Adieu" we read, "Je me revois la peau rongée par la boue et la peste" ("I see myself again, my skin corroded by mud and the plague").[108] And finally in "Vierge Folle" ("Mad Virgin") Rimbaud elaborates the images of tatoos and scarification as metaphors for his text.

> Je suis de race lointaine: mes pères étaient Scandinaves: ils se perçaient les côtés, buvaient leur sang.—Je me ferai des entailles partout le corps, je me tatouerai, je veux devenir hideux comme un Mongol.[109]

> I descend from a faraway race: my fathers were Scandinavians: they pierced their sides, drank their blood—I will make slashes all over my body, I will tatoo myself, I want to become hideous like a Mongol.

"Vierge Folle," which is of one of the most urgent, violent, and driven texts of the collection, offers a large repertoire of exotic masks—from mythical "nègres" to mythical "Scandinaves" from mystic Christians to cannibalistic pagans. But his image of bodily writing, in spite of its debt to literary exoticism, is crucial. It is a writing with one's own "bad blood," writing on the body with body fluids, and also writing as scarification, as a tattoo. It inscribes pain, violence, and split subjectivity. "Je est un autre" ("I is another") reveals a split between the "I" of a cannibal and the "I" of a victim, between the "I" of an artist and the "I" of the art object whose body is covered with tattoos. It is an internalization of exterior violence. For Mallarmé, especially regarding his obsession with fashion, the text can be compared with texture, with the folds of a semitransparent, multilayered dress. For Rimbaud the metaphor is different: the clothes have been disposed of publicly, and the text resembles a naked skin. Each sign, each inscription, is painful and violent.

Perhaps the term inscription, the very movement toward the allegorization of violence, is reductive and dangerous. In many ways the texts of *Une Saison en enfer* are prophetic: they anticipate Rimbaud's life after his stopping writing. In one of the poems Rimbaud talks about traveling "hors du monde" ("outside the world"), which refers to a journey to some utopian exotic place located perhaps in the Orient. There appears to be a

connection between this "hors du monde" and "hors du texte." Both express a similar desire for the extreme and liminal experience, a desire to push everything to the limit—literary genres and ways of living.

In one of Rimbaud's last letters, written a few months before his death, we find again the mention of scars, of "la plaie cicatrisée" ("the cicatrized wound"), which reminds us of the mythical scars from *Une Saison en enfer*.[110] This time, however, the reference is to Rimbaud's body and to his very real physical suffering after the amputation of his leg in the hospital of Marseille. Thus the scars go full circle—from the violent image prophetically anticipating physical pain to the description of this pain in the most matter-of-fact manner, from the text that anticipates Rimbaud's departure from literature to the letter that anticipates his departure from life.

There is an obvious difficulty in deciding which is foremost in our critical enterprise—whether we read Rimbaud's life through his texts (as with the alleged homosexual rape), or whether we read his texts through the later developments of his nonliterary career. The impossibility of drawing clear distinctions between the poeticization of violence and the violence of poetics becomes apparent. At the same time, Rimbaud's writing urges us to reexamine the differences between life and literature and to rethink the limits of textuality.

"La Vraie Vie est absente"

The most crucial element in the myth of Rimbaud is his uncompromising choice of life over literature, his radical challenge of the prestige of the literary institution. If Mallarmé challenged the Romantic myth of the poetic life of the poet, and placed the drama of writing above the drama of life, Rimbaud challenged the myth of a poet without a biography (or rather a poet with an eventless middle-class biography) as well as any myth of the Poet with a capital P.

Life is described and rewritten in many of Rimbaud's literary works. It is Rimbaud's only positive modern heroine, and yet the poet's fascination with life is not entirely original. The opposition of life and writing, and the philosophical obsession with the notion of "individual life," goes back to Rousseau and the German Romantics and reemerges in the writings of Nietzsche, Kierkegaard, and the twentieth-century existentialists. In Nietzsche's "Of the Use and Misuse of History for Life," the valorization of life is linked to the reevaluation of modernity and is opposed to the burden of the historical conscience.[111] According to de Man

Nietzsche's "life" "is conceived not in biological but in temporal terms as the ability to forget what precedes the present situation."[112] For Nietzsche the ability to live is an ability to reestablish the immediacy of experience, to recognize one's "truly human nature," and to lift the heavy burden of cultural metaphors. Life, unlike culture, promises a pursuit of happiness. As a prophet of life Nietzsche follows the pattern of Rousseau's paradox: the desire for life inspires more writing. Here, for example, is one of Nietzsche's glorifications of life:

> We saw that the animal, which is truly ahistorical and lives confined within a horizon almost without extension, exists in a relative state of happiness. We will therefore have to confine the ability to experience life in a nonhistorical way as the most important and the most original of experiences, as the foundation on which right, health, greatness, and anything truly human can be erected.[113]

An interesting and no less obsessive literary elaboration of the same idea can be found in Fyodor Dostoevsky's *Notes from the Underground*. We remember that the spiteful underground hero constantly dreams about "the living life."[114] This living life always exists elsewhere, in a kind of utopian exterior, far away from the artificial prison-refuge of a bitter, ironic writer. The relationship between life and the writer's "underground," however, is not entirely one of opposition. It is precisely the impossibility of a living life that feeds his life as a writer, allowing him to pontificate about his guilt and about nostalgia and to experience sadomasochistic pleasures. Does this living life created in the underground have anything to do with Rimbaud's ideal "vraie vie" hors du texte and hors du monde? What are the myths of the living life, "true" life? Is true life completely independent from literature?

The fact that the ideas of life and action are crucial to Rimbaud is already evident in his first work of prose on the future of poetry—the letter to Demeny. According to Rimbaud, in ancient Greece verses rhymed actions, and the two lived in harmony. Yet for the "poets of newness" this relationship shifts.

> Donc le poète est vraiment voleur de feu. Il est chargé de l'humanité, des *animaux* mêmes; il devra faire sentir, palper, écouter ses inventions . . .
> Le poète définirait la quantité d'inconnu s'éveillant en son temps dans l'âme universelle: il donnerait plus que la formule de sa pensée, que la notation de *sa marche au Progrès!* Enormité devenant norme, absorbée par tous, il serait vraiment un *multiplicateur de progrès!* . . . La Poésie ne rhythmera plus l'action; elle *sera en avant.*[115]

Therefore, the poet is indeed the thief of fire. He is responsible for humanity, and even for *animals;* he shall have to make his inventions felt, palpable listened to . . . The poet must define the quantity of the unknown awakening in his time in the universal soul: he would give more than the formula of his thought, the record of *his march toward Progress!* Enormity becoming the norm, absorbed by all, he would truly be *a multiplicator of progress! . . .* Poetry will no longer rhythm action; it *will be ahead of it.*

Two words that are often capitalized in Rimbaud's letter are poet and progress. The poet is destined to become the herald of modernity and to find the language for this revolutionary march of progress. It is hard to determine which is primary and which is secondary—the march of visionary poetry or the march of progress. The poet is defined in other than literary language: he is "le voyant," "le grand malade, le grand criminel, le grand maudit et le suprême Savant" ("the seer," "the great diseased one, the great criminal, the great accursed one and the supreme Sage") who strives to reach the unknown. The letter is both prophetic and utopian, as is Rimbaud's enthusiastic vision of modern life.

In *Une Saison en enfer* and *Illuminations* we find the same obsession with the idea of life. Life is often used in the plural, for instance, in "Vies," one of the prose poems from *Illuminations,* or in expressions such as "Est-ce-qu'il y a d'autres vies?" ("Are there other lives?").[116] Also in "La Nuit d'enfer" ("The Night of Hell") Rimbaud rewrites the well-known idiom, "C'est la vie" ("That's life"), an affirmation of a commonsensical notion of life, by describing the life of "le grand criminel" and "le grand maudit": "C'est encore la vie! Si la damnation est éternelle . . . C'est la vie encore! Plus tard les délices de la damnation seront plus profondes"[117] ("That's still life! If damnation is eternal . . . It's still life! Later on the delights of damnation will be more profound"). Thus life forms part of Rimbaud's textual play; life, like love, is one of the concepts that Rimbaud wishes to reinvent. "L'Amour est à reinventer" ("Love should be reinvented"). The idea of life is closely linked to Rimbaud's notion of modernity and progress. What are, then, the modern lives that Rimbaud describes in his text?

First, in "Mauvais Sang" ("Bad Blood"), there is the life of the modern hero—the scientist: "La science, la nouvelle noblesse! Le progrès. Le monde marche" ("Science, the new nobility! Progress. The world marches").[118] The image of a march reappears later in the poem in another description of life, the French life par excellence—that of the army. The entire drama from "me tuer" ("to kill myself") to "m'habituer" ("to

get used to") is acted out with passion, urgency, and irony. Here in only one stanza Rimbaud fancies his life and death in combat.

> Assez! Voici la punition. —*En marche!*
> Ah! les poumons brûlent, les tempres grondent,
> la nuit roule dans mes yeux, par ce soleil! le coeur . . .
> les membres . . . Où va-t-on? au combat? je suis faible!
> Les autres avancent. Les outils, les armes . . . le temps!
> Feu! feu! sur moi! Là! ou je me rends. —Lâches!
> Je me tue! Je me jette aux pieds des chevaux!
> Ah!
> —Je m'y habituerai.
> Ce serait la vie française, le sentier de l'honneur![119]

> Enough! Here is your punishment—*Forward march!*
> Ah! My lungs are burning, my temples are roaring,
> night is rolled in my eyes, by this sun! my heart . . .
> my arms and legs . . . Where are we going? To battle? I am weak!
> The others advance. Tools, weapons . . . time!
> Fire! fire! on me! Here! or else I'll give myself up—Cowards!
> I'll kill myself! I'll throw myself under horses' hooves!
> Ah!
> —I'll get used to it.
> That would be French life, the path of honor!

There is also the life of an explorer, traveler, and adventurer, dreamed by many poets including Baudelaire and Mallarmé in their numerous "voyages" and "invitations au voyage." This life is also evoked by Rimbaud in "Vierge Folle": "O, la vie d'aventure qui existe dans les livres d'enfants . . . j'ai tant souffert, me la donneras-tu?" ("Oh, the life of adventures that exists in children's books . . . I've suffered so, will you give it to me?"). Rimbaud's modern voyage can lead away from the modern world, to the wisdom of the Orient, "the primitive fatherland."[120]

The plurality and coexistence of all these lives within the same text adds a certain perspectivism and ironic dimension to Rimbaud's search. In fact, life itself is often described by him in literary, or theatrical, terms, life as a farce to be led by all. In "Vies" the poet sees himself as an illustrator of the "human comedy," which makes him question his own position in time and space and whether he is inside or outside this human comedy, whether he is an author or only a plagiarizer of the artistic ambitions of others (Balzac in this case). Each of Rimbaud's descriptions of life is linked to the idea of escape, evasion, or departure. At the end of

"Vies" Rimbaud pictures himself outside "lives": "Je suis réellement d'outre tombe, et pas de commissions" ("I am actually from beyond the grave, and no messages, please").[121] Thus death is also inscribed in Rimbaud's continuous departures, this imaginary traveling from life to life.

Separate from life as a farce, Rimbaud postulates another life, "la vraie vie" ("the true life") which, as he declares with poetic extremism, "is absent."[122] This enigmatic sentence was paraphrased and reinterpreted by several generations of French avant-garde, from the Surrealists to the students of 1968. For Rimbaud himself the search for true life does not lead him outside Western myths. In his description of "primitive fatherland" he makes an obvious allusion to the Christian myth of Eden, a myth Rimbaud refuses to dismiss in spite of the often sacrilegious character of his text. In the poem symptomatically entitled "L'Impossible," Rimbaud writes: "Tout cela est-il assez loin de pensée de la sagesse d'Orient, la patrie primitive? . . . Les gens d'Eglise diront: C'est compris. Mais vous voulez parler d'Eden . . . c'est vrai; c'est à Eden que je songeais!" ("All of this is far enough from the thought of Eastern wisdom, the primitive fatherland? . . . Church people will say: Understood. But you want to speak of Eden . . . It's true; I was thinking of Eden!").[123] Where does one find the utopian space where the true life is possible?

After having played different roles textually in the theater of modern life, Rimbaud departs from his text; he moves from literary to literal levels. Now he is an actor and not a scriptwriter, but the repertoire of "lives" is quite similar. Rimbaud lives through the period of "la vie maudite" ("the damned life") during his brief sojourn with Verlaine in London, where he experiments with drugs and studies the occult. Then he tries to enlist in the U.S. army but ends up going to the Orient with the Dutch navy. Finally he goes to Abyssinia, which he believed to be "la patrie primitive" of humankind, particularly to the town of Aden, similar in name to Eden. And there he lives among the natives, who turn out to be quite different from the exotic "nègres" described in "Mauvais Sang." He deals in arms and becomes an explorer, writing a short article for the French Geographic Society. He writes Ernest Delahaye for books on chemistry and geography (but the cosmology is omitted).

Rimbaud's letters from Abyssinia are strikingly scarce and spare. In them we hardly encounter any exotic descriptions of the place, romantic accounts of the voyage, or metaphysical reshaping of the traveling experience. A direct, unpoetic, and nonliterary tone is characteristic not only of the letters addressed to Rimbaud's mother and sister, from whom he used to run away early in his writing career, but also of the letters written

to Rimbaud's college friend and long-time correspondent, Delahaye. The letters shock us with what appear to be their omissions, their lack of literariness, and, furthermore, a complete indifference toward literature. Life is discussed in the most pragmatic context, that of material survival—"gagner la vie" ("to earn a living").

One is tempted to speculate (and many critics have) about Rimbaud's lost poems and unknown lovers. But, in fact, we learn from the letters that this undescribable life that Rimbaud leads in Abyssinia is full of unbearable everyday boredom—the much poeticized ennui—and existential routine. Rimbaud describes his unpoetic silences in a letter to his mother and sister.

> Ne vous étonnez pas que je n'écrive guère: le principal motif serait que je ne trouve jamais rien interessant à dire. Car, lorsqu'on est dans des pays comme ceux-ci, on a plus à demander qu'à dire! Des déserts peuplés de nègres stupides, sans routes, sans courriers, sans voyageurs: que voulez-vous qu'on vous écrive de là? Qu'on s'ennui, qu'on s'embête, qu'on s'abrutit, qu'on a assez, mais qu'on ne peut pas en finir, etc., etc., etc.![124]

> Don't be surprised that I don't write: the principal motif would be that I never find anything interesting to say. For, when one is in countries such as these, one should rather ask what to say! Deserts inhabited by stupid natives, without roads, messengers, travelers: what would you have me write from here? That I am bored and annoyed, that I am brutalized, that I've had enough, but that I can't stop, etc., etc., etc.!

Thus the lack of writing is explained not by the excess of life experiences but by the confrontation with a certain emptiness. The letter reveals a destruction of Rimbaud's myth of an exotic primitive fatherland, as well as of the myth of an escape through traveling—the famous modern escape in search of newness proposed at the end of Baudelaire's "Le Voyage." It also challenges the expectations of the reader or critic who often partakes in the same cultural myths and wishes to find reflections of them in the letters. Rimbaud's encounter with emptiness and boredom in the Orient is similar to Mallarmé's encounter with nothingness described in the letter to Henri Cazalis, an encounter that inspired the creation of "Igitur." Rimbaud's more than prosaic representations of his everyday life in Abyssinia anticipate twentieth-century accounts of the existential nausea related by Camus and Sartre. They share the alienated sensibility of Camus's *L'Etranger* (*The Stranger*). Amazingly, in a letter written almost ten years earlier, we encounter the same motifs of

existential boredom. Moreover, Rimbaud often considers ending this unbearable life and resorting to the most radical of escapes, suicide.

> Hélas! moi, je ne tiens pas du tout à la vie; et si je vis, *je suis habitué*
> à vivre de fatigue, mais si je suis forcé de continuer à me fatiguer comme
> à present, et à me nourrir des chagrins aussi véhéments qu'absurds dans
> ces climats atroces, je crains d'abréger mon existence . . . Enfin,
> puissons-nous jouir de quelques années de vrai repos dans cette vie; et
> heureusement que cette vie est la seule, et que cela est évident, puisqu'on
> ne peut s'imaginer une autre vie avec ennui plus grand que celle-ci![125]

> Alas! I am not in any way attached to life; and if I live, *I am used to*
> living from fatigue, but if I'm forced to continue to wear myself out as I do
> at present, and to feed on sorrows as vehement as they are absurd in the
> atrocious climates, I'm afraid I will cut short my existence . . . Well, let
> us enjoy a few years of true rest in this life; luckily this is the only life,
> which is obvious since we couldn't imagine another life filled with more
> ennui than this one!

Here again we notice the correlation between "me tuer" and "m'habituer"; habit produces deadening ennui and saves the writer from suicide.
Thus the search for "true life" and "other life" is not entirely successful
in Rimbaud's flight from literature. Nor did the escape to the Orient—if
it was an escape at all and not a practical decision about how to make a
living—place him closer to his ideal "hors du monde." Rimbaud's escapes only lead to new escapes, always in the plural. They reveal both
the inescapability of life's ennui and the impossibility of the ultimate
comforting evasion, a total rupture. Instead of revealing true life, Rimbaud's experiences in the Orient taught him a sobering lesson (what
Adorno and de Man would call "negative knowledge") about the lives of
this world. In fact, in the excerpt from the last letter, Rimbaud expresses
his doubt regarding the very existence of that mythical other life; he calls
into question the existence of something other than the unbearable everyday routine and ennui. Rimbaud's search for true life turns out to be the
search for a utopian place outside the world and outside the text, a space
which is always by definition elsewhere. Rimbaud's true life can never be
lived, as the Mallarméan ideal book can never be written.

In *Une Saison en enfer* Rimbaud wrote one of his most radical impera-
tives: "Il faut être absolument moderne" ("One must be absolutely
modern"). [126] Absolute modernity is a rupture, an impossible presentness
without representation, a simultaneity of one's multiple estranged "I."

The search for modernity, a desire to participate in the march of progress, led Rimbaud away from literature. In the end he divorced the search for vision, invention, and action from poetry. For Rimbaud the expression "modern poet" is pushed to a radical extreme; it becomes an oxymoron. The kind of modernity Rimbaud aspired to precluded the practice of literature. The aporia of literature and life that is at the heart of modernism led Rimbaud to break with literature and, instead of trying to find a new language, to try to find a new life.

If we look at the signatures on Rimbaud's written documents we find "Arthur Rimbaud, homme de lettres" and later "Arthur Rimbaud, négociant français" on his letters to the Abyssinian king, Ménélik.[127] "Homme de lettres" was not Rimbaud's way of defining himself; it was only one of the cultural myths in which he participated, one of the roles he played in the drama of his life. Rimbaud dealt a heavy blow to the prestige of the literary institution: he demonstrated by his own example that faith in the poet as a prophet of modernity had been shaken from the inside, had been questioned by the poets themselves. Rimbaud participated in many modern cultural myths—the myth of the adolescent communard, of the explorer, of the scientist (although he never quite became one), the myth of the real man ("a man without women," to paraphrase Hemingway) who takes charge of his life, and the myth of the escapist, who ultimately fails to escape himself and his own otherness.

The one myth that Rimbaud defied and never accepted is the myth of a comfortable bourgeois professional writer who leads a supposedly eventless life with his wife and possibly a fashionable mistress. Rimbaud's problematic sexuality, problematic according to the established cultural norms of the time, excluded him from the institution of bourgeois marriage, from living what would be considered a dignified and normal life. And yet, paradoxically, as Mallarmé's insistence on the possibility of erasing biography revealed a certain cultural myth of normative life, so did Rimbaud's search for true life demonstrate the presence of many literary myths, specifically the myth of utopia—be it the modern idea of progress or the belief in the "primitive fatherland" of the Orient. Rimbaud, unlike Mallarmé, did not question the popular modern fascination with action, which led Mallarmé to engage in dialogue with many theorists of modern progress, contesting the separation between writing and acting. Mallarmé regarded writing as a complex "action restreinte" which reveals the constraints of any unproblematic action. Yet Rimbaud saw "l'impossible" as the impossibility not only of pushing oneself to the rad-

ical limit and finding the other life but also of completely divorcing life from the text—the cultural text in a broad sense—which shapes one's literary and nonliterary existence.

Ultimately, Rimbaud did not become a famous revolutionary, explorer, inventor, or soldier. It seems a paradox, but the only social institution that was able to accommodate such an unconventional modern hero was that of literature. The temptation to stop writing, to push textuality to the limit, is inscribed in the modern practice of literature, even when it is not acted out to its radical dénouement as in the case of Rimbaud. Rimbaud became a prototype of the twentieth-century avant-garde artist, an artist who lives out all the discontinuities and ruptures of the modern text, and helps to redefine its limits.

Rimbaud and His Doubles

Rimbaud's two deaths, first that of the poet and then of the man, inspired many legends, from the Russian revolutionary poets to the American Rambo. According to René Etiemble, there were many mythical Rimbauds: Rimbaud demiurge, Rimbaud visionary, Rimbaud poète maudit, Rimbaud adolescent poet, Rimbaud "communard and communist" (the title of Louis Aragon's article), Rimbaud Surrealist, Rimbaud heresiarch, Rimbaud newly born Christian, Rimbaud homosexual, Rimbaud adventurer, Rimbaud African arms and slave dealer, and so on.[128] At the core of Rimbaud's enigma are the notion of being "absolutely modern" and the tension between literature and life, with its many gaps and ruptures usually filled by the interpreter's own imagination. In most cases Rimbaud's story is pushed polemically in one direction or the other, into the myth of life or the myth of literature depending on the critic's ideological preferences. The relationship between the two, their peculiar symbiosis, is not reconsidered.

The criticism on Rimbaud is reminiscent of a detective story; each critic tries to uncover the "true Rimbaud." We remember that in Valéry's creation of the myth of Mallarmé, he attempted to perform a reductive metareading of Mallarmé. In the case of Rimbaud, the critics and writers usually select one exemplary life among the plurality of possibilities offered by the poet. The choice is between ethical and aesthetic (Berrichon and Mallarmé), vital and textual. The critic's desire to fragment the myth of Rimbaud, to select one dimension of it and privilege it over the others, is a reflection upon and reenactment of the modern death of

the author, which in turn is the result of the growing autonomy of literature, the fading role of a poet in the society, and the fragmentation and
separation of the discourses of science, literature, religion, morality, and
so on.

The myth of Rimbaud is exemplary because it goes beyond national
boundaries. There is a Czech Rimbaud—the hero of Milan Kundera's
novel *Life is Elsewhere*, the prophet and victim of another modern utopia,
communist Czechoslovakia.[129] There is also a pair of Russian Rimbauds.
One of them is Vladimir Mayakovsky, especially the way he was envi-
sioned by the French Surrealists Breton and Aragon as the modern revolutionary poet par excellence. The other is the fictional poet/hero described by Vladimir Nabokov in his short story "The Forgotten Poet." The
only similarity between Nabokov's hero and Rimbaud is their "biographical legend." Nabokov's Russian Rimbaud stops writing at an early age
and is believed dead for fifty years.[130] Then he reappears to claim the
money set aside for the construction of his monument, and his nonpoetic
appearance provokes a scandal. The story plays with the idea of author/
impostors and shows how the most radical escapes can be co-opted by
the literary establishment. Nabokov's "The Forgotten Poet" can be read
as a kind of cultural parable about commemoration and oblivion, about
building the poet's monument and forgetting the poet's text.

The most recent pastiche of Rimbaud's criticism is Dominique Noguez's 1986 mock study entitled *Les Trois Rimbaud (The Three Rimbauds)*
which again urges us to reconsider the implications of the figurative and
nonfigurative death of the author.[131] The book is a reaction against the
most recent development in Rimbaud criticism—on the one hand, a
close, textual, often deconstructive, reading of the poems and, on the
other hand, evidence of the reemerging interest in Rimbaud's biography
and existential experiences.

Noguez's *Les Trois Rimbaud* proves on many levels that Rimbaud (and
the fascination with Rimbaud) did not die in 1891. The work claims to be
an analysis of the "profound unity" of Rimbaud's work from the 1870's to
the 1930's (that is, forty years after Rimbaud's death in the hospital in
Marseille). It is written as scholarly research, with all the necessary documentation, including a portrait of Rimbaud in 1921, quotes from
Thomas Mann's letters to Rimbaud in 1931, and photocopies of the man-
uscript of his 1925 chef-d'oeuvre *L'Evangelie Noir (The Black Gospel)*.
Les Trois Rimbaud reenacts all the conventions of academic discourse,
from stylistic mannerisms to excessive bibliographical references. It ob-

viously no longer matters that most of the references are fictional, as long as they are all properly footnoted in proper scholarly style. The scholar/narrator never experiences any crisis of conscience and never transgresses the conventions of academic sobriety. As a result the narration is long, pretentious, and pedantic. The irony of the work is not located entirely on the textual level; rather, the ironic effect emerges from the clash between the reader's prior knowledge of Rimbaud's biographical legend and these new discoveries.

The story opens in the Académie Française: Paul Valéry gives a speech to honor the new academician Arthur Rimbaud, the celebrated author of *Les Nuits d'Afrique (The Nights of Africa)* and *Systèmes de la vie moderne (Systems of Modern Life)*, who is known as "the Patriarch of Charleville." The date is January 1930, and at the time very few people remember the scandalous author of the juvenile poems of *Illuminations* and *Une Saison en enfer*. Since it has become passé to talk about two Rimbauds (one before 1891 and one after 1891), Noguez's fictional scholar claims to demonstrate that there were in fact not "*deux* Rimbauds" but "*des* Rimbauds" ("several Rimbauds"), at least three of them. The new scientific periodization of Rimbaud's work goes as follows: 1870–1875—the now almost forgotten years of juvenilia, sonnets, *Une Saison en enfer* and *Illuminations;* 1875–1891—the years of alleged silence; and finally 1891–1936—the period of intellectual maturity, the disappointment in Futurism and Surrealism, the marriage to Louise Claudel (Camille might have been more appropriate), and his conversion to Catholicism in 1925. In spite of the two ruptures in Rimbaud's life, however, the narrator promises to demonstrate that there is a "profound unity" in Rimbaud's art. To do so he uses not only stylistic but also fashionable, superficially structuralist and psychoanalytical methods. Ultimately he reveals that at the core of this profound textual unity is the dialectical contradiction between the sacred and the profane (a cliché that can be applied to the work of many modern poets).

Yet this profound unity hides more contradictions than the narrator wishes to expose. The search for profound textual unity is one of the obsessions of textual criticism. The critical legend of textual unity goes back to Romantic organic unity and therefore implies that a work of art imitates natural life. In the context of the book, this critical cliché is reduced to absurdity, first because the narrator proclaims a unity between the actual works of Rimbaud, such as *Illuminations* and *Une Saison en enfer*, and the invented works, such as *Les Nuits d'Afrique*. Moreover, the

unity resides exclusively in the poet's texts and is completely lacking from the poet's life, or rather his three lives. One wonders what precedes what in the mind of the critic—Rimbaud's work, Rimbaud's biography, or the critic's own literary and scholarly myths.

If in Nabokov's "The Forgotten Poet" the so-called Russian Rimbaud, Perov, was resurrected to threaten the establishment, the revived Rimbaud of Dominique Noguez has, on the contrary, grown to become a part of it. Rimbaud without the legend loses his place in literary history; his biography as well as his writings become conventional, almost stereotypical "life and works" of the turn-of-the-century French intellectual. From a radical prophet of modernity, Rimbaud turns into a fashionable, modern epigone, a secondary Valéry or Gide without their characteristic singularity of voice. To use again the words of Tomashevsky, if we transform Rimbaud from the "writer with a biography" into "the writer without a biography" he would no longer be Rimbaud. Without his shocking literary persona of the *enfant terrible* who stops writing at the age of twenty and dies at thirty-seven, Rimbaud becomes *personne*, nobody, a simulacrum of the others. One can only speculate how we would analyze the early work of, for instance, Valéry if he had stopped writing in the 1890's and become a famous brain surgeon. What would we think of Mallarmé's sonnets had he died in the Paris Commune? Would we still read Marx if he had continued writing romantic poetry, as he did in his early years, and never started practicing philosophy?

Noguez's *Les Trois Rimbaud*, a reduction to absurdity of the obsessions of contemporary critics, is a rewriting of Borges's ironic scholarly essays on Pierre Ménard. It is another exercise in implausible criticism, another reduction to absurdity of the critical enterprise. At the same time, it provides a powerful insight into not only the institution of literature but also the institution of contemporary criticism, which would happily proliferate Rimbauds and kill and resurrect authors as long as that helps to strengthen the critic's identity and authority.

Les Trois Rimbaud can be read as a parable of the impossibility of distinguishing between literature and biography, which are so closely intertwined in the mind of the reader, since both form a significant part of modern myths. Ultimately, Mallarmé and Rimbaud, the martyr of the ideal book and the martyr of the utopian "true" life, do not appear as opposites but rather as Borgesian uncanny doubles. They are both Borgesian symbols of the modern condition who pushed to the limit the death of the author, be that either endless literary self-effacement or merely stopping writing. Furthermore, the paradoxical pair, Mallarmé and Rim-

baud, makes us rethink the very idea of the death of the author, the modernist myth central to contemporary criticism. In a way Mallarmé, the pure (or purified) poet, never stopped living; he never questioned the conventions of normative bourgeois life. Similarly Rimbaud, the radical rebel of the literary institution, never stopped writing cultural myths; he took very seriously his role in the contemporary mythological drama of action, progress, radical escapes, and other modern absolutes.

Statue of Vladimir Mayakovsky, Moscow. Soviet postcard (right)

· 2 ·

The Death of the
Revolutionary Poet

"Revolutionary Poet": History, Myth, and the Theater of Cruelty

Vladimir Mayakovsky is a poet with a biography par excellence, a poet who is nonexistent without it. He is one of the last in the enfilade of Soviet Russian poet-heroes whose biographical legends became well-known popular fiction. We can count among them Alexander Pushkin and Mikhail Lermontov, who depicted dramatic duel scenes in their novels as if uncannily predicting their own deaths; Sergey Esenin, the "poet-hooligan," who cut his veins in a dusty hotel room and wrote a rhymed farewell note literally in blood (not in the transemotional, metaphorical blood described by Victor Shklovsky, but in nonpoetic actual human blood); and finally Mayakovsky, who put a period at the end of his life, as in his poem, "with the bullet."

Due to peculiar cultural and political circumstances, the reaction against the Romantic myth of the poet was much less pronounced in Russia than, for instance, in France. Thus, for Russian modernism the idea of the death of the author, the disappearance of the subject in the process of writing and the "deromanticization" of the poet's life, was not at all central.[1] The persistent Russian conception of the poet's life is a curious blend of German Romantic ideas of national genius and of Russian patriotism; of the European Romantic conception of the unity of the poet's life and art and of the civic tradition of the Russian intelligentsia embodied in the writings of Vissarion Belinsky. The cult of the poet thrives on political oppression. The poet is supposed to be more than just a poet and to have a cultural mission. He can be a voice and consciousness of the nation, a martyr, dying young, a Christ-like figure, who takes upon himself the sufferings of the people. Willingly or not, every Russian writer confronts this heroic tradition that privileges dead authors and literary martyrs and often "kills" literary texts by subjugating them completely to political, biographical, social, and metaphysical concerns. The worship of the Poet with a capital P is a peculiar form of Russian religion which survives today. Perhaps the most recent manifestation of it was the cult of the contemporary Soviet bard Vladimir Vysotsky, whose untimely death in 1980 provoked the largest spontaneous demonstration in Moscow since the death of Stalin.[2]

"The revolutionary poet" can be regarded as one of the avatars of the poet-hero: it is a distinctly modern phenomenon which presents an alternative to the image of the alienated and effaced poet. The notion of revo-

lution presupposes an acute historical conscience and points to many modern myths, such as the myth of progress—a radical rupture with tradition—the myth of action, and the myth of a man-made justice. Thus the expression revolutionary poet will activate many of the already suggested aporias of modernity that underline the relationship between literature and history, as well as between writing and life. Hegel and many others after him tried to carefully distinguish between "revolution" and "revolt," seeing in the first a collective protest against social injustice and the objective force of history, and in the second the individual reaction of an alienated intellectual.[3] For a poet, someone who constantly experiments with language, both estranging this collective tool of communication and being estranged by it, the relationship between "revolt" and "revolution" is particularly intricate and complicated.

The idea of a revolution that would bring about social justice develops with the process of secularization, when the empire of religion is displaced by the monopoly of politics. It is in the age of Enlightenment that writers, especially the Encyclopedists, enter into a public polemic and often openly criticize the existing social order.[4] The first revolutionary poet par excellence was André Chénier, who—symptomatically—was guillotined during the postrevolutionary (or revolutionary) Reign of Terror. Chénier's *Jambes*, written in prison, for the first time entangles the poet's death with revolution and attempts to affirm the power of writing. In Chénier's first revolutionary poetics *vertu*, *vérité*, and *vers* (virtue, truth, verse) become closely linked: "O mon cher trésor, O ma plume!" ("O my dear treasure, O my pen") and "Toi, Vertu, pleure si je meurs!" ("You, Virtue, cry if I die!"). His verses appeal to the "honnêtes hommes" ("honest men"), the defenders of moral justice, true revolution, and the progress of humanity; they clamor for a kind of "poetic justice," a moral immortality, and protest against the cruelty of the poet's physical death, which is orchestrated by "ink-slingers of the law," bad writers, and false revolutionaries.

The connection between Chénier's political death and his poetic triumph was to become a tragic paradigm in the myth of the revolutionary poet. This paradigm was revived on Russian soil. One of the first writers to suffer for his openly expressed political ideals was Alexander Radishev, author of *A Journey from Petersburg to Moscow*, which depicts a gloomy critical picture of Russian serfdom. He was exiled by Catherine the Great (who also played the role of liberated tsarina and was a penfriend of one of the most celebrated Encyclopedists—Diderot). Radishev later committed suicide.

In the Russian Romantic tradition, the ties between poetry and social protest were further consolidated. Many of the Decembrists, the organizers of the armed rebellion against the absolute monarchy and serfdom in 1825, whom Lenin regarded as "the first Russian revolutionaries," happened to be more or less talented Romantic poets. Among them were Kondraty Ryleev, executed on the personal order of the tsar, and Wilhelm Kuchelbekker and Anton Delvig, Pushkin's schoolfriends who were exiled to Siberia. These poets—Decembrists according to Ginsburg and Lotman—best exemplified the Romantic merging of literature and life by living out their high poetic and revolutionary ideals even at the price of personal sacrifice.[5] Thus in the Russian tradition (which is not exclusive to Russia) the Romantic biographical legend often includes revolutionary activity. Although there were individual cases of a poet's revolt against social norms before Romanticism, the revolutionary poet as a cultural configuration develops as a result of new Romantic self-awareness and the growing awareness of social contradictions. It is no accident that the most famous nineteenth-century theorist of the social revolution, Karl Marx, started as a Romantic poet—a fact that he would later wish to repress from his biography. The mature Marx saw his early flirtation with poetry as an aberration of youth, a shameful and frivolous digression which does not belong to the proper "biographical legend" of a serious scientist of the revolution.[6] Marx's shame of poetry, which he regarded as "blurry" and inappropriate for the expression of social criticism, points to a serious problem of language that any revolutionary poet has to face: the tension between poetic and revolutionary discourses, their rhyming and dissonance, collaboration, and antagonism.

Yet can we consider the configuration of "revolutionary poet" as a cultural myth? Does not the notion of revolution imply rupture and progression, which are inconsistent with mythical consciousness? Jurij Striedter discusses these contradictions and demonstrates how Mayakovsky participates in the "new myth of the revolution."[7] According to Striedter, Mayakovsky's cry for a new myth in his long revolutionary poem *150,000,000* (1919–20) harkens back indirectly to the Romantics' discussion of myths and to Nietzsche's demand for a new myth, which is embodied in the figure of Zarathustra. Mayakovsky's expression "new myth" points to a contradiction between the recurrent mythical consciousness and the modern idea of newness—the contradiction that is embodied even in the etymology of the word "revolution," which at once signifies a rupture and a repetition. What is the relationship between myth and history?[8] Should the two be regarded as opposites? If so, with which of them should we place the figure of the revolutionary poet?

It is well known that Marx himself, and later Lenin, tried to avoid mythicizing the revolution, and that both were consistently in favor of historicizing all discourses, at least in their theoretical pronouncements.[9] Moreover, Marx emphasized the need to unmask bourgeois myths, to show that they are "artificial products of modern history" and not "eternal laws" of nature: "With the inevitability of a *natural* process, capitalist production generates its own negation."[10] Striedter demonstrates how this sentence exemplifies the blind spots of Marx's discourse. The scientist of the revolution displaces the "legend of the theological fall of man" with the "history of the economic fall of man," often unaware that legend and history use the same structures of representation and the same myth-making paradigms. The claim of the *natural* inevitability of the revolution betrays the fact that the revolution itself has turned into the unquestioned myth of the social scientist. In other words, the theorist of the revolution himself shared—among others—the bourgeois myth of the scientist's objectivity, the transparency of his language, which would enable him to describe the "true revolutionary situation." The examination of one of Marx's most crucial statements suggests that it is possible to trace a history of certain myths and the myths of history. As Barthes stressed in the revision of his *Mythologies*, the task of a contemporary student of cultures is no longer to demystify, to demythicize, or to historicize.[11] Rather, the contemporary mythologist must show the hesitation between the mythical and the historic modes of discourse and self-consciously reflect upon the moments when the discourse breaks, challenging yet unquestioned myths of the critic.

The figure of the revolutionary poet, as exemplified by Mayakovsky, reveals traditional mythical patterns, both Christian and Romantic.[12] At the same time the revolutionary poet is a *new* myth, one that makes us rethink the specifically modern aspects of the role of the poet in society. We will examine here how Mayakovsky's spectacular life-creation and death-creation are related to the idea of the revolution. In what way does Mayakovsky's story exceed the Romantic myth of merging life and art? What is specifically modern about his self-fashioning? Lastly, what happens when revolutionary fashions cross the border, specifically, between Russia and France? And how are they altered according to national tastes?

Mayakovsky's life and death were perceived by many contemporaries as a reenactment of the Russian cultural myth of the poet's fate. Mayakovsky was one of the most theatrical, spectacular, and controversial figures on the twentieth-century Soviet Russian cultural stage and definitely the most *visible* Soviet poet in the West. It would be a cultural misrepre-

sentation to limit oneself to a purely textual and formal analysis of Mayakovsky's verse; and it will be demonstrated later that even for one of the founders of Russian Formalism, Roman Jakobson, this task has proved impossible.

Mayakovsky is both more and less than just a poet. Everyone always describes him as a poet plus something else—a qualifying adjective or a suffix. Marina Tsvetaeva writes that even to imagine Mayakovsky simply at the writing desk is "a physical incompatibility."[13] For Tsvetaeva he is "a poet-fighter," a poet "with history." For Boris Tomashevsky, Mayakovsky is a poet "with a biographical legend"; for Yury Tynyanov, "a poet with a new will."[14] In Osip Mandelstam's humorous version, he acquires a feminine suffix—turning from "a poet" into "a poet-ess," an embodiment of excessive subjectivism and emotionalism.[15] Even the expression revolutionary poet, when applied to Mayakovsky by other poets and critics, is frequently qualified. Thus in André Breton's view, a revolutionary poet turns into a surrealist, revolutionary antipoet. For Louis Aragon Mayakovsky is "revolutionary" and "poetic" in accordance with the correct French Communist Party definitions of his time. The tension between the poet Mayakovsky and his multiple qualifying adjectives and spectacular attributes—the tension that might have been at the heart of the mystery of his death—will be key in this chapter.

Mayakovsky's art and life are often seen as a continuous performance on the stage of history, too large and too public for "just a poet." Mayakovsky himself in his early tragedy *Vladimir Mayakovsky* created a theatrical frame and a hyperbolic scale for all his future portraits, allowing the spectators to modify slightly the costumes and props. The only enduring requirement is to make the main hero—the Poet Vladimir Mayakovsky—monumental and immortal.

Boris Pasternak attempts to comprehend the nature of Mayakovsky's modern theatricality and its connection to the poet's suicide. He includes Mayakovsky in his own poetic autobiography, presenting him as his impossible alter ego.[16] Mayakovsky becomes an exemplary poet-phenomenon (*javlenie*) with a "spectacular Romantic biography," an "impure" poet dependent upon brilliant exterior attributes. Mayakovsky's opposite and double is Pasternak himself, an impersonal and untheatrical "pure poet."

Pasternak rebels against the cheap theatricality surrounding the figure of the poet, which he sees in opposition to truly poetic time and space that is both atemporal and atopian.[17] Pasternak shares the antitheatrical

prejudice: for him, the theater is reduced to a superficial public spectacle, a variety show with lustre and heroic affectation. And yet he sees a dangerous vitality in Mayakovsky's drama: "In contrast to playing roles, Mayakovsky played with life."[18] Mayakovsky chose the most difficult pose—the pose of exterior unity, the unity of life and art joined together in a spectacular and heroic romantic legend. He selected his own life "as a plot for the lyrical drama" and intended to make it a work of art.

Although in the framework of Pasternak's poetics, the "spectacular" attributes of the poet's life are diametrically opposed to the "true poetic mystery"—understood as the poet's ability to diffuse himself spiritually in the surrounding world and remain invisibly present without putting on a heroic mask—the case of Mayakovsky goes beyond this simple opposition. Mayakovsky's mystery consists of the *transgressive nature of his theatricality*, which acquires a dangerous vitality and ubiquity, threatening to blur the differences between life and art, as well as between life and death. The doctrine of "life-creation" elaborated by the Russian Symbolists was both parodied and lived out by Mayakovsky. According to Pasternak many Symbolists and Futurists flaunted their poetic makeup, and yet their masquerade remained harmless, "soft," and undisturbing, while that of Mayakovsky "smelled of blood." We may say that Mayakovsky lived out Antonin Artaud's ideal of the Theater of Cruelty, where blood and sacrifice are real—real to the point of vertigo, hyperreal, exposing the endless chain of illusionistic effects.

My focus here will be on the connection between Mayakovsky's "spectacular biography" and his deaths—figurative and nonfigurative. The Romantic mask of a Poet-hero fighting *byt*, or a self-sacrificing revolutionary, lures the poet with a promise of immortality and future resurrection, and at the same time it threatens him with an ultimate murderous depersonalization and a loss of self.

Before viewing Mayakovsky from the position of his Russian and foreign spectators and before attempting to disentangle the contradictory myth of the revolutionary poet, I will examine how Mayakovsky himself tailors his spectacular attire, in whose rich texture the threads of life, art, and politics are interwoven. My emphasis will be on the rhetorical devices and strategies which hold this texture together, specifically on the tension between personification and depersonalization and on Mayakovsky's peculiar use of vital metaphors. I will also explore the ways in which Mayakovsky reinvents and poetically motivates his own name so that its sound patterns become tragically alliterative.

"Vladimir Mayakovsky": Personification and Depersonalization

In Mayakovsky's case it is hard to determine who is more responsible for his biographical legend, the poet or his readers. Mayakovsky was his own image maker and mythologist, the author of many of his own legends; and yet he could not control the diverse reproductions of his image that proliferated in Soviet Russia and abroad after his death.

Most of Mayakovsky's lyric and long poems are written in the first person. Moreover, from the titles of Mayakovsky's early poems one notices a clear opposition between "I," the title of a short poetic cycle (1913), and "You" (in the plural), the title of a 1915 poem that echoes the Romantic opposition between the poet and "the mob." "We" appears in the title of a 1913 poem, referring to the outrageous Futurist-hooligans, and turns into the official optimistic "we, the people" in his postrevolutionary poems, such as "We are on the move" (1919) where "we" means "the carriers of the new faith." [19] Even in the postrevolutionary poems, however, the communal "we" and the overtly personal, lyrical "I" constantly combat each other, and "I" ultimately wins.

Mayakovsky's autobiography is entitled *I, Myself* (*Ja sam*), which reads almost as a pleonasm, an excess of selfhood. At the same time, this double affirmation of the self suggests a discontinuity and results from a kind of fear that there might be an "I" which is not "myself," an "I" which has become a pure poetic convention, or the ideologically unsound "I" of the extravagant Futurist. In his autobiography, written in 1928, Mayakovsky claims to relate only "what has a residue of the words." "I am a poet: that is what makes me interesting." [20] In response to his potential adversaries, who claim that his autobiography is not very serious, Mayakovsky says that "he is not used to nursing his own persona." [21] This is obviously a case of false modesty; Mayakovsky nurses both his poetic and his heroic life personae, fashioning himself in a peculiar telegraphic style, the style of a new myth. Moreover, in Mayakovsky the distinction between person and persona is particularly tenuous: most of Mayakovsky's personal anecdotes have "a residue of words," while the poet's words take on an urgent and vital quality.

Mayakovsky's first person cannot be regarded simply as a poetic convention, a lyrical voice. At times it is a larger-than-life "I" of a megalomaniac, who equates himself with Napoleon, invites the Sun for tea, and amicably addresses Pushkin and Lenin; at other times it is a small private lyrical "I" of a desperate lover. Mayakovsky's overwhelming "I" can be

compared with the "I" of Walt Whitman—one of Mayakovsky's favorite poets—in its ability to seem at once self-glorifying and self-effacing, all-embracing and exclusive. Moreover, many of these diverse "I"s are named Vladimir Mayakovsky, as if the poet deliberately ignores all the noble restrictions and conventions of literary genres by imposing the signature of the author and his almost corporeal presence upon every sentence. The name Vladimir Mayakovsky is used across poetic genres—from the early tragedy *Vladimir Mayakovsky* to the revolutionary poems, the addresses to Pushkin and Lenin, and the conversations with the financial inspector and comrade Kostrov about "the oddness of love." The excessive use of "I" and of the poet's own name point to authorial transgressions that operate in Mayakovsky's theater. It is precisely these transgressions that do not allow one to draw a clear line between the life and the text, leading to the final discontinuity between "I" and "myself" in which one of the two ends up destroying the other.

The role of the proper name, the name of the author, is very carefully examined by the theoreticians of the author's death and resurrection. For Yury Tynyanov, the name of the author is the locus of confusion between literature and *byt* (everyday existence, daily grind, nonliterary discourses in the society), between the "author's individuality"—a set of personal, psychological characteristics, totally irrelevant from the literary point of view—and "literary individuality"—a set of features representing the author in the reader's mind.[22] Then, in parentheses, Tynyanov insists on the necessity of drawing a distinction between the two and on studying exclusively the literary individuality, which is the significant factor in literary evolution. To prove his point, he compares the study of literature with the study of the Russian Revolution: "To discuss the personal psychology of the creator is the same as, when explaining the origin and the importance of the Russian revolution, to claim that it took place due to the personal features of its leaders."[23]

As Peter Steiner remarks, the name of the author for Tynyanov is not a "senseless" mark but a description that places the author in a certain context. It is "a kind of bridge, where impulses coming from the text, meet extra-textual information."[24] On the one hand, the name is "the last limit of the stylistic person's literary specificity," that is, the specific features of style which lead to the formation of the literary persona. On the other hand, the name is linked to the text from the outside, connoting the reader's expectations. Tynyanov pays special attention to the literary pseudonym, which is the name par excellence for the literary personality of the author. If taken to its radical extreme, any name on the cover of a

book should be seen as a pseudonym which just happens to be a homonym of the name of an actual person.

In "What Is an Author?" Foucault argues very much in the same vein. He also notes the peculiarly borderline position of the name of the author and its paradoxical existence. According to Foucault, "the proper name and the name of the author oscillate between the poles of description and designation but cannot be reduced to either of them."[25] Although Foucault chooses to regard the author and his name only as "functions of a discourse" in order to avoid the confusion in the relationship between life and discursive practices, he acknowledges the ambiguity of the author's position. Foucault writes: "The author's name remains at the contours of the texts, separating one from the other, defining their form, and characterizing their mode of existence . . . the author's name is not a function of a man's civil status, nor is it fictional; it is situated in the breach between the discontinuities, which gives rise to new groups of discourses."[26]

In his almost fetishistic obsession with his own name Mayakovsky seems to exceed even the most flexible critical categories and far outstrips the other poets. It is unthinkable for someone like Mallarmé to include his name in his poetry, although the name easily yields itself to puns, some of which have been savored by the critics (*mal-larme, mal-armé, les fleurs de mal-armées*, and so on). Pasternak explicitly states that in poetry a name is always alien (*chuzhoe*), different from one's actual name. Mandelstam includes his name in "The Fourth Prose," but as an insult in the imaginary discourse of his enemies, in the "trial records and other cruel documents": "What sort of fruit is this Mandelstam, how long will he shift around?" Here Mandelstam makes a cryptographic pun on his name playing with the German (Yiddish) etymology of the word "mandelstam," meaning "almond stem." Marina Tsvetaeva often recreates a poetic mythology with her name "Marina"—marine, sea breeze, as well as the name of the "proud Polish woman," Marina Mnishek, the accomplice of the courageous impostor Grishka Otrepiev, Pushkin's heroine. As John Shoptaw has demonstrated, the poet's cryptographic inscription of his or her name in the text is quite common and occurs from the Greeks to the present. Often it is a cipher, or an imprecise anagram, as in Sylvia Plath's use of "plaster." Thus in the very act of poetic writing, self-effacement and self-inscription go together. Moreover, ciphered self-inscription often provides the first impulse for writing.[27]

Yet, Mayakovsky's use of his name is unique. Instead of a cryptographic, indirect cipher we encounter his name in large letters in the

poems' titles and in all possible variations—from the last name alone to the first name and patronymic, Vladimir Vladimirovich. One of the earliest and most striking examples of this is in Mayakovsky's play *Vladimir Mayakovsky*. As Pasternak remarks, "'Vladimir Mayakovsky' should be read not as the name of the author, but as the name of the subject matter."[28] On the cover of the play, the name doubles; it is hard to determine who is the mirror image of whom: Vladimir Mayakovsky the author of *Vladimir Mayakovsky* or vice versa.

In fact, the title of the play emerged almost by accident. Initially, the poet entitled his work "The Rebellion of the Things" ("Vosstanie Veshchej"). However, written in the copy presented to the censor was: "Vladimir Mayakovsky, A Tragedy." Reportedly, the censor took the author's name for the title and approved the tragedy *Vladimir Mayakovsky* for performance.[29] It was a unique case in which the purely accidental displacement of quotation marks on the part of a careless censor provided a brilliant insight into the play, which extremely excited the author himself. Vladimir Mayakovsky was not only the name of the author, the name of the play, and the name of the main character, but also the name of the actor and of the director, at least in the first production of the work in 1913 in the Luna Park theater in St. Petersburg. This interplay between depersonalization and personification, between self-effacement in the act of writing and self-impersonation in the performance, underlines the play on all levels.

Vladimir Mayakovsky can be seen as a monodrama. In its genre it has obvious similarities to Mallarmé's "Igitur."[30] "Igitur," as was demonstrated in the previous chapter, is an antitheatrical, unperformable "play," which heavily depends on syntax, already visible in its title, and can be regarded as a protofilmic game of shadows. Mayakovsky's monodrama is quite theatrical. Its central device is *personification*.[31] As follows from the early title "The Rebellion of the Things," things become personified in their protest against the conventional violence of naming: "And suddenly all the things rushed,/ straining their voices/ throwing off the trappings of worn-out names" ("I vdrug vse veshchi kinulis',/ razdiraja golos/ skidyvaja lokhmot'ja izmozhennykh imen").[32] This drama of the things is echoed by a no less anthropomorphic drama of nature: "The sky is crying,/ desperately/ sonorously/ and the cloud has a little grimace on the wrinkle of its mouth" ("Nebo plachet/ bezuderzhno/ zvonko/ a u oblachka/ grimaska na morshchinke rotika").[33] Moreover, the suicide of the poet described at the end of the prologue is presented as an almost joyful embrace of the poet and an anthropomorphic train: "I will lie down/

light/ in lazy attire/ on the soft bed of real dung/ and the train's wheels will embrace my neck/ while I quietly kiss the knees of the rails" ("Ljagu/ svetlyj/ v odezhdakh iz leni/ na mjagkoe lozhe iz nastojash-chego navoza/ i tikhim celujushchim shpal koleni/ obnimet mne sheju koleso parovoza").[34] The prologue also suggests a link between the death of a poet and the death of poetry in Mayakovsky's proclamation that he may be "the last poet."

The device of personification, as well as that of the apostrophe, as has been noted in recent work on lyric poetry, has double implications: on the one hand, it perpetuates the poet's power over the world, his ability to create a world of his own and to animate it through language, and, on the other hand, the personified things reflect the poet like a mirror, objec-tifying him, asserting the powers of language itself.[35] The character Vlad-imir Mayakovsky, like the rebellious things around him, wishes to throw away "the trappings of the worn-out names." But does this rebellion in-clude his own name? What happens to it in this interplay of depersonali-zation and impersonation?

If there were no other characters in the play, the anthropomorphic drama would still be acted out on the level of language. The characters serve to create a minimum of highly stylized dramatic action, and they are distinguished not so much by speech as by their grotesque visual attributes, for instance, "the old man with dry black cats," "a man with-out an ear," "a man with two kisses," "the woman with a tear," "the woman with a big tear," and "the woman with a little tear." The artist Pavel Filonov who designed the costumes for the play's first production emphasized the flatness of these characters with quite an ingenious visual solution. Instead of costumes, he created drawings that the actors carried in front of them throughout the play. This emphasizes the uniqueness and three-dimensionality of the character Vladimir Mayakovsky, who was acted by the poet himself. Mayakovsky is the only character in the play who appears without a mask, although in the second act he puts on a toga and a laurel crown as though parodying a classical poet. "Ja-poet/ ja raznicu ster mezhdu licami svoikh i chuzhikh" ("I am a poet/ I erased the difference between my people's faces and alien ones").[36] This claim of erasing the difference between himself (or selves) and others suggests many dangerous transgressions—between faces and masks, between ob-jectification and personification—which forebode a dangerous ending to the poet's monodrama. There is always some suspicion that, perhaps, nothing is hidden beneath the many layers of disguises, and that in fact there is no "beneath" at all, only a superimposition of images, revealing the contours of a death mask.

The following extract from the epilogue enhances some of the themes of the play:

Иногда мне кажется—
я петух голландский
или я
—король псковский.
А иногда
мне больше всего нравится
моя собственная фамилия,
Владимир Маяковский.[37]

> Sometimes I think I am a Dutch cock, or I am a king of Pskov. And sometimes, I like best of all my own name—Vladimir Mayakovsky.

This provocative ending reminds us of Nikolay Gogol's "Diary of a Madman," in which the main character overhears dogs' conversations and imagines himself to be the king of Spain. This is Gogol's only text narrated in the first person, the first person being, of course, that of the multifaced schizophrenic, everyman and no-man, a little man and a writer. In the epilogue Mayakovsky declares himself "a blessed fool," evoking an entire tradition of Russian literature in which madness is often seen as lucidity and distorted articulation is construed as insight. The ending of Mayakovsky's epilogue is a kind of schizophrenic paraphrase, or a madman's reading of "Diary of a Madman," in which the king of Spain turns into the more modest king of Pskov.

The last lines of the play present yet another mirroring of the name, the poet's explicit declaration of love to his proper name, not to himself as in *The Cloud in Trousers*.[38] Thus the name of the heroically tragic, larger-than-life poet-character becomes reified, acquires a life of its own. The name turns into a dangerous fetish, a potentially destructive double, reminiscent of Gogol's and Dostoevsky's fantastic characters, who threatens to suck the life out of the man.

The same configuration—the dramatic first person, the proper name, and the theme of a heroic self-sacrifice of the poet—recurs in another prerevolutionary long poem, *Man (Chelovek)*. This is a peculiar personal gospel of Mayakovsky divided into sections—"Mayakovsky's Nativity," "Mayakovsky's Life," "Mayakovsky's Passions," "Mayakovsky's Ascension," "Mayakovsky in the Sky," and "Mayakovsky—to the Centuries." The poem is a mixture of sacrilegious remarks about the official religion and obviously plagiarized Christian myths. Here Mayakovsky is not only a poetic character but also the exemplary man, whose mythical predeces-

sor is Jesus Christ. Thus, in the creation of what Mayakovsky will call in 1919 "the new faith" ("We Are Marching") the poet often usurps the imagery from the old faith, particularly from Christianity.

The use of Christian imagery for revolutionary purposes and its coexistence with a blatant critique of religion, "the opium of the people," have puzzled many readers and scholars. This imagery illustrates again the central issues and paradoxes involved in the new myth demanded by Mayakovsky, the myth first of the rebellious poet and then of the revolutionary poet. In *Man*, "Mayakovsky" is no longer the name of a poet but a name of the myth; "Mayakovsky" vacillates between death and immortality, between anonymity and privileged singularity, between the name of an everyman and the name of a chosen man, a self-sacrificial redeemer of humanity.[39]

In the postrevolutionary poems the use of the first person is only slightly modified. From the very first day Mayakovsky accepts the October Revolution fully, to the point of personal appropriation; "my revolution," he writes in *I, Myself*.[40] Mayakovsky is one of the six writers and artists who arrived at Smolny, Bolshevik headquarters, a few days after the storming of the Winter Palace to participate in the meeting of intellectuals convoked by the new Soviet power.[41] Thus Mayakovsky literally witnesses the making of history and wishes to be one of the first to poeticize the revolution. In 1919 Mayakovsky writes another long poem, *150,000,000* (the population of the Soviet republic at the time), in which he engages or rather flirts with the idea of revolutionary anonymity and joyful effacement of individual authorship.

> 150,000,000 мастера этой поэмы имя
> Пуля—ритм.
> > Рифма—огонь из здания в здание.
> 150,000,000 говорят губами моими.[42]

150,000,000 is the name of the craftsman of this poem, the bullet is the rhythm. The rhyme is the fire from building to building. 150,000,000 are speaking through my lips.

In these opening lines we notice a series of correlations. First, as in the tragedy *Vladimir Mayakovsky*, there is an attempt to identify the name of the author with the title of the work. Then, an analogy is made between the violent action of the revolution and writing verse. One is not simply a metaphor or simile of the other; rather, the relationship between the two is that of an uncompromising equation. Furthermore, there is a claim that

the same unproblematized equation relationship exists between the voice of the first person and that of the 150,000,000. As is characteristic of Mayakovsky's transgressivie poetics, it goes beyond a simple poetic claim. In fact, as Mayakovsky reports in *I, Myself*, he initially published the poem without his own name and wished that each reader would continue writing it.

> Кончил *150,000,000*. Печатаю без фамилии. Хочу чтоб каждый дописывал и улучшил. Этого не делали, зато фамилию знали почти все.[43]

I finished *150,000,000*. I am publishing it without my last name. I want everyone to continue writing it and to improve it. Nobody was doing it. But almost everyone knew the last name.

Thus we see that what could have become an interesting avant-garde project turns into a comedy of false modesty and concealed self-flattery. In fact, whereas in the poem *Man* "Mayakovsky" stands for Everyman and for Christ, here "Mayakovsky" stands for 150,000,000; the name is written between the lines and implied in the minds of the reader as the vox populi. The claim of the revolutionary "death of the author," what appears here as a voluntary self-collectivization, badly conceals a new version of an old myth of invisible divinity.

> Кто спросит луну?
> Кто солнце к ответу притянет—
> чего
>   ночи и дни чините!?
> Кто назовет земли гениального автора
> Так
>   и этой
>   моей
>   поэмы
>   никто не сочинитель.[44]

Who will ask the moon? Who will force the sun to answer?—Why are you sharpening days and nights? Who will name the genius author of the Earth? In the same way nobody is the author of my poem.

The poem recreates the old literary myth, particularly developed by Flaubert, the myth of the author who is ever present and yet invisible like the God of creation, the author of the universe. The only inconsistency here is the word "my" which proudly occupies the line before "nobody."

The tension between "I," Vladimir Mayakovsky, and "I," anonymous nobody, the collective genius of the people, is made visible in many post-revolutionary poems. In the most optimistic of these poems, Mayakovsky often uses the second person plural, a form of the imperative. For instance, in the opening lines of "Left March" we read: "Razvorachivajtes v marshe/ slovesnoj ne mesto kljauze!" ("Rally your ranks in the march, /It's not the place for quibbling!").[45] The speaker of this poem is anonymous, and yet his role is quite prominent. He is the invisible omniscient poet, revolutionary commander-in-chief who tells the sailors and the people in general with which foot they should start marching.

The poem "Anniversary," addressed to Pushkin and written in the midst of deadening official celebrations of the poet's death, can serve as an example of the optimistic and self-glorifying use of the proper name in the postrevolutionary period. In the poem Mayakovsky proudly presents himself to Pushkin: "Alexander Sergeevich, let me introduce myself, Mayakovsky."[46] Moreover, he describes his imaginary chat with Alexander Sergeevich:

> Вот
>   когда
>   и горевать не в состоянии—
> это,
>   Александр Сергеич,
>   много тяжелей.
> Айда, Маяковский!
>   Маячь на юг!
> Сердце
>   рифмами вымучь—
> Вот
>   и любви пришел каюк,
>   дорогой Владим Владимыч.[47]

And when you're not in a condition to grieve, that, Alexander Sergeevich, is a lot worse. Come on, Mayakovsky, drift [*Majach'*] to the South, torture your heart with rhymes. The love has gone sour, dear Vladim Vladimych.

This conversation is faintly reminiscent of Gogol's comic character Khlestakov and his familiarities with "pal Pushkin." At the same time it reveals a real urgency of communication between Pushkin, "alive and not the mummy," and Mayakovsky; breaks up the mummifying conventionality of the lyrical "I"; and lurks "alive" behind the white

page. Mayakovsky not only promises to offer Pushkin a job on the journal of the Left Front of Art (LEF) but even makes him speak like a Futurist, almost turning Pushkin into a double of himself. Thus, "Pushkin" makes puns on Mayakovsky's name: "Aida, Majakovskij *ma*jach' na jug" ("Come on, Mayakovsky, drift to the South"). We find in the poem a curious mirroring; Mayakovsky creates a Pushkin in his own image so that this newly born Pushkin can reveal the poetic quality and the potential suggestivity of Mayakovsky's name.

"Majachit'"—a very interesting colloquial Russian verb meaning to lurk on the horizon, loom, haunt someone like a ghost—is used here unusually, signifying simply "to drift" and pointing to the poet's perpetual homelessness and wandering. And indeed, "Mayakovsky" intrusively does "majachit" in the eyes of the reader, violating many literary conventions. The first person is used with a proper identification, with an autograph signed several times throughout the poem. Mayakovsky's constant "authentification" of the first person is one of the important devices which contribute to the proliferation of biographical legends, inviting the reader to see a continuity and a symbolic relationship between the poet's art and his life. In Mayakovsky's poems the reader is neither a private confidant nor a neighbor-eavesdropper who overhears from the corridor the author's private conversations. The reader is instead invited to enjoy the freedom of speech of the poet's ideal communal kitchen, which then turns into a stage, or a tribune. The name of the author becomes poetically motivated; the reader is asked to motivate it even further by engaging in new word plays. Ultimately, the name "Vladimir Mayakovsky" with its suggestive root *may(j)ak* (beacon) remains as the only stable signpost to the poet's multiple schizoid images.

Moreover, the poem addressed to Pushkin and to the officially worshipped Pushkin monument is about demystifying the official deadening cult of the great poet, in the same way that Mayakovsky's epic poem *Lenin* is aimed against the popular sentimentalization and profanation of the great party leader. Mayakovsky, however, has a personal stake in both demystifications which he performs so obsessively. In fact, in both cases the poet not only demystifies and ridicules the official, stifling, and philistine cult of the two men but also offers his own corrected version of a new myth. Pushkin is slightly more humanized than Lenin, who is presented as a purified embodiment of the objective forces of history. To paraphrase the quote of Marx, they personify the inevitability of the natural laws of history. This is only a new version of the Romantic definition of genius. Mayakovsky actively and aggressively introduces himself in

both poems, inscribing himself on the same page of history as a great poetic and political genius. Thus directly and indirectly, voluntarily and uncannily, Mayakovsky supervises and corrects the frames of his own myth, offering paradigms for a proper revolutionary image.

However, as follows from the Russian fantastic tradition, particularly from Pushkin's "Bronze Horseman" admired by Mayakovsky, the games with statues and the challenging conversations with men of power, tsars or party leaders, tend to end tragically. At the beginning Mayakovsky claimed the revolution for himself, calling it tenderly "my revolution." But gradually it will be the revolution, or a postrevolutionary *byt*, that will consume the poet. We can imagine another drama in which the revolutionary and postrevolutionary things claim: "My Mayakovsky." The tension between appropriating the revolution and being appropriated by it unfolds in many of the poet's works, including his suicide note.

In one of his late and unfinished poems, "At the Top of My Voice" (Vo ves' golos"), Mayakovsky names his revolutionary persona "latrine cleaner and water carrier drafted and recruited by the revolution" and also "agitator, leader, loudspeaker."[48] Again, however, this "loudspeaking" ("gorlan"; from *gorlo*, throat), like the device of personification used in *Vladimir Mayakovsky*, threatens the poet with straining his voice or, to use Mayakovsky's own image, with strangling "the throat of his own song": "No ja/ sebja suirjal stanovjas'/ na gorlo sobstvennoj pesne" ("But I restrained myself, stepping on the throat of my own song"). Here we observe first the splitting of the first person: "I" is restraining "myself." The correlation between "gorlo" and "gorlan" in the next lines becomes apparent: the public loudspeaking is made possible by stifling the personal traditional lyric voice. The throat (*gorlo*) is a synecdoche of the poet's body, the point of poetic articulation and a vital organ. The revolutionary loudspeaker (*gorlan*) is a grotesque and hyperbolic formation, a making of a persona out of one fragile but poetically essential synecdoche. In these lines "the throat" is transferred from the poet to the song itself. The song is made anthropomorphic, personified at the price of violence to the subject. One senses that the poet himself is on the verge of exhausting his powers of personification; he is pushing figuration to dangerous limits, the point where poetic figures of speech become fragile and unstable as if revealing the vulnerability of the poetic subject itself.

Thus the role of the first person and of the author's name in Mayakovsky's work goes beyond the ambiguities and discontinuities described by Tynyanov and Foucault. The name "Mayakovsky" is not simply "at the

contours" of various discourses, nor is it a bridge between literature and *byt*. Marina Tsvetaeva remarks with great lucidity that Mayakovsky always uses "direct speech with a living target."[49] This direct speech threatens to transgress and exceed all the categories of literature and *byt*, life and discursive practices, real name and literary pseudonym, rhetorical figure and the figure of the poet, the body of the text and the body of the author. The poet's potentially murderous loud-speaker is aimed both at himself and at the reader.

A Portrait of the Artist in a Yellow Blouse: Metaphor and Transgression

С Маяковским произошло так ... Он раскрыл рот и сказал—Я!—Его спросили—кто—я? Он ответил—я, Владимир Маяковский.—А Владимир Маяковский— кто?—Я! ... Так и пошло—"Владимир Маяковский, тот кто я." Смеялись. Но "Я" в ушах, но желтая кофта—в глазах—оставались.

This is what happened to Mayakovsky ... He opened his mouth and said: I! They asked him: Who is "I"? He answered: I, Vladimir Mayakovsky.—And who is Vladimir Mayakovsky?—I! And since then that's how it goes—"Vladimir Mayakovsky is who is I." They laughed. But "I" in the ears and the yellow blouse in the eyes persisted.
      Marina Tsvetaeva, "Epics and Lyrics of Contemporary Russia"

We can represent the cultural iconography of Vladimir Mayakovsky in a series of imaginary portraits, a collage of the poet's photographs, paintings, and verbal descriptions. Here is a prerevolutionary Mayakovsky— "the handsome, twenty-two-year-old" Futurist in the yellow blouse, asking the audience "to brush his ears." He is a bit of a dandy, with a long white cigar and a cylinder hat, a passionate poseur with intense dark eyes, a stylish hooligan.

The next portrait is of a Revolutionary poet with a capital R, roaring from the tribune: "Who is there marching to the right?/Left/Left/Left!" His hair is cut short like a soldier's, without even a trace of the unyielding Romantic forelock, revealing only a majestic skull and strong virile features.

Then there is a postrevolutionary Mayakovsky who aspires to become a major Soviet poet and a messenger of Soviet Russia on all continents:

we see him on a vacation boat with the secretary of the Mexican Communist Party, wearing a black bow tie and smoking a cigar, then with his former fellow Futurist, David Burlyuk, near the Brooklyn Bridge, and finally with Lily Brik's sister, Elsa, in a Parisian café.

We see the next Mayakovsky, pre- and postrevolutionary poet-lover, screaming in the streets of the city "about that" in a fit of universal jealousy "to Copernicus." He is part of Alexander Rodchenko's constructivist collage, precariously balancing on a tower of Ivan the Great raised above a modern city, Moscow or New York, with Lily Brik in the foreground and skyscrapers in the background.

Finally, there is Mayakovsky the poet-monument. He wears the official bureaucratic bronze jacket, with an officially Revolutionary Romantic forelock, and guards the streets and squares of Soviet cities.

But these images are not as consistently representational as it might seem. In fact, there is an unusual self-portrait of Mayakovsky that stands out as exceptional and does not correlate with the cultural mythology of the poet. This portrait presents a cubist disfiguration of the face; it is an exercise in representational possibilities, a game in perspectives, and a juxtaposition of different planes to the extent that the individual anthropomorphic features and idiosyncratic attributes become invisible or irrelevant. From the pictorial point of view, the portrait is quite unoriginal: Mayakovsky uses already developed cubist techniques with one important difference, the object of disfiguration is his own persona. Although this self-portrait of the artist and poet is virtually unknown, and in general is rather uncharacteristic for Mayakovsky, we will keep it in mind throughout this discussion. It will allow us to regard all the other figurative and representational images as palimpsests, which betray traces of this self-disfiguring experimentation.

Traditional visual attributes played a crucial role in Mayakovsky's myth making. They correlated with important cultural icons and served as conscious and unconscious "visual propaganda" with which the poet attempted to shock and seduce the reader. I will not trace here the development of Mayakovsky's iconographic attributes from yellow blouse to bronze jacket. Rather, I will concentrate only on the adventures of the famous yellow blouse which will function as an exemplary metaphorical texture that discloses Mayakovsky's strategies of self-creation.

Mayakovsky describes the genesis of the yellow blouse in his autobiography, *I, Myself*. The poet promises to relate only what "has a residue of words" and of course the making of the yellow blouse is one such event.

Костюмов у меня никогда не было были две блузы гну-
снейшего вида . . . Нет денег. Взял у сестры кусок желтой
ленты. Обвязался. Фурор.[50]

I never had any suits. I had two blouses of a most disgusting type . . .
There was no money. I took from my sister a piece of yellow ribbon.
Wrapped it around. A scandal.

The tailoring of the blouse, its color and material are all the result of
accident, and they reflect nothing but the poet's poverty. At first, the
blouse contributed only to the shock effect of the Futurist's happenings.
Subsequently, it became poeticized. In 1914 Mayakovsky dedicates to it
(or to her, since the word blouse in Russian is feminine) a short poem,
"Fop's Blouse" ("Kofta fata"). The poem is a typical example of Mayakovsky's early urban lyric. The poetic persona is a larger-than-life figure
of the Futurist poet who goes to "rape the green springs" and converses
with the Earth and the Sun on equal terms. In the first stanza, the act of
sewing cloth is a significant poetic initiation.

Я сошью себе черные штаны
из бархата голоса моего.
Желтую кофту из трех аршин заката.
По Невскому мира, по лощеным полосам его,
профланирую шагом Дон-Жуана и фата.[51]

I will make myself black pants out of the velvet of my voice. A yellow
blouse out of six feet of sunset. And I'll stroll around the paved stripes of
the Nevsky Avenue of the world like a Don Juan and a fop.

The yellow blouse is no longer made of the prosaic and ordinary cloth
of his sister, but of "six feet of sunset." It is a sign of the poet's communion with the sun. The relationship between the poet's self and cloth
grows more and more intimate. In the last stanza the yellow blouse turns
into an interface between the poet and the outside world.

Женщины, любящие мое мясо, и эта
девушка, смотрящая на меня, как на брата,
закидайте улыбками меня, поэта—
Я цветами нашью их на кофту фата!

Women, who love my flesh, and this girl, looking at me as though I were
her brother, throw your smiles at me, the poet. I'll embroider them like
flowers on my fop's blouse!

The title, "Fop's Blouse" ("Kofta fata"), wraps around the poem, offering us an interesting interpretive thread. It presents a suggestive sound patter. The word "fat" (fop), which designates an outrageous Futurist persona of Mayakovsky's, seems to emerge from "kofta" (blouse) to strengthen the effect of the sound repetition: ko*f-ta fata*. Thus it seems that even before the "I" of the poem takes control and tells us about the exciting creation of the blouse out of the sunset, the persona of the poet himself—"fat"—is already created by the suggestive and seductive sound patterns of the word "kofta." In other words, the cloth poetically motivates the figure of the poet. Moreover, if we displace the accent in the word "*fa*ta" and turn it into "fa*ta*" (a bridal veil)—a gesture that Mayakovsky's poetry invites us to do—we might imagine the creation of "kofta" as an important poetic ritual, a preparation for the futuristic "marriage" to the modern city.

From a seemingly insignificant article of everyday life, the yellow blouse turns into a "literary fact" and then into a cultural emblem which starts affecting the poet's daily existence. Thus, Victor Shklovsky claims that yellow, which by pure chance was the color of the poet's sister's remnant, becomes *the* color of Futurism, and Mayakovsky's yellow blouse becomes its banner. This metamorphosis of the poet's cloth, which gradually acquires a cultural significance, is a vivid example of the vital interaction between art and life.

In the long poem *The Cloud in Trousers* (*Oblako v shtanakh*) (1914–1915) Mayakovsky tries to convince us that the blouse is only a protective disguise: "Khorosho kogda v zheltuju koftu dusha ot ukusov uprjatana" ("It's good when the soul is protected from bites in a yellow blouse").[52] However, it is becoming more difficult to separate the poet's Futurist soul from his Futurist clothing; they become metaphors of each other and drift into each other's territory.

Mayakovsky creates in his various articles a parodic image of a poet in a yellow blouse that stands for Mayakovsky the Futurist. The provocative essay "O raznykh Majakovskikh" ("About the Different Mayakovskys") (1914) begins with the grotesque recreation of his Futurist persona, not only that of a fop but also of a "hooligan and cynic," in which Mayakovsky consciously rejects his Futurist attire for all sorts of bourgeois jackets.

Я-нахал, для которого высшее удовольствие ввалиться, напялив желтую кофту, в сборище людей благородно берегущих под чинными сюртуками, фраками и пиджаками скромность и приличие.[53]

I am a lout, for whom the highest pleasure is to put on my yellow blouse and rush into a gathering of people, who nobly guard modesty and decency under their formal suits, dress coats and jackets.

The essay is a good example of Mayakovsky's ironic criticism, a mixture of self-mockery and self-advertisement. Here the poet masterfully promotes his long poem *The Cloud in Trousers*, both flirting with and provoking the reader. Mayakovsky performs a series of *saltos mortales*, shifting back and forth between "a young man of twenty-two" and the capital *P* Poet, parodying his own image of "a publicity seeker and a scandal maker in a yellow blouse" and glorifying it in the same gesture. In the article "A Drop of Tar" ("Kaplja degtja") (1916), which playfully declares the death of Futurism, Futurism itself is personified and turned into an "eccentric pal with a red forelock" which reminds us of the young Mayakovsky.[54] But it is even more striking that the Futurist movement is personified on its death bed, about to be killed, a proof of the poet's masterful ability to personify and depersonalize, to animate and destroy cultural movements. Mayakovsky parodies and objectifies his literary personae, often to the point of vertigo.

Later, in the programmatic *LEF* article "How Are Verses to Be Made" ("Kak delat' stikhi") (1926), Mayakovsky describes his first encounter with Esenin, wearing peasant shoes and an embroidered peasant blouse like a *muzhik* from an operetta, and compares Esenin's "theatrical props" with his own yellow blouse.[55] As both the essay and the poem written on Esenin's suicide suggest, the Imaginist Esenin is a double of the Futurist Mayakovsky in life as well as death. The descriptions of Esenin's literary persona and of his actual and literary suicide help Mayakovsky to defamiliarize himself from himself and discuss, both directly and indirectly, his own tragic predicament.

In terms of rhetorical tropes, the relationship between the cloth and the skin is that of metonymy, which is a relationship by contiguity rather than by resemblance. More specifically, the yellow blouse can be seen as a synecdoche, a particular kind of metonymy that substitutes a part for the whole and the whole for a part. Paul de Man writes about the peculiar unstable status of synecdoche in the history of rhetoric.

Classical rhetoric generally classifies synecdoche as metonymy, which leads to difficulty characteristic of all attempts at establishing taxonomy of tropes; tropes are transformational systems rather than grids . . . Synecdoche is one of the borderline figures that creates an ambivalent zone

between metaphor and metonymy, and that by its special nature, creates the illusion of a synthesis by totalization.[56]

In the case of Mayakovsky we notice an obvious transformation of a synecdoche into a metaphor, into a kind of fetish-figure, which indeed promises some form of "totalization." In fact, Roman Jakobson developed his theory about metaphor and metonymy in literature using the examples of Mayakovsky and Pasternak.[57] Metaphor, according to Jakobson, emphasizes the relationships of similarity and semantic resemblance over that of syntactic contiguity. Similarity is linked with the tendency toward the symbolic (from the Greek *sum-ballein*, to throw together, to give a token for identification, to compare) which was particularly privileged by the Romantics. In Jakobson's bipolar universe, metaphor characterizes poetry as a genre and Romanticism as a movement, while metonymy distinguishes prose and Realism (although Jakobson is aware of the limitations of his model and the numerous exceptions to it). In a broad sense, the tendency toward metaphor represents the desire to make everything relevant, related, motivated, and signifying and thus to avoid the accidental, contiguous, chaotic, and uncontrollable elements that constitute the metonymic pole, or even point beyond rhetorical figuration as such.

Moreover, metaphor is at the core of what Jakobson later calls "the poetic function," based on the principle of equivalence, "promoted to the constitutive device of the system."[58] The poetic function turns language upon itself, superimposes similarity upon contiguity and forces motivation upon the unmotivated elements by including them in patterns of repetition. Jakobson notes that the poetic function is not solely confined to poetry but can also be observed in various forms of verbal communication. If we push Jakobson's notion even further, perhaps much further than Jakobson himself wished to push it, and regard the poetic function not as a unique property of the poetic text but as a peculiar way of creating meaning through patterning and repetition, then the poetic function exceeds the limits of discourse, the object of both linguistics and poetics. In the case of Mayakovsky, the poetic function, like "literariness," no longer assures the autonomy of literature, but on the contrary becomes transgressive and vital. Mayakovsky wished to motivate his life poetically, presenting it as a series of metaphorical knots in a single design, creating a biography in which each everyday occurrence is written as something significant and signifying. The orientation toward the poetic function, toward the patterning and metaphorization in life and art, promises the poet some form of control over his immortality. It serves as an antidote to the contingency and entropy that he would have to face were

his life only metonymically related to his art.[59] The poetic yellow blouse offers some existential protection, and yet with time it also becomes worn out, full of unpatchable holes.

The figure of metaphor is ambiguous. On the one hand, it seems to assure the transfer of signification and to inscribe the elements of resistance into a pattern, making gaps a part of the ornament. On the other hand, to quote Jakobson, it "deepens the fundamental dichotomy of sign and object."[60] The poet driven by what I will call *"metaphor compulsion"* (analogous with "the repetition compulsion") sooner or later confronts an abyss of displacements and discontinuities and a perpetual noncoincidence of words and things, which for him is tragic. The *metaphor compulsion* does not allow him to account for the heterogeneity and multiplicity of elements in everyday life (the *byt*, the daily grind which the poet saw as his worst enemy), the elements that do not yield to even the most unconventional poetic meters, and to accept with an appropriate balance of humor and wisdom the limitations of human control and the limits of intelligibility. When the lights in the theater go off, the poet is alone in the darkness and there is no space for chiaroscuro.

In the case of Mayakovsky, the metaphor compulsion functions like the Derridean *pharmakon* discovered in Plato's pharmacy: it is both a cure and a poison, it provides some temporary relief from the destructive effects of the untamable and nonsignifying chaos and, at the same time, further aggravates the disease, feeding its very roots.[61] Excessive personification and depersonalization become closely interwoven, and the poet's self-metaphorizing "I" turns into a discontinuous series of personae, in which it is impossible to distinguish between mask and face, cloth and skin.

Hence certain devices in Mayakovsky's poetry—"direct speech with a living target," the intrusive use of his proper name, self-parodying, and an overwhelming use of metaphors, particularly metaphors of the self—contribute to his peculiar understanding of the poet's life and to the genesis of a spectacular "biographical legend." The yellow blouse is only one example of Mayakovsky's transgressive metaphors, the tenor of which is located on the fragile border between literature and life.

Mayakovsky's chef d'oeuvre—the yellow blouse—originally an ordinary item in the poet's life, has become a literary fact and then a critical metaphor. Mayakovsky's contemporaries, his fellow poets and writers, appropriated and altered it in different ways. They, together with the yellow blouse, inherited that contagious *metaphor compulsion* which it provokes. The blouse appears in almost all the articles on Mayakovsky's suicide and serves as a metaphor in various paradigms. Kornely Zelinsky,

one of the Constructivist theorists, remarks that Mayakovsky's yellow blouse is better known than his poetry.[62] The Constructivists see the yellow blouse as a Futuristic atavism that does not allow Mayakovsky to embrace fully Soviet revolutionary art, an anonymous process of production and not an individual subversive act of "épater les bourgeois." Similarly, André Breton, the poet and theoretician of the Surrealist revolution, argues with Lev Trotsky, the practitioner of political revolution and later theoretician of revolutionary art, over the significance of the yellow blouse. Breton tries to convince Trotsky that even if the blouse can be regarded as "bohemian" it is not necessarily "counterrevolutionary."[63] The implied opposition is between the individualistic yellow blouse and the proletarian uniform of the author-producer.

Pasternak places the yellow blouse in yet another series of binary oppositions. Superficially, he contrasts it with the "philistine's jacket," while on a deeper level with the "black velvet of the poet's talent contained within himself."[64] The use of cloth as a metaphor for poetic talent is a curious case of the "textualization" of the poet's "inner self." In the clothing of the inner self we find a parallel with Mallarmé's "Igitur" and the same allusion to Hamlet. It seems that Pasternak himself is affected by the rhetorical powers of the yellow blouse so that, instead of laying bare any poetic talent, he clothes it again in a new metaphoric disguise.

That a blouse is at the center of a serious poetic debate is not as strange as it might appear at first glance. The obsession of male poets with clothes, both literary and actual, has a long tradition. It is enough to remember *le gilet rouge* of the poetic circle *La Jeune France*, the black attire of dandies and *poètes maudits*, Baudelaire's famous praise of makeup, which laid the foundation of modern poetics, and Mallarmé's fashion magazine.

Mayakovsky, in both his poetry and life, was extremely preoccupied with clothing. Perhaps that is one of the reasons why Osip Mandelstam and later Yevgeny Zamyatin derogatively call him a "poetess." In the essay "Literary Moscow" ("Literaturnaja Moskva") Mandelstam writes that "Mayakovsky . . . is in danger of becoming a poetess, which is already half-done."[65] (In the same essay he calls the Formalist School—in Russian it is the feminine "formal'naja shkola"—a woman critic, but grants it a privileged position among the not so flatteringly described poetesses: "It is the only woman who entered the circle of poetry as a new muse.") It is interesting to note that "poetess" is not defined entirely by biology. Rather it is a cultural metaphor of femininity, a metaphor for poetic inferiority, for lyrical indecency and emotional excess, jarring like an ex-

cess of tawdry makeup. The lyrical poet with a spectacular biography is in danger of becoming a poetess, in danger of imitating the female figure of Vanity trying on beautiful, richly embroidered attire before a mirror.

In the essay "Moscow-Petersburg" Zamyatin classifies Futurism, a movement "based on the image," specifically the emotional image, as "feminine." This classification applies primarily to Mayakovsky, who according to Zamyatin could have claimed that "Futurism—is I."[66] According to Zamyatin, the postrevolutionary Mayakovsky never quite overcame Futurist image making; he merely dyed his yellow blouse red: "The inventors of the yellow blouse were the first to win the red mandate—the right *to represent* the Revolution in literature."[67] Here Zamyatin addresses a crucial problem of revolutionary and postrevolutionary representation, whether the Soviet modification of the yellow blouse should be a symbolically red attire, a kind of new "gilet rouge" of the French Romantics, or a colorless and unspectacular worker's uniform. The yellow blouse circulates, therefore, between many paradigms of class, gender, poetics, and politics, intricately tying them together: bohemian blouse vs. bourgeois jacket, feminine blouse vs. masculine shirt, Futurist yellow vs. Revolutionary red, the exteriority of cloth vs. the interiority of the poetic self, the rich black velvet of talent vs. the cheap yellow satin of the poseur, and—most dangerous of all—the remarkable, lively singularity of the yellow blouse vs. anonymity, the absence of mark, the erasure of the image, the death of the poet.

The image of the modern author as producer, a functionary of the state, appears to be absent from Mayakovsky's cultural iconography in spite of his efforts.[68] Only a few weeks before his suicide Mayakovsky organized a photograph exhibition, "Twenty Years of Work," in an attempt to present his new and distinctly Soviet iconography. But again he wished to author his own antiauthorial image, to impersonate the new myth and even document it photographically, in the best of modern traditions. The exhibit offered a carefully documented reflection of his artistic persona as defined by the author himself at the end of his creative period. This persona of the literary "latrine cleaner and water carrier" or "Soviet factory producing happiness" was largely derived from Mayakovsky's association with the organization LEF, which saw itself both as a child of Futurism and its killer. An excerpt from the LEF program, written in the euphoric collective "we" of an avant-garde manifesto, is illustrative.

Раньше мы боролись с быками буржуазии. Мы эпатировали желтыми кофтами и размалеванными лицами. Теперь мы

боремся с жертвами этих быков в нашем советском строе. Наше оружие—пример, агитация, пропаганда.[69]

Before we were fighting against the bulls of the bourgeoisie, jarring [épater] it with the yellow blouses and made-up faces. Now we are fighting against the victims of these bulls in our Soviet regime. Our arms are: setting an example, agitation, and propaganda.

Sergey Tretyakov, one of the ideologues of LEF, suggests the necessity of "rational costume" for "workers of art" (*rabotniki iskusstva*) who should be seen as "psycho-engineers" and "psycho-designers." He argues for what he calls "*the americanization of the writer's personality* [the development of a businesslike, efficient matter-of-factness], which runs parallel to the electrification of the industry."[70] In accordance with Tredyakov's description, Mayakovsky tries to present himself in his last exhibition as a writer as deprived of any Futuristic exhibitionism, a fully integrated functionary of the state working in the artistic industry and cultivating the modern consciousness. And yet there is something threatening about this technocratic model. The anonymity associated with the process of production does not simply jeopardize the possibility of representing the figure of the poet by depriving him of any spectacular attributes; it actually questions the poet's right to exist.

Walter Benjamin, in his famous article "The Author as a Producer," in which he sympathetically describes Sergey Tretyakov as an exemplary "operating writer," draws a parallel between Plato's *Republic*, a perfect community in which the poet is considered to be harmful and superfluous, and the Soviet state: "The Soviet state, it is true, will not banish the poet like Plato, but it will . . . assign him tasks that do not permit him to display in new masterpieces the long-since counterfeit wealth of creative personality."[71] (Benjamin's attitude toward this creative personality is ambiguous. On the one hand, Benjamin is aware that its extreme embodiment is the fascist "superman" mentality. On the other, in its more moderate "liberal" and somewhat anti-Romantic expression, the creative personality can also refer to a figure dear to the critic's heart—a free-floating flâneur, a collector of poetic fragments and urban illuminations, who as Benjamin nostalgically remarks in the essay "Moscow" has turned into an almost extinct species in the revolutionary state.) Thus the murder of the poet-Futurist dressed in spectacular attire is a necessary death, a necessary sacrifice in service of the state for the birth of the new rational "worker of art."

The making of a new Soviet author is linked to the final purge and death of the poet. If the LEF's radical ideas were to be followed consistently, the poet both as inspired Romantic prophet and as subversive avant-garde explorer of language would be replaced by the journalist, the reporter, the propagandist *au service* not of the Revolution but of the post-revolutionary state. Or maybe the poet's replacement would be an "americanized" poet who saves his neologisms and puns for political advertisement. There is a tragic irony in the fact that Tretyakov himself fell victim to one of the first Stalinist purges and died in a camp. Perhaps he, like Mayakovsky, was too much of a poet in his radical rhetoric and vision of the technocratic utopia. The official Soviet death of the poet was more grim and literal than the LEF's and the Constructivists' joyful collective depersonalization through the process of production. Its style was party academism (that is, Socialist Realism), which turned the poet not simply into a reporter but into an informer—in the Soviet sense of the word— and threatened him with both figurative death and actual physical destruction.

The image of the author as a producer, the poet as a Soviet factory producing happiness, was something Mayakovsky both desired and feared. He felt that he was "the last poet," flattering himself with this peculiar singularity. His contemporaries had rightly distinguished the worn-out yellow blouse behind all Mayakovsky's "rational costumes." In Soviet Russian cultural history Mayakovsky's avant-garde and revolutionary repertoire was reduced to traditional literary masks. Tynyanov compared him to Gavril Derzhavin, Jakobson to Pushkin; Pasternak, Lidiya Ginsburg, and others saw him as the new embodiment of the old Romantic spectacular biography. Mayakovsky's obsession with "life-creation" ("zhiznetvorchestvo") links him also to his immediate predecessors—the Symbolist poets Andrey Bely and Alexander Blok. Yet, the historical specificity of Mayakovsky's fate, his confrontation with modern conditions in their peculiar Soviet variation, has to be taken into consideration. His repertoire of cultural masks is much wider than that of the Romantic poet, and much more contradictory and pluralistic. It includes among others the masks of a Futurist-urbanist, of a technology lover (as opposed to the Romantic nature lover), and of an author-producer, a functionary of the technocratic postrevolutionary state.

In his description of the poet on his death bed, Victor Shklovsky returns to Mayakovsky, as a last gift, his bright spectacular attributes and a new blue blouse. In Shklovsky's presentation the dead Mayakovsky is surrounded by an atmosphere of heightened theatricality, heightened to

the point of uncanniness: "There lay Mayakovsky, in a light blue blouse, on a colorful sofa, near the Mexican shawl."[72]

Suicide as a Literary Fact: "Vladimir Mayakovsky" by Roman Jakobson

In 1926 Mayakovsky wrote about the suicide of Sergey Esenin, whose farewell verses were signed in blood: "Esenin's death has become a literary fact."[73] Thus Mayakovsky suggests that the poet's death can be easily fictionalized and mythified. It can be considered a part of literature, a final mysterious dénouement of the poet's work. In a similar way he wrote about Alexander Blok and Velimir Khlebnikov, whose deaths in art and life are closely interrelated. Blok's death, according to Mayakovsky, comes as a result of an exhaustion that is both physical and artistic, as the inability to make a vital choice in the revolutionary whirlpool.

Я слушал его в мае этого года в Москве, в полу-пустом зале, молчавшем кладбищем, он тихо и грустно читал старые строки о цыганском пении, о любви, о прекрасной даме—дальше дороги не было. Дальше смерть. И она пришла.[74]

Last May in Moscow, in a half-empty hall, which was silent like a cemetery, I listened to him: he quietly and sadly read his old lines about gypsy singing, about love, and about the fair lady—there was no further way to go. Further on there was death. And it arrived.

One might suspect that Mayakovsky secretly desires to relegate the master Symbolist with a spectacular biography to the realm of the past. Blok's death is regarded as an inevitable outcome of the impending revolutions in art and politics, which he failed to embrace completely. (Mayakovsky, of course, styles himself as a herald of both revolutions.) On the contrary, Khlebnikov, who died a year after Blok in 1922, is presented as an exemplary modern martyr in life and in language who suffers for the "poetic idea."

Ƃиография Хлебникова равна его блестящим словесным построениям. Его биография—пример поэтам и укор поэтическим дельцам.[75]

The biography of Khlebnikov equals his brilliant verbal compositions. His biography is an example for poets, and a reproach to poetry dealers.

Thus, in both examples the death of the poet and the death of the man are intimately linked and are metaphors of each other.

In 1930 Roman Jakobson, confronted with the tragedy of Mayakovsky's death, uncannily echoes the poet's own words. He writes that the motif of suicide in Mayakovsky's work has become "literature of fact." [76] It contains a curious inversion, an interesting shift in syntax from the suicide in life viewed as "literary fact" to the suicide in poetry considered "literature of fact"—which in the formulation of the LEF theorists meant a document, a vital and timely element that goes beyond the traditional boundaries of the "literary." In the case of the poet's suicide the literary fact and the literature of fact mirror each other, creating an enigmatic chiasmus. Here I will try to delineate the space of this chiasmus, the space between multiple suicides, described and acted out, hypothetical and realized, public and private, revolutionary and counterrevolutionary. Which suicide precedes the other, the suicide in poetry or the suicide in life? Which one is original and authentic? Does suicide, like a Derridean metaphor, exist always in the plural? Who, then, was shot in the Lubyanka office on April 14, 1930? What is the politics of suicide? How is the suicide of the revolutionary poet related to the most obsessive of Surrealist dreams—the dream of practicing poetry and of living out art?

Mayakovsky's final message, "To All of You," together with Esenin's poem in blood, forms a peculiar genre of *auto-moribundia*—to borrow an expression of the Spanish avant-garde writer Ramón Gómez de la Serna. Here is the text of Mayakovsky's suicide note:

To All of You:
  Don't blame anyone for my death, and please, don't gossip about it. The deceased hated gossip.
  Mama, sisters, comrades, forgive me. This is not a good method (I don't recommend it to the others), but for me there is no other way out.
  Lily, love me.
  Comrade Government, my family consists of Lily Brik, mama, sisters and Veronica Vitoldovna Polonskaya.
  If you can, provide a decent life for them. Thank you.
  The verses which I have begun, give to the Briks. They'll figure them out. As they say, the incident is closed.

> Love boat
> has crashed against the daily grind
> I don't owe life a thing
> and there is no point
> in counting over

mutual hurts,
harms
and slights.

Best luck to all of you!

Vladimir Mayakovsky
4/12/30

Comrades from the Proletarian Literary Organization, don't think me a coward. Really, it couldn't be helped.
Greetings!
Tell Yermilov it's too bad he removed the slogan: we should have fought over it.   V.M.

In the desk drawer I have 2,000 roubles. Use them to pay my taxes. The rest can be obtained from the State Publishing House.[77]

In an almost schizoid fashion Mayakovsky displays in a short message to his contemporaries the entire repertoire of his cultural personae. This suicide note is a strange document that consists of verses, solicitations of love, jokes, and promises to pay taxes. It addresses both the poet's lovers and his comrade government with the same intimate and informal *you*, second person singular. What strikes us at first glance is the note's heterogeneity, a clash of different discourses. It contains high poetic diction, contemporary Soviet speech, colloquialisms, and some expressions which seem to come from popular urban romances and sentimental melodramas, linking death with kitsch. Such is for instance the much quoted sentence "Ljubovnaja lodka razbilas' o byt" ("Love boat has crashed against the daily grind"), which does not allow us to distinguish between pathos and irony. (It seems that the English expression "the love boat" with all its television connotations is an adequate cultural translation of this expression in Russian.) Political and poetic effects of Mayakovsky's love boat are discussed with much seriousness by André Breton, while Marina Tsvetaeva describes it rather ironically as an alien vessel on the poet's carefully styled Soviet "ship of modernity." In her poetic epitaph to Mayakovsky she writes: "Lodka-to tvoja, tovarishch, iz kakogo slovarja?" ("That love boat, comrade, what language does it come from?")[78]

Perhaps it is precisely this nontotalizable heterogeneity of Mayakovsky's note, its combination of poetic and antipoetic elements, a very modern, transient matter-of-factness of its discourse—which explains nothing but rather covers up the enigma—that tantalized his contemporaries. The note has many intertextual allusions, mostly to the poetic work of Mayakovsky himself. In this way Mayakovsky the author of poems and

Mayakovsky the author of the suicide note become inseparable. The note reveals the poet's desire to estrange himself from his own death, to fictionalize it. At the same time, it proves the impossibility of that ultimate literary distance in the haunting proximity of the revolver.[79]

"Don't blame anyone for my death, and please, don't gossip about it. The deceased hated gossip," wrote Mayakovsky, as if anticipating the proliferation of gossip and hypothetical explanations of his suicide. The discourse of gossip—from the Russian *spletnja/spletat'* (to intertwine)—whimsically connects the facts from the poet's life and art and the popular fictions about him, helping to generate the biographical legends. Mayakovsky's friends in Russia and abroad tried to separate themselves from the gossipers, but their own versions of the poet's death also present intertwinings of life and fiction, of the voice of the poet and of the critic.

Among those who wrote about Mayakovsky immediately after his suicide were Tynyanov, Trotsky, Shklovsky, Jakobson, Pasternak, Tsvetaeva, Aragon, Rolland, Vallejo, and Breton. Instead of proposing a new, authentic version of Mayakovsky's suicide, I will focus on the interpretative paradigms in some of the versions of the poet's death and the ways in which they set the stage for the tragedy *Vladimir Mayakovsky*—a modern drama of art, life, poetry, and politics, which is translated into different languages.

André Breton wrote in his response to the Surrealist questionnaire on suicide: "Le suicide est un mot mal-fait; ce qui tue n'est pas identique à ce qui est tué" ("Suicide is a badly composed word: the one who kills is never identical with the one who is killed").[80] The root *sui*—"of oneself"—presents an enormous problem, because then the word suicide suggests precisely the impossibility of the oneness of the self, the split between self as subject and "self" as object, between victimizer and victim. Suicide is the moment of the subject's ultimate decentering; the subject turns upon itself, murdering its many mirror images, reestablishing the only possible oneness—the oneness of death.

Emile Durkheim in his sociological study tries to distinguish between "*ego*istic" and "*altru*istic" suicide, the former being modern suicide, a result of the individual's alienation from bourgeois society, and the latter, suicide of primitive societies—an outcome of preindividualistic social integration and conformity to laws.[81] He also points to the contagious character of suicide, its epidemic potential, its ability to elicit imitations and reenactment.

Modern suicide exceeds any precise classification: it is at once a reenactment of certain cultural myths, especially in the case of a poet's suicide, and a result of alienation not only from society, from "others"—

altrui—but also from oneself, within one's own ego, from one's rapidly proliferating masks. Thus, in the case of Mayakovsky, we wonder who was killing whom: the Futurist in the yellow blouse killing the postrevolutionary poet-functionary, the poet-lover killing the poet-bureaucrat, the poet killing the conformist, the man killing the poet, or the reverse of any of these possibilities. Was it an act of a monomaniac, a "Mayakomorphist" as Trotsky once put it, a schizoid lost in his multiple incompatible masks, or else of an artist-aesthete finding the perfect ending to his own eclectic drama? One wonders if the poet's suicide signifies a desire for self-effacement, more radical than "the elocutionary disappearance of the poet," or on the contrary whether it reveals the astute gesture of a myth maker wishing to reenact culturally glorified poetic martyrdom in hopes of resurrection.

The motives of this self-destructive act are equally obscure. It is hardly possible to draw the line between exterior and interior, cultural and individual, reasons for the self-inflicted murder. Moreover, one fails to determine when exactly the suicide begins. Philippe Hamon, in his structuralist analysis of novelistic dénouements, points out that it is extremely difficult to locate the precise place of an ending.[82] He argues that there are certain "strategies of closure," certain patterns that foreshadow the final dénouement, a chain of "false endings" anticipating the "real" one. In a similar way Mayakovsky's suicide, a final dénouement of the poet's novelistic or rather novelesque life, might have been prefigured already in the provocative lines of the futuristic drama *Vladimir Mayakovsky* and by the metaphor compulsion—potentially a death drive—that traverses the poet's life and art.

Then again, there is a chance that the poet's suicide may have been overdetermined only by his critics, who wished to assign meaning to the poet's accidental "gambling with death," something that might have been, as some of Mayakovsky's contemporaries have suggested, just his unlucky turn at Russian roulette. Mayakovsky's suicide, in spite of its seeming factuality, presents an enigmatic "whodunit" which challenges all interpretations and often reveals the interpreter's own closures.

The official Soviet version of Mayakovsky's suicide conveys ideological clarity. The death is seen as a "strictly personal matter," something that has nothing to do with the Soviet Poet of the Masses, Poet-Revolutionary. The journalist Koltsov expresses "public opinion" on the poet's death: "Someone else was shooting; someone who temporarily and by mistake took over the weakening psyche of the poet, the public figure and the revolutionary."[83] The Soviet revolutionary poet has become immortal; he is community property, property of the socialist state. He cannot be ac-

cidentally murdered by the weak and impressionable individual Vladimir Mayakovsky. In the duel between the official Vladimir Mayakovsky and his flickering double, the first always wins. The poet is no longer in control of the dynamic and playful process of self-creation; some of his masks are already "patented" by the literary establishment with all rights reserved.

It is against this cultural background that Roman Jakobson launches a morbid attack on his generation in "On a Generation That Squandered Its Poets." Jakobson's article is not written from the omniscient point of view of the literary scientist. It uses the first person plural *we* and presents a kind of cultural autobiography of the generation that "squandered its poets." In this article the complexities of Jakobson's own perspective become visible: He is both a scholar and a personal friend of the poet, a defender of the Russian revolutionary avant-garde and an émigré from postrevolutionary Russia. The pathos of the essay comes from the clash of those perspectives, from the inability to allegorize the poet's death completely, comfortably enclosing it within the necrological or critical frame; and from the impossibility of defamiliarizing oneself entirely from the subject of analysis, protecting the autonomy of literature and of the literary scientist. The blood of the poet—Shklovsky's favorite Formalist metaphor and a powerful Surrealist image—becomes all too real, tinging the poet's lines with red.

Jakobson's article opens with a set of important dilemmas:

> О стихе Маяковского. О его образах. О его лирической композиции. Когда-то я писал об этом. Печатал наброски . . . Но как писать о поэзии Маяковского сейчас, когда доминантой не ритм, а смерть поэта, когда (прибегаю к поэтической терминологии Маяковского) "резкая тоска" не хочет сменится "ясною осознанною болью"?[84]

> Mayakovsky's poetry—his imagery—his lyrical composition—I have written about these things and published some of my remarks . . . But how is it possible to write about Mayakovsky's poetry now, when the *dominanta* is not the rhythm, but the death of the poet, when (if I may resort to Mayakovsky's poetic terminology) "sudden grief" is not yet superseded by "a clearly realized pain"?

Curiously, even in talking about the poet's death Jakobson uses the literary term "dominanta" and in describing his own very personal grief he resorts to the poetic terminology of Mayakovsky. The essay demonstrates that in Mayakovsky's case it is impossible to separate the strictly

personal and the social, the collective, the public, as well as the personal and the poetic. "Personal motives about the common *byt*" ("Po lichnym motivam ob obshchem byte") was Mayakovsky's poetic motto. The very notion of the strictly personal, of bourgeois individual privacy, is alien to Mayakovsky. (It is interesting to note that the word "privacy" cannot be directly translated into Russian, nor can the word "identity." The Russian culture has never absorbed this "individualistic" jargon.) Mayakovsky vacillates between two extremes, both equally removed from the nineteenth-century bourgeois individual privacy: between the hyperreal, hyperbolic, but always ironic exhibitionism and the constructivist self-effacing uniformity of the process of production—two extremes that intricately converge in the moment of death.

Jakobson describes how Mayakovsky acts out the suicide under different disguises, parodying and glorifying it at the same time. Yet as a critic he disbelieves the superficial histrionics. Revealing his own peculiar antitheatrical prejudice, Jakobson argues against all those who lost "the real Mayakovsky" behind the "masquerade" and remain blind to the only true mask, hardly visible behind the temporal disguises, the tragic death mask. Jakobson attempts to devise an almost archetypal design of the poet's fate, which manifests itself through Mayakovsky's seemingly eclectic repertoire. He describes it in the avant-garde genre of a literary montage:

В душе поэта взрощена небывалая боль нынешнего племени. Не потому ли стих его начинен ненавистью к крепостям быта, и в словах таятся "буквы грядущих веков"? . . . С каждым шагом все острее сознание безысходности единоборства с бытом. Клеймо мучений выжжено.[85]

The poet nurtured in his heart the unparalleled anguish of the present generation. Is that why his verse is charged with hatred for the strongholds of *byt*, and in his words "the alphabet of coming ages" languishes? . . . The hopelessness of his lonely struggle with the strongholds of *byt* becomes clearer and sharper with every step. The brand of martyrdom is burned into him.

The poet reenacts the cosmic drama, a heroically uneven struggle between the future sun's reflections and the earthly strongholds of *byt*. His death is seen as a ritual sacrifice in the ceremony of radical historical change. It seems that behind Jakobson's literary montage of the poet's biography lurks the ghost of Romantic genius, the belief in the ahistori-

cal, archetypal fate of the poet-prophet, poet-messiah, who takes upon himself the brand of martyrdom to redeem the generation that would otherwise be doomed to remain songless, locked forever in the slimy fortresses of *byt*.

The Death of the Poet—the title of the book in which the essay first appeared—echoes the title of Mikhail Lermontov's famous poem on the tragic death of Pushkin, Russian poetry's "slave of honor" who was "slandered by the mob," an exemplary Russian genius. Jakobson's Mayakovsky reenacts the eternal return of the Russian genius, the poet-savior. The critic styles his own, the only "true" and "real," Mayakovsky according to the archetypal tragic mask designed by the Romantics. This heroic rendering covers up many unromantic contemporary details, allowing Jakobson to ignore the concrete circumstances of Soviet history in the late 1920's and early 1930's—the beginning of the ideological persecutions of intellectuals, constant attacks on LEF and the other avant-garde groups, and the malicious critique of fellow Formalists and friends from the OPOJaZ. On the one hand, Jakobson seems to have had very little regard for the historical specificity and the peculiar modernity of the poet's suicide. On the other, this in itself can be seen as a reaction against the official politicization of all the discourses in the Soviet context, be they on literature, life, or an author's death.

In Jakobson's version of the story, Mayakovsky's suicide is something predetermined by the poetic autobiography as a system. Suicide is one of the elements of its grammar—to use Jakobson's later terminology—that is destined to be realized with a greater degree of vitality and less and less literariness. Jakobson writes that "Mayakovsky's poetry from his first verses to the last lines is one and indivisible."[86] Although he sees certain dialectical oppositions behind the motifs of Mayakovsky's poetry—such as between rational and irrational, present and future, "I" and "not I"— the structure of the system and the interrelationship between "the grammar of life" and "the grammar of poetry" seem to remain continuous.

Yet even within Jakobson's argument, the continuity between systems is challenged. His article both perpetuates and blurs the opposition between poetry and personal life, between literary science and biographism. Jakobson demonstrates that the motif of suicide pervades Mayakovsky's corpus and actually transgresses it, losing its literariness.

Этот мотив теряет литературность. Сперва из стиха он уходит в прозу. "Деваться некуда"—ремарка на полях "Про это." Из прозы в жизнь—"мама, сестры простите—это не способ, но у меня выходов нет."[87]

> This motif [of suicide] loses its literariness. First, from the poetic passage it found its way into prose—"there is no way out" turns up as the author's remark on the margins of the long poem *About That*. And from prose it moves to the poet's life—"Mama, sisters, forgive me—this is not a good method, but for me there is no other way out."

The motif of suicide, according to Jakobson, is the most "unpoetic," that is, the least formal and most personal, element in Mayakovsky's work, which makes the literary scientist reconsider the strict boundaries between the disciplines. These statements of Jakobson's comment upon and paradoxically complement his 1919 radical Formalist proclamation that "to incriminate the poet with ideas and emotions is as absurd as the behavior of the medieval audience that beat the actor who played Judas."[88]

The loss of literariness prevents us from drawing a line between the literary mask of the poet and his nonliterary self. Suicide, a voluntary loss of life, is a particularly striking example of the loss of literariness because it entangles art with death and makes the limits of identity less and less tangible. It is no longer clear, therefore, whether the motif of suicide in Mayakovsky's poetry anticipates and predetermines his death or whether the poet's actual suicide allows the critic to reorganize the elements of his poetry and in retrospect see it as dominant and prophetic.

For Jakobson the moment of extreme uncanniness comes when the boundaries of systems are blurred, making it impossible to protect the autonomy of art proclaimed by the Formalists.

> Формализм брал в кавычки лирический монолог, гримировал поэтическое "я" под псевдоним. Непомерна жуть, когда внезапно вскрывается призрачность псевдонима, и смазывая грани, эмигрируют в жизнь призраки искусства, словно в давнишнем сценарии Маяковского—девушка похищенная из фильма безумцем художником.[89]

Formalism placed the lyrical monologue in quotation marks and masked the poet's "I" under a pseudonym. What an unbound horror and uncanniness result when suddenly the elusiveness of the pseudonym is disclosed, and the phantoms of art emigrate into life, blurring all the boundaries— just as in Mayakovsky's scenario *Bound in Film* a girl is captured from a film by a mad artist.

The most dangerous effect of this emigration is that the elusiveness of the pseudonym and the phantoms of art reveal neither the true self nor

the real life of the poet, but a chain of simulacra. Perhaps the source of Jakobson's uncanniness resides not only in the loss of literariness but also in the loss of reality. Or, rather, it suggests a broader notion of literariness that goes beyond Jakobson's early definition, hinting at the complex intertextuality among life, art, and politics. There is a danger that the face of the real or archetypal Mayakovsky clings too intimately to literary and cultural masks—almost to the point of inseparability.

One of the untrue and pseudo-Mayakovskys, a Mayakovsky impostor, that Jakobson tries to exorcise is "the drummer of the October Revolution" glorified in the West. According to Jakobson "the West"—this peculiar Russian generalization is a mixture of provincialism and self-centered patriotism, a unique definition of all the countries lying to the west of the Russian border—knew only Mayakovsky's mask that was created by propagandistic oversimplification, that of a drummer of the October Revolution.

Jakobson satirizes the Western view of Russian culture and presents Mayakovsky as the last tragic genius of Russian and of Western literature, the last inspirer of the generation, the prophet of modernity. Jakobson sees that the division between Russia and the West is not purely geographical; it passes through the same frontier as the division between the literal and figurative meanings of words. In delineating these borders Jakobson juxtaposes by analogy male courtship, the practice of Marxist Leninism, and the poet's Golgotha.

> Есть страны, где женщине целуют руку, и страны где только говорят "целую руку." Есть страны, где на теорию марксизма отвечают практикой ленинизма, страны где "безумство храбрых," костер веры и Голгофа поэта не только фигуральные выражения ... И в конечном счете, особенность России не только в том, что сегодня магически перевелись ее великие поэты, как и в том, что они еще были. У великих народов Запада после зачинателей символизма, думается не было большой поэзии.[90]

There are some countries where men kiss women's hands, and others where they only say "I kiss your hand." There are countries where Marxist theory is answered by Leninist practice, and where "the madness of the brave," the martyr's stake, and the poet's Golgotha are not just figurative expressions . . . In the last analysis what distinguishes Russia is not so much the fact that her great poets have ceased to be, but rather that not long ago she had so many of them. Since the time of the first Symbolists, the West seems not to have had great poetry.

And now we will cross the Russian border and turn to the Western Mayakovskys, who according to Jakobson are much more figurative and unauthentic. We will examine the mask of the revolutionary poet made in France—an inspiring Surrealist *cadavre exquis* who is elaborately made-up and animated.

Poetics of Mistranslation: "Vladimir Mayakovsky" by André Breton

European avant-garde artists and writers regarded Mayakovsky as an exemplary, almost mythical figure, a modern poet who seemed happily to reconcile the important epithets "revolutionary" and "avant-garde," a poet who managed to live out the Surrealist dream of "practicing poetry" in the service of a victorious Bolshevik revolution. The voluntary death in 1930 of the exemplary revolutionary poet in the heart of Soviet Russia challenged the Mayakovsky myth in the West. There was something unreadable in it, something that defied interpretation. Was it, as declared in the official Soviet press, "a strictly personal matter," or, on the contrary, was it the poet's response to Soviet political contradictions, his revolt against what Leon Trotsky called "pseudorevolutionary officialdom"? Was it a sign of counterrevolutionary, bourgeois, individualist weakness, or revolutionary free will? The suicide of a poet always occurs on the borderlines, blurring the frontiers between politics and poetry, art and life, life and death, revolution and repetition.

The Surrealists' response to Mayakovsky's death is particularly interesting because it addresses different aspects of Mayakovsky's myth. André Breton adds some surrevolutionary layers to the old yellow blouse, trying to defend the poet, to save him at least from a figurative death, giving him back his privileged position in society. Louis Aragon, on the contrary, attempts to understand what it means to be first and foremost a revolutionary and only then a poet. He tries on the official Soviet mask— much more hyperbolic than that of Mayakovsky—not the mask of the individualistic anarchist, but that of the Marxist-Leninist proletarian writer following the party line. Finally, René Crevel carries on the enigma of Mayakovsky's death with his own avant-garde act.

The Surrealists' connection with Mayakovsky exposes their own complexities and contradictions, particularly the tensions between politics and poetics in the relationship between Surrealists and Communists. It also forces us to reexamine some vital issues of avant-garde poetics, particularly the conjunction between poetry and revolution, which ex-

emplifies the specifically modern aspects of the poet's death. Is the expression "a revolutionary poet" an oxymoron? Should it be replaced by "the proletarian poet," a poet-producer and functionary of the state, a poet *au service* of the proletarian revolution? Is the revolution, as Jakobson suggests, linked to the death of the poet? What are the contexts of the words revolutionary and avant-garde? From what language are we translating them? What is the role of contexts, frontiers, and frameworks in discussing the politics of the poet's death? Should we frame the poet's death with his life, his life with his art, his art with his politics, his politics with his social and cultural background, or the reverse?

In the year of Mayakovsky's death the Surrealists voted unanimously to change their journal's name from *La Révolution surréaliste* to *Le Surréalisme au service de la Révolution*, stressing the new understanding of the word revolution and its relationship to Surrealism. The central article of the first issue is dedicated to Mayakovsky. Breton gives it a title in Russian—a language he did not know: "Ljubovnaja lodka razbilas' o byt" ("Love boat has crashed into *byt*").[91] (The French title, translation by the sister of Lily Brik, Elsa Triolet, is "La Barque de l'amour s'est brisée contre la vie courante.") It is a quote from Mayakovsky's poem *About That*, which reappears in his final message, "To All of You." The essay is both *article de circonstance* and a programmatic Surrealist document which raises major philosophical and political issues. Like Jakobson's "On a Generation That Squandered Its Poets," it attempts to transgress the necrological frame and place Mayakovsky among "the living intellectuals." It is also written in the first person plural—Breton's privileged *we*, the glorious *we* of "the Surrealist voice" that disguises its single-voicedness behind the collective mask.

The essay is quite eclectic: it juxtaposes almost Shakespearean questions, "to love or not love," with responses to slanderous articles in the Parisian newspapers. It was printed with large margins filled with all sorts of material about and by Mayakovsky. These included the poet's suicide note; the articles of his fellow LEF members, proclaiming Mayakovsky a true "revolutionary proletarian poet" and reenforcing his image as a poet-producer working for the Revolution; fragments from *About That*, a poem about love, suicidal despair, and murderous everyday *byt*; "Notre Dame," a poem which envisions a Russian-style proletarian revolution in Paris; and finally the Surrealists' responses (both in words and fists) to the ignominious articles against Mayakovsky. Breton's essay suggests a parallel, but sometimes conflicting, reading with its marginalia. It proceeds as a polemical dialogue with several interlocutors, including

the anonymous *monsieur*, a kind of generalized image of the petit bourgeois liberal; Trotsky; the editor of the Communist newspaper *Humanité*; and fellow Surrealists.

The framework of the article is very peculiar: on the one hand, Breton presents Mayakovsky from the poetic "inside," that is, from the point of view of an avant-garde poet; on the other hand, it regards the Soviet Russian poet "outside" his immediate historical and cultural context. Breton defines his own fragile ground by fluctuating between different poles. In the realm of politics, he defends Mayakovsky from the bourgeois press, which regarded his suicide as a failure of the revolutionary ideal, and from the Communist *Humanité*, which converged with the former in deploring the voluntary death of the poet. For *Humanité* the suicide was an ultimately counterrevolutionary manifestation, an act that unmasks Mayakovsky as a "bourgeois, who never accepted the ideas of proletarian emancipation." In the realm of poetics, as in the realm of politics, Breton defends the Russian poet on both fronts. Paradoxically, in the polemical discussions of the time Mayakovsky was accused of being at once "too lyrical for a revolutionary poet" and "too engagé" for a lyrical poet. Breton argues against the logic that separates politics and poetry, personal and public personae, revolutionary activities and love— the logic that produces both the bourgeois image of the poet-lover, creator of beautiful lyrical verses, and the ascetic ideal of the Communist revolutionaries. The power of the revolutionary avant-garde poet, according to Breton, resides precisely in his ability to poeticize politics and politicize poetry, thus subverting the fundamental structures of the dominant ideology. Breton argues, both in this essay and in *Misère de la poésie*, that the "poetic drama" and the "social drama" can and must coexist. He desires to create a new Surrealist revolutionary ideal, one that would grant a poet a privileged, active social status.[92]

This Surrealist revolutionary ideal was one of the most beloved and obsessive Surrealist dreams. It represents a heroic attempt to save a poet from imminent modern death, which jeopardizes the very existence of poetry in the new society and questions its necessity. Breton enters into a dispute with Trotsky, who also wrote an article on Mayakovsky's suicide in May of 1930. Trotsky reestablishes his priorities and claims that Mayakovsky never quite merged with the Revolution: "It is not true that Mayakovsky was first of all a revolutionary and after that a poet, although he sincerely wished it were so. In fact Mayakovsky was first of all a poet, an artist who rejected the old world without breaking with it."[93] Breton rightly suspects that Trotsky sees in Mayakovsky first of all a poet in a yellow blouse, who has arrived at the revolution by "a short cut of rebel-

lious bohemia." Yet Breton questions in his "love boat" article the derogative use of the word "bohemian" by the Communists. He compares the bohemian pipe smoke with that of the factory chimneys, trying like Mayakovsky to draw an analogy between the poet's labor and that of the worker. This comparison also reminds us of Walter Benjamin's analogy between the alienation of the factory workers and that of the Baudelairean "flâneur"—a privileged mask of the modern poet, an idle collector of allegorical fragments, who is alienated from and possessed by the metropolitan crowd.[94]

Yet neither Breton nor Benjamin wishes to turn this ambiguous analogy into a prescriptive metaphor. The poet might be *like* a worker in some respects, but the worker cannot be the only model for the poet. The poet exceeds this grid and is irreducible to it, just as the poetic function of language is irreducible to pragmatic linguistics. The poet has a privileged intimate relationship with language—the main tool of social manipulation—and an exceptional receptivity to "objective chance"—the force of that mostly inaccessible, unintelligible, impossibly real world.

Perhaps somewhere between Breton's lines the same ghost of the Romantic poet-genius that haunted Jakobson reappears, but with an important modification. The Surrealist poet is always an antipoet who subverts the established literary institutions and surpasses the autonomous domains of poetry, a poet who stops writing like Arthur Rimbaud or never starts writing like Jacques Vaché, a poet who constantly plays Russian roulette with death and madness. In the Surrealist "republic" the antipoetic poet is not only above the worker but also above the philosopher and the party leader; he is regarded as more "democratic" than they and as antidogmatic, as someone who constantly questions the law and explores the limits of human consciousness in dreams, in "mad love," and in "chance encounters" with the modern marvelous. The poet partakes more fundamentally of human experiences than the others. Besides the power of language, he has an extraordinary ability to love.

Thus Breton does not simply argue against the image of the Futurist Mayakovsky, a bohemian in the yellow blouse; he attempts to reevaluate this image, to redesign the poet's yellow blouse so that it both performs the function of "épater les bourgeois" and serves the revolutionary state. Moreover, he rewrites the notion of the revolutionary poet as a revolutionary Surrealist antipoet and refuses to read it as an oxymoron, as a combination of mutually exclusive adjectives—which would have been the official reading strategy of the French Communist Party at the time. He wishes to preserve a suggestive white space between "revolutionary" and "poet," a mark of independence and irreducibility of one to the other.

A few years after Mayakovsky's suicide, in "La Position politique du surréalisme"—a speech prepared for the International Congress of Writers in the Defense of Culture in Paris, where another poet committed suicide—Breton dreams of a happy marriage of Marx and Rimbaud: "Transformer le monde, a dit Marx, changer la vie, a dit Rimbaud, ces deux mots d'ordre pour nous n'en font que un" ("Transform the world, said Marx, change life, said Rimbaud, these two words of order make only one for us").[95] Then in "Pour un art révolutionnaire independent," written with his former adversary Trotsky, he tries to find a Marxist justification to grant "the anarchist regime of individual liberty" to a poet or an intellectual. The proclamation ends with a new motto: "L'independence de l'art—pour la révolution; la révolution—pour la liberation définitif de l'art."[96] It suggests a creative tension, a double movement between art and revolution which never culminates in a synthesis, but might lead to a tragic rupture in the life of an individual poet.

If in Jakobson's understanding Mayakovsky's suicide is seen as something predetermined by the poetic autobiography and by Russian fate, in Breton's view it becomes the act of a free will, perhaps its ultimate expression: "Sommes-nous au monde, oui ou non, c'est-à-dire y nous avons-nous été mis par des personnes qui s'éntendaient plus ou moins à nous-y mettre et . . . ne pouvons-nous par nous même juger d'opportunité d'y rester ou d'en sortir?" ("Are we in the world, yes or no, that is to say were we put here by those who more or less agreed to put us here and . . . can't we judge for ourselves whether to stay here or to get out?").[97] Suicide clearly plays a very important role in Surrealist discussions. In the second issue of *La Révolution surréaliste* the Surrealists were invited to answer a questionnaire on suicide. Although there is no glorification of suicide, it is viewed as a peculiar liminal experience, a transgression of all boundaries.[98]

For Breton the suicide of Jacques Vaché, a "Surrealist in life," a poet who stopped writing before even starting, was an exemplary Surrealist act. Its subversive force was not only, and not so much, in the act of the voluntary death itself but rather in its joyful, almost accidental, entirely antitragic spirit, in its radical playfulness. As Breton reveals in "La Confession dédaigneuse" ("The Disdainful Confession"), the life and voluntary death of Jacques Vaché had the most crucial impact on him; without it he would have been just a poet and not a poet-antipoet, a surrevolutionary who intends like Rimbaud to "change life."[99] Thus Mayakovsky's suicide fits neatly within the Surrealist grid; with his political activity, it contributes to his image as an antipoet, a sort of Russian version of Rim-

baud—a poet who does not simply describe but practices the discontinuities of life.

If Jakobson's version of Mayakovsky's suicide is a literary montage Russian style, then Breton's is a Surrealist melodrama. Already in the first paragraph Breton develops a contradiction between revolutionary devotion and love and, in the case of Mayakovsky, love for a counterrevolutionary woman. Breton presents his reader (a male reader, an anonymous *monsieur* with whom the author pretends to have a coffee-table chat) with a drama of love, a drama that somewhat resembles a soap opera. The heroine is, as usual, an ideally beautiful woman with ideally beautiful breasts ("des seins trop jolis"). She is one of those unknown beautiful women whose names often appear in Surrealist manifestos at the end of a long list of male poets and artists.

Love, according to Breton, offers an instant resolution of all contradictions, unachievable in a social struggle oriented toward a future utopian society. Love is something that is equally repressed by bourgeois hypocrisy and revolutionary asceticism. Ultimately, what matters for the poet is to be a Surrealist revolutionary, to be in love with love rather than with a specific woman. In Mayakovsky's case the woman happened to be a sort of *femme fatale* who "dans l'incompréhension toute féminine" created obstacles in the revolutionary activities of the man.

> Il va sans dire que la situation faite aux femmes dans la societé contemporaine expose les plus favorisées physiquement d'entre elles à souséstimer l'action révolutionnaire . . . je répète qu'en outre le socialisme pourrait-il changer cela?—elles ont l'horreur congenitale de tout ce qui ne s'entreprend pas pour leur beaux yeux.[100]

> It goes without saying that the situation made for women in contemporary society leads the physically most favored among them to underestimate the revolutionary action . . . I repeat, can socialism, moreover, change this?—they have a congenital horror of all that is not undertaken for their beautiful eyes.

The woman is seen as apolitical if not antipolitical by definition. She and indirectly the society that formed her are found guilty in the poet's tragedy. Breton's popular story of Mayakovsky's suicide hints at the poet's love affair with a Russian émigré, Tatyana Yakovleva, whom Mayakovsky met in Paris. According to Elsa Triolet, Aragon's future wife, Yakovleva appeared "rather anti-Soviet." The relationship between her and Mayakovsky ended half a year before his suicide when the Soviet government

denied Mayakovsky an exit visa; two months later Yakovleva married a French diplomat.

In Breton's account, the story of Mayakovsky's death becomes symbolic. If in Jakobson's version it was the archetypal Russian fate of the poet-prophet, here it is the universal drama of a revolutionary poet in love with a counterrevolutionary woman (of course, this "universal" is based on the French Surrealist model). Mayakovsky is compared with Rimbaud, and his death is inscribed in the French context and examined in the Surrealist discussions of the 1930's on the relationship between love and revolution, poetry, and politics.

The only trace of Russian present is in the title of Breton's essay, which is printed in the Cyrillic alphabet. It is the only foreign sentence in the whole article and Breton curiously mistranslates it. There appears to be a certain tension between the title and the rest of his essay. In the Mayakovsky quote the revolution is not even mentioned; rather it is "la vie courante," the daily grind, that engulfs and destroys the "love boat." The Russian original for "la vie courante" is *byt*—a very common word that according to Jakobson is all too Russian, hence untranslatable, not linguistically but culturally. Jakobson explains:

Творческому порыву в преображенное будущее противопоставлена тенденция к стабилизации неизменного настоящего, его обрастание косным хламом, замирание жизни в тесные окостенелые шаблоны. Имя этой стихии— быт. Любопытно что в русском языке и литературе это слово и производные его играют значительную роль ... а в европейских языках нет соответствующего названия—должно быть потому что в европейском массовом сознании устойчивым формам и нормам жизни не противопоставлено ничего такого, чем бы эти стабильные формы исключались.[101]

Opposed to this creative urge toward the transformed future is a tendency toward stabilization of an immutable present, covered over by a stagnating slime, which stifles life in its tight hard mold. The name of this element is *byt*. It is curious that this word and its derivatives should have such a prominent place in the Russian language, while Western European languages have no word that corresponds to it. Perhaps, in the Western European collective consciousness there is no concept of such a force as might oppose and break down the established norms of life.

Byt is everyday routine, the things surrounding us which are deprived of any aura, of any latent capacity for the illumination of the marvelous.

It is a tantalizing presence of omnipotent ordinariness in its most static and conservative forms, pettiness, philistinism, and slime, that are all too real to inspire any nostalgia. At the same time, there is another, non-Romantic conception of *byt: byt* relates to "byt'" (to be), and in nonpoetic speech it often signifies simply everyday existence. Perhaps, it is this everyday existence that resists the metaphor compulsion and the heroic designs of life-creation.

In many of Mayakovsky's poems about love, death, and revolution, it is *byt* that is the main hero, as Jakobson remarks, a primordial enemy of the poet. *Byt* for Mayakovsky is the most petrifying and deadening force of "la vie courante." *Byt* as his primary "other" appears in both his pre-revolutionary and postrevolutionary poems. In the famous poem "On Trash," Mayakovsky writes: "The revolution is by philistine meshes entangled, the philistine meshes are more dangerous than Vrangler" ("Oputali revoluciju obyvatel'shchiny niti /strashnee Vranglera obyvatel'skij byt").[102] (The Russian for "philistine" is "obyvatel'skij," which shares the same root as *byt*.)

In Mayakovsky's works *byt* appears to be immune to the most radical social revolutions. This uncontrollable sphere of everyday practices and ordinary routines resists both political change and poetic metaphorization. *Byt* creates a gray area between the two poles—revolutionary and counterrevolutionary—complicating the relationship between them. Is the everyday counterrevolutionary and antipoetic by definition? Or does it challenge the utopian political constructs of revolutionary theories and revolutionary poetics? What does it mean to be a *revolutionary* ten years after the revolution? How can one survive the everyday bureaucracy in the country where the Bolshevik revolution was already won and where "revolutionary" discourse has become a discourse of power? Is there any difference between being at the service of the revolution in the country where revolution is still an ideal and serving in the country where revolutionary ideals are merging with philistine *byt* and certain dreams about the future are becoming politically dangerous?

In his book *Theory of the Avant-Garde* Peter Bürger questions whether the revolutionary avant-garde can exist in a socialist society and whether art can be totally integrated into the "praxis of life."[103] He raises this issue, however, only in a footnote, thereby acknowledging it and at the same time placing it outside the main body of his text, in which he elaborates the theory of the avant-garde exclusively on the Western European, particularly Surrealist model. It seems that the "practice of poetry"—to use Breton's term—in the Soviet Russia of the 1930's demonstrates the impossibility of the utopian ideal of a complete integra-

tion of revolutionary art into revolutionary, or rather postrevolutionary, society. The Soviet literary establishment turned to the most conservative "bourgeois" art forms, and the exciting and euphonic word "revolutionary" became part of the official bureaucratic "speak." The gap between being revolutionary "in line" and being revolutionary "beyond the line" became unbridgeable. During Stalin's purges of the mid and late 1930's this seemingly metaphorical delineation of frontiers led to a life-and-death dilemma for many poets and writers.

By staging the drama *Vladimir Mayakovsky* in the Surrealist context, Breton does poetic justice to the Soviet Russian poet, giving him a chance of surrevolutionary resurrection. At the same time, while defending Mayakovsky from both the bourgeois press and *Humanité*, he immerses him completely in the French context; he dresses him as a Soviet Rimbaud, overlooking the cultural and historical specificities of Mayakovsky's suicide. If, as Walter Benjamin says, "the translation is a somewhat provisional way of coming to terms with the foreignness of languages," it is precisely this foreignness that Breton fails to take into account.

I would like to end this discussion of the Surrealist drama *Vladimir Mayakovsky* with a subversive happening—a story of yet another suicide which uncannily repeats that of Mayakovsky. In the first issue of *Le Surréalisme au service de la Révolution*, in which Breton published his essay on Mayakovsky, there appeared an article by René Crevel entitled "Mort, Maladie et Littérature" ("Death, Disease, and Literature"). In it Crevel proclaims the necessity of guaranteeing poets a minimal human right— "the right to despair."[104] The article is a perfect example of Surrealist black humor, with a certain dangerous edge. Among other jokes the writer declares that he will have such a long life that André Breton would hardly have time to write an obituary for him.

René Crevel, in response to the Surrealist questionnaire on suicide, answered much less ironically and indirectly than others:

> Une solution? . . . Oui. On se suicide—dit-on, par amour, par peur, par vérole. Ce n'est pas vrai. Tout le monde aime, ou croit aimer, tout le monde a peur, tout le monde est plus ou moins syphilitique. Le suicide est un moyen de sélection. Se suicident ceux-là qui n'ont point la quasi-universelle lâcheté de lutter contre certaine sensation d'âme . . . une sensation de vérité. Seule cette sensation permet d'accepter la plus vraisemblablement juste et définitive des solutions, *le suicide*.[105]

> A solution? . . . Yes. People say that one commits suicide out of love, fear, syphilis. That's not true. Everyone loves, or think he loves; everyone

is afraid; everyone is more or less syphilitic. Suicide is a manner of selection. Those who don't have the quasi-universal cowardice to struggle with a certain sensation of the soul . . . a sensation of truth. This sensation alone permits one to accept the most just, in all probability, and the most definitive of solutions: suicide.

Crevel committed suicide five years after Mayakovsky, in 1935, in the midst of a new series of controversies between the Surrealists and the Communists. The suicide took place during the International Congress of Writers in the Defense of Culture, where Breton and Aragon (now an active member of the Communist Party and an anti-Surrealist) both gave speeches. As Nadeau reports, the Surrealists were not allowed to give a speech because of a violent incident involving one of the members of the Soviet delegation—Ilya Ehrenburg. Apparently he accused the Surrealists of "pederastic activities" and was "corrected" by André Breton.[106] The day after Crevel's suicide the Surrealists regained the right to speak, but later were slandered again by *Humanité*. Such are the circumstances of Crevel's death as described by Nadeau, while the reasons for it, as the critic remarks, remain "obscure."

In the story of this suicide there is again a strange French-Russian connection and an intermingling of art and politics, of sexual and social issues. The death of Crevel, like the death of Mayakovsky, can be regarded as a political act and can be understood only within a concrete cultural and historical context. And yet there is something in it that exceeds this context and refuses the enclosure. Crevel seems to reenact the enigma of Mayakovsky. Perhaps "le droit au désespoir" gained by the poet creates what Kafka calls the "commentator's despair" and frustrates all our attempts to write "the literature of fact" about the poet's death.

Politics of Mistranslation: "Vladimir Mayakovsky" by Louis Aragon

According to Louis Aragon, it was not enough to rename the journal *Le Surréalisme au service de la Révolution;* the time demanded "poetry on the revolutionary march" and active construction of the "real." In his speech "Le Rétour à la réalité," Aragon states: "Je réclame ici le retour à la réalité, et c'est la leçon de Maïakovski dont toute la poésie est partie des conditions réelles de la Révolution" ("Here I call for the return to reality. It's the lesson of Mayakovsky, for whom poetry is part of the real conditions of the Revolution").[107] Thus, for Aragon, Mayakovsky be-

comes a prophet of a *real* Communist paradise on earth, what he would later call "Soviet nouvelle Arcadie," as opposed to the idealist sur*realist* utopia of dreams.[108] Two different versions of Mayakovsky's myth, Breton's and Aragon's, illuminate the split between Surrealists and Communists, particularly those who diligently followed the official party line, and shed some light on the splendor and misery of poetry on the revolutionary march. In the same way that the encounter with Jacques Vaché turned Breton into a Surrealist antipoet, Aragon's symbolic encounter with Mayakovsky converted him into a realist anti-Surrealist and later a Socialist Realist. Thus Mayakovsky changes: from a Surrealist revolutionary and anti-poet, he becomes a Socialist Realist.

Aragon wrote on numerous occasions about Mayakovsky-alive and Mayakovsky-symbol. He never explicitly addressed the poet's suicide, silencing it as something almost irrelevant, "too personal," and exceeding the iconography of the revolutionary poet. In other words, his view of the suicide, his embarrassment and inability to incorporate it into the Socialist-Realist framework, conforms exactly to the official Soviet interpretation: Mayakovsky is either alive or immortal. The only mention of Aragon in connection with Mayakovsky's suicide was in the margins of Breton's article where Aragon is described as ferociously beating an "insulter of Mayakovsky," the Russian émigré André Levinson, who accused him of being a Communist. But this defense of the dead Mayakovsky on the part of Aragon remained mostly nonverbal, since Aragon in this scene acted more with his fists than with words.

Aragon describes his fortuitous encounter with Mayakovsky at a Montparnasse café in "Voyage sentimental dans la littérature soviétique."

> Le 5 Novembre 1928, dans un de ces cafés de Montparnasse . . . j'entendis une voix étrangère m'appeler par mon nom. Des inconnus, sur la banquette, me regardaient; l'un d'eux se souleva et me dit: "Le poète Vladimir Maïakovski vous demande de venir vous asseoir à sa table . . ." Que savais-je de Maïakovski, sinon la légende? Le poète haut-parlant, ce destin sans pareil, la Révolution et la Poésie melées, la mélodie de millions d'hommes, la voix qui fait se lever le soleil . . . Le géant était là, comme son propre Epinal, assis avec des copains, derrière un crème à la Coupole. Que savais-je . . . de la réalité gigantesque d'où venait cet homme? de ce pays couvert de clameurs contradictoires, cette sorte de rêve sorti d'Hugo ou Dante . . . qu'en savais-je, à part quelques livres, des images, et *Le Cuirassé Potemkine?* Je m'assis à cette table, avec tout ce romantisme au coeur, et l'ignorance vertigineuse de Paris. J'ignorais que, de ce fait, ma vie allait changer de fond en comble. Et le lendemain, dans le

même lieu de confusions et de courants d'air, un peu plus tard . . . je rencontrais Elsa Triolet. Nous ne nous sommes jamais quittés depuis.[109]

On November 5, 1928, in one of those cafés of Montparnasse . . . I heard a foreign voice call me by name. People I didn't know, who were sitting on the bench, were looking at me; one of them got up and said to me: "The poet Vladimir Mayakovsky requests that you come sit at his table . . ." What did I know of Mayakovsky, except for the legend? The loud-speaking poet, that destiny without parallel, Revolution and Poetry inter-twined, the melody of millions of men, the voice which makes the sun rise . . . The giant was there, as his own Epinal, seated with friends, behind a coffee à la Coupole. What did I know . . . of the gigantic reality where this man came from? from that country covered with contradictory cla-mours, some sort of dream out of Hugo or Dante . . . what did I know, other than a few books, pictures, and *The Battleship Potemkin?* I sat down at that table, with all this romanticism in my heart, and the vertiginous ignorance of a Parisian. I was unaware that, because of all this, my life was going to change from top to bottom. And the next day, in the same place of confusion and drafts, a bit later I would meet Elsa Triolet. We've never parted since.

This legend of Mayakovsky begins with the legend of a "drummer of the October Revolution" as described by Jakobson, a poet who comes from an exotic country, like the dreams of Hugo or Dante or the images from *The Battleship Potemkin.* This is a perfect example of revolutionary "orientalism"—to borrow Edward Said's term—which points to the yet unexplored connection between exoticism and radical politics.[110] The al-most Surrealist encounter described by Aragon opens Aragon's "senti-mental journey" into the realm of the "real," that is, into a political en-gagement with the French Communist Party and into Socialist Realism in literature. In his article "Shakespeare and Mayakovsky" (written almost twenty years after their meeting) Aragon attempts to demonstrate how far he had moved from the initial romantic legend and the "ignorance of a Parisian" toward a knowledge of Soviet reality and Mayakovsky's poetic realism. In fact, a large part of the essay is dedicated to the problem of translation and its various traps which can blur the distinctions between true Communist revolutionaries and anarchists, distort the voice of the poet-genius, and misrepresent the "true meaning" of his work. This essay provides a framework to discuss Aragon's poetic tribute to Mayakovsky, "Front Rouge" ("Red Front"), written around the time of Mayakovsky's suicide. I note in passing that Aragon's writings, as well as the writings

of many other Communist intellectuals in the West from the 1930's to the 1950's, are for many reasons respectfully silenced in contemporary criticism, and thus their rereading helps to recover a somewhat blurred page in French cultural history.

The title of the essay, "Shakespeare et Maïakovski," is a rhetorical tour de force. Aragon does not discuss the texts of the two authors (apart from a rather unconvincing parallel between Iago and Pobedonossikov); instead, he compares their "myths" and their significance for their times. The rhetorical twist of the essay involves two steps: first, the conversion of Mayakovsky into "un Shakespeare," a Shakespeare of the twentieth century; and, second, the conversion of Mayakovsky into "un Maïakovski," a new symbol of the Communist revolutionary poet. The first section of the essay ends with an imaginary dispute with the reader, similar to Breton's *petit bourgeois monsieur:* "Oui, si vous voulez savoir, L'Union Soviétique a produit ce que vous appelez 'un Shakespeare.' Il s'appelle Maïakovski" ("Yes, if you really want to know, the Soviet Union has produced what you call 'a Shakespeare.' His name is Mayakovsky").[111] And the article continues with a clever twist: "Un Shakespeare? On dira bientôt, on dit déjà un Maïakovski" ("A Shakespeare? Soon people will say, they already say *a* Mayakovsky").[112] Thus Aragon, following Mayakovsky's own strategy of self-mythification, objectifies the poet's name. Instead of putting it in quotation marks, and writing "an optimistic tragedy"—to borrow the Soviet term—he uses an indefinite article—a device unavailable in Russian, which would not discriminate between *Mayakovsky, a Mayakovsky,* and *the Mayakovsky.*

Who is Aragon's "a Mayakovsky"? This new Community revolutionary idol is "le génie dans le mouvement ascendant de la classe porteuse de l'avenir, porteuse des intérêts de l'humanité" ("the genius in the movement arising from the class carrying the future, carrying the interests of humanity").[113] Several sections of the essay end with sort of a refrain in which Mayakovsky is coupled with Maxim Gorky as "the founder of Socialist Realism."[114]

Aragon is critical of the idealization and varnishing of the poet, which tends in his words "to touch up the image of Mayakovsky." However, his own "a Mayakovsky," the Socialist Realist Mayakovsky, manages to escape the slippery varnishing because of Aragon's emphasis on the poet's "blood connection to life" and his progress on "the road of real life": "C'est la logique de la vie, la dialectique du travail pratique, qui ont fait du futuriste Maïakovski le grand poète Vladimir Maïakovski, l'un des fondateurs du réalisme socialiste" ("It's the logic of life, the dialectic of

practical work, which has made the Futurist Mayakovsky into the great poet Vladimir Mayakovsky, one of the founders of Socialist Realism").[115] Aragon masterfully uses the mass appeal of such words as "reality," "practice," and "life" to authorize his own version of Mayakovsky.

Moreover, Aragon elaborates the French ancestry of Mayakovsky, placing him not in the Russian literary context, but in the French one. Among Mayakovsky's chief precursors are the "critical realist" Victor Hugo and Arthur Rimbaud the "poet-communard." However, Aragon's placement of Mayakovsky is different from Breton's. If Breton views Mayakovsky from the French Surrealist perspective and "frenchifies" the Russian poet, then Aragon, trying to avoid the trap of what could be called—in 1980's critical language—French cultural imperialism, reinterprets the history of French literature from the official Soviet Socialist Realist perspective and "russifies" French writers. In other words, for Aragon Rimbaud becomes potentially "a Mayakovsky" and Hugo, "a Gorky" of the French nineteenth century. The obvious "bad guys," the precursors of formalism, modernism, and other dangerous "isms"—Surrealism, Futurism, and so on (as opposed to the ideologically correct "isms," realism and patriotism)—are in Aragon's view Théophile Gautier, who boasted that during the 1848 revolution he was composing *Emaux et Camées* (*Enamels and Cameos*), and Mallarmé, the infamous advocate of "art for art's sake," verbal formalism, and "the neutral tone."[116] Hugo is an important ideological choice. Aragon tries to differentiate between Hugo of the French Academy, and "the true Hugo," "la préfiguration dans la poésie de ce que nos amis soviétiques ont appellé *le réalisme socialiste*" ("the prefiguration in poetry of that which our Soviet friends called *Socialist Realism*").[117] Hence Aragon translates Hugo not simply into Russian, but into Soviet.

Rimbaud is one of the few Surrealist ancestors whom Aragon attempts to rescue both from the Surrealists and from Paul Claudel's Christian interpretation. For radical thinkers, *a* Rimbaud is too powerful, too revolutionary, too appealing a myth to be easily discarded. According to Aragon Rimbaud is created in the image of Mayakovsky and in turn Mayakovsky the Futurist is shaped in the image of Rimbaud. Rimbaud, like Mayakovsky, is considered to be a follower of Hugo's critical realism, a communard, and the author of "Les Mains de Jeanne-Marie." Had the Commune won, Rimbaud would have been the French drummer of the Revolution, the proto-Mayakovsky. In Aragon's view, it is not Rimbaud's poetic suicide that is important for twentieth-century writers, but his revolutionary life.[118] The same could be said of Mayakovsky's poetic and

nonpoetic suicide, about which Aragon, to use his words from a different occasion, "lies by omission." Mayakovsky's suicide is simply not discussed by Aragon, because it defies the newly established canons of revolutionary optimism and violates the laws of genre. The poet's suicide does not fit with the happy ending required by the Socialist Realist iconography and Communist teleology. It does not point to the collective bright future.

Later Aragon remarks that as a new myth "a Mayakovsky" is far superior and far more revolutionary than "a Rimbaud." "Maïakovski est à la fois le dernier poète du passé et le premier poète de l'avenir, il est le liquidateur de l'alchimie du verbe, le *fondateur de la poésie debout dans l'humanité en marche, aidant cette marche* . . . le fondateur du réalisme socialiste en poésie" ("Mayakovsky is at the same time the last poet of the past and the first poet of the future; he is the liquidator of the alchemy of the word, the *founder of poetry standing in humanity on the march, helping this march* . . . the founder of Socialist Realism in poetry").[119]

And where is Louis Aragon in this march of the prerevolutionary and revolutionary poets? Is he trying to create "an Aragon?" Who is hiding behind his collective *we? Vox populi?* Aragon defends Mayakovsky's hypertrophic use of "I": "il était *un moi* qui traduit infiniment mieux *le nous de son temps* que la prétention 'objective' de la troisième personne" ("He was *a me* which infinitely better translated *the we of his time* than the 'objective' pretention of the third person").[120] The "I" of the progressive revolutionary poet is both an "I" of the masses and a very concrete and *real* "I" of Mayakovsky the person, and not that of his literary persona.[121]

Aragon does not wish to see the differences and tensions among Mayakovsky's various "I's." For him, between literature and life, between the "we" of the masses and the "I" of the lyric poet, there is a perfect continuity—not a metaphorical relationship, but a transparency; they simply coexist in reality, the reality authorized by Aragon's own rather pervasive "I." The ideal "I" of Aragon mirrors the idealized "I" of Mayakovsky. Aragon wishes to become a French Mayakovsky, or a Hugo of the twentieth century. His "a Mayakovsky" is constructed in his own purified image. Thus as a former Surrealist and a Communist-Stalinist at the time of writing of his essays, Aragon glorifies Mayakovsky's break with Futurism and his desire to become the official Soviet poet. Aragon, the author of *Paysan de Paris*, does however praise the Futurist Mayakovsky for one thing—his urbanism, his discovery of the modern city. Aragon, the author of the passionate love poems "to a real woman—Elsa," celebrates Mayakovsky grandiose love poetry "to the real woman," Elsa's sister Lily Brik.

Aragon wishes to relive Mayakovsky's drama but with a happy ending, avoiding the poet's suicide. Instead of the drama The Revolutionary Poet Falling Tragically in Love with a Counterrevolutionary Woman, it would be the story of A Revolutionary Poet Happily in Love with a Revolutionary Woman, with all the revolutionary romanticism and optimism of the best traditions of Socialist Realism. It would be a story with two positive characters, a New Man and a New Woman, the poet and the poet's companion and colleague. Elsa Triolet was in fact partly responsible for Aragon's conversions, both political and artistic. Her preference for twentieth-century critical realism over avant-garde literary experimentation and her own realistic writing influenced and shaped Aragon the novelist. Hence the point of the essay—the glorification of "a Mayakovsky"—is also a glorification of "an Aragon," who does not wish to follow the model of le père surréaliste, André Breton, but that of le beau-frère, Socialist Realist Mayakovsky. So the question remains who imitates whom? How does one poet's self-mythification elicit the same from another poet? What happens in the "transport of the revolution" both politically and poetically? Does it lead to internationalism, or to mistranslations? What was the intellectually more responsible position during the difficult time of the 1930's: the active revolutionary idealism, sometimes tinged with idealization, of the poets au service de la révolution who joined the pro-Stalinist French Communist Party and supported Soviet Stalinism, or the vacillations and double movements of the Surrealist intellectuals who sought their own tortuous path of opposing the official French bourgeois culture as well as Stalinism and Fascism?

In the essay on Mayakovsky, Aragon pays special attention to poetic translation, which in turn raises the issues of the survival of poetry, its translatability, and the ideological consequences of mistranslation. Aragon vehemently argues against the Soviet practice of rhymed translation.[122] He sees translation in verse as more harmful than prose translation because it distorts more the singular, original voice of the poet's "I" by emphasizing what he calls the "formalist" elements in poetry rather than the "sense." His two primary examples are the rhymed mistranslations of Mayakovsky into French (to which he opposes much more faithful prose translations by Elsa Triolet) and, following the obvious analogy, the poetic translations of Aragon into Russian, in which the French poet fails to recognize his own voice. According to Aragon, it is important to recognize "la préeminence du contenu sur la forme poétique." The content of poetry is defined as the "antiformalist" aspect of the poems and the way in which the author has said "what he wanted to say."[123] Once the Surrealist experiments with the unconscious, automatic writing, and

the illogic of dreams are forgotten or repressed, Aragon turns back to the Cartesian conception of the rational self and the Romantic notion of the poetic genius, modernizing them with the jargon of "scientific materialism," Marxist Leninism, and Socialist Realism (Stalinism in brackets). The genius of the triumphant revolution, whose "I" reflects the "we" of our time, knows and is able to say what he really wants to say. (In this context one begins to see the subversive potential of Mallarmé's "Restrained Action.")

The translation of Mayakovsky's famous 1918 poem "Left March"—an example of "la poésie en marche révolutionnaire"—exposes the dangers of the "formalist" approach. Here is the beginning of the poem in Russian with the French verse translation quoted by Aragon:

Разворачивайтесь в марше!	Allons, en marche à tour de rôle!
Словесной не место кляузе.	Assez de chicane bavarde!
Тише ораторы!	Silence orateurs!
Ваше	La parole
Слово,	Prends-la
Товарищ маузер.	Mauser, bon camarade!
Довольно жить законом,	Assez de loi, vieilles et fausses
данным Адамом и Евой.	Depuis Eve et Adam,
	bancroches!
Клячу истории загоним.	Cavale-toi, Histoire, eh! rosse!
Левой!	Tous gauche,
Левой!	Gauche!
Левой!	Gauche![124]

Rally the ranks into a march!
This is not the place for quibbling!
Silence, you orators!
You've got
the word
Comrade Mauser!
Enough of living by the laws
given by Adam and Eve.
Put yourself to pasture, history! You old nag!
Left!
Left!
Left!

Aragon claims that a minor rhetorical slippage in the French, made for stylistic purposes—the substitution of Mayakovsky's "the laws given

by Adam and Eve" by "the laws" in general—jeopardizes the ideological meaning of the poem; it transforms Mayakovsky from a Bolshevik Marxist revolutionary into an anarchist. This slippage reveals the incredible fragility of the Marxist-Leninist-Bolshevik, scientifically materialist, Socialist Realist, "true sense" of the poem—to use the list of Aragon's "politically correct" epithets—since it shows how easily the sense can be obscured with a simple syntactical substitution. "Left March," according to Aragon, has to be controlled: by marching too far to the left, one can become vulnerable to formalist and idealist attacks, falling victim to the arms race of rhetoric.

From Mayakovsky's "Left March" mistranslated into French I would like to move to Aragon's own poetic march, written in the year of Mayakovsky's death. In it Aragon desires to give a true and ideologically correct translation of Mayakovsky's poetry in the revolutionary march, which ensures the poet's immortality and his permanent revolutionary role of commander-in-chief—to use Mayakovsky's image—of the "army of art."

The Aragon poem in question is "Front Rouge," published in 1931 in the journal *La Littérature de la Révolution mondiale* (*Literature of the World Revolution*). It was written in the Soviet Union during the Second International Congress of Revolutionary Writers in Kharkov, at which Aragon and Georges Sadoul were supposed to present the political positions of the Surrealists, but instead ended up denouncing the Surrealists, Trotskyites, and Freudians as dangerous counterrevolutionary idealists. When Aragon returned to France he continued playing a double game between the Surrealists and Communists, on the one hand ensuring fellow Surrealists that he never put his signature to any declaration and on the other providing all signs of loyalty to his comrades in the French Communist Party. The poem sparked controversy not only between the conservative bourgeoisie and the revolutionary intellectuals but also between different ideologues of the revolution. The French bourgeois press regarded it as politically subversive and threatened Aragon with a trial. In this respect, *l'affaire Aragon* is a revealing art scandal that can teach us to question the seemingly peaceful coexistence of autonomous art and autonomous politics in Western European countries as well as in the United States.

Breton, while defending Aragon from the accusations of subverting the regime and simply trying to save his friend from going to jail, criticized the poem for not being artistically subversive. According to Breton, "Front Rouge" is "a poem of circumstances," "the return of the exterior and particularly passionate subject," which does not present "the poetic

drama" alongside "the social drama" and "does not open a new voice for poetry."[125] Aragon's poem and Breton's *Misère de la Poésie*—at once a defense of Aragon and an attack on "Front Rouge"—explores what is at stake in the conflict between artistic and social revolution and calls into question the myth and mystique of the revolutionary poet.

It is difficult to approach *l'affaire Aragon*, and the poem that sparked it, exclusively from the point of view of textual criticism. The frames of the poem—political and ethical, French and Soviet Russian—are responsible for its scandalous effect, and it is this *effect* that conditions our readings. The *affair* problematizes the relationship between the written text and the act and resists our attempt to establish critical distance. How can we read "un poème de circonstances" outside its circumstances? Can we read a poem "on trial" without taking a political position? The poem on trial puts its reader on trial, forcing the reader to confront her or his own ideological biases and preconceptions. My own bias leads me to examine the Russian subtext and context (the two are in this case closely intertwined) of "Front Rouge" and its link to the death of the most famous of Russian revolutionary poets—Vladimir Mayakovsky.

The lyrical persona of "Front Rouge" tries on Mayakovsky's mask of the poet, "agitator of the masses" and "loud-speaker." We witness Aragon's change of make-up: a covering up of the Surrealist split subject—that of a semiawake automatic writer—with the confidence of a proletarian poet, at once a participant in the revolutionary march and its leader.

> J'assiste à l'écrasement d'un monde hors d'usage
> J'assiste avec enivrement au pilonnage des bourgeois . . .
> Je chante la domination violente du Prolétariat sur la bourgeoisie.[126]
>
> I participate in the destruction of a world beyond use
> I participate with intoxication in the hammering of the bourgeois . . .
> I sing the violent domination of the Proletariat over the bourgeoisie.

The poet optimistically projects both a feeling of continuity between his aspirations and those of the revolutionary proletariat and a sense of perfect reconciliation between his art and politics. As Breton stated "le sens littéral ne se présente pas" ("the literal sense doesn't present itself") in this poem. "Front Rouge" has a skillful rhetorical construction: it is built on the principle of *symmetry and analogy*. Each section acts out the conversion, or the correct ideological translation from French into Russian: from URSS into SSSR—the Russian abbreviation of the Union of Soviet Socialist Republics. SSSR, SSSR, SSSR serves as a refrain at the

end of each section. Aragon attempts to simulate the whistling sound of
the name of the revolutionary state.

> SS un air joyeux comme le fer
> SS/SR un air brûlant c'est l'es/perance
> c'est l'air
> SSSR c'est la chanson d'Octobre aux fruits éclatants
> Sifflez sifflez
> SSSR
> SSSR
> La patience n'aura qu'un temps
> SSSR
> SSSR
> SSSR. [127]

> SS a joyous air like iron
> SS/SR burning air it's de/sire
> it's air.
> SSSR, it's the October song of bursting fruits
> Breathe breathe
> SSSR
> SSSR
> Patience will have only one time
> SSSR
> SSSR
> SSSR.

There appears to be a perfect continuity between the French sound and
the Russian, a continuity between the triumphant Russian Revolution
and the imminent French Revolution, between the revolutionary and the
postrevolutionary struggle against traitors and conspirators.

The poem proceeds through a number of iconic poster-like images,
characteristic of Russian poetry of the 1920's and of the art of visual
propaganda. Here everything is in black and white, or rather in red and
white. The "bad guys" are an aristocratic Parisian lady, a cliché embodiment of the ruling classes, and the "traitors of the revolution"—a whole
bestiary of them: "the wise bears of social democracy" and "the wolves,"
who together with "the dogs" enter into an antiproletariat conspiracy. The
image of the victorious Communism also has a carefully elaborated iconography: "Marx et Lenin dans le ciel/rouge comme l'aurore" ("Marx and
Lenin in the sky/red as the dawn") and the Revolution whose "yeux bleus
brillent d'une cruauté nécessaire" ("blue eyes shine with a necessary

cruelty"). In the fourth section there is a metapoetic moment in which the poet defends his program against the epigones of pure art with "some simple words." What follows is a documentary fragment—a reminder of the LEF's insistence on the "literature of facts"—a story of foreign conspiracy and General Vrangler's plans of invasion.

The rest of the poem is quite different from a straightforward documentary, however. Furthermore, the usage of some of the historical references is quite problematic. For instance, there is an image of marching soldiers of Budenny—the hero of the Russian Civil War of 1918–20—who are "the Proletariat's conscience in arms" and the heralds of "the Universal Revolution." In the 1930's, however, ten years after the Civil War, the Stalinist slogan to continue the revolutionary attacks, repeated by Aragon in his appeal to fight those who endanger the October conquests and threaten to sabotage the five-year plan, acquires a different meaning. At that time the struggle was not often against the abstract "lady" and the bourgeoisie but instead against the fellow revolutionaries, particularly the revolutionary intellectuals, who were accused of all kinds of conspiracies allegorized by Aragon. Among them were fellow writers from Mayakovsky's LEF—Tredyakov, the "engineer" of the "author as a producer" image, for instance—many of whom were accused of cosmopolitanism and formalism.[128] It is sadly ironic that in the year of Mayakovsky's death Aragon, in his sincere desire to adopt the Russian poet's revolutionary mask, in fact ends up repeating the official postrevolutionary clichés, foreshadowing the Stalinist paranoia that led to the epoch of great purges. This only proves Jakobson's idea of a political division between the literary and metaphorical meanings of a word: what is an outrageous avant-garde metaphor, or an expression of naive idealist revolutionary enthusiasm, in bourgeois France is a grotesque reality in Stalinist postrevolutionary Russia. "Front Rouge" stands on a peculiar frontier between bourgeois France and Stalinist Russia, a frontier on which the song of liberation turns into a glorification of oppression.

The necessary cruelty of the Revolution deserves special attention. It is not the Surrealist theater of cruelty, but a programmed revolutionary violence, violence "in the line." It is interesting to note that the Marxist critic Roger Garaudy in his *L'Itinéraire d'Aragon* criticizes the poem for what he calls "Surrealist anarchism"[129]—precisely that anarchism which Aragon feared the most in the mistranslations of Mayakovsky. Indeed we see in the poem a certain intoxication with the "A bas" ("Down with") slogan which sometimes leads to quite unexpected syntactical paradoxes. For instance at the very end of the poem we read: "A bas l'impérialisme

à bas/SSSR SSSR SSSR" ("Down with imperialism down/SSSR SSSR SSSR").[130] It is, of course, highly unlikely that Aragon would like to proclaim "down with" the revolutionary state which he glorifies throughout the poem. This is revolutionary poetic zeal reduced to absurdity.

In reaction to Surrealist automatic writing and linguistic experimentation, Aragon turns to automatic copying of the officially sanctioned revolutionary, or rather postrevolutionary, conventions which had a murderous effect not only on language but also on people's lives. According to some contemporary critics, such as John Berger and Julia Kristeva, this systematic "murder of the poetic language" that occurred in Russia in the 1930's and the consolidation of the official bureaucratic language were two "poetic" reasons for Mayakovsky's suicide.[131] This was perhaps what Jakobson meant by pointing at the mysterious "conspiracy" between the Revolution and the death of the poet, the conspiracy that blurs the features on Mayakovsky's revolutionary mask.

Forty-five years after the publication of "Front Rouge" Aragon called it "un poème que je déteste" ("a poem which I detest").[132] This confession appears in his complete works in "Une Préface morcelée" ("A Carved-up Preface"), a commentary about Mayakovsky and the events following his long-silenced suicide. It is here that we find the striking passage in which Aragon tries to give an account of the background of "Front Rouge" and of his own never quite "fixed" "double vertigo." The syntax of this autobiographical confession is far less coherent than that of the poem.

Ce n'est pas ici que je vais raconter ce congrès ni le voyage aux chantiers du Dniepropetrovsk qui l'a suivi; comment nous avions cru gagner la partie . . . Comment Georges et moi, à nôtre retour, en décembre, nous avions, retrouvant les nôtres, mesuré l'incommunicabilité de ce par quoi tous deux nous avons passé "d'autre côté du monde," de ce double vertige de là-bas et d'ici . . . mais je ne vais pas me mettre à expliquer ça . . . (et ça ne suffisait donc pas de pouvoir dire que la revue *La Révolution Surréaliste* venait changer de titre pour s'appeler *Le Surréalisme au service de la Révolution*) . . . pris entre cela et, une fois à Paris . . . objets de notre double passion . . . c'est une de ces phrases qu'on ne termine pas, et il va y avoir de cela quarante cinq années, je n'y peux penser sans vertige.[133]

Here I won't tell about that congress, nor about the trip to the yards of Dnepropetrovsk which followed; how we thought we had won the game . . . How, finding our people again upon our return in December, Georges and I measured the incommunicability of that by which we had together

passed from "the other side of the world," of this double vertigo from there and from here . . . but I am not going to start explaining that . . . (and thus that wasn't sufficient to be able to say that the review *The Surrealist Revolution* came to change titles in order to be called *Surrealism in the Service of the Revolution*) . . . taken between this and, once in Paris . . . objects of our double passion . . . it's one of those sentences which one never finishes, and it is going to be forty-five years since then but I can't think about it without vertigo.

This passage with its numerous significant ellipses, incoherences, and vacillations recovers both the moral, poetic, and political drama erased from the revolutionary optimism and the joyful self-confidence of the engaged proletarian writer of "Front Rouge." The belated double vertigo is the payment for the incurable intellectual nostalgia for the *lost reality* and a desire to recover it as promptly as possible. If this autobiographical confession marks a kind of return to reality—to paraphrase Aragon's speech—this return to reality is fashioned in opposition to the earlier one. The vertigo enacted in this passage reveals the complexities and contradictions of the situation, as well as all the difficult compromises which the poet preferred to conceal in his "Front Rouge" and only forty-five years later was able to confront with proper intellectual honesty and engagement. There is a dizziness involved in trying to fit one's face to the shape of the idealized mask of the revolutionary poet, seen through the rose(*rouge*)-colored spectacles of revolutionary exoticism.[134]

I would like to end the international Socialist Realist march of Vladimir Mayakovsky and Louis Aragon with a circle dance scene. It takes place literally between Russia and France—in Czechoslovakia. We recognize the familiar protagonists: one dead poet and another reciting verses about love and freedom; one poet brutally murdered and hanged in the public square and another singing about Communist paradise and the international solidarity of the revolutionary youth. This scene—from Milan Kundera's novel *The Book of Laughter and Forgetting*—describes the ex-French Surrealist Paul Eluard's visit to Czechoslovakia in June 1950, the time when Milada Horakova, a representative of the Socialist Party, and the Czech Surrealist Zavis Kalandra, an old friend of Breton and Eluard, were executed as "enemies of the people"—only to be posthumously rehabilitated seventeen years later.

Knowing full well that the day before in their fair city one woman and one Surrealist had been hanged by the neck, the young Czechs went on dancing and dancing, and they danced all the more frantically because their

dance was a manifestation of their innocence, their purity that shone forth so brilliantly against the black villany of the two public enemies who had betrayed the people and its hopes. And Breton did not believe that Kalandra had betrayed the people and its hopes, and called on Eluard . . . to protest the absurd accusations and to save their old Prague friend. But Eluard was too busy dancing in the gigantic ring encircling all the Socialist countries, and all the Communist Parties of the world; too busy reciting his beautiful poems about joy and brotherhood. After reading Breton's letter Eluard took two steps in place, one step forward, he shook his head, refusing to stand for a man who betrayed his people.[135]

Kundera remarks that revolution and Stalinist terror were the reign of the hangman and the poet—the revolutionary poet, marching in a line and dancing in a ring, singing of paradise and gulag. This is yet another, rather grim conjunction of poetry and revolution.

The Revolutionary Poet: Oxymoron or Tautology?

Mayakovsky's spectacular figure continues to fascinate the audience of both poets and critics, in the Soviet Union and in the West. It tempts the imagination with its numerable knots of unresolvable contradictions, the paradoxes of what Trotsky called "Mayakomorphism": multiple layers of modern masks and an uncanny flatness of image; brilliant verbal inventiveness of verse and a relative simplicity and straightforwardness of philosophy and logic (in what can be called the poet's syntax); a combination of loud declamatory rhetoric and the most fragile vulnerability in poetry and life. "Vladimir Mayakovsky" strikes us with a clash of styles: a Romantic drama and a Socialist-Realist march, elements of kitsch and of high tragedy. The endless variety of theatrical props, *trompe l'oeil* effects, masks, disguises, blouses in different colors—is disrupted by the cruel and all-too-real ending of the poet's suicide. After all, who was the *real* Mayakovsky? What imposters should be dethroned and killed, and who should be resurrected?

Mayakovsky's wide international repertoire can be presented as a proliferation of derivatives of the root *real*, using all the possible linguistic tools—prefixes and suffices ("sur-real" or "real-ist"), qualifying adjectives ("socialist" or "critical"), or the powerful rhetorical strategies of persuasion. Those who appropriate Mayakovsky's story assert their authority by claiming a privileged access to that evasive, enigmatic, and alluring domain of "the real." Metaphor compulsion—the most powerful

drive in Mayakovsky's art and life—nurtures in survivors the desire to find the *real* Mayakovsky, a "Vladimir Mayakovsky" without quotation marks, to fix the metaphorical vertigo, to reinvent the *real* once and forever.

In Mayakovsky's case the understanding of "the real" is closely linked to our understanding of "the revolutionary." The word revolutionary, as has been noted many times, contains a paradox of inscribing both repetition ("turning or rotating motion around the axis, a single complete cycle of such orbital or axial motion") and rupture ("a sudden or momentous change in any situation" or "a sudden political overthrow or seizure of power brought about from within the political system").[136] Obviously, if we consult a Soviet dictionary, the third meaning would be given first priority, and in fact in contemporary Russian this word is employed exclusively in the political context; in the scientific context it has been supplanted by terms from a different root (*vrashchenie*) in order to eliminate the possibilities of dangerous wordplay. This reveals again the politics of word usage and the collective cultural biases of dictionaries, which are supposed to be "neutral" and "scientific."

The expression "revolutionary poet" is rich in contradictions, cultural and political ambiguities interwoven with etymological ones. Indeed, might it be an oxymoron, since the poet in order to remain poetically free cannot engage himself in any political service? In this case the "poetic drama" is defined as a drama of defamiliarization and disengagement from the immediate demands of society.[137] Or is "revolutionary poet" a tautology, that is, a "needless repetition of the same sense in different words, a redundancy"? In other words, to be a poet is already to be a revolutionary in the sphere of language, meaning that to be subversive in any society is to engage in a revolutionary struggle against the conservative forces of *byt*. These questions seem to be an undercurrent of the resurrections of Mayakovsky in the Soviet Union and in the West during the past decade, which contribute to the contemporary debates in literary theory.

But before the conclusion we have to pay tribute to the official Soviet Mayakovsky, the "poet-monument." "I don't give a damn for the monumental bronze, I don't give a damn for the marble slime. Let socialism, built in struggles, be our common monument," wrote Mayakovsky.[138] It turned out, however, that it was much easier to build a monument to the revolutionary poet than to build socialism itself. Edward Brown entitles the conclusion to his book on Mayakovsky "Not in Heaven," suggesting that the resurrected Soviet Mayakovsky "was enshrined by *byt*."[139] But

such an explanation of the poet's official immortality might seem a bit too Romantic: the Poet, even posthumously, remains the victim of *byt*. Indeed, Mayakovsky is "not in heaven" but occupies an important place in the Soviet version of "paradise on earth" which he allegorized in his verses.

Since Stalin's declaration that "Mayakovsky was and remains the greatest poet of our times" Mayakovsky has been commemorated in the streets and squares of Soviet cities. In Moscow, which was supposed to be the exemplary Communist city (a dream from the 1930's that was resurrected during the 1980 Olympic Games), Mayakovsky stands in the square named after him parallel to Pushkin Square, facing the main thoroughfare, Gorky Street. Thus the urban iconography of the Soviet capital illustrates Soviet Russian literary history from critical realism to Socialist Realism with the impressive bronze figures of canonical geniuses. The Mayakovsky monument embodies Aragon's "a Mayakovsky" and represents the true Socialist Realist with a romantic forelock wearing a bronze jacket and looking optimistically into the Communist future. Mayakovsky is also the hero of the Underground, the official underground system, the subway. In Leningrad, for instance, one can easily go literary sightseeing from Pushkin Station to Mayakovsky Station, and from there to Lenin Square by changing at Insurrection Square. The subway map presents an interesting allegory of the official Soviet strategies of reading.[140]

There are no monuments in the Soviet Union to Khlebnikov, Tsvetaeva, Mandelstam, Akhmatova, Pasternak, and many other poets who were neither less talented nor less modern than Mayakovsky, but perhaps were less visible, less spectacular. The deaths of the other poets were even more tragic than his, tragic in the most cruel, unromantically Soviet way, but until very recently they received little attention in the West because they lacked the exotic Russian revolutionary aura. We can only dream of creating a new underground in the Soviet cities, an underground underground where the deaths of these poets would be commemorated. Mayakovsky is one of the canonized Soviet poets, one whose works are required reading for Soviet high-school children, one who is not known so much from the books as from the words of the school teacher or pioneer leader. Fragments from the poems "Very Good," "Vladimir Ilich Lenin," and "At the Top of My Voice" are learned by heart and enthusiastically recited at oral exams. They form part of the common Soviet cultural text, together with Pushkin's "I Loved You," Lermontov's "And Dull and Sad . . . ," Marx's *Communist Manifesto*, and numerous quotes from Lenin.

Gorbachev's policies of glasnost and perestroika are only beginning to

affect the Soviet school program. However, the artists who partake in the emerging new experimental movement, which includes literary and performance groups, do not put Mayakovsky among their predecessors. This clearly distinguishes the artists of the 1980's from those of the 1960's, the poets of the "thaw generation," Evgeny Evtushenko, Robert Rozhdestvensky, and especially Andrey Voznesensky, who earlier tried to save Mayakovsky's provocative Futurist poetics from official monumentality. Instead the artists of the late 1980's have chosen to recover poets such as Daniil Kharms of OBERIU, the avant-garde absurdist group of the 1920's and 1930's, poets who were the uncompromised martyrs of the official culture. The contemporary Leningrad poet Alexander Kushner provided evidence of this trend when he remarked during his visit to Cambridge in 1989, "Mayakovsky is not read now."

Whether the official Soviet resurrection of Mayakovsky should be seen as the poet's most tragic death, for which, as Pasternak suggested, he is not to be blamed, or whether it is a kind of life after death that the poet dreamed of remains to be seen. In any case, each Soviet or Soviet émigré writer who discusses Mayakovsky's death and resurrection today responds to the Soviet myth of Mayakovsky incarnated in the official poet's monument. The critics in the West tend to ignore the official Soviet hero in the bronze jacket, or simply do not pay it tribute. And yet unknowingly many of them are victims of the monument. In fact, it is the monument that gave Mayakovsky a peculiar visibility in the Soviet Union and abroad, not an innocent visibility but a visibility at the expense of others. Many foreign critics confuse the most spectacular Soviet poet with the most talented, the most experimental, the most revolutionary, or the most representative one.

Among the most symptomatically provocative recent studies of Mayakovsky's death written by unofficial Soviet or Soviet émigré critics are the article by Alexander Zholkovsky "On Genius and Evil, or On Baba and All-Russian Scale" and Yury Karabichevsky's *Mayakovsky's Resurrection*.[141] The aim of Zholkovsky's insightful and original study is "to suggest a fresh, independent from the critical myths reading of Mayakovsky's poetry." Zholkovsky is aware that this freshness is relative and yet attempts a "revisionary demystification" of the poet through the scholarly analysis of certain less well known features of Mayakovsky's poetics. He warns the reader that he is not talking about Mayakovsky personally, but about his "literary persona" and the "implied author." In the present examination of Mayakovsky's unescapable mythifications and self-mythifications, we have observed how the claims of "demystification," as

well as the more modest claims of a "neutral scholarly objectivity," can become problematic.

Zholkovsky's essay offers a fascinating and fresh structural analysis of the theme of violence, particularly violence against women; a repeated rape under different disguises permeates Mayakovsky's poetry, raising crucial questions about the role of gender in the avant-garde and in revolutionary poetry. However, the critic's choice of paths through Mayakovsky's work, although quite original and meaningful, seems to be ideologically predetermined. From violence toward women, Zholkovsky moves easily toward "violence against language" and ends up linking Mayakovsky with the forces of evil (paraphrasing Pushkin in "Mozart and Salieri" that "genius and evil are incompatible"). The critic creates a pedigree for his "revised" Mayakovsky, including Raskolnikov, Nietzsche, Smerdyakov, Limonov's Edichka, and the heroes of A Clockwork Orange. Moreover, Mayakovsky becomes a loudspeaker for the devilish modern trinity "Extremism/Avant-Gardism/Terrorism."[142] In this way, the critic, while demystifying the official Soviet monument Mayakovsky, as well as Jakobson's Mayakovsky, a poet who commits a tragic suicide which redeems him in the eyes of the "liberal intelligentsia," perpetuates certain antimodernist biases of the (often not so "liberal") émigré intelligentsia, particularly the bias against the mythical evil three-headed dragon of modernity—extremism/avant-gardism/terrorism.

Yury Karabichevsky's "demystification" moves in a similar direction. The critic also wants to convince us and himself of his untendentiousness (nepridvzjatost' i bespristrastnost'), but he too acknowledges the difficulty of objectively analyzing the poet's work because Mayakovsky has become not only a literary fact but also a fact of Soviet everyday life. Indeed, the most interesting part of his book is precisely the critique of the official Mayakovsky myth. But the critic is caught up in the framework of Romantic poetics and Christian allegories. Gradually his Mayakovsky turns into the most dangerous carrier of the contagious virus of modernist aesthetics, a kind of modern "devil-seducer" with an "ironic mask instead of self-expression, grammatical complexity instead of depth of images, and on the part of the readers, admiration of the technical virtuosity of the verse, instead of the co-creation, and catharsis."[143] This leads Karabichevsky to claim that Mayakovsky is alive today—as Joseph Brodsky, with his emotional emptiness and superficial verbal elegance. (According to the critic, there are also a few pseudo-Mayakovskys in the Soviet Union: Rozhdestvensky, Voznesensky, and Evtushenko who inher-

ited Mayakovsky's external brilliance and his antihumanist moral vacuum.) In spite of their radical ideological differences, the rhetorical process in Karabichevsky's book is similar to that in Aragon's article: it is based on the same shift from Mayakovsky singular to Mayakovsky plural, from Mayakovsky to *a* Mayakovsky. Again, while exorcising the myth of the Soviet Mayakovsky in the bronze jacket, Karabichevsky reveals his own cultural or countercultural myths including the antimodernist bias. Thus, for the alternative-thinking Soviet or ex-Soviet intellectuals, "revolution" is overshadowed by postrevolutionary terror in the same way as, for the alternative-thinking Western intellectuals, postrevolutionary "deviations" are often excused or overlooked for the sake of revolutionary utopia. For Zholkovsky and Karabichevsky, a revolutionary poetry—if it is "true poetry"—can only be an oxymoron; poetry and the Bolshevik Revolution are as incompatible as genius and evil.

If we borrow a Christian metaphor from the Soviet-born critics educated in the official spirit of "scientific atheism," we might say that our move to the West will also be a move toward a more angelic image of Mayakovsky, who from a Soviet demon might become an antibourgeois apostle and martyr. This possibility reveals an interesting ideological flexibility of the figure of Mayakovsky; it stimulates each new interpreter to criticize his or her own culture. I will concentrate on two recent Western European versions of Mayakovsky's death that symptomatically disclose their own cultural myths. One is by the British art critic, poet, and fiction writer John Berger, and the other is by the Bulgarian émigré and French critic Julia Kristeva.

John Berger is first and foremost an art critic, an explorer of *visibility*. Thus perhaps his choice of Mayakovsky as the most original and representative Soviet poet is due both to ideological considerations and to Mayakovsky's spectacular nature. In his article, co-written with Anya Bostock, "Mayakovsky: His Language and His Death" Berger proposes to regard Mayakovsky "as an example central to any thinking about the relation between revolutionary politics and poetry."[144] For Berger, the revolutionary nature of Mayakovsky resides not in his "romantic legend" but precisely in his use of language which "has so far proved very hard to translate." (It seems that it has become commonplace to criticize the "legend of Mayakovsky" and to exorcise Mayakovsky the Impostor, a "mistranslated Mayakovsky," before starting the interpretation.) Berger writes: "Mayakovsky's story and tragedy concern the special historical relation which existed between him and the Russian language. To say this is not to de-politicize his example but to recognize its specificity."[145]

According to Berger, in the specific historical moment of the Revolution, as a result of the extensive literacy campaign launched by the Soviet government and the creation of a working-class "virginal" reading public, the Russian language demanded poetry, and Mayakovsky responded to this demand. Berger sees the death of Lenin as a turning point, poetic and otherwise, in "the betrayal of the Revolution." He describes this postrevolutionary (or counterrevolutionary) shift almost as a fall from the Communist paradise into the world of linguistic deception: "From the period of NEP [New Economic Policy] onwards the language of the Revolution began to change. At first, the changes have been almost imperceptible—except to the poet/performer like Mayakovsky. Gradually, words were ceasing to mean exactly what they said. (Lenin's will-to-truthfulness was exceptional and his death now appears as a turning point.) Words began to hide as much as they signified." [146] Thus when the revolution stopped being revolutionary, the revolutionary poet had to commit suicide, to respond with silence to the purge of the paradisiacal poetic language.

In this fascinating account of Mayakovsky's death there is a perfect continuity, almost an interchangeability of the words "poetic" and "revolutionary"; the figurative death of the poet leads inevitably to his actual suicide. At the same time we notice a clash between the Marxist notion of the priority of historical and social "objective" demands over the poet's subjectivity and a disguised Romantic notion of genius. Berger describes Mayakovsky and his poetic endeavor as completely unique, "too original to be easily defined by comparison with the other poets." Mayakovsky is an unprecedented, exotic Russian genius who stands completely outside the literary tradition and has a unique rapport with the unspoiled unwritten language of the people. In spite of the many fascinating insights characteristic of all John Berger's writings, there are some striking erasures in this spectacular retailoring of Russian literary history. From Berger's story one might assume that there were no pre-Mayakovskian revolutionaries of the poetic language, no Khlebnikov, for instance, and no history of interdependence of poetics and politics, as in Pushkin, Lermontov, Nekrasov—to name just a few nineteenth-century examples. Moreover, Berger's version of Mayakovsky's death erases the fact that the controversy between the social revolutionaries and the poetic revolutionaries started immediately after the Revolution, and that Lenin himself, highly praised between parentheses in the essay, confessed that he never understood Mayakovsky and had much preferred Pushkin. [147]

Julia Kristeva like John Berger ignores in her "Ethics of Linguistics"

"the flowers of evil" at the pedestal of the Soviet monument to Mayakovsky and prefers to disregard the poet's posthumous Stalinist resurrection. Her essay is an attempt to reread Jakobson's article on Mayakovsky's suicide as a lesson in ethics for contemporary linguistics. It leads her to question the epistemological foundations of contemporary linguistics, its desire to "hem in" ("suturer"—another term from the vocabulary of the yellow blouse) the field of study, dissociating the problem of truth in linguistic discourse from any notion of "speaking subject."[148] What has often been perceived as Jakobson's apolitical stance, his opposition of poetics and politics, turns out to be a subversive political position of Russian Formalism, that is, the Formalists' attempt to see how the over-politicized Marxist discourse "is made" and how it can become "murderous." The depoliticization of Russian Formalism by the French Structuralists and the American old New Critics was the effect of yet another cultural mistranslation. (Formalism was perceived in the Soviet Union as extremely dangerous politically and as a result was carefully purged.) Being a poet in Soviet society, a carrier of the subversive "poetic function" able to capture "the pre-trans-logical" rhythm of death and the future, was Mayakovsky's most revolutionary activity. Kristeva's Mayakovsky joins the French "revolutionaries in the poetic language" Mallarmé and Artaud, with their gift to "hear and understand the signifier as such—as ciphering, as rhythm, as a presence that precedes the signification of object or emotion," their dangerous gift "to make language perceive what it does not want to say."[149] Developing further Jakobson's opposition of the Poet and *byt*—in its Romantic poetic definition as a stabilizing conservative force—Kristeva states: "On the eve of Stalinism and fascism a (any) society may be stabilized if it excludes poetic language."[150] Kristeva continues the ethical challenge of Jakobson's "we"— the eruption of the critic's subjectivity which forces us to confront the unavoidable question: "If we are not on the side of those whom society wastes in order to reproduce itself, *where are we?*"[151] This dilemma makes us experience Aragon's repressed vertigo, an unfixable ethical vertigo from the repetition of "revolutionary situations," poets' sacrifices, and critical choices. If we push Kristeva's suggestive analysis further we can perform an important critical leap, from focusing on a suspiciously happy marriage or a suspiciously violent divorce between politics and poetics to a reconsideration of the broader issue of ethics that underlines writing and acting, making poetry and love as well as making and unmaking the self.

For the sake of what is the poet sacrificed? Is it to destabilize, desa-

cralize, subvert, and contaminate *byt* with the revolutionary poetic virus? Or to provide a necessary dialectical/dramatic/dialogical tension in a (any) society, avoiding totalitarian closure or disclosing the cultural myth of an illusionary "bourgeois" open-endedness? Is it possible to talk about a (any) society? Can there be a society in which the most self-sacrificial poets go unnoticed, and the news of their death is given only a thirty-second spot on television squeezed in between the story of drunk drivers and a "how-do-you-spell-relief" commercial?

We can also engage an alternative line of questioning: Are we to preserve the opposition between a poet and *byt* foregrounded by Mayakovsky himself as well as by many critics, or should we regard it as one of Mayakovsky's reductive metaphors? Is this opposition only a convenient Romantic construct, while in fact *byt* can be quite poetic in its modest quotidian way and a poet quite "conservative," conventional, and compromisingly embedded in social and linguistic clichés? Or to push the question further, does *byt* have to be seen as "conservative," or can it be regarded as a source of potentially subversive micropractices? Is it an alternative force that might provide a comic relief from the seriousness of the transgressions and excesses of both poets and revolutionaries, poetic revolutionaries and revolutionary poets?

Mayakovsky fascinates his spectators with a dazzling performance in language and death. Perhaps he is a revolutionary predecessor of the "postmoderns," with his love for advertisement and fashion. The story of Mayakovsky's suicide yields itself to many "theoretical fables"—of figurative and actual deaths linked to one another, of a left march turning into a *marche funèbre*, of "left" becoming "right," and a song of liberation becoming a glorification of oppression; of the ethics of linguistics and the linguistics of ethics; of the dangers of both excessive engagement and excessive defamiliarization, as well as of hypocritical moderation; of the murderous vitality of metaphors; of literary criticism converging with autobiography; of the transgression of genres in art and life; of the poet's gunshot, both enticing and resisting allegorization.

E. E. Kruglikova, Silhouette of Marina Tsvetaeva (right)

· 3 ·

The Death of the Poetess

The "Poetess": Lack, Excess, and Aesthetic Obscenity

Адалис и Марина Цветаева пророчицы, сюда же и София Парнок. Пророчество как домашнее рукоделие. . . . Женская поэзия продолжает вибрировать на самых высоких нотах, оскорбляя слух, историческое, по-этическое чутьё.

Adalis and Marina Tsvetaeva are prophetesses, and so is Sophia Parnok. Their prophesy is like domestic needlework . . . Feminine poetry continues to vibrate at the highest pitch, offending the ear, offending the historical, poetical sense.

Osip Mandelstam, "Literary Moscow"

Вошла комсомолка с почти твердым намерением взять, например, Цветаеву. Ей, комсомолке, сказать, сдувая пыль с серой обложки—Товариш, если вы интересуетесь цыганским лиризмом, осмелюсь вам предложить Сельвинского. Та же тема, но как обработана! Мужчина.

The Komsomol girl came in with a strong intention to get, for instance, Tsvetaeva. One should tell her, the Komsomol girl, blowing away the dust from the gray book cover: "Comrade, if you are interested in gypsy lyricism, I would dare to offer you Selvinsky. The same topic, but look how well it is done! In one word, done by a man."

Vladimir Mayakovsky, "Let's Wait before Accusing the Poets"

"Иинтеллпгентный человек"—Марина?—это почти такая же глупость, как сказать о ней "поэтесса." Какая гадость!

How can one call Marina a member of the intelligentsia? This is almost as stupid as to call her a "poetess." What a disgusting thing to say!

Marina Tsvetaeva, *The Tale of Sonechka*

The word "poetess" is derived from "poet"; poet plus a feminine suffix, an excess, a mark of "bad taste," a sign of cultural inferiority. In our culture the texts written by a "poet" are read differently from those written by a "poetess." In the mind of the reader, the word "poet"—grammatically masculine—is often perceived as culturally neutral, unmarked, while the word "poetess" is embarrassingly gendered. In the essay "Literary Moscow," Mandelstam poetically synthesizes the attributes of the cultural mask of the poetess, which include excessive lyrical exaltation, abusive use of metaphor, and the lack of a sense of history or

historical responsibility.[1] The poetess is ahistorical, extremely subjective, and incapable of stepping out of her little emotional home into the disinterested objectivity of language. She is an exalted literary weaver, who by mistake picked up the wrong textures/textiles for domestic knitting—words instead of threads.

The poetess is not merely another eccentric Russian heroine; rather she reflects a commonly shared European and American cultural myth that developed in the nineteenth and early-twentieth centuries and still survives today. In this context, the poetess embodies neither the essential features of a woman-poet nor those of feminine/feminist/female writing. Instead, like the revolutionary poet, the poetess is viewed as a cultural mask, the mask of a not-so-glamorous heroine in the contemporary commedia dell'arte, or the theater of the cruelty of modern culture. In my approach to femininity I provisionally agree with Julia Kristeva that "a woman is never that" ("la femme ce n'est jamais ça").[2] And yet there are certain attributes chosen from the plurality of feminine that are reified and become a cultural myth. This myth can be traced through the superimposition of a number of representative texts from Russian and European literature. Moreover, the cultural myth does not merely affect the artistic representation of women; it also, in more general terms, shapes our aesthetic tastes and value judgments.

Mandelstam regards literary femininity as a peculiar way of unconsciously parodying poetic invention and collective memories that constitute the very kernel of true (virile) poetry.

> На долю женщин в поэзии выпала огромная доля пародии, в самом серьезном и формальном смысле слова. Женская поэзия является бессознательной пародией, как поэтических изобретений, так и воспоминий. Большинство московских поэтесс ушиблены метафорой. Это бедные Изиды, обреченные на вечные поиски куда-то затерявшейся второй части поэтического сравнения, долженствующей вернуть поэтическому образу Озирису, свое первоначальное единство.[3]

> To the fate of women in poetry has fallen a tremendous share of parody, in the most serious and formal sense of the word. Feminine poetry is an unconscious parody of both poetic inventions and remembrances. The majority of Muscovite poetesses have been hit by the metaphor. These poor Isises are doomed to an eternal search for a forever-lost second part of the simile, which would return to the poetic image Osiris its primordial unity.

The poetess becomes an unconscious parody of a poet. Parody was at the center of attention among both Russian Formalists and the Bakhtin circle. Tynyanov, for instance, saw it as part of the driving force of literary evolution, as a rhetorical device indicating evolutionary shifts in genres and discourses.[4] Bakhtin regarded parody as a privileged form of double-voiced speech, as a dialogue that helps to estrange the authorial pretensions of parodized discourse.[5] And yet Mandelstam's poetess does not call into question the authorial pretensions of what he calls a poet. Mandelstam's use of "unconscious" is very significant here; the poetess lacks precisely the authentic artistic subjectivity that would enable her to turn upon the poetic tradition and critically comment on it.

In the European and American traditions, women in poetry, by nature, or rather perhaps by culture, play the role of muses, addressees, or beautiful love *objects*, but almost never that of speaking *subjects*. To paraphrase Edgar Allen Poe, the most poetic subject in the world is the death of a beautiful woman, and any woman-poet is forever haunted by the beautiful corpse of a female heroine, over whom she often has to step in order to write.

Mandelstam's poetess presents a grotesque conglomeration of *lack* and *excess*. The poetess's excessive use of metaphor and propensity for exalted love songs is based on her cultural uprootedness, her radical and irretrievable lack—a loss predating possession—of the primordial unity of the masculine image Osiris. One remembers that according to the legend, the missing part of Osiris that the goddess never recovered was his phallus. Hence a curious intertwining of sexuality and aesthetics (and a specific culturally dominant version of both female aesthetics and female sexuality) becomes more and more obvious and one cannot help making an analogy between the "penis envy" of Freud's "normal woman" and the poetess's "pen's envy," an analogy that has already engendered many critical puns.[6] A woman according to Freud is an unconscious parody of a man, a nonsubversive parody which does not question but rather consolidates penile powers.

In his controversial essay "On Femininity," Freud claims to approach his subject not from the literary or stylistic point of view, but on the basis of "sexual functions." He defines femininity in a structurally similar way, as a combination of lack—lack of penis and lack of inventiveness, originality, and social responsibility—and excess—a propensity for hysteria, from the Greek word for uterus, the womb with its overwhelming theatrical manifestations, fantasies, and love obsessions.[7] The only inventions Freud credits to women, incapacitated by their "genital deficiency," are those of plaiting and weaving, which supposedly stem from their obses-

sion with pubic hair. We recognize here the familiar metaphor of weaving, or in Mandelstam's words of "domestic needlework," with which we started the examination of the textual idiosyncrasies of the poetess. In this cultural paradigm women can excel only in *textiles*, but not in *texts*. At the end of his essay Freud himself confesses his doubts and advises the audience to "turn to poets" and consult them on the subject of femininity before "science can give deeper and more coherent information." Freud's own argument constantly vacillates between anatomy and psychology, between biological and cultural considerations, between literary and scientific methods, as if he is unable to locate the precise place where femininity resides. Femininity remains a riddle in which sexual functions and cultural preconceptions, scientific observations and poetic mythifications, are intimately interwoven. In this vicious circularity of cultural myths, it is impossible to discern what is primary and what is secondary, what is literary or extraliterary, poetry or biology.

The major lack of the poetess, ciphered in Mandelstam's expression "man's force and truth," the lack that she hides behind the manneristic folds of her dress, can be defined in literary terms as a lack of genius. The word shares a root with genre, gender, genetics, and genitalia. The poetess is by definition not a genius; she is a sort of literary *nouveau riche* who lacks the genetic blue blood of the artistic aristocracy. Genius is a sign of genetic artistic superiority, crucial to the genesis of "true" poetry and available to one gender only. In the European Romantic and post-Romantic traditions genius has been conceived as quintessentially virile.[8] Hence the word poetess inscribes an oxymoronic relationship between its suffix and its root: poetess is therefore something less than a poet, something that lacks a root—the authentic artistic identity, the genius.

Obviously, the notion of "poet" is not at all monolithic. It is rewritten differently by each major poet and in each artistic manifesto. In terms of gender, however, there seems to be a good deal of agreement; the poet is either virile or asexual (the latter has acquired the poetic name "spiritual androgyny," that is, above and beyond sexual difference). Masculinity is described by Mandelstam with much less playfulness and humor than femininity.

В отличие от старой гражданской поэзии, новая русская поэзия должна воспитывать не только граждан, но и "мужа." Идеал совершенной мужественности подготовлен стилем и практическими требованиями нашей эпохи. Все стало тверже и громаднее, поэтому и человек должен стать тверже

... Гиератический, то есть священный характер поэзии
обусловлен убежденностью, что челонек тверже всего оста-
льного в мире.[9]

> In contrast to the old civic poetry, the new Russian poetry has to edu-
> cate not simply citizens, but "men." The ideal of perfect manliness is
> prepared by the style and the practical demands of our time. Everything
> has become firmer and more immense, so a human being has to become
> firmer . . . The hieratic, i.e., sacred, character of poetry is conditioned
> by the conviction that a man is firmer than anything in the universe.

The image of "manliness"—which reminds one of a perfect Greek
statue with a classical fig leaf—intertwines ancient ideals and Russian
cultural prejudices. It is characterized by a peculiar hieratic firmness
and by epic dimensions. For Mandelstam, femininity and masculinity are
not so much specific references to the poet's gender but are cultural metaphors. They are matters of style and taste more than of biology or anatomy. Thus, in the same article Mandelstam indicates that Mayakovsky,
with his excessive futuristic lyricism, is in danger of becoming a "poetess," and goes on to suggest that some literary movements—for instance, Symbolism, or even Futurism—can be regarded as feminine, as
lacking the historicity and cultural and linguistic attentiveness of a more
virile, more classical Acmeism, the latter in Mandelstam's idiosyncratic
view being more in tune with the revolutionary epoch. Literary femininity
is often regarded as a stylistic aberration even in the sympathetic accounts of women writers and poets. It manifests itself in what Emily Dickinson names "inversion in the sentence" and what Virginia Woolf describes as "the atrocity" that women writers committed in "natural prose"
of the nineteenth century, turning "man's sentence" into a "clumsy
weapon."[10] Literary femininity, at least the way it is engendered by
nineteenth-century aesthetics and is carried out far into the twentieth
century, is doomed to a peculiar "stylistic miscarriage," which at the
same time is irreducible to matters of style. Paradoxically, the problem
with the poetess is not only that she is not properly stylish but also that
she never goes beyond the mannerisms of style.

Harold Bloom, in a seminar at Harvard University in 1987, used the
term "aesthetic dignity" in relation to the poetics of Wallace Stevens.
When asked to define the term, he hesitated to do so. It seemed that the
term did not require a precise critical definition; it referred to a certain
myth of modernist poetics, the myth of unaffected "good taste," which is
supposedly "naturally" shared by the sophisticated literary community.
Hence in this tradition, literary femininity is a loss of this undefinable

aesthetic dignity, a transgression of literary propriety, an aesthetic obscenity. For a woman to be a poet (or a writer or an artist, for that matter) is not simply absurd, as Blok put it, but also obscene. The etymology of the word "obscene" is obscure: it can relate either to the Latin *ob* (on account of) + *caenum* (pollution, dirt, filth, vulgarity) = *obcaenum* or to *ob* (in relation of tension) + *scena* (scene, space of communal and ritual enactment, sacred space) = *obscenum*. "Obscene," therefore, is defined as something "in relation of tension" to the (aesthetic) scene.[11] In the context of my work it points to something that has been perceived as culturally marginal and marginalized, as something played offstage with respect to the performance of a virile genius. The dictionary defines "obscene" first as "offensive to accepted standards of decency or modesty" and second as "inciting lustful feelings, lewd."[12] Perhaps it is the exposed genderedness of the poetess's writing, the laying bare of sexual difference, that offends the accepted universal standards of literary decency. Barthes suggests in *A Lover's Discourse* that contemporary obscenity is not pornography or shocking transgression, but sentimentality, sentimentality that is less strange and therefore even more "abject" than the Marquis de Sade's classic example of transgression—the story of the pope sodomizing a turkey.[13] It is this sentimental "lover's discourse," this excess of affect and lack of structure, that disrupts the aesthetic dignity of literary discourse and shapes the modern cultural myth of writing in the feminine.

My wish is not to marginalize further the poetess, secluding her within an exclusive, restrictive frame, but rather to disclose the presence of this frame around every literary figure. The portrait of the poetess will help to lay bare the very device of framing, even when a cultural effort is made to hide it with various illusionistic devices, including the mask of universality. In other words, the "-ess" of poetess will ultimately make visible a conspicuous absence of suffix (or suffix zero, as linguists would call it) in the word poet.

As we recall, "the revolutionary poet" was also an excessive construct, but in that case the excess was a touch of glamour, a heroic garb—from yellow blouse to bronze jacket. In our theoretical fables the death of the revolutionary poet—as tragic as it might have been—culminates with the creation of the poet's monument. As for the poetess, she hangs herself in a complete uncompromising anonymity, and the exact location of where her body is buried remains unknown. The dress of the poetess is gaudy and unmonumental; her underwear is a deadening, unreadable white, and her overcoat might easily become the straitjacket of a hysteric.

The poetess is like the heroine in a masquerade who covers up her real face—or lack of one—with many layers of disguises, flaunting her inauthenticity. In her repertoire are multiple travesty masks of female male impersonators—the trousers and male pseudonyms of George Sand, for instance—and of male female impersonations, that is, male images of literary women, from the "blue-stocking with an itch for scribbling" to a little virgin all in white to a dazzling Romantic heroine. Marina Tsvetaeva, in her essay on the poet and critic Maximilian Voloshin, describes one of the acts of making, or rather of making up, the poetess. She tells the story of the young, modest school teacher Elizaveta Dmitrieva, who was handicapped and not conventionally beautiful and who possessed the "unmodest and cruel gift of poetry, which wasn't lame and like Pegasus flew above the earth." [14] Yet if she appeared in the salon in unglamorous attire, she would remain unloved by men, and go unpublished.

As the story unfolds, Voloshin, trying to help Dmitrieva, decides to manipulate the cultural myths and invents for her a dramatic persona, that of Cerubina de Gabriak—foreign, exotic, Catholic, rich, beautiful, suffering, romanesque. Cerubina de Gabriak, in her Romantic legend, eventually conquers St. Petersburg and becomes the most popular poet of *Apollon*, the fashionable literary journal of the time. To preserve her myth and mystique, she remains invisible, like Psyche, or a Muse. In other words, Cerubina de Gabriak the poetess becomes a Romantic heroine and the recipient of letters and flowers from male admirers. She is a beautiful dream object of male love—ideal, absent, disembodied, and almost unsexed, who as an extra activity, a pleasant extravagance or stylish eccentricity, happened to write "feminine poetry." Woman-as-subject-of-writing was appropriated by a much more culturally accepted image, woman-as-object-of-courtly love. Hence, the poetess has been murdered by the Romantic heroine.

Tsvetaeva reports the mysterious death of Cerubina de Gabriak somewhere in Turkestan and confesses that she was the only one who was repelled by "the narrow purple envelope, sharp handwriting, and strong perfume" of Cerubina. She gave three reasons—as a woman, as a poet, and as anti-aesthete—"I did not love the proud foreign woman, but precisely the modest school teacher Dmitrieva with Cerubina's soul, but why should Cerubina care about my love?" [15] A woman-poet reflected in the eyes of another woman-poet is beyond the official cultural "scopophilia." Only this self-reflective feminine gaze might redeem the otherwise completely vaudevillelike character of the poetess.

We see that the very existence of the poetess-as-subject is fragile: she

is always in danger of being objectified and murdered by one of the female cultural "monsters," be it a Romantic heroine, a femme fatale, or an "angel in the house," Virginia Woolf's ironic definition of the ideal Victorian woman. Her theater is represented as a cheap vaudeville, or a provincial melodrama, and not a visceral theater of cruelty open only to male geniuses. Virginia Woolf writes about a peculiar "desire to be veiled," a "desire for anonymity" that runs in the blood of women writers.[16] According to Woolf, this propensity for anonymity could enable women writers to accept more easily modernist aesthetics—the aesthetics of depersonalization and distance. At the same time, this tradition of anonymity signals the extreme vulnerability of a woman as a writing subject and might be interpreted as her lack of personal voice, a lack of genius. It would not be seen as a conscious aesthetic position, as an attempt at the depersonalization of a fully accomplished artistic personality, but as a revisitation of the eternal feminine deficiency.

It is not surprising that in the works of women writers and poets, the poetess turns from a comic character into a tragic one. The poetess's infamous lack, her exalted emptiness, is filled with suffering, with memories of painful silence, or even with her sacrificial death. Two such examples are Virginia Woolf's story of the suicide of the exemplary poetess Judith Shakespeare and the mythical tale of Procne and Philomela which is often used as an allegory for "maddened and grotesque female artists" who make "absurd, grotesque, and pitiful" sounds and was later revised in a feminist manner by Sandra Gilbert and Susan Gubar.

Thus, the poetess's distorted voice, her hysteria and ahistoricity, her mannerisms and emotionalism, might be a cover-up not for a lack but for an excess of painful memories. The ritual sacrifice, that of Judith Shakespeare, Procne, Philomela, and others, is a sacrifice at the very root of articulation which is responsible for that peculiar "anxiety of authorship" experienced by any woman artist. The feminine discourse, as it is engendered in our culture, is situated on a fragile boundary between kitsch and tragedy.

As Mayakovsky demonstrates in "Let's Wait before Accusing the Poets," it is very easy, especially for a male artist, to perform the rhetorical movement from a critique of literary femininity to insults directed at the woman-poet. The example of Marina Tsvetaeva, a woman-poet and writer so often accused of being too much of a "poetess," a woman-poet with an unconventionally tragic biography, will lead us to explore the relationship between cultural predestination and individual resistance. Here again I will employ the half-mask strategy, playing textual analysis

against multiple contextual configurations. The duel between the woman-poet and her female pedigree is at the center of this chapter. Can she in her writing escape the ghosts of cultural metaphors of femininity? How does she redefine her literary identity against (or rather, together with and against) the cultural myth of female creativity? Can she escape that touch of a "bad taste" that marks the discourse of a poetess? The continuous dialogue between the poet and his or her multiple qualifiers, adjectives, suffixes, and derivatives can help to unveil enigmas which appear at the root of poetry and writing itself.

The Poetess's Self-Defense:
Close Reading and Clothes Reading

Самоохрана торчества. Чтобы не умереть—иногда нужно убить (прежде всего в себе).

The self-defense of creativity. In order not to die, one has to murder something or someone (first and foremost in oneself).
Marina Tsvetaeva, "The Poet and His Times"

Tsvetaeva's story does not yield to a series of glamorous portraits as Mayakovsky's did, except perhaps for the first image of Tsvetaeva as a poet, which is imbued with conventional Romantic potential. We imagine the portrait of seventeen-year-old Marina, the daughter of the founder of the Pushkin Art Museum in Moscow, happily married to the hero of her dreams, Sergey Efron. Her first book of artful girlish verses, *The Evening Album*, has just been published and praised by Valery Bryusov for its "uncanny intimacy." She seems the perfect incarnation of a Romantic heroine/poetess, a gifted femme-enfant.

Then the scenario changes. Tsvetaeva was too much in love with love and poetry to remain within conventional frames. She had love relationships with most of the major poets of the time: Osip Mandelstam, Sophia Parnok, Anna Akhmatova, Boris Pasternak, and Rainer Maria Rilke. Some of these relationships were platonic and others were more than platonic—for Tsvetaeva the difference between the two was never crucial. Her propensity for love can hardly be confined to the exalted passion of the poetess. Rather, she was always in need of an *erotic intertextuality* that would nurture her life and her art—neither a power struggle for survival nor an oedipal rivalry with other poets, but what can be called a "structure of love."

Her politics were as unconventionally passionate as her love relation-

ships. She did not accept the Revolution, and wanted to remain faithful to her romantic vision of White Russia. But neither did she join in the anti-Soviet spirit of the Russian émigrés in Paris. She always wrote against the grain. While still in Soviet Russia she glorified the White officers, twentieth-century Romantic heroes, and in France she dedicated a cycle of poems to the official Soviet revolutionary poet Mayakovsky, provoking a scandal among the émigrés. She herself emigrated twice, in opposite directions, and remained an outcast both times. First she left Russia for Czechoslovakia and then later moved on to France, where she was artistically and personally alienated from the émigré literary circles because of her nonconformist writings and the ambiguous position of her husband, who turned out to be a KGB agent. And yet Tsvetaeva's life was neither the romantic (or modernist) story of a poet fleeing Soviet oppression, nor a Hollywood spy drama featuring a woman with a mysterious Slavic accent as undercover double agent. Furthermore, it did not become a Socialist-Realist optimistic epic of the "return of the prodigal daughter." Tsvetaeva left France and returned to the Soviet Union in 1939, following her husband and daughter, only to find herself a complete foreigner in the country of her childhood and never to learn the peculiarly Soviet way of practicing hypocritical silence, adopted by and forced upon her fellow poets.[17]

As for sexual politics, Tsvetaeva never claimed to be a feminist, although all her life she materially supported her husband and was in love with the mythical Amazon. She even wrote the controversial "Letter to the Amazon" addressed to the founder of the famous women's salon in Paris, Nathalie Barney, in which she polemically states that there is only one kind of love "more perfect than love between women"—the maternal. At the same time, she was always accused by her friends and enemies of being a "bad mother," too negligent or too obsessive, too maternal, or not maternal enough.

Marina Tsvetaeva hanged herself on August 31, 1941, just two months after the declaration of war, in the little Siberian town of Elabuga where she had been evacuated. There were no obituaries in either Soviet or foreign newspapers, no one accompanied her body from the funeral, and the exact place of her burial remains unidentified. For almost twenty years she was unpublished in the Soviet Union and abroad, for somewhat similar reasons—the ambiguity of her politics—and was only posthumously declared one of the major Russian poets of the twentieth century. Just as her poetry participates in but does not conform to any movement or school, avant-garde, modernist, or otherwise, neither does her life lend itself to any grid or set pattern. And yet both her poetry and her life

partake of the same economy, an erotic intertextuality that makes them inseparable. They are determined by the central feature in Tsvetaeva's poetics—"immoderation (excess) in the world of measures" ("bezmernost v mire mer"), that excessiveness, obsessiveness, and passion that were often culturally codified as the mannerisms of the poetess. Instead of confining Marina Tsvetaeva to the mask of the poetess, I will demonstrate how it both entraps and liberates her, opening for her new poetic options and possibilities for play.

As follows from Tsvetaeva's essay "The Poet and His Times," the "self-defense of creativity" calls for the poet's metaphorical murder, often a suicide, the murder of one of his or her own problematic alter egos. It is regarded as a sacrifice that nourishes the creative process. The poetess, a woman-poet's seductive look-alike, is one of Tsvetaeva's sacrificial victims who would later be resurrected as her beloved. The story of Tsvetaeva's art and life can serve as a perfect theoretical fable that intertwines figurative and nonfigurative deaths and problematizes the relationship between writing and its cultural makeup. My discussion will move from a figurative death to the actual one, from Tsvetaeva's own poetics of death to the responses to her suicide.

To be faithful to Tsvetaeva's intertextual designs, I propose the alternating strategies of *close reading* and *clothes reading*. Cloth—the essential poetess attribute—can be read as both a theme and a trope, a frame and a part of the portrait, a surface and a fold, a literary element and an element of *byt*, an element of style and a social marker. M. H. Abrams, in his celebrated book *The Mirror and the Lamp*, remarks that starting in the eighteenth century, "style was regarded as a dress of thought." [18] Thus, in our close reading and clothes reading we will address again the relationship between style and thought and pay close attention to the cultural intertwining of the problems of style and gender. Moreover, instead of the established cultural paradigm that opposes text and textiles, the former being an emanation of virile genius and the latter a clumsy disguise of feminine uninventiveness, we will combine the two and show their mutual co-dependence, which can be observed in both male and female writing.

My focus will be on Tsvetaeva's critical essays and prose in which the poetess often appears as a character. These writings, composed for the most part in the 1920's and 1930's during Tsvetaeva's exile in Czechoslovakia and France, received very little critical recognition; and they were denounced in quite a hyperbolic manner. D. S. Mirsky for instance calls her prose "the most pretentious, unkempt, hysterical and altogether the worst prose ever written in Russian." [19] In other words, some of these texts

were accused of what I call aesthetic obscenity, which is worth investigating since it will help us understand what constitutes critical dignity and its limitations. Moreover, Tsvetaeva's prose offers interesting intergeneric hybrids, which are best suited for my intergeneric criticism examining biographical legends and combining clothes readings and close readings.

Thus, there is something in the very structure of Tsvetaeva's prose works, especially *The Tale of Sonechka*, that insults the notion of "good taste" and shocks so many literary critics.[20] This element reveals itself in excessive "hysteric" lyricism, overflowing subjectivism, and the impossibility to distinguish between writing about the self and writing about others. The interferences go both ways: Tsvetaeva's critical and fictional writings become autobiographical to the same extent that her more conventionally autobiographical writings are both critical and fictional. Tsvetaeva's prose goes beyond all acceptable boundaries of genre and does not allow us to draw comfortable distinctions between criticism and autobiography, prose and poetry, fact and fiction, author and narrator, person and persona.

Tsvetaeva's ambivalent attitude toward the cultural myth of femininity manifests itself in a series of self-defensive performances: on the one hand, the female narrator often attempts to distance herself from the traditional feminine heroine, whether "a beautiful woman or a poetess," and on the other hand, she becomes infatuated with aesthetically obscene, "oversweet," and overly romantic "feminine" discourse which she tries to reinvent despite all critical taboos. The poetess as a character in Tsvetaeva's writings appears both as a distinctly separate entity, another woman artist, and as a curious alter ego of the narrator herself. I will argue that in *The Tale of Sonechka* the aesthetic obscenity is no longer treated as a shameful feminine disease requiring a cure. On the contrary, in this story which presents the complex intertwining of genre and gender, all the aesthetic excesses and deviations are self-consciously explored and enjoyed.

In the essay "Hero of Labor" Tsvetaeva describes "an evening of poetesses" organized by Valery Bryusov in 1920. Bryusov defines femininity as a cultural curiosity and an exoticism: "Woman, Love, Passion . . . From the very beginning women could only sing about love. Outside of love, woman in poetry is nothing" ("Zhenshchina. Ljubov'. Strast' . . . Zhenshchina s nachala vekov umela pet' tol'ko o ljubvi. Vne ljubvi zhenshchina v tvorchestve nichto").[21] "Woman, Love, Passion," this amorous triangle predictably enough precludes any social or revolutionary preoccupation and reduces the whole scope of feminine literature to

"crimes of the heart." The suffix "-ess" becomes much more important than the root. Curiously, Bryusov not only describes but also reenacts the stylistic features of parodic literary femininity in his own writings. He published a collection, *Nelly's Poems*, which as Tsvetaeva suggests betrays its author; it mimes the poetess's mannerisms but lacks her "soul" or what we might view as her tragic transgressiveness.

Bryusov's evening of poetesses is an interesting event. The number of poetesses is nine, as in the nine Muses of antiquity ("What a pseudoclassic!" mocks Tsvetaeva). They are viewed as the ornaments and inspirers of their male mentor Maecenas, Valery Bryusov, the widely acclaimed and established poet with whom they hardly share equal rights. As Tsvetaeva remarks, the evening of poetesses is more like "a bridal show" for male audiences than a serious poetry recital. Tsvetaeva's attitude toward the event is contradictory: she is both sarcastic and sympathetic; she mocks with a great deal of humor the very idea of such an event. At the same time, nonetheless, she consents to participate in it. She claims that she has always been appalled by anything that bears the mark of "female separatism . . . and the so-called women's question," except for "its military resolution" in the legendary kingdom of the Amazons and the no less legendary Petrograd Women's Battallion. As Karlinsky points out, "Tsvetaeva might have wanted to dissociate herself from any kind of feminism in response to the trend in the Soviet Union towards segregating women poets into a somewhat inferior critical category." [22] Yet, Tsvetaeva is not ashamed of femininity, like some other famous women-poets— Zinnaida Gippius among them. She quickly qualifies her response, saying that there are no "women's questions" but there are "women's answers to 'human' questions": those of Sappho, St. Teresa, Bettina Brentano, Marie Bashkirtseff, and Rosa Bonheur.

In describing the poetesses, Tsvetaeva's gaze fluctuates between the audience and the participants; she is both a spectator and an inspected object, both a part of the spectacle and an observer. Laura Mulvey, in her essay on film theory, discusses a complex identification of the female spectator with the male gaze, which makes the female gaze culturally "bisexual." [23] The "bisexuality" of the gaze is very characteristic for Tsvetaeva. On the one hand, she objectifies the poetesses, regards them as heroines from a cheap melodrama. On the other, she shares a warm female complicity with them. Tsvetaeva's description of the other poetesses (except that of Adalis, to whom she dedicates special attention) is primarily *visual*. She sees them as carnival characters; or not even characters, but masks and attributes—"whitish blots—faces; red inkspots— lips; black *circonflexes*—eyebrows." She not only objectifies them but

also presents them in a kaleidoscope of metonymic details—the poetess Poplavskaya's dancing little tails of fur, pearl-like teeth, and cocaine pupils; Malvina's stylist blue glass beads; someone's crimson beret; Bonar's "Gavroche" hair cut.

The description ends with a Georgian countess, beautiful, with verses that "did not seem so bad," and a certain Susanna, "a beauty, without any verses whatsoever."[24] Thus, the poetesses' masquerade reaches its logical conclusion: the poetess is murdered by feminine beauty, from a speaking subject she becomes a mere object of sight. Perhaps Susanna is actually the truest poetess in Bryusov's sense, the most hyperbolic incarnation of his patronizing definition. Beautiful herself, she need not write about beauty.

The beautiful poetess without poems is a reduction to absurdity of the grotesque image of the female artist. It is Tsvetaeva's ultimate parody, aimed not so much at Susanna herself but at the male artists' hypocrisy hidden behind women-loving attitudes in literature. Tsvetaeva estranges herself from the poetesses by poetically undoing their images, by turning them into an assemblage of metonymic details, by depicting their statements as statements on fashion and not on poetry. At the same time, she describes their "feminine kindness" and tolerance toward her anarchic, nonconformist self.

We have already observed the connection between clothes and rhetoric in the discussion of Mayakovsky: the revolutionary poet transformed his favorite yellow blouse from an insignificant synecdoche into a powerful poetic and revolutionary metaphor. One of the "facts of life" became a "literary fact" and vital cultural symbol. In her description of poetesses Tsvetaeva capitalizes on the synecdochic details, but never turns these synecdoches of appearance into a signifying metaphor. She refuses to create a single, totalizing figure of the poetess, neither a sympathetic one nor a caricature. Her description preserves a playful kaleidoscopic quality, defying and deferring generalizations about the poetess's real or inauthentic self.

The question of style and mannerism, good and bad taste, disguise and the self (or lack thereof), is at the heart of the poetess's problem. Tsvetaeva herself was often a victim of insults directed against literary femininity. Even Anna Akhmatova, the most influential woman-poet of the time, who was also accused of writing "chamber poetry" (a subspecies, a limited, feminine "lyrical diary"), found much of Tsvetaeva's poetry too romantic and "in bad taste."[25] In describing herself, humorously as she described others, Tsvetaeva emphasizes the "unfeminine" character of her clothes, which were supposed to challenge and provoke the

audience with their poverty and certain politically dangerous attributes, such as the tsarist army lieutenant's belt.

Я в тот день была явлена "Риму и миру" в зеленом, вроде подрясника,—платьем не назовешь (перефразировка лучших времен: пальто), честно . . . стянутом не офицерским даже, а юнкерским . . . ремнем . . . Ноги в серых валенках, хотя и мужских, по ноге, в окружении лакированных лодочек, глядели столпами слона. Весь же туалет, в силу именно чудовищности своей, снимал с меня всякое подозрение в нарочитости.[26]

That day I was presented "urbi and orbi" in green, in some kind of cloth—which could not even be called a "dress" (in better times it would be euphemistically called an "overcoat"), honestly . . . with a tight officer's, or rather cadet's, belt . . . On my feet I wore common felt boots, although not men's boots—they were my size—but they resembled elephant hooves in the presence of the patent leather pumps. My whole costume, due to its very monstrosity, freed me from any suspicion of pretentiousness.

Unlike Mayakovsky, Tsvetaeva in this description does not glamorize her own clothes, as if she is afraid to lose her poetic self in the gaudy skirts of the poetess. Her peculiar antiaestheticism especially in her later work is a protective shield and a reaction against the cultural overaestheticization of femininity. The woman-poet wants to kill the traditional feminine heroine in herself as an act of self-defense so that this heroine will not in turn be able to kill the poet in her. For in our culture a self-reflective male poet is compared with the artist Narcissus, while a woman-poet with a looking glass is immediately equated with a figure of Vanity, desperate for male approval.

Tsvetaeva writes against and in spite of the other's gaze. The use of her own clothes in her writings (except in the early collections of poems *The Evening Album* and *Magic Lantern*) is often parodic: her clothes are often depicted, as in the description just cited, as extravagantly ugly, unpretentious, and antifeminine. They represent the poet's material poverty, rather than a style. In fact, one of Tsvetaeva's longest descriptions of dress occurs in her letter to Teskova, in which she asks her woman friend to send her any sort of secondhand, relatively clean dress, because she simply had nothing to wear.[27]

Tsvetaeva's antiaestheticism, as well as the clothes she wore at the

evening of poetesses, however, are obviously an artistic statement and not a sign of neutrality. (It is hard to imagine any "neutrality" in clothes. Indeed, how can one be *clothesless*, when nakedness itself makes a stronger statement than the most outrageous apparel.) Tsvetaeva describes the other poetesses as dressed "in accordance with the themes and meter of the verses—freely." In a curious way, Tsvetaeva's own free-spirited attire reflected the style of the poems she chose to recite.

The essay "The Hero of Labor" is full of intended and unintended ironies, both on the part of Bryusov and on the part of Tsvetaeva. Bryusov, for instance, persists in addressing poets, whom he has selected entirely on the basis of their gender, with the Soviet neutral term "comrade" ("tovarishch"), which he always pronounces after a meaningful pause. "Comrade" is one of those grammatically masculine words which are supposed to be semantically neutral and proclaim the revolutionary equality of rights, but in fact mask a new (or an old new) revolutionary ideal of virility which must be adopted equally by men and women.

Bryusov's "comrade poetess" is a curious oxymoron which disguises a subtle or not so subtle condescension. "Comrade Tsvetaeva" as a participant in the evening of poetesses is a peculiar character with quite an ambiguous political and sexual makeup. Let us look at the poem with which Tsvetaeva ends her performance at the recital, a poem intended as a radical subversion of the "comrade-poetess" mask. She claims to recite these "feminine poems" without "I," and without love, in order to demonstrate that "reciting poetry to the audience makes no sense" and, finally, to tell the Red Army soldiers "the truth of the wife of a White officer." Thus, she aims at being not only antifeminine but also anti-Soviet. An interesting example of authorial framing of a poem, it is preceded by descriptions of authorial intention, of her mode of recitation, and of the clothes she is wearing. However, this authorial framing is in itself a part of Tsvetaeva's modernist prose, a part of her self-mythification, a part of her biographical legend. The poem is a revision of old myths about femininity and rebellion and a transgressive rewriting of Tsvetaeva's authorial claims.

"Кричали женщины ура! и в воздух чепчики
    бросали . . ."

Руку на сердце положа,
Я не знатная госпожа!
Я—мятежница лбом и чревом!

Каждый встречный, вся площадь—все!—
подтвердят, что в дурном родстве
Я с своим родословным древом.

Кремль черна чернотой твоей!
Но не скрою, что всех мощей
Преценнее мне пепел Гришки!

Если ж чепчик кидаю вверх,—
Ах! не так же ль кричат на всех
мировых площадях—мальчишки?!

Да, ура!—За царя!—Ура!
Восхитительные утра
Всех, с начала вселенной, вьездов!

Выше башен летит чепец!
Но—минуя литой венец
На челе истукана—к звездам![28]

"The women shouted hurrah and tossed their little bonnets
    up in the air . . ."

Resting my hand on my heart,
I am no distinguished lady!
I am a rebel in mind and in womb!

Everyone I meet, the whole city square,
will affirm that I am on bad terms
with my genealogical tree.

Kremlin! I am black with your blackness!
But I won't hide the fact that of all the relics,
Grishka's ashes are the dearest to me!

And if I toss my little bonnet up in the air—
Oh, but don't street boys yell the same
on all the squares of the world?

Yes, hurrah!—Here's to the tsar! Hurrah!
The splendid mornings of all entrances
since the beginning of the universe!

The bonnet flies up past the towers!
But—passing the crown on the head of the statue
it flies upward to the stars!

The poem begins with an excerpt from the famous nineteenth-century play by Alexander Griboedov *The Misfortune of Being Clever*. It is the

ending of Chatsky's famous monologue "And who are the judges," which satirizes "fathers of the fatherland" and represents women exclusively as wives and daughters who are even more grotesque in their "passion for the uniform."

In Tsvetaeva's poem, the caricatural and pathetic women throwing their little bonnets into the air in a fit of official patriotic exaltation become female rebels. Moreover, the perspective shifts from the anonymous third person plural to the first person singular. In spite of Tsvetaeva's claim, we encounter here a strong and passionate "I," which is definitely female but antifeminine in Bryusov's sense. However, it is not the "I" of the wife of the White officer. Rather, the speaker in the poem is an anarchic female rebel, "on bad terms" with her pedigree and in a discontinuous relationship with history. Her hero is the impostor Grishka Otrepiev, the pseudo-Dmitry, unsuccessful pretender to the Russian throne—a perfectly heretic genealogical tree for a female rebel. Tsvetaeva's promise is fulfilled: this is not a "love poem." And yet it is extremely passionate in its diction, its numerous exclamations and Tsvetaeva's characteristic disjointed syntax.

The use of female attire in this poem is very interesting. The infamous little bonnet (*chepchik*) of Griboedov's pathetic wives and daughters, an ultimate feminine attribute of "the angel in the house," by the end of the poem loses its deprecatory diminutive suffix and becomes "chepec," a bonnet-banner of fresh rebellion against the authorities. Moreover, Tsvetaeva's bonnet is always linked to flight—a theme that will be developed later in my discussion of the essay on Nataliya Goncharova. The act of tossing it up in the air is compared with the boyish enthusiasm found in all the squares of the world, a kind of universal enthusiasm of revolt.

The poem is both politically subversive and romantically ahistorical. Its famous lines, dangerously provocative when read in front of the Red Army soldiers three years after the revolution—"Da, Ura!—za carja!—Ura!" ("Yes, hurrah! Here's to the tsar! Hurrah!")—rhyme with the romantic "voskhititel'nye utra" ("splendid mornings") of eternal entrances, a fact that immediately erases the historical specificity of the first line. In typical Tsvetaeva fashion, the stereotyped political slogan is set next to an ungrammatical construction (the plural of "mornings" [utra] does not exist in Russian) as a peculiar affirmation of poetic liberty.

With a similar poetic liberty, Tsvetaeva both transgresses and reaffirms the "feminine" frames of reference in the poem. On the one hand, the poem features an unconventional heroine who participates in the rebellious enthusiasm of the street boys. On the other hand, it ends up retailoring and making a fetish of the old bonnet of Griboedov's wives and

daughters. In spite of Tsvetaeva's passionate claims in her article, the poem she read at the evening of poetesses does not completely escape feminine trappings. But the trappings certainly appear altered and reshaped, far beyond Bryusov's conventional design.

In her essay "Nataliya Goncharova," Tsvetaeva again addresses the question of the relationship between art and gender.[29] At the center of the essay is a contrasting juxtaposition of the two Goncharovas. Nataliya Goncharova, the wife of Pushkin and Lanskoy, was an exemplary feminine beauty (*krasavica*), empty and wordless.[30] Hers is an everyday biography (*zhitejskaja biografija*), that is, a biography consisting entirely of the events of everyday life. The other Goncharova, her distant relative, the artist—to quote Tsvetaeva—"did not condescend to beauty, as Natasha Rostova did not condescend to the intellect." Hers is a "purely masculine" biography (*chisto muzhskaja*), a biography of the creator through the creation.

Tsvetaeva writes that the opposite of beauty is not the beast ("la belle et la bête") but "the essence, the personality, the mark" ("sushchnost', lichnost', pechat'"). This quote curiously paraphrases some of Flaubert's pronouncements, in which he contrasts the artist and the woman. Unlike a woman, who is intuitive, natural, voiceless, and entirely absorbed in everyday life, the artist has to be a monster in everyday life, an *homme-plume* (man-pen), a martyr of writing. According to Tsvetaeva, the opposite of female beauty is "essence," which suggests universality, atemporality, a space beyond gender distinctions, and is equated here with the purely masculine.

Tsvetaeva's emphasis on "pure" rather than impure, vulgar, macho-type masculinity is interesting. It emphasizes the metaphoric dimension of her discussion and is analogous to Mandelstam's notion of ideal or idealized virility, described in his essay "On the Nature of the Word." Tsvetaeva internalizes gender distinctions in art. And yet her "pure masculinity" is exemplified by female artists and writers (Goncharova, George Sand, and others). It is the purely masculine side of the split female personality that she values most, which provokes a tension, a contradiction, a suspension of the conventional cultural mask.

Tsvetaeva relates a famous episode of Goncharova's exhibitionism— her walks around St. Petersburg half-naked, with her face painted with avant-garde flowers. But she carefully differentiates between the artist's paint and female makeup. She stresses that Goncharova neither "put on rouge" nor covered up wrinkles, but decorated ("ne krasila, a izukrashivala") her face, like a canvas. It was the act of an artist, not of a woman.

The bonnet of Griboedov's wives and daughters reappears here with an

even more radical alteration. The image that in Tsvetaeva's imagination links her with Goncharova is that of Goncharova's grandmother swinging in Tsvetaeva's yard (they happened to be neighbors in Moscow) because she did not wish to meet potential fiancés.

> Бабушка, качающаяся на качелях, потому что не хочет женихов! Бабушка, не хотящая женихов, потому что качается на качелях! Бабушка, от венца спасающаяся в воздух! Не чепец кидающая в воздух, а самое себя! . . .
> Мои пятнадцатилетние стихи—не Гончаровой ли бабушки качели?[31]

The grandmother is swinging on the swing in the garden because she does not want any fiancés! The grandmother who does not want fiancés because she is swinging on the swing in the garden! The grandmother escaping from a wedding into the air. Tossing not the bonnet but her own self into the air! . . . My verses written at age fifteen, aren't they the swing of Goncharova's grandmother?

Here a bonnet, a piece of clothing, a synecdoche and potentially a metaphor for femininity, is poetically and ideologically transformed. It does not simply stand for something else; rather, it is linked to flight itself and thus to *the very process of metamorphosis or metaphorization.* The flying bonnet turns into a flying self, a feminine self flying away from traditional feminine roles, or not even flying *away* from something but simply enjoying flight for its own sake. This flight is the foreplay for writing poetry; it offers a chance to turn away from the feminine heroine, not necessarily "to kill her off" but to leave her behind. In one gesture Tsvetaeva turns a metonymical connection with Goncharova's grandmother—who was Tsvetaeva's neighbor—into a metaphorical one; she wishes to adopt Goncharova's grandmother, to become her impostor granddaughter, her granddaughter-in-art (not in-law) and a blood sister of Nataliya Goncharova. The Nataliya Goncharova of Tsvetaeva's essay incarnates her exemplary artist—a female artist who kills the heroine in herself, or simply flies away from her, a female artist with a purely male biography. The peculiar kind of artistic bisexuality that Tsvetaeva advocates here is female virility, a flight away from the fragile poetess with her seductive disguises that were designed by sympathetic, patronizing poets.

In *The Tale of Sonechka* Tsvetaeva's duel with a poetess turns into a love encounter. In this tale of love, theater, and revolution, Tsvetaeva stages a large repertoire of gender roles and plays many of them herself. To quote Sonechka's nanny: "It's a revolution now, a great cataclysm . . .

One does not distinguish men from women, especially among the deceased" ("Sejchas revoljucia, velikoe sotrjasenie, muzhchin ot zhenshchin ne otlichajut, osobenno pokojnikov").[32] In fact, most of the characters in the novella, who happen to be professional actors or poet-playwrights, have ambiguous sexual identities, and the relationships between them are, at the very least, triangulated. Hence it is possible to talk not only about bisexuality but also about the general fluidity of sexual identities.

At the center of the tale is Tsvetaeva's ideal tragic couple, a poet and an actress—the poet-playwright Marina and Sonechka, "a woman, an actress, a flower, a heroine." For Marina Sonechka exemplifies true femininity, unidealized, unbridled, unstructured, excessive. And this is why Sonechka is "unloved by men": her peculiar, deeply feminine intelligence goes beyond "pseudo-feminine pseudo-Beatrice and pseudo-Carmen." Even her name, a diminutive of Sophia, appears significant, almost symbolic. It is one of those unpremeditated, uncanny coincidences that easily yield to allegorization. According to the Russian philosopher Vladimir Solovyov, Sophia is the name of the Eternal Feminine, Feminine Wisdom, the Symbolist Muse, which then metamorphosed into Blok's famous "belle dame." The name "Sonechka," flaunting its endearing diminutive suffix ("umen'shitelivo-laskatel'nyj"), belongs to a different discourse.[33] It is a feminine term of endearment, an element of feminine language that is inappropriate for a beautiful, incorporeal, ideal *belle dame*. The name is part of Sonechka's own discourse, which, as Tsvetaeva writes, is full of diminutive suffixes—diminutive, imploring, and endearing.

Marina recreates by memory the long monologues of her beloved, which form almost one third of the tale.

> И вот, Марина, так любя ваши стихи, я безумно, безнадежно, безобразно, позорно, люблю—плохии ... такие, Марина которых никто не писал и все знают ... "крутится, вертится шар голубой,/крутится, вертится над головой/ крутится, вертится, хочет упасть/ка-ва-лер барышню хочет украсть." Нет, Марина, не могу! Я вам это—спою! (Вскакивает, заносит голову и поет то же самое ...) А теперь, скажите, Марина, вы это—понимаете? Меня такую, можете любить? ... Потому что это просто—блаженство (речитативом, как спящая)—Шар—в синеве—крутится, воздушный шар монгольфьер, в сетке из синего шелку, а сам—голубой, и небо—голубое, и тот на него смотрит и безумно боится, что—бы он не улетел совсем! А шар от взгляда нач-

инаег еще больше вертеться, и вот-вот упадет и все монго-
льфьеры погибнут!³⁴

And Marina, while loving your poems so much, I madly, hopelessly, dis-
gustingly, shamefully love bad verses—those verses, Marina, which nobody wrote but everyone knows, like "the blue balloon is turning and
spinning,/turning and spinning overhead/turning and spinning and wishing to fall/a young man wishes to kidnap a girl." No, no, Marina, I can't,
I'll sing it to you . . . (She jumps, tosses her head and sings the same.)
And now, tell me, Marina, do you understand it? Can you love me the way
I am? Because it's just bliss (she recites as if asleep)—a balloon—in the
blue of the sky—is spinning, a fire balloon, in the net of blue silk, and it
itself is blue, and the sky is blue, and one looks at it and is scared to
death that it might fly away forever! And from his glance the balloon is
beginning to spin more and more, and it is about to fall down and all the
fire balloons will die!

Sonechka's speech reveals all the mannerisms of the actress and poetess: extremely passionate diction, immoderation, excessive use of exclamations, repetitiveness, and flights of fancy. It curiously intertwines different clichés from literary and popular culture (paraphrasing Pushkin,
"I madly, hopelessly love") and popular "cruel romances" in one line.
Sonechka is a professional actress, and a potentially exemplary poetess,
since the poetess is seen primarily as an actress, a heroine, the opposite
of the antitheatrical, solitary, and self-effacing author. We could call her
"a poetess in life," paraphrasing Breton's famous statement that his friend
Jacques Vaché was "a Surrealist in life," even though he never wrote
poetry. Sonechka's monologues display genuine poetic insights, emotional generosity, and a passion for cheap melodrama which comes from Dostoevsky's hysterical and sentimental heroines that she impersonated on
stage. As Karlinsky remarks, it is possible that Tsvetaeva never read
Netochka Nezvanova, since she was generally not interested in Dostoevsky, and yet the discourse of Dostoevsky's that exalted girls in love with
each other—one of the first of such instances in Russian literature—
enters the novella through Sonechka's speeches.

In Sonechka's confession of her love for "bad poetry"—passionate
gypsy songs and cruel romances of what is often called philistine (*me-
shchanskaja*) urban culture—we see a connection between feminine aesthetic obscenity and notions such as Peter Brook's "melodramatic imagination" and kitsch. The aesthetic obscenity is produced by heightened
theatricality, unrefined emotionalism, and the nontranscendental sentimentality and sympathy that does not allow one to construct an autono-

mous, self-reflective, and self-reliant self who can give birth to sublime artistic creations.

Yet Marina appears charmed and inspired by Sonechka's obscenity. She gives her a symbolic feminine gift—the dresses of her grandmother which carry "the burden of four female generations."[35] Marina dresses up Sonechka, giving her a part of her own past, establishing, as with the artist Nataliya Goncharova, not a metonymic relationship but a blood relationship. In the tale the clothes circulate between the narrator and her heroine/poetess as a token of sympathy, affection, and tenderness, and not as a shameful masquerade disguise. Thus, feminine fashions in clothes do not produce the famous figure of Vanity—a woman in front of a mirror, a moralistic portrait created by male artists—but rather a figure of Sympathy.

For Marina the poet (not the poetess, as Sonechka argues) Sonechka becomes a living embodiment of all the empty, ideal female addressees of the male lyric, the Muses and the beloved. The relationship between Marina and Sonechka, however, goes beyond the traditionally unbalanced relationship between the eloquent poet and his ideally silenced beloved, the female beauty—the first Nataliya Goncharova. Unlike her brother poets, Marina's relationship with her female addressee is not based on the lyrical appropriation of the beloved by the poet, but rather on a creative dialogue with her. The element of being in love with the language of the beloved is characteristic of many of Tsvetaeva's infatuations, although most times she was infatuated with well-known poets of the time such as Parnok, Mandelstam, Akhmatova, Pasternak, and Rilke. What distinguishes *The Tale of Sonechka* is the fact that its language of the beloved is culturally ostracized and clearly marked by the poetess's bad taste. Moreover, creative dialogue is realized in it to a much larger degree than in any of Tsvetaeva's other love stories. Tsvetaeva lowers her voice and allows us to hear Sonechka's own speech with all its childish cuteness, diminutive suffixes, sighs, and exclamations. Marina starts as a playwright writing parts for Sonechka and ends up speaking in Sonechka's voice, letting the aesthetically obscene feminine discourse dominate the story.

The verbal intercourse between the two women goes two ways: as Marina's voice becomes contaminated by Sonechka's heightened theatricality, Sonechka becomes infatuated with Marina's poetry. Sonechka talks constantly about her works and exposes Marina's poetic credo. A similar device is used in Gertrude Stein's fictional *Autobiography of Alice B. Toklas*, in which the fictional Alice praises "Gertrude Stein" and talks about

her "philosophy of composition." Sonechka makes a number of crucial statements about Marina. On the one hand, she protests calling Marina "a poetess," which is as absurd as calling her "a member of the intelligentsia" ("intelligentnyj chelovek").[36] On the other hand, Sonechka claims to be personally offended when Marina is called "a remarkable poet"or "a poet of genius."

> Я всегда обижаюсь, когда говорят что вы "замечательный поэт," и пуще всего, когда "гениальный." Это—Павлик "гениальный," потому что у него ничего другого за душой нет, у вас же—все, вы вся. Перед вами, Марина, перед тем что есть—вы, все ваши стихи—такая чу-уточка, такая жалкая кро-охотка.[37]

> I am always offended when people say that you are "a remarkable poet," and especially, "a poet of genius." Pavlik is "a poet of genius" because there is nothing more to him. But as for you, Marina, you have everything, you are whole . . . In comparison to what you are, your poems are such a tiny thing, such a minuscule thing.

According to Sonechka, Marina is more than just a poet, if a poet is simply one who writes verses. She is a poet in life; she has the genius of personality, not simply the genius for versification. This statement echoes one of the crucial statements of Tsvetaeva's poetics, which is expressed in her programmatic article "Art in the Light of Conscience." Here, she distinguishes between a major poet, a great poet, and a lofty poet.[38] A major poet (bol'shoj poet) is one who has a good poetic gift, the lofty poet is one whose spiritual qualities are more important than his often modest poetic gift, while in the great poet the genius for writing and the genius of personality are harmonically balanced: "For a great poet the biggest [poetic] gift is not enough; he needs equal gifts of personality: of mind, of soul, and of will, and an aspiration toward a definite goal."[39] Tsvetaeva shares a Romantic view of the poet, envisioning a poet who both lives and writes poetically. According to her, this "genius of personality" is more often encountered in women, particularly among women who practice love and art with equal intensity, an intensity that often leads to a tragic catharsis.

The radically modified relationship between the poet and her addressee, as well as the continual transvestism of all the characters, influences the very structure of the tale. In fact, Tsvetaeva writes: "In my tale there were no characters. There was love. It controlled the action"

("Dejstvujushchikh lic v moej povesti ne bylo. Byla ljubov'. Ona i dejstvovala licami").[40] Thus, the tale is not structured like any other literary genre; it is structured, or rather obsessively unstructured and potentially destructive, like love itself. Tsvetaeva's prose exceeds the conventions of every literary genre. It is full of contradictions: it is both excessively lyrical and novelistically polyphonic; addressed to Sonechka, to her early avatars, like Vera, and to herself; written in Russian and in French. It consists of seemingly disjointed fragments (from diaries, letters, and postcards), multiple parenthetical remarks, and discontinuous recollections. It participates in many genres—the epistolary novel, the memoir, the essay, the novella—but does not belong to any one of them.

Thus, there is something in the very structure of Tsvetaeva's prose work—its "hysteric" lyricism, overflowing subjectivism—something excessively feminine or excessively poetic, that insults the very notion of "good taste" and provokes passionate critical insults. However, Tsvetaeva's writing cannot be called an "unself-conscious parody" of good writing, as Mandelstam suggested. Tsvetaeva herself is quite aware that the structure of love goes against the grain of conventional literariness.

(Знаю, знаю, что своей любовью "эффект" "ослабляю," что читатель хочет сам любить, но я тоже, как читатель, хочу "сама любить," я, как Сонечка, хочу сама любить, как собака—хочу сама любить . . . Да разве вы еще не поняли, что мой хозяин—умер и что я за тридевять земель и двудевять лет—просто—вою?!)[41]

(I know, I know, that with my love I "diminish" the "effect," that the reader himself wants to love, but I too, like a reader, want to love, like Sonechka, I myself want to love, like a dog, I myself want to love. Do you still not understand that my master is dead and that I am miles and ages away, and I am just howling?!)

Her writing with the urgency of love seems more like an emotional exorcism, a lament, than a composition of a work of art. The logic of the tale is what in Russian is called scornfully "feminine logic" (*zhenskaja logika*)—an expression commonly used to characterize something irrational, illogical, anarchic, capricious, inconsistent, paradoxical, hysterical, or excessively emotional. But in Tsvetaeva's writings this cultural stigma—"feminine logic"—is reevaluated. Her works do not simply exceed, but transgress the gentlemen's etiquette of literary good taste. However, in terms of Tynyanov's concept of literary evolution, defined as a

continuous shifting of the boundaries between literature and *byt*, Tsvetaeva's prose appears to be very innovative. It questions the established notion of literariness and mixes literary and popular genres, including examples of bad verse, philistine cruel romances, and the excessively emotional, "feminine" speeches of Sonechka. Driven by some kind of female complicity or compassion—a "feminine logic," perhaps—the tale becomes aesthetically obscene or, as Tsvetaeva self-consciously remarks, "oversweetened." Sonechka is not only Marina's Muse, but also an author, an exemplary poetess often ridiculed and insulted by poets. The playwright Marina no longer censors the voice of the poetess; instead she falls in love with it.

Even when the poetess is reflected in the loving mirror of a female gaze, however, she cannot escape her tragic wrapping. The love between the playwright and the actress is unconsummated and doomed; Sonechka, as Marina remarks, "chooses a feminine destiny—to love a man, whomever, and him alone," and ends up leaving Marina abruptly without a final farewell. Moreover, Tsvetaeva wrote the tale during her exile in France, where she received news of Sonya Holliday's death. To use Tsvetaeva's Orphic image, the story is a fictional attempt to bring the dead beloved back from Hades, a resurrection that is doomed because of the inscrutable "laws of fate," and perhaps because of the laws of genre too. The love dialogue between poet and poetess is based on the tragic impossibility of any final synthesis, consummation, or fusion; it is a dialogue from exile, conducted through numerous spatial and temporal discontinuities; it takes place almost twenty years after the described events, partly in a foreign language, and after the death of the main protagonist.

Maximilian Voloshin once suggested to Tsvetaeva that she adopt a male pseudonym—like Petukhov, who authored poems about Russia—or even several pseudonyms—like the genius brother and sister Kryukov twins, the creators of Romantic verses.[42] Unlike many famous women-poets of the time who started writing under male pseudonyms, Zinnaida Gippius and Sophia Parnok among them, Tsvetaeva refused to do so. She wished to keep her female identity, but stretch it, push it to the limit, deviating from and violating the established conventions of both literary femininity and literary masculinity. Hers was always a nonconformist one-woman show.

Many critics of Tsvetaeva's work have discussed her problematic relationship to her femininity. Antonina Gove demonstrates how Tsvetaeva gradually goes beyond traditional feminine stereotypes and "transcends

the realm of social roles."[43] Anja Kroth suggests that at the center of Tsvetaeva's "dichotomous vision" is the notion of androgyny, the expression of the ultimate "sexlessness of the soul," a desire for ultimate reconciliation of the terrestrial sexes in one transcendental being.[44] The concept of androgyny, as it persists in the Western tradition—dating back to Plato's *Symposium* and Ovid's *Metamorphosis*—is a very controversial one. The primary root of both androgyne and hermaphrodite always remains male. As Hélène Cixous pointed out, the desire for androgyny is often a veiled desire to devour the other in oneself, to eliminate the difference.[45] Androgyny suggests a final reconciliation of the sexes, the absence of conflict, tension, dialogue, an ultimate self-complacency and self-sufficiency. The Platonic and Romantic "total being" is a disguised Narcissus, who hides his infatuation with his own sex under the mask of universality and wholeness. The infatuation of female artists and critics with the figure of androgyne is a peculiar *Narcissus envy* and often a disguised shame about their femininity, what might be called an *Echo complex*. In fact, Virginia Woolf, the literary mother of the archetypal "poetess" Judith Shakespeare, aspired toward a tranquil aesthetic detachment, a "room of one's own" where the androgynous writer can escape the excessive anger (even when justifiable) of one's always already wounded and hysteria-prone femininity.[46]

Tsvetaeva's theoretical pronouncements, which are tinged with Romantic Platonism, might suggest a figure of androgyne—an embodiment of the desire to transcend cultural sexual stereotypes. However, true to her defiant spirit, Tsvetaeva often deviates from her own critical pronouncements, and her writings remain controversially and unconventionally gendered. They stage multiple gender roles and introduce many unusual transvestites, challenging the very notions of reconciliation and transcendence of conflicts. Tsvetaeva's gender theater is not necessarily "dichotomous" or "dualistic," but rather truly dramatic, characterized by—to use Bakhtin's term—"heteroglossia," what we might call sexual multivoicedness or *polysexuality*. This polysexuality, like Dostoevsky's "heteroglossia" that Bakhtin celebrates, is not devoid of cultural prejudices and myths; in Tsvetaeva's case, it reveals many conflicting attitudes, especially with regard to the relationships between women. And yet it is possible to say that *The Tale of Sonechka* is one of the most unconventional love stories ever written in Russian, one that recovers many culturally repressed feminine dialects and challenges the reader's aesthetic principles. What Tsvetaeva gains is not the disinterested distance of an androgyne, but a peculiar "bisexuality of gaze," a polysexual-

ity that signifies neither the erasure of differences nor the aestheticizing of indifference, but a passionate interplay of distance and involvement, "the multiplication of the effects of the inscription of desire."[47] The gender and genre theater of the self-conscious poetess is much wider than that of the poet; there are many more clothes, disguises, and forms of makeup at her disposal. Aware of her potential repertoire, she can play different roles—tragic and comic, conformist and nonconformist—constantly reifying and demystifying herself as a heroine and as a poet, and never reaching a happy denouement. Tsvetaeva's transgressive practice of aesthetic obscenity presents a serious and self-conscious cultural parody on the aesthetic purism of a poet with no "-ess," a poet lacking the suffix.

The Death of the Poet: Emigration beyond Gender?

Marina Tsvetaeva wrote no suicide note, either in verse or in blood. The two letters that she sent to her close relatives were not preserved. Thus, the only documents we have that might unravel the mystery of her death are her texts, and the peculiar mythology of life and death they elaborate. Again we are engaged in a double movement between literature and biography: Tsvetaeva's suicide highlights certain dangerous paths in the maze of her texts, pointing out crucial patterns and repetitions. At the same time, these patterns in turn shed some light on her final act—if not explaining it, then at least offering us some perspectives from which we can begin to understand it.

Unlike Mayakovsky, Tsvetaeva was not obsessed with the theme of suicide. We could not say, paraphrasing Jakobson, that the motif of suicide had been dominant in her work. On the contrary, as Karlinsky remarks, her poetry is life-asserting, compassionate and not self-destructive.[48] However, Mayakovsky and Tsvetaeva do share certain poetic devices and a similar conception of the poet's poetic life. These allow us to regard Mayakovsky's and Tsvetaeva's suicides as "literary facts," linking in metaphorical chains the death of the revolutionary poet and the death of the poetess.

Like Mayakovsky, Tsvetaeva believed in the Romantic version of the poet's life, emphasizing the importance of the genius of personality, which goes beyond the narrowly understood concept of "literariness." "Life" for her is not just metaphorically related to "work"; it also offers the poet a blood test that exposes the real geniuses, in Tsvetaeva's unconventional sense of this word. To use a Surrealist metaphor, life and art are

seen as "communicating vessels" which are always at the verge of breaking. Also, like Mayakovsky's "I," Tsvetaeva's first person has hyperbolic dimensions. However, there are subtle nuances in the use of this hyperreal first person that distinguish the two poets.

Tsvetaeva resists creating multiple autobiographical icons in a frank Mayakovskian manner—like the beautiful twenty-two-year-old poet, the fop in a yellow blouse, the dramatic poet-hero "Vladimir Mayakovsky," and the revolutionary water carrier and latrine cleaner—and promoting constant self-objectification, but like Mayakovsky she imbues everything with her overflowing subjectivism. A peculiar feature of Tsvetaeva's poetics, which she herself defined as an "excess in the world of measures," a "transgressive element," "hysterical element," or "structure of love," is precisely what fosters communication between the vessels of art and life; they are constantly overflowing onto each other, exchanging fluids, becoming inseparable. Is this excess a part of feminine poetics? If so, is it poetics of a poetess, according to male poets, or a "revisionist" feminine poetics, reevaluated by women writers? Is this "-ess" just another "-ism," a mannerism of style, or is it something more visceral, as Tsvetaeva tried to persuade us? Should we try to inscribe this excess into our critical discourse, or on the contrary let it exceed?

Tsvetaeva's poetics of excess is reflected in her treatment of death, as is demonstrated in the following short poem.

> Вскрыла жилы: неостановимо,
> Невосстановимо хлещет жизнь.
> Подставляйте миски и тарелки!
> Всякая тарелка будет—мелкой,
> Миска—плоской.
> Через край и *мимо*—
> В землю черную, питать тростник.
> Невозвратно, неостановимо,
> Невосстаносимо хлещет стих.[49]

> I have opened my veins: life gushes out,
> Unrestrained, unrestorable.
> Go ahead, bring bowls and plates!
> Every plate will be too shallow,
> every bowl too flat.
> Spilling over the edge, and beyond—
> into the black earth, to feed the reeds.
> Irretrievable, unrestrained,
> unrestorable, verse gushes out.

"I have opened my veins" belongs to the Russian tradition of verses written in blood, among them the suicide poems of Esenin and Maya-kovsky. In the poem figurative death is linked to the excess of life. The poet's blood/ink gushes out, breaks and overflows all possible containers and vessels—veins, plates, bowls, and lines on the page. The connection of the Russian *stikh* (verse) and *stikhija* (element, or source of both verse and life) is suggested in many of Tsvetaeva's poems. The typography of the sixth line of this poem dramatizes the excess, emphasizing it through repetition: the blood gushes out not only *over* the edge but also *beyond* it. As Gove states, there are indirect references to the "woman's *byt*" in the images of "mundane domestic utensils," and there is an obvious use of the feminine in the first person: "I opened (fem.) my veins" ("vskryla veny").[50]

The poet's death is not depicted as such in this poem; it is only hinted at in the image of excessive life giving and nurturing, in the poet's self-sacrificial maternity. Suicide and maternity, the gushing out of poem and life (in Russian, "life" is feminine and "verse" is masculine) and the bursting into blood and ink, overflowing all vessels—all these contradic-tory images are intertwined in the poem, exceeding many critical grids for the discussion of death. In my search for the poetics of death in Tsve-taeva's work, or rather in my search for the threads that might lead to the mystery of her own suicide, I will keep in mind this notion of excess and avoid confining it to any particular critical vessel. I will try to open up the controversial possibilities of different genres and genders of death, as well as demonstrate how the excess of life invades Tsvetaeva's writings and how the poetic function shapes her life, and its tragic ending.

In Tsvetaeva's writings, death is regarded as a transcendence and as a transgression, as a feat and a feast, as an escape into the poet's incorpo-real paradise and as a reenactment of feminine tragedy. The passing away of Mayakovsky and Rilke affects Tsvetaeva's poetics of death. Tsvetaeva writes about Mayakovsky's "suicides"—always in the plural, juxtaposing figurative and actual death and showing how in certain critical circum-stances a poet's suicide can reaffirm his or her poetic identity.

Владимир Маяковский, двенадцать лет подряд верой и прав-дой, душой и телом, служивший—"Я тебе отдаю, атакующий класс!/Всю свою звонкую силу поэта"—кончил сильнее, чем лирическим стихотворением—лирическим выстрелом. Дв-енадцать лет подряд человек Маяковский убивал в себе Маяковского-поэта, на тринадцатый поэт встал и человека убил.[51]

Vladimir Mayakovsky, who truly and faithfully served for twelve years, with his body and soul—"I am giving to you, the attacking class, all my sonorous power of the poet"—ended more powerfully than with a lyric poem—with a lyric shot. For twelve years in a row Mayakovsky the person was murdering in himself Mayakovsky the poet, and in the thirteenth year, Mayakovsky the poet stood up and murdered the person.

Mayakovsky is a controversial figure in Tsvetaeva's poetic world: "poet among heroes, hero among poets," "epic poet" for lyric poets like Pasternak, and a lyric poet when confronted with epic times. He is a "revolutionary poet," according to Tsvetaeva, and not simply "a poet of the revolution" ("le Chantre de la révolution"—Tsvetaeva is probably referring to André Chénier), because he combined in himself poetic and heroic elements. And yet the act of suicide is regarded as a victory of the poet, as an ultimate *poetic* transgression, and a subversive political gesture, subversive precisely due to its artistic anarchism. With the "lyric shot," her Mayakovsky declares his poetic independence from the Soviet revolutionary officialdom.

Besides critical essays, Tsvetaeva wrote a poem, a cycle of poems, dedicated to Mayakovsky in which she develops some of the same themes. Curiously, Tsvetaeva's response to Mayakovsky's suicide alienated her from both the Parisian White émigré community and from Soviet sympathizers. As usual, she was able to make enemies in both camps with one stroke of the pen. The verses she dedicated to Mayakovsky represent her poetic attack against narrow political delimitations.

The poem has an unconventional structure of address. The "I" almost does not appear—which is quite uncommon for Tsvetaeva. Instead the poem incorporates many voices and discourses—colloquial speech, common Soviet discourse, quotes from the émigré papers, and folkloric refrains, especially in the conversation of the two suicide poets Mayakovsky and Esenin. Suicide is inscribed in the poem precisely as a subversion of different discourses, the breaking of the vessels of art and life. Here again, as in the poem "I have opened my veins," the ruptures in Tsvetaeva's syntax and in the poem's typography reflect the peculiar unstable and transgressive status of death as a poetic figure. The poem starts with the image of blood on the front page of a literary newspaper, blood breaking through the typographic line.

Литературная—не в ней
Суть, а вот—кровь пролейте!

Выходит каждые семь дней.
Ушедший—раз в столетье![52]

> The literary—the heart of the matter
> is not in it—shed the blood!
> The newspaper comes out every seven days.
> The departed—once a century!

Pushkin once remarked that *krov'* (blood) always demands *ljubov'* (love), and indeed love appears in the next poem again as a transgression of literary conventions. Tsvetaeva uses as an epigraph the line from Mayakovsky's poem that appeared in his final message—"Ljubovnaja lodka razbilas' o byt" ("Love boat has crashed against the daily grind"). This line, as I demonstrated in the previous chapter, was mistranslated by many foreign admirers of the Russian revolutionary poet. Tsvetaeva notes that the words used in this line belong to a different vocabulary and sound "un-Mayakovskian," that is, not conforming to the official image of the "Comrade Mayakovsky" mask. She addresses Mayakovsky ironically, parodying the pseudo-folk rhythms of official Soviet poetry: "One wouldn't give a half-penny/For such a ringleader./That love boat, comrade, what language does it come from?" ("I polushki ne postavish'/Na takogo glavarja,/Lodka-to tvoja, tovarishch, iz kakogo slovarja?").[53] This transgression of the officially "censored" Mayakovskian vocabulary is reflected in Mayakovsky's final act itself.

Вроде юнкера, на Тоске,
Выстрелевшего—с тоски!
Парень, не по-маяковски
Действуешь: по шаховски! . . .

То-то же как на поверку
Выйдем, стыд тебя заест
Совето-российский Вертер,
Дворяно-российский жест.[54]

> Like the cadet in *Tosca*
> who shot out of grief,
> fellow, you are acting un-Mayakovskian,
> you are acting like a lord . . .

Fellow, when we check you out,
you will surely burn with shame,
you, Soviet Russian Werther
with your Russian gentry act.

Suicide makes Mayakovsky a Romantic hero, a Soviet Russian Werther and a poet whose pedigree is no longer that of a Soviet "comrade." In this poem Tsvetaeva does a clothes reading of Mayakovsky. In the first poem of the cycle we encounter Mayakovsky's by now infamous yellow blouse, which is then supplanted by the "ordinary dark costume" and "tough boots" of a macho revolutionary. In the other poem prefaced by Mayakovsky's epigraph about the "love boat," the poet's costume reveals "White-class layering," white as opposed not so much to yellow but to the revolutionary red. ("White" was frequently romanticized by Tsvetaeva, who often described the White officers as the last Romantic heroes.) Mayakovsky's white layering, disclosed by Tsvetaeva, is an alien texture in his otherwise perfectly revolutionary outfit.

The last poem of the cycle describes an interesting post-mortem tête-à-tête between Esenin and Mayakovsky, a man-to-man, poet-to-poet, suicide-to-suicide talk over a glass of vodka, in which the two poets decide to blow up the world. Tsvetaeva's relationship to her hero is ambiguous. Her tone is that of ironic comraderie, rather than of the peculiar, almost uncanny intimacy that characterized Mayakovsky's own poem to Esenin, or Tsvetaeva's poems to Rilke. It is unclear whether Tsvetaeva was aware of Mayakovsky's attacks on her; in any case this poem can hardly be accused of any elements of "literary femininity." It is more of a man-to-man talk—reflections of an elder brother, perhaps—at once sympathetic and ironic. At the same time, Tsvetaeva's addresses to Mayakovsky are imbued with some maternal intonations: "So that our dear country would not die out/for lack of restless fellows,/go ahead, baby Volodimer,/you can have (*volodej*) the whole world" ("Chtoby kraj rodnoj ne vymer/Bez otchajannykh djadej/Bud', mladenec, Volodimer/Celym mirom volodej").[55]

In her own unconventional, poetic way, Tsvetaeva motivates Mayakovsky's suggestive name. The poet's last name has already become his official Soviet signature. "Mayakovsky" is the name of Tsvetaeva's enemy, "my dear enemy," as she warmly addresses him, making it almost a term of endearment. But the poet's first name—"Vladimir," his name as a child—is still unspoiled by the official language. "Volodimer" is poetically correlated with"volodej"—a stylized Slavonic form of the verb

"vladet," to possess. Tsvetaeva's first lines sound like a lullaby; she writes to the poet/child Volodimer, wishing that he live and possess the world, because without restless and desperate poets the world itself will die out. Hence in Tsvetaeva's tragedy, "Vladimir Mayakovsky" ("Volodimer") murders "Mayakovsky," and among other possibly tragic endings (between two evils, in Russian) this is a happy one.

Death erupts and disrupts language; it is the wildest poetic trope, pointing to the limits or limitlessness of poetry. In the poem "New Year's Eve," dedicated to Rilke, Tsvetaeva tries to find every possible linguistic, stylistic, and poetic framing for the word "death."

> С наступающим! (Рождался завтра!)—
> Рассказать что сделала узнав про . . . ?
> Тссс . . . оговорилась по привычке.
> Жизнь и смерть давно беру в кавычки,
> как заведомо пустые сплеты.[56]

> Happy coming year! (Born tomorrow!)—
> Should I tell what I did when I found out about . . . ?
> Ssh . . . I misspoke as usual.
> I have long put life and death in quotation marks,
> like fabrications known to be empty.

Thus, she introduces the news of Rilke's death in the ellipsis, as if afraid to distort the tragic fact irretrievably by naming it. The poet's death can be easily trivialized with "ordinary language." In the next strophe she proposes a different typographic element for death—an asterisk.

> Жизнь и смерть произношу с усмешкой
> Скрытою—своей ее коснешься,
> Жизнь и смерть произношу со сноской,
> звездочкой . . . [57]

> Life and death I pronounce with a secret
> smile—you will touch it with your own.
> Life and death I pronounce with a footnote,
> with an asterisk . . .

"Death" is a *reference* or a *transference* to another level; like an asterisk it *defers* the absolute ending. Finally, Tsvetaeva discovers a poetic motivation for Rilke's death: "There is an inner rhyme—'Rainer is dead'" ("Vnutrennjaja rifma—Rajner umer"). However, this murderous

internal rhyme makes the verse bleed from inside, disturbing the everyday routine (*byt*) of the living poet: "What am I to do in the New Year's noise with this inner rhyme: Rainer—dead?" ("Chto mne delat′ v novogodnem shume s etoi vnutrenneju rifmoi: Rajner—umer?").[58] In the very last strophe the word "smert′" (death) abruptly cuts the last line; it stands out by itself, as a wound on the poetic organism, a wound for which there is no cure, no rhyme. And yet the poet suggests that perhaps there are rhymes for the word "smert′," always in plural, but that they exist in a foreign language, in a new language of poetic paradise.

Tsvetaeva's poetic paradise is quite different from the conventional Christian paradise. It is an ideal place for writing, where the poet no longer worries about a good table ("table for an elbow"), a good pen, and some spare time—the bare essentials for poetry which Tsvetaeva herself often lacked. The poet's paradise is not a final resting place; it is a fantastic theater, an amphitheater, with many levels. (Note that the word for paradise in Russian is "rai"—the first syllable of the name "Rainer.")

> Рай не может не амфитеатром
> быть (а занавес над кем-то спущен . . .)
> Не ошиблась, Райнер бог—*растущий*
> баобаб? Не золотой Людовиг—
> Не один ведь бог? Над ним другой ведь
> бог?[59]

> Paradise can only be an amphitheater
> (And the curtain has fallen on someone . . .)
> Am I right, Rainer? God is a *growing*
> Baobab? Not a gold Louis—
> There is not just one God, right?
> Above him there must be another
> God?

"God," like the rhymes to "death," exists only in the plural. The poet is always a polytheist, or even a *poettheist* for whom "God" is a fantastic creature that can be compared only to the ever-growing "baobab."[60] "Baobab" is poetic babble; it contains two letters of the word "God," *bog*, the word which, like the word "death," is for the poet a profanation, a sacrilege committed in the naming of something unutterable. So "baobab" functions like a cipher in a children's game, a magical, nonsensical *bog-baba-baobab* that evokes God (*bog*), woman (*baba*), and an exotic plant (baobab). The poem estranges the discussion of death from

both the everyday and religious contexts, and suspends its trivialization.

Joseph Brodsky writes in his brilliant analysis of the poem that Tsvetaeva was not interested in traditional theology, but rather in poetic cosmogonies.[61] She shares a certain poetic version of "eternal life" that has no beginning or end. This optimistic version of poetic infinity can be compared with the Bakhtinian notion of the unfinalizability of dialogues. Poetic communication continues beyond entropy and chaos. The poet's dialogical paradise is a kind of theater *ad infinitum*, where the curtain periodically falls, and then rises again for a new drama.

Death is not a final arrival or a final departure, but rather the most far-removed stop in the poet's "emigration," a vantage point from which earthly "bellevues and belvederes" would seem ridiculous. In the middle of "New Year's Eve" Tsvetaeva uses a motif from Baudelaire's "Voyage," one of her favorite poems, which she translated into Russian. She echoes Baudelaire's ending, the apostrophe to "Old Captain Death," expressing the desire to "plonger au fond du gouffre, Enfer ou Ciel, qu'importe?/Au fond de l'Inconnu pour trouver du *nouveau!*" ("to plunge into the depth of the abyss, Hell or Heaven, doesn't matter/Into the depth of the Unknown to find the *new!*").[62] Tsvetaeva rewrites these lines as:

> Значит жизнь не жизнь есть. Смерть не смерть есть.
> Значит—тмится, допойму при встрече!—
> Нет ни жизни нет ни смерти—третье,
> Новое.[63]

> That means life's not life. Death's not death.
> It means—it vanishes, I'll seize it when I meet it!—
> There's neither life nor death—there's a third thing,
> Something New.

The poetic journey consists of crossing and recrossing the boundaries between "life" and "death," rewriting these words with different syntax and punctuation, searching for "newness" and innovation. In the essay "The Poet and Time," Tsvetaeva writes:

> Всякий поэт по существу эмигрант, даже в России. Эмигрант царства небесного и земногн раяприроды . . . Эмигрант из бессмертья во время, невозвращенец в свое небо.[64]

> Any poet is, in fact, an émigré, even when he is in Russia. An émigré from the kingdom of heaven, and from nature's paradise on earth. An émigré from eternity to time, a defector from his heaven.

The poet is "always already" an "émigré"—with all the possible political connotations of the word. In the verses to Rilke, Tsvetaeva tries to blur the boundaries between the figurative and literal meanings of the word "emigration," presenting death as a border crossing not radically different from any voyage to a foreign land. Death is both a transgression of the borders of "this world" (from "etot svet" to "tot svet") and a transcendence, never the final one, but only a step up from one balcony to the next in the poetic cosmogonic amphitheater.

The word "emigration" also crops up in Jakobson's essay on Mayakovsky in his description of the "unbound horror" and "uncanniness" that result when "the phantoms of art emigrate into life." Both Jakobson and Tsvetaeva wrote about emigration, in the most commonsensical meaning of the word, during their own experience of it, and both attempted to "allegorize" their political situations, to imbue the word with a "poetic function."

Tsvetaeva's poetic description of the "emigration to death," however, betrays the impossibility of final allegorization. Her poem unfolds on the edge of diction itself, on the verge of crying. It is a desperate attempt to burst into language in order not to burst into tears. Yet the abruptness of the lines and the peculiar intonation of lamentation characteristic of the poem betray the repressed tears. As Brodsky remarks, Tsvetaeva's diction, her peculiar word/death play, is an example of *emotional formalism*. This might be compared to the structure of love in *The Tale of Sonechka*, and it is possible to imagine one of the unfriendly critics of Tsvetaeva's time using the adjective "feminine" to characterize her peculiar brand of formal experimentation.

"Emotional formalism" and "structure of love" might appear oxymoronic, but not for Tsvetaeva. For her, both terms reflect a truly poetic logic. In her essay "The Poet on Criticism," Tsvetaeva criticizes both "the formal method" and the trivialized Romantic notion of the poet's "spark of inspiration."

> Так например на утверждения: "никакого вдохновения—одно ремесло" (формальный метод, то есть видоизмененная базаровщина)—мгновенный отклик из того же лагеря . . . "никакого ремесла—одно вдохновенье" . . . И поэт ничуть не предпочтет первого утверждения второму и второго—первому. Заведомая ложь на чужом языке.[65]

To such statements as "there is no inspiration—only craft" (a formal method is a new form of Bazarovshchina [after Turgenev's hero, the eccen-

tric materialist and nihilist Bazarov])—there is a response from the same camp: "there is no craft—only inspiration" . . . The poet cannot prefer the first one to the second or vice versa. These are both deliberate lies in a foreign language.

It seems that the very genre of this apostrophe to deceased poets points beyond the gender difference; or rather, the gender difference is not staged in the foreground here. Rilke becomes Tsvetaeva's ideal addressee, with whom she has an ideal poet-to-poet talk in a paradisiacal setting. Death appears to be a precondition of poetic fraternity; it invites one to read the masculine noun "poet" as finally radically neuter, precluding even the possibility of a feminine suffix.

Death in the Feminine: The Amazon's Severed Breast

The word "poet" is grammatically masculine in Russian; the word "death" (*smert'*) is feminine.[66] In Tsvetaeva's poem addressed to Rilke the latter is used as if it were a neuter noun and is never accompanied by feminine adjectives. In her essay "Art in the Light of Conscience," however, Tsvetaeva suggests a specific feminine version of death, for which she uses a neologism—*mra* (from the masculine *mor*, meaning "pestilence"). *Mra* is associated with the craft of writing.

> Темная сила!
> Мра—ремесло!
> Скольких сгубило
> Как малых—спасло.
> . . . Мра . . . беру как женское окончание, звучание—
> смерти.[67]

> The dark force!
> *Mra*—the craft
> has ruined so many!
> And saved so few!
> I take *mra* for a feminine ending—a sounding of death.

If Tsvetaeva finds an internal rhyme—"Rajner umer" and "Rajner-raj" (*raj* means "paradise")—by analogy we can find an internal rhyme between "mra" and "Marina"—a tragic alliteration. Tsvetaeva plays with her name in a somewhat different way from Mayakovsky. She associates it with historical characters, as in her cycle of poems about Marina Mnishek, the lover of the famous impostor Grishka Otrepiev. But more often

she completely depersonalizes her name, relating it to the sea (using the Latin etymology of the word) or attaching personal poetic images to it—"farewells" (*razluka*) in the poem "Farewell," for example. In *The Tale of Sonechka*, she describes the name "Marina" using Sonechka's articulation; it sometimes sounds long and musical ("Maa-riina") and sometimes abrupt, like the French "Marne." "Mra"—death with a distinctive feminine ending—betrays a peculiar connection with the poet's own name.

In Tsvetaeva's poetics, there appear to be two different tropes for "death"—"smert'" and "mra." If the "death of the poet" should be translated as "smert' poeta"—the title of Lermontov's poem written on the death of the greatest Russian poet, Pushkin, and then echoed by Jakobson—the "death of the poetess" should perhaps be translated with Tsvetaeva's neologism—"mra poetessy" (*mra* of the poetess). Tsvetaeva believed that she had inherited a distinctly feminine tragic ending from the women in her family. It is interesting that to describe her feminine inheritance she uses the word "genius"—"genius of the female pedigree" ("genij roda zhenskogo"). In Russian, the root "rod" in "genij roda" signifies gender, pedigree, family line. In a letter to her Czech friend Anna Teskova, Tsvetaeva states:

Гений нашего рода? (у греков гений и демон одно). Гений нашего рода—женского—моей матери рода—был гений ранней смерти и несчастной любви . . . Я четвертая в этом роду и в ряду, и несмотря на то что вышла замуж по любви и уже пережила всех—*тот* гений рода—на мне.[68]

The genius of our gender [family]? (Greek has the same word for genius and demon.) The genius of our gender—feminine—the genius of my mother's family line—was a genius of early death and unhappy love . . . I am the fourth in our family, and even though I married for love, and I have *already* outlived all of them—*that* genius of the family—is upon me.

Tsvetaeva employs the word "genius" in its German Romantic sense, that is, poetic genius, as well as in its original Latin sense, genius of the family. The first meaning can be seen as masculine (according to Tsvetaeva in her essay on Nataliya Goncharova, although in other writings she tends to view genius as genderless), while the second refers mostly to the poet's female pedigree, both in life and in literature.

Tsvetaeva's mother, who was nearly a literary heroine in the poet's autobiographical writings, is Tsvetaeva's primal tragic ancestor.[69] Her

early death affected Tsvetaeva as a daughter and as a poet. The mother is portrayed by her daughter as an exemplary "female reader" of Russian literature. According to Tsvetaeva, "female" is an important clarifying adjective because women had a peculiar way of reading literature by living it. In Tsvetaeva's semifictional description, her mother lived out the tragic predicament of one of the most famous and most beloved "truly Russian" heroines—the self-sacrificial Tatyana Larina from Pushkin's *Eugene Onegin*. In the end Tatyana casts aside her love for Onegin and remains faithful to her never-loved husband.[70] Her final words to Onegin, "But I am given over to the other and will be forever faithful to him" ("No ja drugomu otdana, i budu vek emu verna"), served as a motto for Tsvetaeva's mother, who rejected her first love and married a widower, following her father's order. She also rejected her other great passion—the passion for music—and in spite of her talent, never became a professional musician.

Marina, the eldest daughter (and, as she considered herself, perhaps unjustly so, the "unloved" daughter, the daughter who was born instead of the much-expected son) defines herself in contrast to her mother. At the same time, she always searches for her mother's unattainable love and wishes to make the mother her own ideal reader. For example, the little "Musya," as the mother calls Tsvetaeva in the autobiographical writings, dares to read literature differently by refusing to identify with the much-glorified, noble, and self-sacrificial heroines of Russian novels. At the age of five she shocks her mother by telling her that she is in love with "Tatyana and Onegin," pronouncing them almost as one word. As a little girl, who is remembered and reconstructed by the mature poet Marina Tsvetaeva, Musya is in love with love itself, especially with the poetic wording of it: "I fell in love not with Onegin, but with Onegin and Tatyana together—maybe a bit more with Tatyana—I was in love with both of them, in love with love."[71] Her perspective is not that of a naive reader—and not at all that of a "female reader"—but rather that of a future poet. Little Musya's writing emerges as a reaction to her mother's music, as a poetic protest, a desire for creative independence. However, as it follows from Tsvetaeva's chapter "The Mother's Tale," which describes Musya's comic, childish interruptions of her mother's fairy tale about a noble robber, the future poet needs to write between the lines of her mother's story. The mother's tale becomes her indispensable grid, which both restricts and inspires. In a similar way, her mother's own life story—her unhappy love, her early tragic death, and her repressed artistic talent—was intimately inscribed into her daughter's poetics. Curiously, in the description

of her mother's influence upon her, Tsvetaeva uses the same imagery as in the poem "I have opened my veins."

> Мать поила нас из вскрытой жилы лирики, как и мы потом, беспощадно вскрыв свою, пытались поить своих детей кровью собственной тоски . . . После такой матери мне оставалось только одно—стать поэтом. [72]

> Mother was feeding us from the open vein of the Lyric, just as we later tried to feed our children the blood of our grief after having mercilessly opened our own vein. After such a mother I had only one way out—to become a poet.

Tsvetaeva the poet inherited her mother's tragic genius as a peculiar feminine birthmark, which is visible in many of her writings and elsewhere as well.

As has been noted many times, Tsvetaeva often gives voice to the famous feminine heroines of world literature and rewrites their stories. Most of Tsvetaeva's favorite heroines—the Amazon, Cleopatra, Eurydice, Ophelia, Phaedra, Tsar-Maiden—die a tragic death, and it is precisely this tragic dénouement of their stories that Tsvetaeva wishes to revise. In her poetic imagination myths intertwine with a peculiar liberty, revealing certain telling tragic patterns. Thus, her Ophelia couples with Orpheus, first metonymically through the "communion by water," in which their dead and immortal bodies float, and second by the "internal rhyme" of their names. But the Shakespearean insane hysterical virgin and the archetypal poet of the Western world (and Rilke's mythical alter ego) do not unite to form a grotesque or idealized androgyne. Instead, they float side by side, touching upon different sides of Tsvetaeva's poetic persona: "So as an unselfish sacrifice to the world/ Ophelia—offers leaves,/ Orpheus—his lyre,/ And me?" ("Tak—nebesckorystnoju zhertvoju miru/ Ofelija—list'ja/ Orfej—svoju liru/ A ja?). [73]

In Tsvetaeva's world, Ophelia is not simply an insane virgin, a female character in the hero's background; she establishes a female complicity with Hamlet's mother, the Queen (see the poem "Ophelia Defending the Queen") and adopts Phaedra as her tragic stepmother. In this way female suicide is reinterpreted: it is not simply a tragedy of love, but a tragedy of maternity. Remembering Jakobson's words about the motif of suicide in Mayakovsky's poetry, one might say that the metaphor of maternity is one of the most vital, informal, and unpoetic ones in Tsvetaeva's work. It is a metaphor of authorship, both biological and literary, a link between

the poet and the woman by analogy and not by some hierarchical subject/object relationship. The mother is neither a poet's addressee nor his or her Muse, but the poet's equal, a poet-in-life.

Contemporary theorists try to reevaluate the mother figure, to rescue her from paternal or filial silencing. Particularly significant is the work of Julia Kristeva who creates new poststructuralist mythologies of the repressed archaic mother.[74] Kristeva attempts to transform the position of the mother from that of a privileged fetish object, both feared and desired, to that of a writing subject. In Tsvetaeva's work the glorification of maternity goes side by side with tragedy, revealing the vulnerability of the mother's position as subject. Maternity, like writing, provides an enormous pleasure of authorship, of procreation, of forgetting one's self. At the same time, it produces a dangerous excess of love that can easily lead to tragedy. This is best exemplified in Tsvetaeva's idiosyncratic revision of *Phaedra*.

In Tsvetaeva's version of the play, the tragedy of maternal love and the conflict between different feminine forces is enacted several times. Hippolyta (or Antiope), the famous Amazon who according to myth dies defending Athens from her own tribe because of her love for Theseus, is presented differently by Tsvetaeva. In a draft of the play Tsvetaeva writes: "The image of Hippolyta, who does not love her husband, but who fights for her son [Hippolytus], is more valuable. Hippolyta remains in the feminine kingdom up to the very end. Theseus is her enemy up to the very end. Hippolyta did not love anyone except her son."[75]

The figure of the Amazon, as it has been frequently argued, is central to Tsvetaeva's poetic mythology. The Amazon-mother is Tsvetaeva's peculiar hybrid creation that seems to emphasize the conflict of two culturally incompatible feminine images—the mother and the warrior. Hippolyta's breasts—one, the severed breast of the Amazon, also seen in the shape of the bow, and the other, the full breast of the mother—recreate the tragic feminine curve, the tragic paradigm of Tsvetaeva's drama of femininity.[76] On the one hand they represent the ideal virility of a woman-warrior, or a woman-artist (compare this with "Nataliya Goncharova"), and on the other they depict the "excessive" femininity that realizes itself in maternity. This *asymmetrical curve of Hippolyta's breasts* presents a geometric design for the conflict of the play. Phaedra herself does not act on her own will, but rather reenacts the tragic predicament of the maternal line of her family, the line of Pasiphae, who was punished for her love for a monster. Moreover, as her nurse remarks, Phaedra's love for Hippolytus, most often referred to as "the Amazon's son," is a reflection of

her own impossible maternity—as impossible as any self-expression, or authorship.

Apart from the tragic chain of mother suicides, the play offers a chain of female "directors," orchestrators of the whole drama. At first it appears that Phaedra's nurse and surrogate mother, who actually makes Phaedra conscious of her love for Hippolytus, is a *maîtresse* of the theatrical ceremony. But as the play unfolds we discover it is the "anger of Aphrodite" and the conflict between the two goddesses Artemis and Aphrodite that is reflected in the drama of the characters. Again, the text is shaped by the paradigm of confrontation between the goddess of love—the embodiment of ideal femininity—and the virile goddess/virgin, huntress and warrior. This confrontation is central to Tsvetaeva's gender theater, in which, in opposition to Shakespearean theater, both masculine and feminine roles are played by female actors. Antonina Gove writes that Tsvetaeva's play reveals different attitudes toward women and "betrays the identification of the poet with her characters."[77] I think it stages the conflict of a female artist; it betrays the one-woman show behind the multiple characters of the play. The play is a perfect example of Tsvetaeva's problematic gender theater, another attempt to write and stage the excessive *structure of love*.

There is one detail in the description of Phaedra's death, however, that might suggest an reverse identification between her and the playwright. Tsvetaeva steps away from the neoclassical view of Phaedra's suicide through poisoning—she is reading Racine at the time—and returns to Euripides' version: her Phaedra hangs herself. Whether Tsvetaeva knew it or not, in classical antiquity hanging was considered an exclusively feminine mode of suicide. Eva Cantarella argues in her essay on the "dangling virgins" that it dates back to the rituals of the vestal virgins, who preferred death to marriage, or to the abandonment of sacred vows, and hanged themselves as part of a communal ceremony.[78] The poet, like one of her heroines, the woman-prophet Sybil, uncannily predicts her own death. Besides describing her own "tragic maternal bloodline,"she creates a fictional line of heroine suicides, an account of women who act out "death in the feminine," in the poetic *mra*.

A bisexuality of gaze is reflected here again; Tsvetaeva's gaze shifts from that of the female director to that of the heroine. She is always in love with two characters at once—with Phaedra and Hippolyta, or with Aphrodite and Artemis. She is both a playwright of a drama from classical antiquity and an actress in her own life, which turned into an unconventional kind of modern tragedy.

Postmortem: Poetess without Quotation Marks

На Одисеевском корабле ни героя ни поэта не было. Герой тот, кто и несвязанный устоит, и без воску в ушах устоит, поэт тот, кто и связанный бросится, кто и с воском в ушах услышит, то есть опять-таки броситься.

Единственное отродясь непонимаемое поэтом—полумеры веревки и воска.

On the Odyssean ship there was neither a hero nor a poet. A hero is one who would persevere without being tied, who would persevere without wax in his ears. A poet is one who would throw himself into the water even when tied up, who would hear with the wax in the ears, that is, once again he would throw himself into the water.

The only thing never understood by poets is the half-measure of ropes and wax.

Marina Tsvetaeva, "Art in the Light of Conscience"

It is rumored that a few days before her suicide Marina Tsvetaeva, having already been evacuated to Elabuga, submitted an application for the position of dishwasher in the local House of Soviet Writers. Her application was refused, perhaps for two reasons—her lack of experience and her excess of qualifications. Again she fell victim to the same dangerous *conjunction of lack and excess* that had haunted her all her life. Whether the story is true or not, it remains very telling, adding one more excessive detail to Tsvetaeva's biographical legend. If we wish to imagine her as some kind of *poète* or *poétesse maudite*, an archetypal struggling artist, this would definitely constitute a very unstylish detail, one that exceeds the cultural iconography of even a poet-pariah.[79] The dish-washing job in the House of Soviet Writers is too "impure" for any poet. The unsavory domestic details and elements of *byt* permeate Tsvetaeva's story, not allowing us to enclose it within any "high" poetic genre.

If Marina Tsvetaeva failed to become a dishwasher in the House of Soviet Writers, she definitely did not fail to end her life's odyssey as a true poet on her own terms. For her the ropes of Phaedra and Odysseus stopped being poetic tropes in the narrow sense of the word. If one were to mythologize the means of the suicide, one would see that Tsvetaeva, perhaps unconsciously and uncannily, chose the ropes, the preferred method of the great heroines of antiquity—the great weavers Phaedra and Antigone. As Margaret Higonnet remarks, "Classically, an Antigone as a weaver of her own destiny hanged herself."[80] Marina Tsvetaeva hanged herself on August 31, 1941, while her son, Mur, and other resi-

dents were not home. Before committing her act, she locked the door and covered it with ropes attached to the wall—a necessary precaution to prevent "a half-measure," an interrupted suicide. This is how Anastasia Tsvetaeva imagines her sister's suicide twenty years later.

> Веревками она замотала дверь обо что-то в стене, хотя был запор, но зачем же ломать запор бедным хозяевам—в военное время все так трудно достать. А пока снаружи размотают целый ворох затянутых веревок—смерть доделает свое дело. Она не ошиблась. Ничего не упустила. Всесторонне, человечно готовилась, и может была вдохновенность в ее действиях—она делала только самое нужное.[81]

> She secured the door with ropes, although there was a lock. But why would she break the lock of the poor landlady—it is so hard to get things in wartime. And while they would try to disentangle the heap of ropes from the outside—death would take its course. She was not mistaken. She took care of everything. She prepared for it with her whole being. Maybe there was even an inspiration in her actions—she was doing only what was necessary.

Anastasia Tsvetaeva proposes a purely personal and "feminine" reason for her sister's suicide in her tragic maternity. Mur was said to have told his mother, during a family quarrel, that one of them would be carried out of the house dead. Anastasia states that Marina's suicide, which "in an uncanny way tied her son and herself together," was a "sacrifice" in order to rescue him. Thus we have a reenactment of the Amazon Hippolyta's and Phaedra's story—the tragedy of a self-sacrificial maternity. While the suicide of the revolutionary poet Mayakovsky was regarded as a strictly personal (and not political or poetic) affair, his drama was pictured as a drama of Romantic unrequited love. Here the story of the poet's suicide turns into an ancient tragedy of maternal sacrifice. Anastasia Tsvetaeva was very distant from her sister during her last years. Her explanation of the suicide, which was officially accepted in the Soviet press, might be another of her "ceaseless strivings to exculpate Soviet society and history for ever being wrong in any way."[82] It remains, however, an interesting example of a "feminine" explanation of the suicide—the suicide of a woman, and not of a poet.

Should we then regard Tsvetaeva's tragic dénouement as in a feminine paradigm and compare it to the suicides of other women poets and writers of the twentieth century—Virginia Woolf, H.D., Anne Sexton, Sylvia

Plath, and others? What is the relationship between *mra* and the suicide of the revolutionary poet?

Margaret Higonnet proposes a fascinating theory of the feminization of suicide in the Romantic period. She starts with an enigmatically suggestive sentence: "Suicide, like woman and truth, is both fetish and taboo."[83] For her, suicide is an important cultural sign, a reflection of cultural myths. If in antiquity suicide was seen mostly as a political measure, toward the end of the eighteenth century it gradually became depoliticized and feminized. "The feminization of suicide was also prepared by the eighteenth-century cult of the Man of Sensibility, which reformulated the Greek congeries of meanings around *pathos:* passion, passive suffering, pathos."[84] The nineteenth-century perception of voluntary death as a "crime of the heart" moves from effeminate male heroes like Werther to self-destructive female heroines—Hedda Gabler, Emma Bovary, Anna Karenina. If we follow this theory consistently, the very view of suicide as "a strictly personal matter"—the official Soviet explanation for both Mayakovsky's and Tsvetaeva's deaths—is a cultural "feminization" of suicide, which is again regarded as a private gesture of passion.

In the Soviet Union many attempts have been made to depoliticize Tsvetaeva's tragic story. Yet in her own poetics, as well as in many denouncing critical remarks about her work, her "literary femininity" is often linked to political anarchism. The critic Vishnyak, for instance, likens Tsvetaeva's mentality to "either the consciousness of an anarchist or that of an irresponsible, capricious poetess."[85] In this way, the last capricious gesture of the poetess, who like her beloved heroines of antiquity finally becomes a "weaver of her own destiny," can be seen as politically subversive, even revolutionary. In the act of suicide, the revolutionary poet and the poetess are tied together.

There are in fact several purely political explanations for Tsvetaeva's suicide. Kiril Henkin proposes that Tsvetaeva was driven to the brink when an agent of the local NKVD (the KGB of Stalin's time) "in a misguided belief that he was helping Tsvetaeva to consolidate her position in the eyes of the Soviet authorities, ordered her to report on the other evacuated writers," thus becoming an unofficial NKVD informer.[86] This seems quite plausible, although it is as much based on rumor as Anastasia Tsvetaeva's version of self-sacrificial maternity.

Everyone in the celebrated poetic quartet—the four major Russian postsymbolist poets Akhmatova, Tsvetaeva, Pasternak, and Mandel-

stam—was in different ways and to different extents persecuted by the authorities, excluded from the official Soviet canon, and turned into unofficial cultural legends. Only Akhmatova and Pasternak survived the war and the Stalinist purges. The deaths of the two other poets—Mandelstam's murder in a Stalinist camp and Tsvetaeva's suicide—became a poetic mirror for their survivors, a reminder, a voice of artistic and civic consciousness. If the poetic apostrophes to canonized "geniuses" like Pushkin or Mayakovsky usually seek to undo the official monument, any postmortem address to Marina Tsvetaeva is haunted by her unmarked grave, her remarkable absence—not only of a monument but of a marked place of burial. Hence Pasternak's poem is about a ritual carrying of her ashes from the unmarked grave in Elabuga.

> Ах, Марина, давно уже время,
> Да и труд не такой уж ахти,
> Твой заброшенный прах в реквиеме
> Из Елабуги перенести.
>
> Торжество твоего переноса
> Я задумывал в прошлом году
> Над снегами пустынного плеса,
> Где зимуют баркасы во льду.[87]

> Oh, Marina, it's time all right,
> and it's not a big effort at all
> to carry from Elabuga
> your abandoned ashes in a requiem.
>
> Last year I started planning
> the solemnity of your transport
> over the snow of the deserted beach
> where the boats winter in the ice.

Marina's absent, disembodied body is a poetic body par excellence, which can serve as an ideal poetic guide to the mystery of death. In the last solemn ritual, the living poet wishes to follow the dead one in her spectral emigration. Since it is impossible to recover the loss and to disentangle the enigma of death, the only way to partake of this mystery is to transport the poet's ashes, her only metonymical earthly remains, to the verge of metaphor (*metaphorein*, to transfer). The poem creates a space inside which writing about death becomes possible. In an early version of the poem Pasternak uses the image of Pushkin's fantastic heroine the Queen of Spades, the uncanny and threatening ghost of an old

woman who haunts all Russian literature from Pushkin to Dostoevsky and beyond.

> Ты б в санях переехала Каму
> В час налетчиков и громил.
> Пред тобой, как пред Пиковой дамой,
> Я б от ужаса лед проломил.[88]

> You would cross the Kama in a sleigh
> in the time of invaders and thugs.
> And before you, as before the Queen of Spades,
> out of horror, I would break the ice.

In the later version, Pasternak discards this comparison between the woman poet and the fantastic, implacable, and horrifying female apparition. And yet even in the verses of the final poem the living poet appears to be haunted by the ghost of the dead one, haunted by her silence in which he reads a promise of resurrection and a reproach of those who did not live out their poetic destiny uncompromisingly. Tsvetaeva's omnipresent absence stirs up Pasternak's guilty conscience, one of a Soviet poet/survivor left with only half-words, half-measures, and linguistic deceptions.

Similarly, in Anna Akhmatova's poem "Komarovo Sketches" ("Komarovskie nabroski") "Marina" reappears as the voice of poetic conscience, a peculiar *genius loci*.[89] Marina Tsvetaeva and Anna Akhmatova, two leading Russian women-poets, had a peculiarly unequal relationship. Tsvetaeva dedicated to Akhmatova a cycle of poems, which opens with a poetic motivation for Akhmatova's name; the stress is put on the first syllable "Akh" (Oh!), which ciphers Tsvetaeva's admiration for her fellow woman-poet. The poems present a good example of Tsvetaeva's *erotic intertextuality*. Akhmatova, for her part, was quite reserved in her attitude toward Tsvetaeva. In the 1920's she regarded Tsvetaeva as too much of a poetess, with her romantic love for Rostand, and her "tastelessness," while she herself practiced restraint and poetic elegance.

Yet, in spite of their crucial aesthetic differences, in the poem written after Tsvetaeva's return from exile in 1940 Akhmatova sees in Tsvetaeva her double, "an invisible girl, a double, a mocking bird." The suicide of one woman-poet was perceived by another as her alternative destiny, her unrealized tragic potential, her "road not taken."[90] "Marina" was interiorized by Akhmatova as her own alter ego, her other extreme, the edge to which she never pushed herself out of a desperate instinct for self-

preservation. Thus, Tsvetaeva's unmarked grave became an uncanny poetic monument that challenges living poets. "Marina" continues her intertextual existence, reappearing at the ends of lines, threatening to break the poetic syntax—something she loved to do so much in her own poems.

Tsvetaeva's absence of general visibility, the absence of her effigy on the streets and squares of cities, and her subversive and "anarchist" politics, neither pro-Soviet nor anti-Soviet, make her much less known in the West than for instance Mayakovsky. Her not belonging to any schools or movements (characteristic of many women artists in general), the polygeneric (or intergeneric) nature of many of her writings, and her peculiar, transgressive *emotional formalism* create difficulties in approaching her life and work.[91]

Akhmatova wrote that Tsvetaeva always remained "dolphin-like"; "one element [*stikhija*, which is related to *stikhi*, verses] was never enough for her."[92] She had to float between the surface and the depths, between life and art, life and death, between genders and genres. Ultimately her death, as well as her writings, yields to many interpretations, to feminine, masculine, and neuter endings. Once again it dramatizes all the conflicts between the root and the suffix of the word "poet," making us finally agree with Sonechka's provocative statement that the title "poet," in spite of its great cultural prestige, could not describe "Marina's" transgressive nature.

Perhaps the word "poetess," if we free it from cultural inhibitions and shame, would ultimately be better suited for Tsvetaeva; it challenges and embarrasses the conventions of academic purism, and it haunts readers with its anarchic, revolutionary, and excessive suffix. But if that is the case, "poetess" has to be rewritten and reinvented to resist all cultural insults and condescendingly precautionary quotation marks.

Conclusion: The Death
of the Critic?

IN THE 1980'S WE WITNESSED not only the death of the poet but also the death of the critic. I use "the death of the critic" here both literally and metaphorically. On the one hand, it refers to the recent passing away of three major theorists of the figurative "death of the author"—Barthes, Foucault, and de Man—and on the other hand, it points to the need to reconsider the cultural myth of the literary critic. In fact, the literary critic has hybrid origins and "impure" blood. Among his or her ancestors are the Encyclopedists of the eighteenth century, salon critics, Romantic philosophers, *hommes/femmes de lettres*, flâneurs, and intellectuals of the nineteenth century. The repertoire of cultural masks of the literary critic include "failed" poets, philosophers, or scientists, socialites, professional academics, teachers by vocation, free-lance intellectuals, and lovers of discourse in any form. What is the relationship between the critic's text and the critic's myth? How can the contemporary practice of literary criticism incorporate this diversity of cultural repertoire and elaborate an interdisciplinary strategy of interpretation?

The deaths of de Man, Barthes, and Foucault touch upon urgent political and ethical issues of our time, including anti-Semitism, AIDS, and homosexuality. Each posthumous publication by the critic or about him points to the limits of textuality and the limitations of the culturally accepted practice of discourse.

The recent discovery of Paul de Man's essays that were written during World War II for a pro-Nazi newspaper and contain anti-Semitic remarks sparked a controversy among professional academic literary critics and gave rise to many sensational journal articles. De Man's story challenged the American myth of a professional academic critic, whose biography and history is comfortably limited to the two conventional sentences on the book cover. Any intrusion of further biographical and historical information threatens the very nature of the institution of academic learning, which is based on fixed boundaries between personal and professional, subjective and scholarly. The necessity to put together the two lives of Paul de Man, in Europe and in America, makes it difficult to draw a trans-Atlantic cultural distinction between the ethical and historical responsibility of a European intellectual and the scholarly and professional responsibility of an American academic. (Incidentally, the very notion of "intellectual" was born in France during another scandalous affair that involved anti-Semitism—the Dreyfus Affair.)

The recovery of de Man's problematic past is an ironic revenge of biography and history upon someone who posited autobiography as defacement and claimed that the bases for historical knowledge are not empiri-

cal facts but written texts, "even if these texts masquerade in the guise of wars and revolutions."[1] Although, the new *facts* about de Man are found in his own journalistic *texts*, the reaction to these texts brings forward their serious political and ethical implications, revealing the impossibility of completely textualizing and disfiguring one's personal and historical memory.

The death of the critic, as well as the death of the poet, serves for the survivors and interpreters as a pretext to capitalize upon their own views. Thus the "de Man Affair" has been heavily manipulated by journalists who used it to voice their fashionable anti-intellectualist critique of the academy, often missing the point—according to Derrida—that the very nature of journalistic writing with its polemical and arrogant superficiality could be at the core of de Man's war-time essays.[2] For many professional critics the recovery of de Man's unknown works has served as a pretext to launch their prefabricated antideconstructionist attacks, while for others it has triggered the impulse to rethink both the shortcomings and the potential of deconstructive reading strategies.[3]

From "a critic without a biography," de Man becomes "a critic with a biography." Now a reader of de Man must read the critic's texts together with or in opposition to his "biographical legend," which can no longer be ignored or erased as neutral. With de Man's biographical legend in mind we can see how the whole corpus of his writings obsessively dramatizes the tension between a radical, modern ahistoricity and the painful burden of history, between defacement and memory. De Man usually desires to privilege the first part of the opposition over the second, and yet the intellectual openness of his late theoretical writings with their complex often paradoxical insights invite the reader to explore various ironic possibilities, including those repressed by the critic himself.

The de Man controversy proves that the relationship between texts and life remains a vitally critical issue. At the same time, it reveals the lack of a comprehensive interpretative strategy or a critical genre that would allow for the incorporation and superimposition of the ethical, historical, biographical, and textual issues. The polemic surrounding de Man raises several crucial questions central to my study. Do the "complete works" of any writer present an organic whole or a collection of fragments? In other words, should we see a continuity or a break between de Man's writing in Europe during the war and his theoretical writing in the United States? Analogously, in what way are we to read a personal history: as a sequence of disruptions, shifts, and discontinuities—as de Man taught us—or as a unified trajectory? How does one distinguish between personal and

theoretical stakes, between desires and repressions operating in text and in life? What is the relationship between theoretical discontinuity and the responsibility of an intellectual? How are we to deal with wars and revolutions that refuse textualization and leave unhealed emotional wounds in readers' minds?

Unlike de Man, who was mainly known in academic circles, Barthes and Foucault were exemplary European intellectuals, who crossed the boundaries between many disciplines, as well as the boundaries between theory and practice of both discourse and politics (especially Foucault). And yet their tragic deaths went beyond the acceptable cultural transgressions. Soon after his mother's death, Roland Barthes was run over by a dairy truck in the Latin Quarter, in his beloved and familiar part of Paris. It was a tragic and somewhat mythical death of a Baudelairean flâneur, a collector of fragmentary insights, a death that was interpreted by many as suicide. The posthumous collection of Barthes's notes and essays entitled *Incidents* appeared a few years after his death. The book includes an article about the light of Barthes's native town Bayonne, observations from travels in Morocco, his "Soirées de Paris," personal notes recounting lonely evenings in Parisian cafés, and failed love stories with young boys.[4] The publication of *Incidents* provoked a serious controversy in France, since many of Barthes's notes were considered to be strictly private and not intended for print.

Again in the center of the polemic are questions about the ethics of writing and publishing. What is our responsibility to the critic's memory? Where do we draw the limits of a critical *corpus?* What discursive (and not only discursive) practices exceed even the most flexible limits of professional ethics? Where should the distinction between private and public, personal and professional, be traced and what myths are behind this cultural censorship?

Barthes's "Soirées de Paris" relates frustrated amorous encounters, neither significant enough nor sufficiently accidental to make it into his book *A Lover's Discourse*. These stories are combined with ordinary and unglamourous observations about the critic's own self, neither flattering nor shocking enough to be included in *Barthes by Barthes*. In other words, judging from the responses to the book, what shocked many readers was the fact that *Incidents* seem to disclose the *obscenity* of Barthes's corpus. And here obscenity refers not so much to the subject matter of "Soirées de Paris" as to its aesthetic quality, or what many critics perceived as a "lack of literary merit." "Soirées de Paris" exposes a raw material of writing, a banal body of the critic and his unaestheticized

everyday life. The sentimental triviality of some of the notes and their unadorned personal character were considered to be excessive even for the seemingly all-inclusive discursive styles of Barthes. In a way these notes defy literariness; they suggest a different, private use of discourse, a need to record everyday eventlessness, to jot down the inessential drifting of the body that, as Barthes's later works suggest, challenge rigid modernist metanarratives.

The death of Foucault, a celebrated historian of textuality, sexuality, and madness, provoked a similar shattering of discourse. Many (although not all) newspapers reported the cause of his death as a brain tumor, which was a sort of euphemistic silencing of the incomprehensible and incurable disease of the 1980's—AIDS. AIDS is an abbreviated name of a syndrome, the name of something that is lacking. And yet in spite of its medical incomprehensibility—in many ways similar to the incomprehensibility of madness—this disease has already been culturally codified; it is associated with practices still considered transgressive, such as drug abuse and homosexuality. Thus the critic, who explored the possibilities of modern disfiguration and the limitations of the institutions of knowledge, at the moment of his death uncannily reacquires a body, an individual body in pain, the body victimized by a new disease that progresses more rapidly than medical science.

We notice from these examples that not only is the poet destined to live through mythifications, immoderations, self-fashionings, and defacements, but so is the critic. In the present theoretical fables of the poet's and the critic's death I have elaborated a series of hinge concepts that allow us to confront the complexity of the relationships among text, life, and culture in each particular case. All of them resulted from the specific textual/contextual elaboration of the initial theoretical premise to trace the tension between cultural myth and the individual practice of writing, between self-fashioning in life and self-fashioning in text.

We have observed how Mallarmé acts out suicidal disfiguration in writing as a kind of preventive therapy to avoid suicide in life. In a similarly paradoxical manner he emphasizes the metonymical relationship between text and life and at the same time practices what I call an *erotics of impurity* that allows him to fold writing and fashioning together.

Rimbaud employs a strategy of disruption, a *violence in (of) poetics* that makes him heroically live out the myth of modern life—only to be absorbed by the literary institution as an exemplary subversive avant-garde figure. As a result, in the interpretation of many literary scholars Rimbaud's peculiar *violence in (of) poetics* is on the verge of becoming

a *poetics of violence*, which then tends to eradicate Rimbaud's scarred body.

Mayakovsky is a figure with *spectacular attributes*—whether Futurist yellow blouse or Soviet bronze jacket—a poet whose life and text seem to take the shape of a single monodrama (even if it is eclectic and modern in style). In his case we observed the so-called *metaphor compulsion*, a tendency to make significant and signifying all elements of everyday existence, which allows us to establish a dangerous connection between literary suicide and suicide in life.

The problem of relating the poet's political engagement and the poet's gender (which is best exemplified in the *revolutionary poet* and the *poetess* but is not confined to these two) further complicates an attempt to see every relationship in terms of the figures of classical rhetoric. In the case of Tsvetaeva I discussed several seemingly oxymoronic terms such as *aesthetic obscenity, emotional formalism*, and the *structure of love*. All of them emphasize the irreducible excess that one encounters in trying to create any interpretative grid around Tsvetaeva's work or life. And yet it is precisely this excess that offers the most revelatory insights into the nature of writing and living.

Most of these contextual *hinge concepts* draw on traditional rhetorical figures and devices (*metonymy, metaphor, personification*) or literary terms (*formalism, structure, poetics*) but are not reducible to them. Rhetorical figures present in a condensed version the working mechanisms, drives, and tendencies that operate in discourse, while the literary terms (which mostly come from the tradition of literary science from Russian Formalism to French Structuralism) allow us to reconsider the boundaries of the literary discipline and different conceptions of the text. At the same time, while relying on both, I have tried to show what are the *breaking points of rhetoric*—the moments of disfiguration, immoderation, and obscenity—as well as the fissures of *discourse* in violence, love, and death.

My analysis has not been confined to the study of the rhetoric of cultural mythification and self-fashioning or to the proofs of the literariness of life. I have also wished to turn the tables on both rhetoric and discourse and demonstrate their *historicity* and cultural conditioning. "Literature," "discourse," "life," "history," and "culture" are often considered to be separate subjects of analysis of different academic disciplines, such as literary criticism/theory, anthropology, history, psychology, and so on. The *hinge concepts* do not investigate the relationship of elements within one academic discipline, rather they focus precisely on the tensions between the traditional disciplines. They allow us to discuss the borderline

cases which are usually dismissed in the face of their methodological complexity. I have attempted to concentrate on those complexities, the gray areas and knots of contradictions, occasionally disentangling them and more often simply making them visible, preserving their aesthetic and vital intensity.

In spite of my own, professionally conditioned drive toward "literariness" I wish to preserve the *difference* between text and life and to avoid subjugating one to the other. In order to open and explore this space of difference we have to trace the ways in which the artistic constructs can, on the one hand, form and inform ordinary experiences and, on the other hand, be deformed and defied by them. This double movement invites us to see literariness or a creative aesthetic impulse in everyday life and to liberate these aesthetic experiences from the confines of "literature" and literary institutions. At the same time, it helps us to deaestheticize literature somewhat and defamiliarize again the violence, pain, and love that it contains.

This study is an exercise in what can be called a *performative criticism*, a kind of criticism that emphasizes the interplay between different disciplines and genres of writing and highlights the transgressive theatricality of lives and texts. "Performative" refers to Austin's and de Man's distinction between "constative" and "performative" utterance. Here it signifies an interactive criticism that both analyzes its subject matter and creatively and rigorously "unlearns"—to use Barthes's term—its own methodology, making visible the gaps in the critical discourse. Also, "performative" can be freely associated with the 1980's genre of "performance arts" which is essentially eclectic and combines different styles, media, and improvisation techniques. Early in the twentieth century a strong emphasis was placed on the elaboration of distinctions between disciplines. Literature was to be "literary," science "scientific," painting "pictorial," and the life of action "absolutely lively" and divorced from fiction. Now it is time to see what has been left behind (out) by the ideal machine of modernism and to retrace the scars and interstices not mapped out by rigidly systematic conceptual grids.

Finally, the figure of death with its multiple incarnations, such as "the death of the author" and the anatomy of criticism, as subversive and suggestive as it might have been, should not be the central privileged metaphor of literary theory. Opening some of the quotation marks around the word "death" might allow us to drift to another, not yet sufficiently explored space where aesthetic experience is not necessarily linked to the death of the subject, and where the making of the literary corpus has

more to do with the individual body than with the corps. Perhaps what the current *fin de siècle* demands is not an apocalyptic or panic criticism predicated on death but a critical rethinking of the process of living and making, not what Jean Baudrillard celebrates as "theoretical violence" but a theoretical sympathy and intersubjective communication. In short, we have to recover a certain kind of nontotalizable and antiauthoritarian ethics that helps to put together the making of poetry, love, and criticism, as well as the making and unmaking of the self. It might be excessive to ask that literary criticism have an obscene and immoderate *structure of love*—Tsvetaeva herself ironically remarked that it could "oversweeten" the story. Nevertheless, necrophilia should no longer be our main scholarly drive.

Notes

Index

Notes

Introduction

1. Jorge Luis Borges, "De alguien a nadie," in his *Otras Inquisiciones* (Madrid: Alianza Editorial, 1979), pp. 143–147. As far as my use of he, he or she, or she is concerned, I neither preserve "he" as a linguistic convention nor use "he or she" everywhere as a mere sign of critical awareness. Rather, I use "he" for the poet or the author, when "he" is culturally implied, as in Foucault's and Barthes's "death of the author." I examine further the notion of linguistic convention and its cultural implications in Chapters 1 and 3 on Mallarmé and Tsvetaeva. "He or she" is used in reference to the contemporary reader or to the poets I selected for the discussion.

2. Stephen Greenblatt, *Renaissance Self-Fashioning* (Chicago: University of Chicago Press, 1980), p. 4. Exceptions do exist: the "vitae" of the Provençal and Catalan troubadours reveal close links to medieval hagiography, and the "proto-Romantic" lives of Christopher Marlowe and François Villon—to name just two examples—are full of heroic and dramatic accomplishments but nevertheless escape cultural sentimentalization and preserve instead a crude picaresque flavor, characteristic of the moeurs of their time. Since my study focuses on the modern period, I cannot fully explore the complexities of the premodern relationship between writing and the making of the self. I would only suggest an extremely thought-provoking quote from Michel Foucault: "It seems to me that all the so-called literature of the self—private diaries, narratives of the self, etc.—cannot be understood unless it is put into the general and very rich framework of these practices of the self. People have been writing about themselves for two thousand years, but not in the same way. I have the impression—I may be wrong—that there is a certain tendency to present the relationship between writing and the narrative of the self as a phenomenon particular to European modernity. Now, I would not deny it is modern, but it was also one of the first uses of writing." *The Foucault Reader*, ed. Paul Rabinow (New York: Pantheon Books, 1984), p. 369.

3. M. H. Abrams, *The Mirror and the Lamp* (London: Oxford University Press, 1980), p. 226.

4. F. V. D. Schleiermacher, *Monologen*, ed. Karl Schiele and Günter Mulert (Leipzig, 1914), p. 22; quoted in ibid., p. 227.

5. The Soviet critic Lidiya Ginsburg cites Shan Girey describing his friend the exemplary Romantic poet Lermontov as "good humored and good natured in domestic life," despite his culturally accepted tragic image as a bitterly disillusioned man of the post-Decembrist generation. The good-natured side of Lermontov's character lies outside the Romantic cultural repertoire, and, as a result, it did not register in the readers' historical memory. This personal fea-

ture is seen as a surprising deviation, which does not fit into Lermontov's "biographical legend." Lermontov's example demonstrates the highly selective character of the Romantic self-stylization which must not be confused with the actual life of the author. See Lidiya Ginsburg, *O psikhologicheskoj proze* (Leningrad, 1977), pp. 25–26.

6. Yury Lotman, "The Decembrist in Daily Life," and Lidiya Ginsburg, "The Human Document and the Formation of Character," in *The Semiotics of Russian Cultural History*, ed. Alexander D. Nakhimovsky and Alice Stone Nakhimovsky (Ithaca: Cornell University Press, 1985).

7. Ibid., p. 197.

8. For the notion of "self-creation" (*zhiznetvorchestvo*), as developed in Russian literary and critical tradition, see V. F. Khodasevich, *Nekropol'* (Paris: YMCA Press, 1976); Ginsburg, *O psikhologicheskoj proze* (partly translated in Nakhimovsky and Stone Nakhimovsky, *Semiotics of Russian Cultural History*; and Victor Zhirmunsky, *Voprosy teorii literatury* (Leningrad, 1928). Of particular interest is the recent work of Irina Paperno, who offered me kind advice. See Irina Paperno, *Chernyshevsky and the Age of Realism* (Stanford: Stanford University Press, 1988). For an interesting analysis of poetic self-fashioning in the Russian tradition, see Gregory Freidin, *Coat of Many Colors: Osip Mandelstam and His Mythologies of Self-Presentation* (Berkeley: University of California Press, 1987). Freidin examines Mandelstam's "mythologies of self-presentation" and the myth of a "charismatic author" in the Russian tradition. Freidin's illuminating and provocative analysis, however, does not focus on the tension between Mandelstam's modernist textuality, the poets' insistence on discontinuities, gaps, and the decentering of the self (especially in *The Egyptian Stamp)* and myth making. Instead, Freidin stresses "the narrative continuity" or even unity in the poet's self-presentation (pp. ix–x).

9. Here I do not distinguish between the "natural school" in Russia; "realism" the way it was developed by the French writers of the 1850's, Champfleury, and others, who I believe were the first to coin the term; and the great "critical realists" of the Russian tradition. For my purpose, I stick to Lotman's and Ginsburg's usage of the term, with their emphasis on the "realist" shift in the ways of looking at the relationship between literature and life.

10. Donald Fanger, *Dostoevsky and Romantic Realism* (Cambridge, Mass.: Harvard University Press, 1967).

11. Charles Augustin Sainte-Beuve, *Nouveaux Lundis*, III, July 22, 1862; reprinted in *Selections from Sainte-Beuve*, ed. Arthur Tilley (Cambridge: Cambridge University Press, 1924), p. 167. Translation mine.

12. Marcel Proust, *Contre Sainte-Beuve* (Paris: Gallimard, 1954).

13. Paul de Man ironically remarks, "There is nothing particularly modern about the concept of modernity" (de Man, "Literary History and Literary Modernity," in his *Blindness and Insight*, Minneapolis: University of Minnesota Press, 1983, p. 144). The usage of the word goes back to the fifth century of our era, then becomes particularly urgent at the turn of the past three centuries: wit-

ness the "Quarrel between the Ancients and the Moderns" in France at the end of the seventeenth century, the debates of the German Romantics and Rousseau at the turn of the eighteenth century, and finally the explosion of what we now call "modernist movements" at the turn of the twentieth century. For the intellectual history of the term "modern," see also Matei Calinescu, *Five Faces of Modernity* (Durham: Duke University Press, 1987).

14. Peter Bürger elaborates a rather general but illuminating paradigm of the shifting function of art in Western society prior to modernization which ultimately leads to the modern alienation of the artist. According to Bürger, in ancient Greece and Rome, as well as during the High Middle Ages, art is fully integrated as a social institution: it forms part of a sacred ritual and is mostly produced and experienced collectively. Next, a shift occurs from "sacred" to "courtly" art, which develops under the patronage of the tsar, king, or prince. Art is still integrated into the everyday life of courtly society, but the sacred ritual turns into a social ritual. Art becomes increasingly secularized, the artist develops his individuality, but the reception remains collective. See Peter Bürger, *Theory of the Avant-Garde* (Minneapolis: University of Minnesota Press, 1984), p. 48.

15. Ibid., p. 46. On the notion of "autonomy of art," see Theodor Adorno, *Aesthetische Theorie*, ed. Gretel Adorno (Frankfurt: Suhrkamp, 1970).

16. See especially Roman Jakobson, "The Newest Russian Poetry," in *Major Soviet Writers*, ed. and trans. Edward J. Brown (New York: Oxford University Press, 1973) and "What Is Poetry," trans. Michael Heim, in *Semiotics of Art*, ed. Ladislav Matejka and Irwin Titunik (Cambridge, Mass.: MIT Press, 1976).

17. Roman Jakobson, "Poetics and Linguistics," in his *Fundamentals of Language* (The Hague: Mouton, 1956).

18. In *Rewriting the Renaissance*, ed. Margaret Ferguson (Chicago: University of Chicago Press, 1986), Nancy Vickers does a fascinating comparative study of the contemporary rock culture and Renaissance court poetry challenging our ways of reading both classic poetry and popular culture.

19. For a theoretical discussion of death, see the forthcoming volume *Departures: Death and Representation*, ed. Sarah Goodwin and Elizabeth Bronfen, which includes the work of Mieke Bal, Ellie Ragland-Sullivan, Margaret Higonnet, Regina Barreca, and others. The volume is based on the colloquium "Representations of Death" organized by Margaret Alexiou, Margaret Higonnet, and Elizabeth Bronfen at Harvard University in October 1988.

20. Roman Jakobson, "O pokolenii rastrativshem svoikh poetov," in his *Smert' Vladimira Majakovskogo* (Berlin: Petropolis, 1931). In English it appeared as "On a Generation That Squandered Its Poets," in Brown, *Major Soviet Writers;* reprinted in Jakobson's *Language in Literature*, ed. Krystyna Pomorska and Stephen Rudy (Cambridge, Mass.: Harvard University Press, 1987).

21. A unique contribution in this respect is Lawrence Lipking, *The Life of the Poet* (Chicago: Chicago University Press, 1981). It examines "poetic careers, poetic vocations, poetic destinies" and focuses specifically on three stages of the

poet's life as a poet which are not to be associated with "the stages of human life in general"—"the moment of initiation, the moment of summing up and the moment of passage." Lipking was one of the first to notice the inadequacy of critical vocabulary for the gray area between biography and textual criticism: "We know far more about the facts of the poets' lives, their quirks, torments, their singularities than we do about the life that all poets share: their vocation as poets . . . Thus most biographies of poets present the development of the hero, his struggle to find a poetic identity, as if it were the product of his own individual will—a unique self-making. Yet no poet becomes himself without inheriting an idea of what it means to be a poet. The same patterns recur again and again; the same excited discoveries lead to the same sense of achievement . . . If the lives of the poets tend to be peripheral to the inside of poems, the life of the poet is often the life of the poem" (p. viii).

My study responds to the same critical problems that Lipking's book raises, but my approach, areas of examination, and most of my examples, except for that of Mallarmé, are significantly different. Instead of focusing on the life of the poet in the singular, the life which supposedly most poets share, I examine the plurality of cultural myths of the poet(ess) in the context of European Modernism, placing my readings within (but not reducing them to) the more general problematics of the modernist making of the self. Hence I sever completely neither the ties between "human life" and "poetic life," nor those among poetic, prosaic, and everyday texts of the poets which include personal letters, suicide notes, and fashion magazines; rather I attempt to reexamine the very limits of textuality. My emphasis is on the rhetorical strategies developed in these diverse texts and the ways in which they shape both the relationship between writing and life and the figuration of human and poetic death.

22. T. S. Eliot, "Tradition and the Individual Talent," in *Selected Prose*, ed. Charles Hayward (London: Penguin Books, 1953), pp. 26, 30. See also Maude Ellman, *The Poetics of Impersonality* (Brighton, Sussex: Harvester Press, 1987).

23. W. K. Wimsatt, *The Verbal Icon* (Lexington: University of Kentucky Press, 1954).

24. Ibid., p. 10.

25. On the newest reappraisal of the New Critics, see Chaviva Hošek and Patricia Parker, eds., *Lyric Poetry beyond New Criticism* (Ithaca: Cornell University Press, 1985).

26. See Jonathan Arac, "Afterwords: Lyric Poetry and the Bounds of New Critics," in ibid., pp. 345–357.

27. Maurice Blanchot, "Mort du dernier écrivain," in his *Le Livre à venir* (Paris: Gallimard, 1959); Roland Barthes, "The Death of the Author," in his *The Rustle of Language*, trans. Richard Howard (New York: Hill and Wang, 1986); Michel Foucault, "What Is an Author?" in *Language, Counter-Memory, Practice*, ed. Donald F. Bouchard (Ithaca: Cornell University Press, 1977); Paul de

Man, "Autobiography as De-Facement," in his *The Rhetoric of Romanticism* (New York: Columbia University Press, 1984).

28. De Man, "Autobiography as De-Facement," p. 69.

29. Ibid., p. 80.

30. Ibid., p. 81. The art of cinematography may serve as a useful metaphor to illustrate my critique of de Man. Film is the most lifelike form of art because of the way that it manipulates the viewer with an illusion of reality, what André Bazin calls "the myth of the total cinema." At the same time, it is based on "cuts," disruptions, and montage to a larger degree than any other art form. Thus it seems that the intensity of illusion is dependent upon the degree of discontinuity and vice versa. The two are correlated, and it is precisely the tension between them that is at the core of the cinematographic image, of its mystique and its power. A "close-up" of the discontinuity would hardly explain film's cultural manipulation, because it is precisely the visual pleasures, the playful enjoyment of lifelikeness, that stimulate it. It is important to create a montage of "shots" that "lay bare the device" and of ones that exploit it—an interplay between disfiguration and proliferation of culturally accepted or, on the contrary, culturally exorcised figures. Perhaps this would provide a less pure, less sublime, less systematic, but also less reductive and less predictable picture of the artist's art, life, and death.

31. Foucault, "What Is an Author?" p. 138.

32. Barthes, "The Death of the Author," p. 52.

33. Ibid., p. 49.

34. Michel Foucault, *History of Sexuality*, II (New York: Vintage Books, 1978), pp. 11–13. See also his "On the Geneology of Ethics," in Rabinow, *The Foucault Reader*, pp. 340–351.

35. Roland Barthes, *Le Plaisir du texte* (Paris: Editions du Seuil, 1973), pp. 45–46. Translation mine.

36. Roland Barthes, *Roland Barthes*, trans. Richard Howard (New York: Hill and Wang, 1977), p. 125. I develop Barthes's idea of the "subject subtracted from the book" in my essay "Obscenity of Theory: Roland Barthes' 'Soirées de Paris' and Walter Benjamin's *Moscow Diary*" (forthcoming in *Yale Journal of Criticism*) where I examine the tensions between everyday writing of the self and theoretical writing, as well as the relationship between body and subjectivity.

37. Barthes, *Roland Barthes*, p. 150.

38. Roland Barthes, *Mythologies* (Paris: Editions du Seuil, 1957).

39. This difference resides in the illusion of pure denotation, "the resistance to meaning . . . in the name of a certain mythical idea of Life" with which the image tempts and manipulates us (Roland Barthes, "Rhetoric of the Image," in his *Image, Music, Text*, trans. Stephen Heath, New York: Hill and Wang, 1978, p. 32). Also what fascinates Barthes about the image is its "obtuse meaning," what in *Camera Lucida* he calls "punctum"—something that punc-

tuates and pierces common cultural codes and the limits of intelligibility. (See Roland Barthes, "The Third Meaning," in *Image, Music, Text*; and Roland Barthes, *Camera Lucida*, trans. Richard Howard (London: Fontana Paperbacks, 1984).

40. Roland Barthes, "The Image," in *The Rustle of Language*, pp. 350–359.

41. Roman Jakobson, *Novejshaja russkaja poezija* (Prague, 1921). In English it appeared as "The Newest Russian Poetry," in Brown, p. 66.

42. Victor Shklovsky, *O Teorii prozy* (Moscow, 1925), p. 192.

43. For the best studies of Russian Formalism see Jurij Striedter, "Zur Formalistischen Theorie der Proza und der literarischen Evolution," in *Texte der Russichen Formalisten*, I, ed. Jurij Striedter (Munich, 1969); Jurij Striedter, *Literary Structure, Evolution, and Value: Russian Formalism and Czech Structuralism Reconsidered* (Cambridge, Mass.: Harvard University Press, 1989); and Peter Steiner, *Russian Formalism* (Ithaca: Cornell University Press, 1984). For a history of the movement see Victor Erlich, *Russian Formalism* (New Haven: Yale University Press, 1965).

44. Yury Tynyanov, "Literaturnyj fakt," "O literaturnoj evoljucii," "Blok," and "O parodii," in his *Poetika, Istorija literatury, Kino* (Moscow: Nauka, 1977). Some of these essays have appeared in English in *Readings in Russian Poetics*, ed. Ladislav Matejka and Krystyna Pomorska (Ann Arbor: Michigan Slavic Publications, 1973). The translation of all Tynyanov quotes is mine. In Russian the term *literaturnaja lichnost'* relates to *lik, oblik*, and *lico*—face; and *oblichie*—mask (persona). Thus, it links face, in de Man's sense of defacement, with personality.

45. Tynyanov, "Literaturnyj fakt," p. 259.

46. Ibid.

47. Tynyanov writes: "There are certain phenomena of style that lead to the persona/face [*lico*] of the narrator. One can observe it to some extent in a simple tale, in the peculiarities of diction, syntax, and especially, in the pattern of phrases and intonation . . . They suggest certain elusive but specific features of the narrator. When the story is oriented toward the speaker, or told from his point of view, these features become specific to the point of palpability. (Obviously this specificity is far from a picture image . . .) The ultimate extreme of the stylistic specificity of this stylistic persona is the *name*" (ibid., p. 268).

Here Tynyanov senses a crucial tension—which I will discuss throughout this book—between the verbal and visual representation of the author. It is exemplified in his essay by the words *oblik* (look, aspect, impersonation, appearance) and *nazvanie* (name). For Tynyanov, it is the name of the author (or his or her literary pseudonym) and not his or her portrait which incarnates "literary personality."

48. In the essay "Blok" Tynyanov distinguishes certain "phenomena of style" which stimulate the creation of the biographical legend. The most important among them are the confessional intonations and the primitive, emotional, and

musical forms of his poetry, often borrowed from sentimental and heart-breaking urban romances (p. 118).

49. Boris Tomashevsky, "Literature and Biography," in Matejka and Pomorska, *Readings in Russian Poetics*, pp. 255–270. It is interesting to note that after the official Stalinist "purge of Formalism" Tynyanov, Tomashevsky, and Ei-khenbaum wrote more conventional biographies of Pushkin and Tolstoy, while Tynyanov published popular historical novels—*Kjukhlja* (1928) and *The Death of Vazir Mukhtar* (1929). It would be worth tracing how similar critical preoc-cupations are developed in different genres of writing practiced by the critics themselves throughout their careers, but that remains beyond the scope of this study.

50. Ibid., p. 55.

51. Ibid., p. 52. Therefore, certain biographical facts that did not become "liter-ary facts" might be irrelevant, while some fictions of the self would prove more helpful "for the literary historian in an attempt to reconstruct the psychological milieu surrounding the literary work."

52. Roland Barthes, "Authors and Writers," and "Writers, Intellectuals, Teach-ers," in *A Barthes Reader*, ed. Susan Sontag (New York: Hill and Wang, 1982), pp. 185, 378.

53. Ginsburg, *O psikhologicheskoj proze*.

54. Yury Lotman, "Poetics of Everyday Behavior in the Eighteenth-Century Rus-sian Culture," and "Decembrist in Daily Life," in Nakhimovsky and Stone Nakhimovsky, *The Semiotics of Russian Cultural History*. Also see his "Prob-lems in the Typology of Culture," in *Soviet Semiotics*, ed. David Lucid (Balti-more: Johns Hopkins University Press, 1988).

55. Yury Lotman, *Pushkin: Biografija pisatelja* (Leningrad, 1983), p. 250.

56. Boris Gasparov, "Introduction," in Nakhimovsky and Stone Nakhimovsky, *The Semiotics of Russian Cultural History*.

57. Barthes, *Mythologies*. The quoted essay is reprinted as "Myth Today," in Son-tag, *A Barthes Reader*.

58. See Roland Barthes, "Change the Object Itself," in *Image, Music, Text*, pp. 165–170.

59. Mikhail Bakhtin, "Iz zapisej, 1970–1971" and "Problema teksta v lingvistike, filologii i drugikh gumanitarnykh naukakh," in his *Estetika slovesnogo tvor-chestva* (Moscow: Khudozhestvennaja literatura, 1979).

60. The figure of the cultural mythologist can be compared to Benjamin's flâneur. This is a twentieth-century flâneur, however, who can no longer limit himself or herself to the Parisian Passage and instead crosses the boundaries of real and imaginary maps and switches the channels of international cable televi-sion.

61. The notion of "theatricality" underlines Lotman's concept of culture as a sys-tem of codes, which determines the "script" of individual performance. If in Saussure's linguistics the central metaphor is the game of chess, in Lotman's

semiotics it is the theatrical stage. One wonders if in the discussions of post-modern self-fashioning a cinematic or video metaphor would be more appropriate.

62. Bari Rolfe, *Behind the Mask* (Oakland: Personabooks, 1977), p. 10.

63. Actors have reported that wearing a mask in a theater performance makes one aware of the theatricality of everyday life and teaches one to regard one's face as one disguise among others. In this respect, the advice that the director Mikhail Chekhov gave his actors is particularly relevant: he recommended that they "wear the face as if it were make-up" (ibid., p. 6).

64. Charles Baudelaire, "Le Peintre de la vie moderne," in *L'Art Romantique, Oeuvres complètes*, IV (Paris: Gauthier, 1923).

65. Elizabeth Burns, *Theatricality* (New York: Harper and Row, 1972). For the uses of the theatrical metaphor in psychology see Erwing Goffman, *The Presentation of Self in Everyday Life* (New York: Doubleday, 1959).

66. Burns, *Theatricality*, p. 63.

67. Jonas Barish, *The Antitheatrical Prejudice* (Berkeley: University of California Press, 1981). This prejudice is reflected in ordinary language in the peculiar use of many theatrical metaphors, which, unlike metaphors borrowed from the other arts, tend to be "hostile and belittling." Here are a few examples: "to be theatrical," "to put on an act," "to make a scene," "to play to the gallery," or in French simply that an action is "du théâtre." These and many other expressions in European languages reveal vestiges of a prejudice against the theater that is as old in European history as the theater itself. See also David Marshall, *The Figure of Theater* (New York: Columbia University Press, 1986) in which he discusses the theatricality involved in publishing a book and in the relationships between authors and readers in eighteenth- and nineteenth-century examples.

68. For the reading of Plato's and Mallarmé's theater see Jacques Derrida, *Dissemination*, trans. Barbara Johnson (Chicago: University of Chicago Press, 1971). See Chapter 1 for a fuller discussion.

69. Interestingly in Barthes's discussion of the traditional Japanese theater, which he constructs as an imaginary other, a space for staging cultural difference, he describes the Japanese mask as a kind of writing on the face and celebrates this ultimate escape from Western naturalist theatricality. (Roland Barthes, *Empire of Signs*, trans. Richard Howard, New York: Noonday Press, 1982.)

70. De Man, "Literary History and Literary Modernity," p. 147.

71. Greenblatt, *Renaissance Self-Fashioning*, p. 2.

72. Ibid. Rather than appear in the traditional biography, this life in quotation marks surfaces in biographical fictions such as Vladimir Nabokov's *The Real Life of Sebastian Knight*, Jorge Luis Borges's "Borges and Myself," Milan Kundera's *Life Is Elsewhere*, and Christa Wolf's *The Quest for Christa T.*

73. Ginsburg, *O psikhologicheskoj proze*, p. 32.

1. The Death of the Author

1. Arthur Rimbaud, "Lettre à Demeny," in *Oeuvres complètes*, ed. Antoine Adam (Paris: Gallimard, Bibliothèque de la Pléiade, 1972), p. 252.

2. Stéphane Mallarmé, "Igitur," in *Oeuvres complètes*, ed. Henri Mondor and Jean Aubry (Paris: Gallimard, Bibliothèque de la Pléiade, 1945), p. 442. All further references to Mallarmé are from this edition. All translations from the French are Lilly Parrot's and mine.

I am grateful to Professor Jeffrey Mehlman whose course on Mallarmé and psychoanalysis taught at Boston University in 1983 initiated me into the practice of reading Mallarmé.

3. All Valéry's writings on Mallarmé are collected in Paul Valéry, *Ecrits divers sur Stéphane Mallarmé* (Paris: Editions de la N.R.F., 1950). They will be discussed later in the chapter.

4. André Breton, *Manifestes du surréalisme* (Paris: Gallimard, 1973), pp. 38–39, 110–111.

5. See Charles Mauron, *Introduction à la psychoanalyse de Mallarmé* (Neuchâtel: La Baconière, 1950) and Jean-Pierre Richard, *L'Univers imaginaire de Mallarmé* (Paris: Editions du Seuil, 1961).

6. Leo Bersani, *The Death of Stéphane Mallarmé* (Cambridge: Cambridge University Press, 1982), pp. 4–5.

7. Jacques Derrida, "Double Session," in his *Dissemination*, trans. Barbara Johnson (Chicago: University of Chicago Press, 1981), p. 201.

8. Ibid., p. 201.

9. Jacques Derrida, "Outwork," in ibid., pp. 3–57.

10. Jacques Derrida, "Freud and Beyond," in his *The Postcard*, trans. Alan Bass (Chicago: University of Chicago Press, 1987).

11. Paul de Man, "Lyric and Modernity," in his *Blindness and Insight* (Minneapolis: University of Minnesota Press, 1971).

12. Ibid., p. 181.

13. Ibid., p. 175.

14. The phrase "radical Möbius-strip–like continuity" is Barbara Johnson's, and I am grateful for her comments on my section on de Man and Derrida.

15. Derrida, "Double Session," p. 180.

16. Barbara Johnson, lecture on de Man, Harvard University, February, 8, 1988.

17. Barbara Johnson, *Défigurations du langage poétique* (Paris: Flammarion, 1979), p. 172.

18. Ibid., p. 172.

19. Ibid., p. 173.

20. Bersani, *The Death of Stéphane Mallarmé*, pp. 5–6.

21. Mallarmé, "Autobiographie," p. 665.

22. Ibid., p. 663.

23. Ibid., p. 661.

24. Ibid., p. 664.

25. Ibid., p. 663.

26. The difficulty in reading Mallarmé consists precisely in the impossibility of enclosing him entirely within any specific context, for instance, within the context of bourgeois ideology. If we do that, we then have to perform a double movement, examine the revolutionary rhetoric of the ideological text itself and question the cultural assumptions behind the notions of "ideology" and "bourgeois." Mallarmé's life is shaped by the bourgeois environment and has all the obvious bourgeois trappings. Yet, it points to a radically discontinuous conception of the self and to the disruptive relationship between the self and language. These notions may explode the very foundation of the bourgeois household.

27. Mallarmé, "Autobiographie," p. 663.

28. Ibid.

29. Ibid., p. 664.

30. Mallarmé, "Igitur," p. 433.

31. Jonas Barish, *The Anti-Theatrical Prejudice* (Berkeley: University of California Press, 1985), p. 337.

32. Mallarmé, "Crise de vers," p. 366.

33. As Robert Greer Cohn remarks, the name "Igitur" and the name from the subtitle "Folie d'Elbehnon" "were chosen, in part because they included reminiscences of Hamlet, Poe, Beckford, Villiers and also contained effective sound and visual symbolism, as well as some interesting harmonies or overtones in the French language (including the trisyllabic 'Mallarmé')" (*Mallarmé's Igitur*, Berkeley: University of California Press, 1981, p. 25). According to Cohn, Elbehnon can refer to a Hebrew word meaning the son of Elohim, emissary of the Creator, the personification of the creative force (p. 22), or it can be associated through sound patterns with "la nuit ébénéenne," recalling Poe's "Raven," "l'oiseau d'ébène," or Hamlet's castle, Elsinore (p. 24). This is only to demonstrate the procreative and suggestive powers of Mallarmé's language.

34. Mallarmé, "Le Mystère dans les lettres," p. 385.

35. Mallarmé, "Hamlet," p. 300.

36. Ibid.

37. Mallarmé, *La Dernière Mode*, p. 763.

38. Mallarmé, "Igitur," p. 447.

39. Cohn, *Mallarmé's Igitur*, pp. 42–58.

40. Mallarmé, "Sur le livre illustré," p. 878.

41. Mallarmé, "Igitur," p. 433.

42. Walter Benjamin, "The Image of Proust," in his *Illuminations*, trans. Harry Zohn (New York: Schoken Books, 1969).

43. See Peter Demetz, *Marx, Engels and the Poets* (Chicago: University of Chicago Press, 1967).

44. Mallarmé, "Action restreinte," p. 370.

45. Ibid., pp. 370–371.

46. Julia Kristeva, *La Révolution du langage poétique* (Paris: Editions du Seuil, 1974), pp. 480–491.

47. There he ironically quotes his own early text, "Une Symphonie littéraire," which presents a beautiful description of a not-so-disfigured classical poet. First, young Mallarmé writes that Banville "n'est pas quelqu'un mais le son même de la lyre" ("is not anyone but the sound of the lyre itself") (Mallarmé, "Une Symphonie littéraire," p. 264). But after this declamatory depersonalization, Mallarmé amorously creates the picture of the poet, while remembering his own pleasure in reading about the luminous sobbings of long-haired women. The prince of poets is represented as "the invincible classical poet in submission to the goddess and living amidst the forgotten charm of heroes and roses" (pp. 264–265). Although the quote from the earlier text is framed rather ironically by the older and wiser poet, he still calls Banville "Sylphe suprème" and "le prince des lettres." The inclusion of a one-page quote from the earlier text is an interesting device. It is Mallarmé's comfortable and sophisticated way of both dissociating himself from a traditional and trivial figuration of the poet and yet indicating that that picture, even if somewhat naive, is still dear to his heart.

48. It is interesting that the debate about classicism and whether it is a specific cultural style or part of the collective memory of universal archetypes continued in the 1980s, specifically in the criticism of postmodern architecture. The persistence of this critical issue shows how strong the desire is to conflate one's individual Western cultural memory with universal archetypes.

49. Mallarmé, "Edgar Poe," p. 531.

50. Carl Paul Barbier, ed., *Correspondance Whistler–Mallarmé* (Paris: Nizet, 1964), p. 257. Whistler writes: "Je suis enfin toujours seul—seul comme a du être Edgar Poe, à qui vous m'avez trouvé d'une certaine resemblance" ("I am finally always alone—alone like Edgar Poe must have been, in whom you have found a certain resemblance to me").

51. As follows from Whistler's letter, he loved Mallarmé's sonnet, particularly the rhyming of his own name and the reference to "noir vol de chapeau." This image combines synecdoche and synesthesia; blackness is transposed from the hat to the flight itself, as if dissociated from the specific piece of clothing to color the atmosphere symbolically. Whistler's letter begins: "Vous devez savoir, mon cher ami, que j'ai été ravi en lisant le joli sonnet! 'la rue sujette au noir vol de chapeaux'! splendide!! Tout le monde est enchanté et nous sommes bien fier—surtout moi! . . . 'puisse l'air/De sa jupe éventer Whistler'! est assez superbe et *dandy!*" ("You must know, my dear friend, how delighted I was

in reading the pretty sonnet! 'The street subjected to the black flight of hats'! Splendid!! Everyone is enchanted and we are quite proud—especially me! . . . 'May the air be able / With its skirt to fan Whistler'! is quite superb and *dandy!*"). Ibid., p. 77.

52. Michel Lemaire, *Le Dandysme de Baudelaire à Mallarmé* (Montreal: Presses de l'université de Montréal, 1978), p. 9. On the myth of the dandy see also Emilien Carassus, *Le Mythe du dandy* (Paris: Armand Colin, 1971).

53. Charles Baudelaire, *Oeuvres complètes*, ed. Claude Pichois and Jean Ziegler (Paris: Gallimard, 1975).

54. Ibid., p. 711.

55. In spite of his "effeminate" habits and tastes a dandy is masculine, radically masculine. In fact, in Baudelairian terms a woman can never be a dandy because her relationship to "loi" and "esprit" is totally different. It is curious that Baudelaire describes "the woman" as a different cultural myth from that of the dandy, rather than as a biological entity. A woman in Baudelaire—not an entirely idiosyncratic view but a reflection of the contemporary myth of femininity—is "une espèce d'idole, stupide, peut-être mais éblouissante," while a dandy is "une espèce d'idole," spiritual, ironic and self-conscious, whose femininity is not predetermined but self-imposed.

The dandy's aristocratism as well as his femininity is paradoxical. The dandy is an aristocrat by choice, which is a contradiction in terms since an aristocrat historically is defined by his ownership of land and/or by his pedigree. The dandy may lack both. What makes him resemble an aristocrat is his lack of definite occupation and his excess of free time. According to Baudelaire, a dandy is 3-D: "déclassé, dégoûté, désoeuvré" (ibid.). Obviously, the dandy is not poor; he needs to have a certain economic base to allow himself all the cultural luxuries of aristocratic self-fashioning. But this economic base might, in fact, be minimal; it is more mythical than actual. The dandy belongs to the peculiar urban stratum that defies specific class definitions: he is the aristocrat's simulacrum, a master image-maker who challenges the economically based class theory.

56. Lemaire, *Le Dandysme*, pp. 106–108.

57. See Bari Rolfe, *Behind the Mask* (Oakland: Personabooks, 1977).

58. Mallarmé, "Le Livre, instrument spirituel," p. 378.

59. Ibid., p. 381.

60. Ibid., p. 382.

61. Some of these insights were developed with my student and friend Richard Murphy who wrote an exciting senior honors thesis in literature entitled "Writing on the White Dress: Politics of Fashion in Mallarmé and Dickinson" (Harvard College, March 1988).

62. Quoted in Mallarmé, *Oeuvres complètes*, p. 1627.

63. Mallarmé, *La Dernière Mode*, p. 716.

64. "Un livre est tôt fermé, fastidieux et on laisse le regard se délasser dans ce

nuage d'impressions qu'à volonté dégage, comme les anciens dieux, la personne moderne pour l'interposer entre les aventures banales et soi" (ibid., p. 717).

65. Ibid., p. 762. Italics mine.
66. Ibid., p. 799.
67. See especially the early conception of Hélène Cixous, who could have considered Mallarmé together with Jean Génet the first representatives of "écriture feminine," in her often quoted essay, "The Laugh of the Medusa," trans. Keith Cohen and Paula Cohen, in *Signs* 1 (Summer 1975), 875–893.
68. Mallarmé, *La Dernière Mode*, p. 881.
69. Ibid., p. 764.
70. Paul Valéry, "Lettre sur Mallarmé," in his *Variété 1 et 2* (Paris: Gallimard, 1978), p. 290.
71. Paul Valéry, "Lettre à Gide," in *Ecrits divers sur Stéphane Mallarmé*, p. 143.
72. Ibid.
73. Ibid., p. 145.
74. Paul Valéry, "La Dernière Visite à Stéphane Mallarmé," in *Variété 1 et 2*, p. 272.
75. Ibid., p. 275.
76. Ibid., p. 274.
77. Paul Valéry, "Stéphane Mallarmé," in *Variété 1 et 2*, p. 259.
78. Ibid.
79. Valéry, "Lettre sur Mallarmé," p. 289.
80. Paul Valéry, *Monsieur Teste* (Paris: Gallimard, 1986), pp. 11–12.
81. Valéry criticized his initial conception of M. Teste as a purely individual intellect in "Yalou," where he emphasizes more the role of tradition, exposing views similar to those later expressed by Eliot in "Tradition and the Individual Talent." Valéry continued to work on M. Teste, however, and never abandoned the project completely.
82. Valéry, *Monsieur Teste*, p. 44.
83. Ibid., p. 39.
84. Jorge Luis Borges, "Valéry como símbolo," in his *Otras Inquisiciones* (Madrid: Alianza, 1979), pp. 76–78. The depersonalization of the author is a central preoccupation in many Borges stories, including "Everything and Nothing," "Borges y yo," "El sueño de Coleridge," "Kafka y sus precursores," and "De alguien a nadie." All translations from the Spanish are mine.
85. Jorge Luis Borges, "Pierre Menard, autor del Quijote," in his *Ficciones* (Buenos Aires: Emecé, 1956), p. 54–55. See Alicia Borinsky, "Repetitions, Libraries, Museums: J. L. Borges," in *Jorge Luis Borges*, ed. Harold Bloom (New York: Chelsea House, 1986). I am grateful to Alicia Borinsky for introducing me to Borges.
86. Borges, "Valéry como símbolo," pp. 77–78. Susan Suleiman has suggested

that Valéry was the only symbolist poet who during the Dreyfus affair assumed an anti-Dreyfus position. This is only one of many historical details that Borges prefers to omit in his description of Valéry.

87. Mallarmé, "Arthur Rimbaud," p. 515.

88. Ibid., p. 513.

89. Quoted from Rimbaud, *Oeuvres complètes*, p. 786.

90. Arthur Rimbaud, *Une Saison en enfer*, in his *Oeuvres poétiques* (Paris: Flammarion, 1964), p. 139. I am very grateful to Norbert Bonenkamp for an inspiring discussion of Rimbaud.

91. Arthur Rimbaud, "Alchimie du verbe," in *Oeuvres poétiques* p. 132.

92. Yury Tynyanov, "O literaturnoj evolucii," in his *Poetika, Istorija literatury, Kino* (Moscow: Izdatelstvo Nanka, 1976).

93. Arthur Rimbaud, Lettre à Banville," in *Oeuvres complètes*, p. 236.

94. Rimbaud, "Lettre à Demeny," p. 250.

95. Shoshana Felman, "Tu as bien fait de partir, Arthur Rimbaud," *Littérature* 11 (October 1973), 3–22.

96. See the original and illuminating study by Kristin Ross, *The Emergence of Social Space: Rimbaud and the Paris Commune* (Minneapolis: University of Minnesota Press, 1988), which came to my attention after this book was already completed. It is an attempt to give a "geopolitical" reading of Rimbaud as a poet of the Commune, to examine Rimbaud not so much in the context of literary history as in the context of changing structures of everyday life, juxtaposing his poems with the other voices of the oppositional culture of the 1870's. I completely concur with the author's insistence on reading Rimbaud "dans tous les sens" and the need to historicize Rimbaud's "poetic devices." On the whole, however, my area of investigation is quite different. I do a more "vertical" analysis of Rimbaud and do not privilege Rimbaud of the Commune over Rimbaud the arms dealer in Abyssinia, the writer of many unliterary letters with descriptions of everyday ennui. Moreover, rather than focus on a single "exceptional" (even if extremely formative and crucial) event in French history and in Rimbaud's life and writing, I attempt to point at a history of shifting cultural myths of the poet and shifting relationships between the literary and the everyday. In this respect, there exists a history of representing Rimbaud not only as a "poète maudit" but also as a revolutionary poet, as "communard and communiste." I will examine fragments of this often quite problematic history of politicizations of Rimbaud in Chapter 2.

97. Rimbaud, "Lettre à Demeny," p. 248. Emphasis mine.

98. Ibid., p. 249.

99. Arthur Rimbaud, "Le Coeur volé," in *Oeuvres poétiques*, pp. 68–69.

100. Arthur Rimbaud, "Lettre à Izambard," in ibid., pp. 249, 1074n.

101. See Colonel Godshot, *Arthur Rimbaud Ne Varietur* (Nice, 1936) and Enid Starkie, *Rimbaud* (New York: Norton, 1938).

102. Antoine Adam, "Notices, Notes, et Variants," in Rimbaud, *Oeuvres complètes*, p. 889.

103. Tzvetan Todorov, "A Complication of the Text: The Illuminations," in *French Literary Theory Today*, ed. Tzvetan Todorov, trans. R. Carter (Cambridge: Cambridge University Press, 1982).

104. For Rimbaud's use of obscenities see "Les sturpa" and "Album zutique," in his *Oeuvres complètes*. For a discussion of these texts see Ross, *The Emergence of Social Space*.

105. Ferdinand de Saussure, *Course in General Linguistics*, trans. Wade Baskin (New York: McGraw Hill, 1966), pp. 66–67.

106. Rimbaud, "Alchimie du verbe," p. 130.

107. Rimbaud, "Lettre à Demeny," p. 251.

108. Arthur Rimbaud, "Adieu," in *Oeuvres poétiques*, p. 140.

109. Arthur Rimbaud, "Vierge folle," in ibid., p. 127.

110. Arthur Rimbaud, "Lettre à Isabelle Rimbaud," in *Oeuvres complètes*, p. 682.

111. Friedrich Nietzsche, "Vom Nutzen und Nachteil der Historie für das Leben," in *Unzeitgemässe Betrachtung*, II, ed. Karl Schlechta, *Werke*, vol. 1 (Munich, 1954), pp. 232–233; quoted in Paul de Man, "Literary History and Literary Modernity," in his *Blindness and Insight* (Minneapolis: University of Minnesota Press, 1971), pp. 144–145.

112. De Man, "Literary History and Literary Modernity," p. 146.

113. See Nietzsche, "Vom Nutzen und Nachteil," p. 215; translation from de Man, "Literary History and Literary Modernity," p. 147.

114. Fyodor Dostoyevsky, *Notes from Underground*, trans. Mirra Ginsburg (New York: Bantam Books, 1974).

115. Rimbaud, "Lettre à Demeny," pp. 250–251.

116. Arthur Rimbaud, "Mauvais Sang," in *Oeuvres poétiques*, p. 122.

117. Arthur Rimbaud, "La Nuit d'enfer," in ibid., p. 124.

118. Rimbaud, "Mauvais Sang," p. 119.

119. Ibid., p. 123.

120. Arthur Rimbaud, "L'Impossible," in *Oeuvres poétiques*, p. 137.

121. Arthur Rimbaud, "Vies," in ibid., p. 153.

122. Rimbaud, "Vierge folle," p. 126.

123. Rimbaud, "L'Impossible," p. 137.

124. Arthur Rimbaud, "Lettre aux siens," February 28, 1890, in *Oeuvres complètes*, p. 611.

125. Arthur Rimbaud, "Lettre aux siens," May 25, 1881, in ibid., p. 330. Emphasis mine.

126. See Felman, "Tu as bien fait de partir, Arthur Rimbaud."

127. Arthur Rimbaud, "Lettre à Ménélik," in *Oeuvres complètes*, p. 620.

128. René Etiemble, *Le Mythe de Rimbaud* (Paris: Gallimard, 1952).

129. Milan Kundera, *Life Is Elsewhere*, trans. Peter Kussi (London: Penguin Books, 1986).
130. Vladimir Nabokov, "A Forgotten Poet," in his *Nabokov's Dozen* (Freeport: Books for Library Presses, 1958).
131. Dominique Noguez, *Les Trois Rimbaud* (Paris: Editions de Minuit, 1986).

2. The Death of the Revolutionary Poet

1. As late as the first third of the twentieth century the consistent critique of Romantic biographical myths is still offered in the writings of Mandelstam and Pasternak, which however did not significantly affect the Russian cultural consciousness. Moreover, Mandelstam and Pasternak themselves, in spite of their desire to be "poets without a biography," as expressed in their theoretical writings, were transformed into "poets with a biography."
2. In Europe and in the United States the Romantic cult of the poet disappeared with the heroic deaths of Byron, Hugo, Leopardi, Rimbaud, and Whitman, yet on a smaller scale it persists in Spanish-speaking countries with Federico García Lorca and Pablo Neruda as its main twentieth-century representatives. Every Russian poet, willingly or not, has to respond to this unwritten but widely shared Russian-Soviet cultural myth, to this heroic tradition that privileges dead poets and deemphasizes the literariness of literature.
3. Friedrich Hegel, *Phenomenology of Spirit*, trans. A. V. Miller (Oxford: Oxford University Press, 1977), pp. 111–118. See also Pierre Miquel, *La Révolte* (Paris: Bordas, 1971), p. 17.
4. Miquel, *La Révolte*, p. 4.
5. See Yury Lotman, "The Decembrist in Everyday Life," and Lidiya Ginsburg, "The Human Document and the Formation of the Character," in *The Semiotics of Russian Cultural History*, ed. Alexander Nakhimovsky and Alice Stone Nakhimovsky (Ithaca: Cornell University Press, 1985).

   Obviously, not all Russian Romantic poets followed a single model. For instance, Zhukovsky offers quite a different example of the relationship between life and art.
6. Andrew Parker elaborated on this point in his lecture at Harvard University, Fall 1986, and in his *Re-Marx* (Madison: University of Wisconsin Press, forthcoming). On Marxism and poetry see also Peter Demetz, *Marx, Engels and the Poets* (Chicago: University of Chicago Press, 1967).
7. Jurij Striedter, "The 'New Myth' of Revolution—A Study of Mayakovsky's Early Poetry," in *New Perspectives in German Criticism*, ed. Richard Amacher and Victor Lange (Princeton: Princeton University Press, 1979).
8. Striedter's definition of myth is slightly different than Barthes's: he defines it as "groups of motifs and narrative schemata that can be derived as a common core from traditional myths and legends" (ibid., p. 364).
9. Ibid., p. 380.

10. Karl Marx and Friedrich Engels, "Die sogenannte ursprüngliche Akkumulation," in *Werke*, XXIII (Berlin: Dietz, 1957), p. 791; discussed in ibid., p. 381.

11. Roland Barthes, "Change the Object Itself," in his *Image, Music, Text* (New York: Hill and Wang, 1978), pp. 165–170.

12. See the discussion of the "poet's Golgotha" in Roman Jakobson, "O pokolenii rastrativshem svoikh poetov," in his *Smert' Vladimira Majakovsogo* (Berlin: Petropolis, 1931), p. 5. In English it appeared as "On a Generation That Squandered its Poets," in *Major Soviet Writers*, ed. and trans. Edward J. Brown (New York: Oxford University Press, 1973). I have made my own, more literal, translation of this essay.

13. Marina Tsvetaeva, "Epos i lirika sovremennoj rossii," in *Nesobrannye Proizvedenija*, ed. Günter Wytrzens (Munich: Wilhelm Fink, 1971), p. 661.

14. Boris Tomashevsky, "Literature and Biography," in *Readings in Russian Poetics*, ed. Ladislav Matejka and Krystyna Pomorska (Ann Arbor: Michigan Slavic Publications, 1973), pp. 47–56; Yury Tynyanov, "O Majakovskom. Pamjati Poeta," in *Poetika, Istorija literatury, Kino*, ed. V. A. Kaverin and A. S. Myasnikov (Moscow: Nauka, 1977), pp. 196–197.

15. Osip Mandelstam, "Literaturnaja Moskva," in *Sobranie sochinenij*, II (New York: Inter-Language Literary Associates, 1971), p. 329.

16. Boris Pasternak, "Okhrannaja gramota," in his *Vozdushnye puti* (Moscow: Sovetskij Pisotel', 1983). Pasternak's paradoxical love-hate relationship with Mayakovsky's literary persona allowed him to define his own literary identity, find his own romantically anti-Romantic "originality." On the comparison between Pasternak and Mayakovsky see Tsvetaeva, "Epos i lirika sovremennoj rossii," and Roman Jakobson, "Randbemerkungen zur Proza des Dichters Pasternak," *Slavische Rundschau* 7 (1935), 357–374.

17. Pasternak, "Okhrannaja Gramota," p. 273.

18. Ibid. On "life-creation" among the Symbolists see Vladislav Khodasevich, *Nekropol'* (Paris: YMCA Press, 1976).

19. Vladimir Mayakovsky, "My idem," in his *Sobranie sochinenij*, I (Moscow: Pravda, 1978), p. 191. All further references to Mayakovsky are from this edition. All translations from the Russian are mine.

20. Vladimir Mayakovsky, *Ja sam*, I, p. 43.

21. Ibid., p. 60.

22. Yury Tynyanov, "Literaturnij Fakt," in *Poetika, Istorija literatury, Kino*, p. 269.

23. Ibid.

24. Peter Steiner, *Russian Formalism* (Ithaca: Cornell University Press, 1984), p. 133.

25. Michel Foucault, "What Is an Author?" in *Language, Counter-Memory, Practice*, ed. Donald F. Bouchard (Ithaca: Cornell University Press, 1977), p. 121.

26. Ibid., p. 123.

27. John Shoptaw, "Elegy and Cryptography," lecture, Harvard University, May 1988. It is interesting to observe that in the recent outburst of graffiti art in the New York subway, the most typical representation was of the name of the artist, either in initials or a nickname.

28. Pasternak, "Okhrannaja gramota," p. 264.

29. For notes to the play see Vladimir Mayakovsky, "Primechanija," IX, p. 297.

30. Edward Brown has pointed out that *Vladimir Mayakovsky* is similar in genre to the Greek tragedy, Symbolist drama, and particularly German Expressionist drama. See his *Mayakovsky: A Poet in the Revolution* (Princeton: Princeton University Press, 1973), pp. 98–99.

31. For more on the device of personification in Mayakovsky see Striedter, "The 'New Myth' of Revolution," pp. 370–371.

32. Vladimir Mayakovsky, *Vladimir Mayakovsky*, IX, p. 6.

33. Ibid.

34. Ibid., p. 7.

35. On apostrophe and personification see Chaviva Hošek and Patricia Parker, eds., *Lyric Poetry: Beyond New Criticism* (Ithaca: Cornell University Press, 1985).

36. Mayakovsky, *Vladimir Mayakovsky*, p. 12.

37. Ibid., p. 24.

38. Vladimir Mayakovsky, "Oblako v shtanakh," I.

39. Striedter distinguishes between the adoption and reshaping of particular motifs, techniques, and structures of traditional myths, dispensing with the mythical view of life, and the intention to revive this "mythical view of life." In the first case, one often employs the classical myths, while in the second, the structure of Christ's myth, which in its own time was "a new myth," prevails. Furthermore, Striedter shows the connection between the ideas of moral and of social justice, of a rehabilitation of a particular form of Christianity and the awakening of a revolutionary conscience in the writings of Pierre Prudhon and Georges Sorel, who exerted influence on Russian literature, especially on Dostoevsky and indirectly on Mayakovsky himself. See Striedter, "The 'New Myth' of Revolution," pp. 360–368.

40. Mayakovsky, *Ja sam*, p. 57.

41. Among the others were Larisa Reisner, Alexander Blok, who was abandoned to die of hunger in 1921, and Vsevolod Meyerhold, who was murdered in one of Stalin's camps in 1940.

42. Vladimir Mayakovsky, *150,000,000*, I, p. 317.

43. Mayakovsky, *Ja sam*, p. 57.

44. Mayakovsky, *150,000,000*, p. 317.

45. Vladimir Mayakovsky, "Levyj marsh," I, p. 185.

46. Vladimir Mayakovsky, "Jubilejnoe," III, p. 38.

47. Ibid., p. 41.

48. Vladimir Mayakovsky, "Vo ves' golos," VI, pp. 175–180.

49. Tsvetaeva, "Epos i lirika sovremennoj rossii," p. 642.

50. Mayakovsky, *Ja sam*, p. 54.

51. Vladimir Mayakovsky, "Kofta fata," I, p. 89.

52. Mayakovsky, "Oblako v shtanakh," p. 242.

53. Vladimir Mayakovsky, "O raznykh Majakovskikh," II, p. 70.

54. Vladimir Mayakovsky, "Kaplja degtja," II, p. 74.

55. Vladimir Mayakovsky, "Kak delat' stikhi," XI, p. 248.

56. Paul de Man, *Allegories of Reading* (New Haven: Yale University Press, 1979), p. 63n.

57. Jakobson, "Randbemerkungen zur Proza des Dichters Parsternak" and Roman Jakobson, "Two Aspects of Language and Two Types of Aphasia," in his *Fundamentals of Language* (The Hague: Mouton, 1956).

58. The Soviet semioticians Pyatigorsky and Uspensky would call this phenomenon "a semiotic type of behavior," which is characteristic of a type of personality that tends to transform "nonsign elements into signs." See A. M. Pyatigorsky and B. A. Uspensky, "The Classification of Personality as a Semiotic Problem," in *Soviet Semiotics*, ed. David Lucid (Baltimore: Johns Hopkins University Press, 1988), p. 140.

59. For more on metaphor and metonymy see de Man, *Allegories of Reading*.

60. Roman Jakobson, "Poetics and Linguistics," in *Fundamentals of Language*, p. 356. In "White Mythology" Jacques Derrida writes that metaphors "exist only in plural": "If there were only one possible metaphor, the dream at the heart of philosophy, if one could reduce their play to the circle of family or group of metaphor, that is to one 'central,' 'principal' metaphor, there would be no more true metaphor, but only through the one true metaphor the assured legibility of the proper" (in his *Margins of Philosophy*, trans. Alan Bass, Chicago: University of Chicago Press, 1971, p. 268). But since there can be no "assured legibility" in the process of designing artistic patterns, the poet, while yielding to repetition compulsion, or metaphor compulson, is inevitably faced with the impossibility of fulfilling his poetic desire.

61. Jacques Derrida, "Plato's Pharmacy," in his *Dissemination*, trans. Barbara Johnson (Chicago: University of Chicago Press, 1981).

62. Kornely Zelinsky, "O konstruktivizme," in *Literaturnye manifesty*, I, ed. Karl Eimermacher (Munich: Wilhelm Fink Verlag, 1969).

63. See André Breton, "Ljubovnaja lodka razbilas' o byt," *Le Surréalisme au service de la révolution* 1 (1930). Also reprinted in his *Point du Jour* (Paris: Gallimard, 1934).

64. Pasternak, "Okhrannaja gramota," p. 262.

65. Mandelstam, "Literaturnaja Moskva," p. 327.

66. Yevgeny Zamyatin, "Moskva-Peterburg," *Novyj Zhurnal* 72 (June 196-). In English it appeared in Mirra Ginsburg, ed. and trans., *A Soviet Heretic* (Chicago: Chicago University Press, 1970). Obviously, one should take into account that both Mandelstam's essay of 1922 and Zamyatin's essay of 1933,

written in exile in Paris, reflect the attitudes of writers who were culturally marginalized from a much more officially accepted "revolutionary poet." In their way, they attempt to subvert Mayakovsky's own argument—his flaunting Futurist virility as opposed to the Symbolist "effeminization"—and turn it upside down.

67. Ibid., p. 147. Italics mine.

68. On Mayakovsky's image making see Halina Stephen, "The Myth of the Revolutionary Poet: Mayakovsky in Three Modern Plays," *SEEJ* 30 (Summer 1986).

69. Sergey Tredyakov, "Lef," in Eimermacher, *Literaturnye manifesty*, I, p. 235.

70. Ibid., p. 242.

71. Walter Benjamin, "The Author as a Producer," in *Reflections*, trans. Edmund Jephcott, ed. Peter Demetz (New York: Harcourt Brace Jovanovich, 1979).

72. Victor Shklovsky, *O Majakovskom* (Moscow, 1940), p. 220.

73. Jakobson, "O pokolenii rastrativshem svoikh poetov," p. 2.

74. Vladimir Mayakovsky, "Umer Aleksandr Blok," II, p. 149

75. Vladimir Mayakovsky, "V. V. Khlebnikov," II, p. 151.

76. Jakobson, "O pokolenii rastrativshem svoikh poetov," p. 25.

77. Vladimir Mayakovsky, "To All of You," trans. Edward Brown, in Brown, *Mayakovsky*, p. 352. The tone of the note is somewhat similar to the tone of Mayakovsky's letters, which reflect a peculiarly modern telegraphic way of letter writing. Mayakovsky's letters, particularly those addressed to Lily Brik, are not letter-essays with a declaration of major poetic principles. They are not written for posterity, but rather for the pleasure of the moment. However, in these letters Mayakovsky invents many neologisms—mostly derivations of Lily's name, Lilenok, Lisenok, and so on—which are terms of endearment. Moreover, Mayakovsky hardly ever signs them with his full name, which has become a worn-out literary pseudonym, but rather with little nicknames, such as "Shchen" ("Doggy").

78. Marina Tsvetaeva, "Majakovskomy," in *Nesobrannye proizvedenija*, p. 56. See Chapter 3.

79. Edward Brown writes that "the note is a kind of re-capitulation of his life and work, composed during the period of deep peace . . . The poet is calm and self-possessed; and though almost all of his other poems express a towering and intransigent egotism, in this one he attends entirely to the 'others': Lily Brik, mama, sisters, Polonskaya, his new 'comrades from RAPP' and even 'Comrade Government'" (Brown, *Mayakovsky*, p. 352).

80. For the Surrealists' interpretation of suicide see *La Révolution surréaliste* 2 (1925).

81. Emile Durkheim, *Le Suicide* (Paris: Félix Alcan, 1930).

82. Philippe Hamon, "Clausules," *Poétique* 6 (1975), 495–526.

83. Quoted in Jakobson, "O pokolenii rastrativshem svoikh poetov," p. 29.

84. Ibid., p. 8.

85. Ibid., p. 25.

86. Ibid., p. 10.

87. Ibid., p. 25.

88. Roman Jakobson, *Novejshaja russkaja poezija* (Prague, 1921). In English it appeared as "The Newest Russian Poetry," in Brown, *Major Soviet Writers*, p. 66.

89. Jakobson, "O pokolenii rastrativshem svoikh poetov," p. 28.

90. Ibid., pp. 32–33.

91. Breton, "Ljubovnaja lodka razbilas' o byt."

92. André Breton, *Misère de la poésie: L'Affaire Aragon devant l'opinion publique* (Paris: Editions Surréalistes, 1932).

93. Leon Trotsky, "The Suicide of Vladimir Mayakovsky," in *On Literature and Art*, ed. Paul Siegel (New York: Pathfinder Press, 1970), p. 177.

94. Walter Benjamin, "Some Motifs in Baudelaire," in his *Illuminations* (New York: Schoken Books, 1969).

95. André Breton, *La Position politique du surréalisme* (Paris: Saggitaire, 1935), p. 36.

96. André Breton, "Pour un art révolutionnaire independent," in *Documents surréalistes*, ed. Maurice Nadeau (Paris: Editions du Seuil, 1964), p. 337.

97. Breton, "Ljubovnaja lodka razbilas o byt," p. 18.

98. See *La Révolution surréaliste* 2 (1925).

99. "Sans lui j'aurais peut-etre été un poète" (André Breton, "La Confession dédaigneuse," in his *Les Pas perdus*, Paris: Gallimard, 1924, p. 9).

100. Breton, "Ljubovnaja lodka razbilas o byt," p. 17. On the myth of femininity in Surrealism, see Xavière Gauthier, *Surréalisme et sexualité* (Paris: Gallimard, 1971); Ferdinand Alquié, *Philosophie du surréalisme* (Paris: Flammarion, 1977). On the representation of women, particularly in Surrealist photography and painting, see Mary Ann Caws, "Ladies Shot and Painted: Female Embodiment in Surrealist Art," in *Female Body in Western Culture*, ed. Susan Rubin Suleiman (Cambridge, Mass.: Harvard University Press, 1986).

101. Jakobson, "O pokolenii rastrativshem svoikh poetov," p. 12.

102. Vladimir Mayakovsky, "O drjani," I, p. 212.

103. Peter Bürger, *Theory of the Avant-Garde*, trans. Michael Shaw (Minneapolis: University of Minnesota Press, 1984), p. 114n.

104. René Crevel, "Mort, maladie et littérature," *Le Surréalisme au service de la révolution* 1 (1930).

105. For responses to the questionnaire, see *La Révolution surréaliste* 2 (1925), 13.

106. Maurice Nadeau, *Histoire du surréalisme* (Paris: Editions du Seuil, 1969), p. 158.

107. Louis Aragon, "Le Retour à la réalité," speech pronounced at the International Congress of Writers in the Defense of Culture, Paris, 1935; published in his *Pour un réalisme socialiste* (Paris: Denoël et Steele, 1935), pp. 69–89.

108. In his Marxist account of Aragon's itinerary, Roger Garaudy discusses Ara-

gon's symbolic relationship with Mayakovsky in the chapter entitled "Comme si le démon se colletait avec l'ange"—a title that reveals a Marxist sentimental attachment to biblical metaphors. Indeed, as Aragon himself confesses, Mayakovsky was a symbolic figure for him, a savior, who showed him "le retour à la réalité" and fostered his Communist realist conversion. Thus Aragon, following Mayakovsky, continues to elaborate the Christian elements in the "new myth" (Roger Garaudy, *L'Itinéraire Aragon*, Paris: Gallimard, 1963).

109. Louis Aragon, *Littératures soviétiques* (Paris: Denoël, 1955), p. 20.

110. It is interesting to note the role of cinematography in spreading information and exotic myths, both positive and negative, about Soviet Russia. Ferdinand Alquié based his critique of the Stalinism of 1932 on the Soviet film *The Road of Life*, in which he observed the traits of official "cretinism." Thus both Aragon's myth of Russia and the Surrealist critique of the Stalinist situation derive from cinematic representation, be it Eisensteinian ideological montage or Stalinist optimistic Socialist Realism.

111. Louis Aragon, "Shakespeare et Maïakovski," in *Littératures soviétiques*, p. 299.

112. Ibid., p. 358.

113. Ibid.

114. Ibid., pp. 300, 307. Mayakovsky might "turn in his grave," if he found out about his being equated with Gorky, since he in many of his poems criticized Gorky for his unresponsiveness to revolutionary experimentation in art and for his prolonged stay on Capri during the crucial years of constructing socialism in Soviet Russia.

115. Ibid., pp. 306–307.

116. Ibid., p. 354.

117. Aragon, "Hugo réaliste," in *Pour un réalisme socialiste*, p. 66.

118. Aragon, "D'Alfred de Vigny à Avdeenko," in *Littératures soviétiques*, p. 23.

119. Aragon, "Shakespeare et Maïakovski," p. 334.

120. Ibid., p. 341.

121. "Mais je sais bien, ce que je veux dire: c'est que de même que le Je, le Moi de Maïakovski est bien le Je, le Moi, d'un homme né le 7 juillet 1893 à Bagdadi, Géorgie . . . et de personne d'autre" (ibid., p. 352).

122. This tradition was due in part to the lack of a free verse tradition and in part to practical considerations: for many great poets, such as Pasternak, Tsvetaeva, and Mandelstam, at that time, translation was the major source of income since their own poems were not published.

123. Aragon, "Shakespeare et Maïakovski," pp. 331–332.

124. Ibid., p. 330.

125. Breton, *Misère de la poésie*.

126. Louis Aragon, "Front Rouge," quoted from ibid., p. 25.

127. Ibid.

128. In Paris Aragon harassed several Russian émigré artists and writers, including the Dadaist Ilya Zdanevich. Among other things Aragon blackmailed Matisse to sabotage his artistic collaboration with Zdanevich. Taking into account recent critical interest in the intellectuals who contributed to the Nazi (or collaborationist) newspapers, it is curious how little attention is now given to the leftist intellectuals' collaborations with Stalinism. In fact, both Aragon and Rolland were asked several times to intervene on behalf of the arrested poets and some former Soviet leftist artists, including Mandelstam, Tredyakov, and others, but they repeatedly refused to do so—a fact that many of them later deplored. Although Aragon criticized his own position during the 1930's and 1950's, this belated self-critique does not exempt his writings and activities during the twenty years of Stalinism from a careful intellectual examination.

129. Garaudy, *L'Itinéraire Aragon*, p. 229. As an example of Aragon's "Surrealist anarchism" Garaudy refers to "the anarchist theme of the destruction of churches" prominent in the poem. This example is incorrect. In fact, this is one of the most real and documentary elements of the poem, a "literature of fact" when regarded in connection with the not so Surrealist Soviet reality of the 1930's. Aragon's statement was prophetic. On the personal order of Stalin, many churches, which apart from their religious function were important architectural monuments, were demolished in the process of constructing the new Communist Moscow—among them the Passion Monastery right in front of Pushkin's monument. It was considered inappropriate for the great Russian genius and Lenin's favorite poet to face the citadel of religion, so Pushkin was turned around and the old monastery pulled down.

Here is a more recent twist on the theme of the destruction of churches. It is unfortunate that in Gorbachev's Soviet Union this tragic fact was used by Russian nationalists as an example of infamous "Jewish conspiracy." If in Stalin's time Jews were accused of capitalist and petit-bourgeois conspiracies, now they are accused of making the Russian revolution and of supposedly destroying the Russian national heritage. Thus in the Russian and Soviet culture, anti-Semitism precedes both revolutions and conspiracy theories and survives all the perestroikas.

130. Aragon, "Front Rouge," p. 28.

131. Julia Kristeva, "Ethics of Linguistics," in *Desire in Language*, trans. Thomas Gora, Alice Jardine, and Leon Roudiez and ed. Leon Roudiez (New York: Columbia University Press, 1980); John Berger, "Mayakovsky: His Language, His Death," in his *The Sense of Sight* (New York: Pantheon Books, 1985).

132. Louis Aragon, "Une Préface morcelée," in his *L'Oeuvre poétique*, V, (Paris: Livre Club Diderot, 1975), pp. 145–152.

133. Ibid., p. 143.

134. It is ironic but also revealing that in the late 1960's Aragon, as if compensating for his harassment of the Soviet émigré artists in the 1930's, defends some of the Soviet dissident writers, among them Andrey Sinyavsky (literary pseudo-

nym Abram Tertz) the author of the famous article on Socialist Realism. In the article Sinyavsky discusses Socialist Realism as one of the most "unrealistic" combinations of Classicism and Romanticism and sees Mayakovsky as the most consistent "Socialist Realist" because he pushed its antirealistic side to the limit ("Chto takoe socialisticheskij realizm" in Abram Tertz, *Fantasticheskie povesti*, New York: Inter-Language Literary Associates, 1967, pp. 399–446).

135. Milan Kundera, *The Book of Laughter and Forgetting*, trans. Michael Heim (New York: Penguin Books, 1987), p. 66.

136. *American Heritage Dictionary* (Boston: Houghton Mifflin, 1982), p. 1058.

137. Curiously, among synonyms of the word "engaged" we find "meshed, interlocked, involved, affianced, betrothed, busy, plighted, contracted, etc." and among antonyms the word "free" (*The Merriam-Webster Thesaurus*, New York: Pocket Books, 1978, p. 195). This reveals again the interpenetration of the cultural and linguistic definitions of these terms, as well as a peculiar understanding of "freedom" and "engagement" in the Anglo-American context.

138. Mayakovsky, "Vo ves' golos," p. 179.

139. Brown, *Mayakovsky*, p. 369.

140. On the poet's monument in the Soviet Union and its cultural mythology see Svetlana Boym, "Inscriptions on the Poet's Monuments," *Harvard Review* 1 (Fall 1986), 65–81.

141. Alexander Zholkovsky, "O genii i zlodejstve, o babe i vserossijskom masshtabe," in *Mir Avtora i struktura teksta*, ed. A. K. Zholkovsky (New Jersey: Ermitage, 1986); Yury Karabichevsky, *Voskresenie Majakovskogo* (Munich: Strana i mir, 1985).

142. Zholkovsky, "O genii i zlodejstve," p. 278.

143. Karabichevsky, *Voskresenie Majakovskogo*, p. 256.

144. Berger, "Mayakovsky," p. 226.

145. Ibid., p. 227.

146. Ibid., p. 235.

147. See "Novoe o Majakovskom," *Literatunoe nasledstvo* 65 (Moscow, 1958); as quoted and discussed in Michael Holquist, "The Mayakovsky Problem," in *Literature and Revolution*, ed. Jacques Ehrmann (Boston: Beacon Press, 1970), pp. 126–137.

148. Kristeva, "Ethics of Linguistics," p. 24.

149. Ibid., p. 31.

150. Ibid., p. 32.

151. Ibid., p. 31.

3. The Death of the Poetess

1. Osip Mandelstam, "Literaturnaja Moskva," in his *Sobranie sochinenij*, II (New York: Inter-Language Literary Associates, 1971), p. 327.

2. Julia Kristeva, "La Femme n'est jamais ça," interview, *Tel Quel* (Autumn 1974).

3. Mandelstam, "Literaturnaja Moskva," p. 328. All translations from the Russian are mine unless otherwise indicated.

4. Yury Tynyanov, "O parodii," in his *Poetika, Istorija literatury, Kino* (Moscow: Nauka, 1977), pp. 284–310.

5. Mikhail Bakhtin, *Problems of Dostoyevsky's Poetics*, trans. Caryl Emerson (Minneapolis: University of Minnesota Press, 1984), p. 195.

6. For a detailed discussion of these issues see Sandra Gilbert and Susan Gubar, *The Madwoman in the Attic* (New Haven: Yale University Press, 1979).

7. Sigmund Freud, "On Femininity," in *New Introductory Lectures on Psychoanalysis*, lecture 33 (New York: W. W. Norton, 1965).

8. The list of examples from major European authors is inexhaustible. I will suggest only a few to show how Mandelstam takes part in general European cultural myths. For instance, Proudhon proclaims that "genius is a virility of spirit and its accompanying powers of abstraction, generalization, creation and conception: the child, the eunuch and the woman lack these gifts in equal measure" ("La Justice," in *Oeuvres complètes*, VIII, Paris: Jacques Rivière, 1923). Flaubert, in his correspondence with Louise Colet, a woman of extreme intelligence, claims that the artist and the woman are extreme opposites, the artist possessing the "monstrosity" of self-consciousness and the "woman" being "natural," that is, completely lacking creative, self-reflective subjectivity (*Correspondance*, Paris: Librairie de France, 1928, pp. 322–323). Mandelstam's elder contemporary, Alexander Blok, told Anna Akhmatova, who was to become one of the major twentieth-century woman-poets, that "for a woman to be a poet is absurd." Ironically, Akhmatova incorporated these words into one of her poems dedicated to Blok, whom she admired and considered to be her mentor ("V poslednij raz my vstretilis' togda," in her *Stikhi i proza*, Leningrad, 1976, p. 63). In response to the criticism of Akhmatova calling her a "chamber" and a feminine poet, see Boris Eikhenbaum, "Anna Akhmatova," in his *O proze O poezii*, (Leningrad, 1986).

9. Osip Mandelstam, "O prirode slova," in *Sobranie sochinenij*, p. 258.

10. Virginia Woolf, *A Room of One's Own* (London: Granada, 1977), p. 79.

11. I am grateful to Leslie Dunton-Downer for sharing with me her thoughts on the etymology and changing signification of the "obscene." See her "Language of the Obscene" (Ph.D. diss., Harvard University, 1991).

12. *The American Heritage Dictionary* (Boston: Houghton Mifflin, 1982), p. 858.

13. Roland Barthes, *A Lover's Discourse*, trans. Richard Howard (New York: Hill and Wang, 1987), p. 175.

14. Marina Tsvetaeva, "Maximilian Voloshin," in her *Proza* (New York: Chekhov, 1955), p. 350.

15. Ibid., pp. 151–153.

16. Woolf, *A Room of One's Own*, p. 52.

17. For the best biographies of Tsvetaeva see Simon Karlinsky, *Marina Tsvetaeva* (Cambridge: Cambridge University Press, 1986); Jane Taubman, *A Life through Poetry: Marina Tsvetaeva's Lyrical Diary* (Columbus: Slavica, 1989). In Russian see Anna Saakyants, *Marina Tsvetaeva: Stranicy zhizni i tvorcestva* (Moscow: Sovetskij Pisatel', 1986); and the forthcoming biography by Viktoria Shweitzer.

18. M. H. Abrams, *The Mirror and the Lamp* (Oxford: Oxford University Press, 1953), p. 230.

19. Quoted in Simon Karlinsky, *Marina Cvetaeva: Her Life and Art* (Berkeley: University of California Press, 1966), p. 272. In the late 1920's and early 1930's several major Russian poets, including Mandelstam and Pasternak, turned to a variety of prose often presenting a poet or a writer as a fictional character, dramatizing the changing literary conventions. In this respect, Tsvetaeva's shift to prose around the same time is not unique; her writings form part of an unconventional and interesting intergeneric tradition of poet's prose, one of the most interesting developments of postrevolutionary Russian and Soviet prose, which for better or worse has not yet been canonized by either Soviet or Western critics. These writings defy easy critical classifications and academic course descriptions.

   The American Association for Advancement of Slavic Studies and other Slavic conferences in recent years have demonstrated an increasing interest in Tsvetaeva's poetry and prose in the work of many American Slavists: Olga Peters Hasty, Catherine O'Connor, Cathy Ciepiela, Greta Slobin, Stephanie Sandler, Anna Tavis, Jane Taubman, Laura Weeks, Pamela Chester, and others.

20. Marina Tsvetaeva, *Povest' o Sonechke*, in her *Neizdannoe* (Paris: YMCA Press, 1974). To the best of my knowledge the novella has not been translated into English.

21. Marina Tsvetaeva, "Geroj Truda," in *Proza*, p. 242.

22. Karlinsky, *Marina Tsvetaeva*, p. 97. Perhaps "feminism" in Tsvetaeva's understanding was as hyperbolic and parodic as the conventional mask of the poetess. "Female questions," according to her, reestablish the narrow boundaries of the separate "female world." In other words, they reestablish what "women lack" and reconfirm the centrality of "male questions." In calling for "female answers" to "human" questions she attempts to get outside the feminine ornamental frame and postulates "a poetics outside of gender," which as we shall see remains utopian and problematic.

23. Laura Mulvey, "Visual Pleasure and Narrative Cinema," in *Film Theory and Criticism*, ed. Marshall Cohen and Gerald Mast (Oxford: Oxford University Press, 1985). Carol Heilbrun, in her *Towards the Recognition of Androgyny* (London: Victor Gollanz, 1974), writes that for the Greeks, "eyes and seeing are in general 'masculine'—the contrast is between Apollonian light and Dionysian darkness." Female powers lie in the "dark" realm of the intuitive, irrational, interior, tactile. The persistence of this view in Western culture made

it possible for Freud to make a "leap of faith" from oedipal self-blinding to castration (in the reading which equates eye*balls* and testicles), while in fact blinding can be regarded as a recognition of a "dark wisdom," of coming to terms with an intuitive and interior gaze, the regaining of a "feminine principle."

24. Tsvetaeva, "Geroj Truda," pp. 239–240.

25. Quoted in Vsevolod Rozhdestvensky, "Marina Tsvetaeva," introduction to Marina Tsvetaeva, *Sochinenija*, ed. Anna Saakyants (Moscow: Khudozhestvennaya literatura, 1988), p. 36.

26. Tsvetaeva, "Geroj Truda," pp. 240–241.

27. Marina Tsvetaeva, *Pis'ma k Teskovoj* (Prague: Academia, 1969), p. 28. Letter writing is essential for Tsvetaeva. Unlike Mayakovsky's antipoetic letters, hers definitely belong to the genre of poetic letters (especially the ones addressed to Pasternak and Rilke); they continue the epistolary tradition of the German Romantics. Moreover, it seems that the practice of letter writing informs and shapes Tsvetaeva's autobiographical and critical prose. *The Tale of Sonechka* for instance, contains fragments from diaries and letters.

28. Quoted in Tsvetaeva, "Geroj Truda," p. 245.

29. Marina Tsvetaeva, "Nataliya Goncharova," in *Moj Pushkin*, ed. A. Efron and A. Saakyants (Moscow: Sovetskij Pisatel', 1981).

30. The sharp opposition between female beauty and genius is developed in Tsvetaeva's numerous autobiographical writings. She tries to present herself as "a lonely girl" in contrast to "a beautiful girl." A beautiful girl is an object of desire, and a lonely girl is a writing subject. In the essay dedicated to Bryusov, Adalis remarks that Bryusov "appreciated Tsvetaeva as a poet, but could not stand her as a woman." According to Tsvetaeva's aesthetics, this comment could have been a compliment.

31. Tsvetaeva, "Nataliya Goncharova," p. 117.

32. Tsvetaeva, *Povest' o Sonechke*, p. 265.

33. It has also been argued that the diminutive suffix is used throughout in order to distinguish Sonechka Holliday from Sonya Parnok. See Sophia Polyakova, *Nezakatnye ony dni* (Ann Arbor: Ardis, 1979); and Karlinsky, *Marina Tsvetaeva*.

34. Tsvetaeva, *Povest' o Sonechke*, p. 308.

35. Ibid., p. 318. Some critics regarded this scene as an allusion to Tsvetaeva's relationship with Sophia Parnok, since one of the dresses described was in fact hers. Sophia Polyakova reads the novella as Tsvetaeva's "theater of oneself" and a revenge on Sophia Parnok (see her *Nezakatnye ony dni*). Karlinsky in a similar vein infers from the novella that Tsvetaeva's relationship with Sonechka Holliday took the "form of a passionate school-girl crush" and did not have the "dimension of unbridled sensuality" that characterized Tsvetaeva's relationship with Parnok. Diana Burgin has rightly observed that Tsvetaeva attempted to conceal her relationship with Parnok by never publishing the poetic cycle

"Podruga" that was dedicated to her. Indeed one can contrast Sophia Parnok, a strong woman poet, and Sonechka, the imaginary, emotional poetess. However, my focus here is on Sonechka, who embodies the culturally ostracized feminine figure, neither a meek Dostoyevskian woman, her namesake, nor an emancipated, strong woman artist. I would suggest that Tsvetaeva's novella has many artistic and erotic dimensions and can hardly be reduced merely to revenge against her old female lover and poet. On the one hand, the novella, as all Tsvetaeva's semiautobiographical writings on love, is a "theater of oneself" in the sense that it is an exercise in personal mythification. On the other hand, this theater is not monologic. It is permeated by the other's erotic presence. Burgin is currently completing a book on Sophia Parnok that will help us understand her powerful but often concealed presence in Russian cultural life. Meanwhile see Burgin's paper "Silver Age Critical Perceptions of Lesbian Sexuality in Sophia Parnok's First Book of Verses, *Poems*," presented at the recent symposium on Bodies, Stories, Images: Representations of Sexuality in Russian Culture, Amherst College, September 1989.

36. Tsvetaeva, *Povest' o Sonechke*, p. 293.

37. Ibid., p. 304.

38. Marina Tsvetaeva, "Iskusstvo pri svete sovesti," in *Proza*, p. 389.

39. Ibid.

40. Tsvetaeva, *Povest' o Sonechke*, p. 304.

41. Ibid., p. 227.

42. Tsvetaeva, "Maximilian Voloshin," p. 225.

43. Antonina Filonov Gove, "The Feminine Stereotypes and Beyond: Role Conflict and Resolution in the Poetics of Marina Tsvetaeva," *Slavic Review* 36 (June 1977), 231–255.

44. Anja Kroth, "Dichotomy and Razminovenie in the Work of Marina Tsvetaeva" (Ph.D. diss., University of Michigan, 1977). See also her article "Androgyny as an Exemplary Feature in Marina Tsvetaeva's Dichotomous Poetic Vision," *Slavic Review* 38 (December 1979), 563–582.

45. Hélène Cixous, "The Laugh of the Medusa," trans. Keith Cohen and Paula Cohen, *Signs* 1 (Summer 1976), 254.

46. Among contemporary feminist critics there is an ongoing debate about Virginia Woolf and the relationship between feminism and modernism. See Toril Moi, *Sexual/Textual Politics* (London: Methuen, 1985); and Elaine Schowalter, *Literature of Their Own* (Princeton: Princeton University Press, 1977).

47. Cixous, "The Laugh of the Medusa," p. 254.

48. Karlinsky, *Marina Cvetaeva: Her Life and Art*, p. 285.

49. Marina Tsvetaeva, "Vskryla zhily," in *Sochinenija*, I, p. 315.

50. Gove, "The Feminine Stereotypes and Beyond," p. 254.

51. Marina Tsvetaeva, "Epos i lirika sovremennoj Rossii," in *Nesobrannye proizvedenija*, ed. Anna Saakyants (Munich: Wilhelm Fink, 1971), p. 661.

52. Marina Tsvetaeva, "Majakovskomu," in ibid., p. 564.

53. Ibid., p. 566.

54. Ibid., p. 567.

55. Ibid., p. 564.

56. Marina Tsvetaeva, "Novogodnee," in *Sochinenija*, I, p. 261. Translation by John Henriksen.

57. Ibid.

58. Ibid., p. 263.

59. Ibid., p. 264.

60. It is interesting to compare "Novogodnee" with the following early poem of Khlebnikov's:

> Бобоэби пелись губы,
> бэээоми пелись взоры,
> пиээо пелись брови,
> лиэээй—пелся облик,
> Гзи-Гзигээо пелась цепь.
> Так на холсте каких-то соответствий
> Вне протяжений жило Лицо.

> Boboebi sang the lips,
> beeomi sang the eyes,
> pieeo sang the eyebrows,
> lieeey sang the image,
> gzi-gzigeeo sang the chain.
> So on the canvas of such correspondences
> beyond dimensions lived the Face.

Here the capitalized "Lico," "the Face," also emerges from alliterations of the transsensual language. This is an interesting case of intertextuality in the description of an unconventional poetic divinity. Velimir Khlebnikov, *Tvorenija* (Moscow: Sovetskij Pisatel', 1986), p. 54.

61. Joseph Brodsky, "Ob odnom stikhotvorenii," introduction to Tsvetaeva, *Stikhotvorenija i poemy*, I (New York: Russica, 1980), p. 75.

62. Charles Baudelaire, "Le Voyage," in *Les Fleurs du mal*, ed. V. Pichois (Paris: Le Livre de Poche, 1972), p. 177.

63. Tsvetaeva, "Novogodnee," p. 265.

64. Marina Tsvetaeva, "Poet i vremja," in Saakyants, *Nesobrannye proizvedenija*, pp. 624–625.

65. Marina Tsvetaeva, "Poet o kritike," in ibid., p. 589.

66. In "Androgyny as an Exemplary Feature in Marina Tsvetaeva's Dichotomous Poetic Vision," Anya Kroth writes that in Tsvetaeva a "gender can be considered a stylistic device if the reader consciously or unconsciously transfers male or female characteristics to an object as a result of its grammatical gender. We can see it as Tsvetaeva's poetic motivation of ordinary language" (p. 570).

67. Tsvetaeva, "Iskusstvo pri svete sovesti," p. 395.

68. Tsvetaeva, *Pis'ma k Teskovoj*, p. 110.

69. Marina Tsvetaeva, "Mat' i muzyka," in *Sochinenija*, II, pp. 86–110. For a discussion of Tsvetaeva's autobiographical prose see Janet King, "Marina Cvetaeva's Mythobiographical Childhood" (Ph.D. diss., Harvard University, 1978).

70. On women in Russian literature and the Russian cultural tradition in general see Barbara Heldt, *Terrible Perfection* (Bloomington: Indiana University Press, 1987).

71. Tsvetaeva, *Moj Pushkin*, p. 316.

72. Tsvetaeva, "Mat' i muzyka," p. 91.

73. Marina Tsvetaeva, "Po naberezhnym, gde sedye derev'ja," in *Sochinenija*, p. 264.

74. Julia Kristeva, "Stabat Mater," trans. Arthur Goldhammer, in *The Female Body in Western Culture*, ed. Susan R. Suleiman (Cambridge, Mass.: Harvard University Press, 1986). See also Julia Kristeva, *Histoires d'Amour* (Paris: Denoël, 1983).

75. Quoted in Marina Tsvetaeva, "Kommentarii," in *Sochinenija*, I, p. 538.

76. Compare this image with the image of the Amazon's breasts in Tsvetaeva's "Amazonka," in ibid., p. 180. The image of the Amazon has been frequently discussed in the criticism of Tsvetaeva, especially by Karlinsky and Gove, and also in the papers by Laura Weeks and Stephanie Sandler presented at the AATSEEL Conference, San Francisco, December 27–30, 1987.

77. Gove, "The Feminine Stereotypes and Beyond," p. 252.

78. Eva Cantarella, "Dangling Virgins: Myth, Ritual, and the Place of Women in Ancient Greece," in Suleiman, *The Female Body in Western Culture*, pp. 57–68.

79. Karlinsky, *Marina Cvetaeva: Her Life and Art*, p. 283.

80. Margaret Higonnet, "Speaking Silences: Women's Suicide," in Suleiman, *The Female Body in Western Culture*, p. 71.

81. Anastasia Tsvetaeva, *Vosspominanija* (Moscow: Sovetskij Pisatel', 1984), p. 758.

82. Karlinsky, *Marina Tsvetaeva*, p. 244.

83. Higonnet, "Speaking Silences," p. 68.

84. Ibid., p. 70.

85. Quoted in Karlinsky, *Marina Cvetaeva: Her Life and Art*, p. 285.

86. Ibid., p. 244.

87. Boris Pasternak, "Pamjati Mariny Tsvetaevoj," in *Izbrannoe*, ed. E. V. Pasternak (Moscow: Khudozhestvennaja literatura, 1985), p. 344.

88. Ibid., p. 512.

89. Anna Akhmatova, "Pozdnij otvet," in *Sochinenija*, I. ed. V. A. Chernykh (Moscow: Khudozhestvennaja literatura, 1986), p. 247. Akhmatova dedicated to Tsvetaeva two poems in her cycle "Venok mertvym" ("The Crown for the

Dead"): "Posdnij otvet" ("The Late Answer" [1940]) and "Nas chetvero" ("There Are Four of Us" [1959]).

90. Anna Akhmatova, "Tsvetaeva," in *Sochinenija*, II, p. 208.

91. It is ironic that during my early research I discovered Tsvetaeva listed in the card catalogue at Harvard's Widener Library under her husband's name as "Efron, Marina Ivanovna." This is an interesting "corrective gesture," an attempt to find a respectable way of classifying quite an unrespectable woman-poet, one that appeals to the institution of marriage, which she so many times transgressed. In spite of her on-and-off love for her husband, she never used the name "Efron," and in many ways it is the opposite of her name as a poet(ess).

92. Akhmatova, "Tsvetaeva," p. 209.

Conclusion

1. Paul de Man, "Literary History and Literary Modernity," in his *Blindness and Insight* (Minneapolis: University of Minnesota Press, 1983), p. 165.

2. For an exemplary journalistic treatment of de Man see David Lehman, "Deconstructing de Man's Life," *Newsweek* (Feb. 15, 1988). See also Jacques Derrida, "Paul de Man's War," *Critical Inquiry* 14 (Spring 1988), 590–652; now collected in *Responses: On Paul de Man's Wartime Journalism*, ed. Werner Hamacher, Neil Hertz, and Thomas Keenan (Lincoln: University of Nebraska Press, 1989).

3. See Geoffrey Hartman, "Blindness and Insight," *New Republic* (March 7, 1988); and Christopher Norris, "Paul de Man's Past," *London Review of Books* (February 4, 1988).

4. Roland Barthes, *Incidents* (Paris: Editions du Seuil, 1987).

Index

D0853852